Giovanni Andrea Scartazzini, Arthur John Butler

A Companion to Dante

Giovanni Andrea Scartazzini, Arthur John Butler
A Companion to Dante
ISBN/EAN: 9783743320567
Manufactured in Europe, USA, Canada, Australia, Japa
Cover: Foto ©ninafisch / pixelio.de

Manufactured and distributed by brebook publishing software (www.brebook.com)

Giovanni Andrea Scartazzini, Arthur John Butler

A Companion to Dante

A COMPANION TO DANTE

FROM THE GERMAN OF

G. A. SCARTAZZINI

BY

ARTHUR JOHN BUTLER

London
MACMILLAN AND CO.
AND NEW YORK
1893

All rights reserved

TRANSLATOR'S PREFACE

DR. SCARTAZZINI needs no introduction to students of Dante. Since Witte's death it may safely be said that no name has been more constantly prominent in their view. Owing to the circumstance that, as an Italian citizen of what must rank as a German commonwealth, he owns practically two mother tongues, he has been able to secure the attention of two audiences, besides having access, unhampered by the usual preliminary linguistic obstacles, to the two most copious literatures of the subject. From Chur, from Milan, from Leipzig, he has for the last quarter of a century poured forth editions, handbooks, *adversaria* of all sorts, with an assiduity 'non vista mai fuorche alla prima gente,' if we may so designate the age immediately succeeding the poet's own. With these every serious student of Dante is bound to make himself acquainted. The present work,[1] as the author tells us, is the result of frequent requests for a German version of his *Prolegomeni della Divina Commedia*, published three years ago. Instead of merely translating this he preferred, however, to write an independent work, treating its predecessor merely as one among other authorities to be consulted in its composition.

[1] *Dante-Handbuch* (Leipzig, Brockhaus, 1892). Unfortunately the author's small *Manuale Dantesco* (Milan, Hoepli) having been already translated in America, the natural title of *Handbook* was not available for the present translation.

New works had appeared in the interval since its publication; further study had placed new aspects on existing evidence; on various points the writer had seen reason to modify his opinion. It was therefore better to face a new fire of criticism, and write a new work.

Those who have read the *Prolegomeni* will trace in the writer a distinct advance in the direction of that scepticism, perhaps almost better called negative dogmatism, which is now in fashion among some of the leading Dante scholars on the Continent. This, though no doubt safer than the phase which preceded it, under which Dante was assumed to have done anything that it was nice to think he had done, if he could not be proved not to have done it, may be carried a little too far. Most readers will probably be inclined to think that the author has carried it a little too far—or been carried a little too far by it—more than once in the present volume, and the reader must always bear this tendency of the author's in mind. On the subject of Beatrice, her identity, her symbolical function in Dante's writings, and indeed on most points connected with her, Dr. Scartazzini's interpretation seems at times perverse to the point of grotesqueness. The 'Frau Bardi, geb. Portinari' way of treating the question seems to have taken possession of him to the exclusion of earlier and surely saner methods. It is no doubt true that 'the conscience of the historian can take no account of subjective wishes'; but this is perfectly consistent with some regard to historical perspective and some allowance for differences in the matter of social and sentimental conventions between the thirteenth century and the nineteenth. Some of the arguments employed in part iii. chap. i. to prove that Beatrice was not Beatrice, 'but another person of the same name,' to borrow the phrase of the German who performed a like office for Shakespeare, seem hardly serious. I have called attention in a footnote here and there to some of the more remarkable instances of what I can only think misplaced ingenuity. To use his own words with regard to another writer, 'now and again the effect is less to convince the reader than to rouse him to opposition.'

But after all, conclusions are not of much importance in a work of this sort. If a scholar likes to take his fling now and then, and diversify his labours with a little paradox, why should we grudge him the amusement? The great question is, does he show us facts, and stimulate us to seek for more ourselves. Now no one will deny that Dr. Scartazzini knows his Dante as well as any man, and Dante literature, especially that of the last hundred years, in all probability better than any man; while, in spite of an occasional outbreak of Italian vivacity which has an odd effect in a German dress, he states his facts with precision and accuracy, and quotes authorities almost in superfluity. A copious bibliography is given at the end of almost every chapter. These I have not thought it necessary to reproduce, since the majority of the books named would be hardly accessible, and certainly not interesting, to English readers. A selection of a few of the more important will be found at the end of this preface. It should be mentioned that the last two chapters of the original have been a good deal abridged, and compressed into one.

The translator would like to say one word on his own account, which is, that the process of 'explaining Dante by Dante' (first begun by the old commentators, who, when they came to an unknown name, informed their readers that A. B. was a person notorious for pride, envy, or as the case might be) would seem, as indeed the present book shows, to have now been carried at least to the point beyond which little further result can be expected from it. Discussion is passing into hair-splitting, originality into paradox. If any more light is to be thrown on the obscurities, of which plenty still remain, it will rather be from the outside. It is almost impossible to read more than a page or two of any work of the twelfth or thirteenth century without coming upon some passage which one feels certain that Dante must have read. In those days it must be remembered one writer had no more scruple about borrowing a phrase or an image from another than a builder had about using the stones of a Roman temple, or than Dante's countrymen have ever since had about borrowing from him. Many obscure allusions, many apparently unaccountable turns of phrase were, we may be sure, borrowed by Dante in this way from the books he read; and by reading the same books, we may eventually succeed in finding their origin and therewith their explanation. It is in this direction rather than in the reading and re-reading (whether to follow them or to contradict them) of commentaries which have reproduced each other with ever-decreasing intelligence for six hundred years, that Dante research will in future have to proceed.

LIST OF COMMENTARIES AND OTHER WORKS[1]

Petri Allegherii super Dantis ipsius genitoris Comoediam Commentarium (*sic*) nunc primum in lucem editum consilio et sumtibus G. J. Bar. Vernon. Florentiae apud Guilelmum Piatti MDCCCXXXV. (The Commentary of Dante's son Peter: of considerable value, indeed probably the most useful of all those edited by Lord Vernon.)

Boccaccio's Commentary (Italian). Frequently printed. A convenient edition is Lemonnier's in two volumes. Florence, 1863. The comment extends only to H. xvii. 17.

Benvenuto Rambaldi of Imola (Latin). Edited in five volumes (Florence, 1887) by Sir James Lacaita and Mr. W. W. Vernon. Extremely useful.

Cristoforo Landino. With the text, first edition, Florence, 1481; and often reprinted in the following century.

Alessandro Vellutello of Lucca. First edition, Venice, 1544; and with Landino 1564, 1578, 1596.

Bernardino Daniello of Lucca. Venice, 1568.

Baldassarre Lombardi, Rome, 1871; and often since.

Brunone Bianchi, Florence, 1854; and often since.

Philalethes (King John of Saxony); translation (German) and notes. Dresden and Leipzig, 1839-1849; and several later editions.

Carl Witte; translation (German) and notes. Berlin, 1876. Dante-Forschungen; 2 vols. Heilbronn, 1869-1879.

L. G. Blanc; notes on certain difficult passages, down to Purg. xxvii. (*Versuch einer blos philologischen Erklärung*),

---

[1] This list of course is a mere selection of such works relating to the *Commedia* as seem most likely to be useful or accessible to English students.

Halle, 1860-1865; and Dictionary, of which an Italian translation (*Vocabolario Dantesco*) by G. Carbone is published by Barbéra, Florence.

G. A. Scartazzini; edition (Italian) in three volumes, with notes, and one volume of *Prolegomeni*, Leipzig, 1874-1890; and edition in one volume, Milan, 1892.

H. F. Cary; verse translation with notes. London, 1814, and repeatedly since.

H. W. Longfellow; verse translation with notes. Boston, 1867, and often since.

A. J. Butler; edition in three volumes, with prose translation and notes. London, 1880-1892.

E. H. Plumptre; verse translation in two volumes, with notes and dissertations. London, 1886-1887.

C. E. Norton; prose translation in three volumes, Cambridge (Mass.) and London, 1891-92.

J. A. Carlyle; prose translation of *Hell* only, with text and notes. London, 1849, and several times since.

M. F. Rossetti; *A Shadow of Dante*. London, 1871, and frequently since.

J. A. Symonds; *An Introduction to the Study of Dante*. London, 1872 and 1893.

F. Hettinger (translated by H. S. Bowden); *Dante's Divina Commedia, its Scope and Value*. London, 1887. Interesting but inaccurate in details.

E. Moore; *Contributions to the Textual Criticism of the Divina Commedia*. Cambridge, 1889.

A. Bartoli; *Delle Opere di Dante Alighieri* (in *Storia della Letteratura Italiana*). Florence, 1887-1889.

CONTENTS

	PAGE
INTRODUCTION	1

PART I

DANE IN HIS HOME

CHAPTER I

SOURCES OF INFORMATION AND AIDS TO STUDY	19

CHAPTER II

ORIGIN	31

CHAPTER III

TIME AND PLACE OF DANTE'S BIRTH	40

CHAPTER IV

INMATES OF DANTE'S HOME	47

CHAPTER V

STUDIES	51

CHAPTER VI

MILITARY SERVICE 61

CHAPTER VII

FAMILY LIFE 71

CHAPTER VIII

POLITICAL ACTIVITY 80

CHAPTER IX

EXILE 97

PART II

DANTE IN EXILE

CHAPTER I

THE COMPANY OF THE WICKED 111

CHAPTER II

STUDENT OR TEACHER ? 125

CHAPTER III

DANTE'S WANDERINGS 133

CHAPTER IV

LOFTY HOPES 142

CHAPTER V

UNDECEIVED 152

CHAPTER VI

THE LAST REFUGE 159

PART III

DANTE'S SPIRITUAL LIFE

CHAPTER I

BEATRICE 175

CHAPTER II

ON THE WRONG ROAD 198

CHAPTER III

GOING ASTRAY 214

CHAPTER IV

ANOTHER AND YET THE SAME . . 239

CHAPTER V

ATTITUDE TOWARDS POLITICAL PARTIES . 251

CHAPTER VI

DANTE'S PERSONALITY 260

PART IV

DANTE'S SMALLER WORKS

CHAPTER I

	PAGE
LYRIC POEMS . . .	. 269

CHAPTER II

| THE *VITA NUOVA* . . . . | 279 |

CHAPTER III

| THE *CONVITO* . . . . . | 288 |

CHAPTER IV

| *DE VULGARI ELOQUENTIÂ* . . | . 301 |

CHAPTER V

| *DE MONARCHIÂ* . . . . | 318 |

CHAPTER VI

| THE LETTERS . . . . | . 341 |

CHAPTER VII

| APOCRYPHAL WORKS . | . 364 |

PART V

THE 'DIVINA COMMEDIA'

CHAPTER I

ORIGIN OF THE POEM	373

CHAPTER II

CONTENTS	386

CHAPTER III

THE FORM	411

CHAPTER IV

THE PURPORT OF THE POEM	440

CHAPTER V

EXPOSITION AND DISSEMINATION	464

INDEX	489

ERRATA.

Page 7, line 30, *for* "is murdered" *read* "murders," and in next line *delete* "by."
,, 34, ,, 24, *for* "son" *read* "father."
,, 61, heading of Chapter VI., *for* "science" *read* "service."
,, 92, line 12, *for* "as" *read* "a."
,, 346, ,, 18, *for* "to" *read* "from."
,, 359, ,, 30, *for* "thirteenth" *read* "fourteenth."
,, 392, ,, 13, *for* "donatism" *read* "donations."

INTRODUCTION

DANTE ALIGHIERI'S marvellous poem, unique and unapproached as it stands in the literature of the world, has for more than five centuries enjoyed a reputation of perhaps wider extent than any other literary work. At the present day we know of more than 500 early MSS., and who can guess how many have perished by lapse of time, or how many yet lie somewhere hidden? Thus even before the invention of printing the book had an extraordinary circulation. Since that time it has been printed more than three hundred times in the original, two hundred and fifty of them in the course of the present century.[1] It has been translated into all civilised languages; into some—as English, French, and German—by twenty or thirty various translators, some of whose works have gone through several editions, and are yet in vogue. So that in the original or in translations this book has been printed perhaps a thousand times, and every year sees a material increase in these figures.

Yet the great poem is very obscure, and the comprehension of it very difficult; so obscure and so difficult that the work of exposition began immediately upon its publication,

---

[1] So in the original—but it was certainly printed many more than fifty times before 1800. The British Museum has some 60 editions earlier than that date.

has gone on through all these centuries, and at the present moment is pursued more zealously than ever. So obscure and difficult that even an educated man often finds himself unable to understand it if he does not call in the aid of one or another expounder. And yet it is read far and wide by hundreds of thousands, which seems to show that it must possess some special value, and its study must be of exceptional importance. What, then, is this value, this importance?

Not unfrequently, even in our century, has Dante's work been sadly ill treated. People have forged a weapon out of it to champion party interests—religious, political, or social. The poet has been pressed into the glorification now of the Catholic, now of the Protestant Church. On one side he has been represented as the most faithful son of Rome, on the other as a witness to evangelical truth, a precursor of the Reformation. People have praised him or inveighed against him, according to their point of view, as a secret adherent of the Albigenses or some other sect of the period, as a freemason, as a bitter revolutionist, as a good republican, as a socialist, as the prophet of the modern State, as the apostle of the political unity of Italy, and so forth. This sort of thing flourished particularly in Italy from the second decade of our century onwards. Each party inscribed Dante's name on its banner, each took to itself credit for striving after that for which he had striven. This abuse of his name had at any rate no small influence in making the poet far more popular in his own country than he had ever been in former ages; but therewith it also largely contributed to obscure the right understanding of his noble work, and render it yet more difficult.

The significance of Dante and his works, including his great poem, is manifold. It involves aesthetics, social and general history, theology, philosophy, philology, ethics : so that all the faculties, to use the expression in its technical sense, have ever interested themselves in this poet, and will continue to do so.

It is hardly necessary to say anything about the moral value of the *Divine Comedy*, for it is universally recognised. Of those who honour the poet the greater number admire and value him for the sake of his incomparable beauty of language, the completeness, the charm, and the picturesque intuition of his pictures, the convincing accuracy of his descriptions, the beautiful symmetry of the whole and of individual parts, the unsurpassable perfection of form which his poem displays on all sides. Goethe's verdict on the famous episode of Count Ugolino—'the few tercets in which Dante has related the death of Ugolino and his sons by starvation are among the highest things which the poetic art has produced. For this very laconic limitation, this reticence, brings before our minds the tower, the hunger, and the utter despair'—applies equally well to each one of the hundred cantos of which the poem consists. That Dante holds the first place among the poets of modern times can admit of no contradiction.[1]

Like his coeval, Roger Bacon, Dante was the precursor of the new culture. His work, a faithful mirror of his time, with all its thoughts and wishes, its emotions and its efforts, its loves and hates, its sorrows and joys, its endurance and its hope, is one of the most conspicuous monuments of the development of human culture. It combines in a marvellous representation the whole history of his time, of his fatherland in the widest and narrowest sense, the scholastic and mystical theology and philosophy of the Middle Ages

---

[1] This is a statement which countrymen of Shakespeare will hardly accept without protest.

transfigured in noble poetry. Here the deepest questions of philosophy and the highest flights of theology are discussed in a fashion up to that time undreamt of, and since then never attained. The most eminent philosophers and theologians have ever since occupied themselves profoundly with this marvellous work of art. Schelling[1] and Hegel,[2] no less than Döllinger[3] and Hettinger,[4] have materially enriched with their contributions the literature of Dante.

When in 1755 Nicolaus Ciangulo edited the first text of the *Hell* that ever appeared in Germany, he deemed it necessary to recommend the book with the observation: 'No one who would with any right claim to be even a little conversant with Italian can dispense with a Dante.' Nowadays a recommendation of this kind seems naïve to the point of childishness: the philosophic value of the poem and its place in the history of literature are fully recognised here and freely expressed. None the less does it remain true that it is and will remain to all time the noblest and highest monument of the Italian language and literature.

Next and highest in importance we place the ethical qualities of the *Divine Comedy*. In contrast to many other poems, this great epic satisfies not only the claims of aesthetic art, but exercises inevitably an ennobling moral effect on whosoever steeps himself with full enjoyment in it. Not only was the poet himself conscious of the significance of his work in this respect; he expressly sets forth that the moral elevation of his readers was the main object sought by his labour. In the letter (of somewhat doubtful genuine-

---

[1] An essay, *Ueber Dante in philosophischer Beziehung*, is printed in his collected works. (Stuttgart, 1859.)

[2] *Lectures on Aesthetic.* (Berlin, 1838.)

[3] *Essays*, translated by Margaret Warre. (Murray, 1890.)

[4] *Dante's Divina Commedia*, translated by Father Bowden. (Burns and Oates, 1887.)

ness) to Can Grande, we read: 'The end of the whole and of the part is to withdraw those who are living in this life from a state of misery, and to lead them to a state of happiness.' Even if these words are not his own, they were undoubtedly inscribed on his mind and heart. In the poem he says with noble self-consciousness, by the mouth of Cacciaguida:

> What though, when tasted first, thy voice shall prove
> Unwelcome; on digestion it will turn
> To vital nourishment.

CHRONOLOGICAL VIEW OF THE HISTORY OF THE PERIOD.

1215. *Origin of the Guelf and Ghibeline parties in Florence.*—Dante's contemporary, the historian John Villani, relates this as follows [v. 38]: Messer Buondelmonte dei Buondelmonti, a noble citizen of Florence, was betrothed to a lady of the house of the Amidei. As he was riding through the city one day a lady of the house of the Donati uttered remarks depreciatory of his betrothed, and said, 'I have been keeping my daughter for you.' Overcome by the young lady's beauty, Buondelmonte broke his pledge and married her. The Amidei were very angry, and with some of the other noble families planned vengeance. While they were debating whether they should kill or merely chastise Buondelmonte, Mosca dei Lamberti uttered the ill-omened sentence, 'Cosa fatta capo ha.' On the morning of Easter Day the conspirators met in the house of the Amidei, and as Buondelmonte in his brave holiday attire was riding from the other side of the river, as he reached the hither side of the Ponte Vecchio, he was thrown from his horse and assassinated. In a moment the city was in an uproar, and from that moment the townsmen were divided into two parties, the partisans of the Buondelmonti taking the Guelf side, those who held with the Uberti and Amidei representing the Ghibelines. 'Whence,' says the historian, 'resulted much havoc and ruin to our city, as we shall hereafter mention, and it is believed that it will have no limit if God does not make an end of it.' Not only Florence but all Tuscany suffered from these dissensions for more than a century, and Dante himself fell a victim to them. He has more than once alluded to the circumstance, e.g. H. xxviii. 103; P. xvi. 136.

1215-50. *Frederick II., Emperor.*—In the imperial court at Palermo Italian poetry begins to flourish in the so-called Sicilian school, cf. H. x. 119; xiii. 58 sqq.; xxiii. 66; Pg. xvi. 117; P. iii. 120.

1237. Building of the bridge over the Arno, called at first Ponte Rubaconte, afterwards Ponte alle Grazie, Pg. xii. 102.

1248. The Ghibelines, with the support of Frederick II., expel the Guelfs from Florence. See Villani, vi. 33; H. x. 48.

1249. Peter de Vineis, poet and minister of Frederick II., dies in prison, H. xiii. 58 sqq. About this time flourished the poets Guido dalle Colonne and Giacopo da Lentino, nicknamed 'the notary,' cf. Pg. xxiv. 56; De Vulg. El. i. 12.

1250. Frederick II. died at Ferentino, Dec. 13, succeeded by his son Conrad IV. First popular constitution in Florence. Villani, vi. 39.

1251. The banished Guelfs return to Florence, Jan. 7, cf. H. x. 49. The Guelfs change their arms from a white lily on a red field to a red lily on a white field. The Ghibelines hold to the old ensign. Villani, vi. 43; P. xvi. 154.

1253. Conrad IV. takes Naples and founds the University of Salerno. Villani, vi. 44.

1254. Conrad IV. dies. Manfred, natural son of

Frederick II., takes the sovereignty of Naples and comes into conflict with Innocent IV. and Alexander IV. Pg. iii. 112.

1258. The Ghibelines are expelled from Florence. Villani, vi. 65.

1260. Ezzelin of Romano, son-in-law to Frederick II., dies from wounds received in the battle of Cassano. Villani, vi. 72; Pg. ix. 29. Battle of Montaperti, Sept. 4. The banished Ghibelines supported by King Manfred and the Sienese win a brilliant victory under the leadership of Farinata degli Uberti which puts Florence and the whole of Tuscany into their hands. Villani, vi. 78; H. x. 75 sqq.; xxxii. 80. On September 13 the Guelfs fly and surrender Florence to the Ghibelines.

1263. Urban IV. summons Charles of Anjou to oppose Manfred. Villani, vi. 88; Pg. xx. 67.

1265. Dante born in May.

1266. Battle of Benevento and death of Manfred, Feb. 26. Villani, vii. 2-10; H. xxviii. 16; Pg. xiii. 105. The Guelfs return to Florence, the Ghibelines are driven out; and all Tuscany except Pisa and Siena becomes Guelf.

1268. Battle of Tagliacozzo, August 23. Conradin the last of the Hohenstaufen is defeated by Charles of Anjou and captured in his flight through the treachery of Frangipani. Vill. vii. 27. Conradin beheaded, October 29. Ib. id. 29.

1269. The Sienese and other Ghibelines under Provenzano Salvani and Count Guido Novello defeated by the Florentines at Colle in Valdelsa in June. Vill. vii. 31; Pg. xi. 121; xiii. 115.

1271. Gregory X. elected Pope. Vill. vii. 39. Charles of Anjou's deputy in Tuscany, Guy of Montfort, is murdered in the Church of Viterbo by Henry, son of Richard of Cornwall. H. xii. 118. King Enzo, son of Frederick II., dies in prison at Bologna.

1272. Henry III. of England dies, Nov. 16, succeeded by Edward I. Pg. vii. 130.

1273. Gregory X. passes through Florence in July on his way to the Council of Lyons, and sets on foot a reconciliation between Guelfs and Ghibelines. The peace lasts four days only, and then the Ghibelines are driven out again. The Pope leaves the town in anger, and places it under an interdict; quarrelling also with Charles of Anjou. Vill. vii. 42. Rudolf of Habsburg elected Emperor. Pg. vii. 91.

1274. Thomas Aquinas dies at Fossa Nuova, March 7. Pg. xx. 69 : P. x. 99 ; xii. 111. The Lambertacci, Ghibelines of Bologna, driven out, June 2. St. Bonaventura, 'the Seraphic Doctor,' dies July 15. P. xii. 127.

1275. Count Ugolino and the Guelfs driven out of Pisa. Malatesta of Rimini and the Bolognese defeated by Count Guy of Montefeltro at San Brocolo. Peter della Brosse, Secretary to Philip III. of France, put to death. Pg. vi. 19. The Ghibelines driven out of Florence again. Branca d' Oria murders his father-in-law Michael Zanche in order to get possession of the jurisdiction of Logodoro in Sardinia. H. xxii. 88; xxxiii. 136.

1276. The Pisans defeated by the Florentines and Lucchese at Pontedera; Count Ugolino and the Guelfs return to Pisa. Gregory X. dies at Arezzo. The poet Guido Guinicelli of Bologna dies. Pg. xxiv. 92. The Della Torre are driven out of Milan and the Visconti regain the chief power.

1277. Hadrian V. is succeeded in the Papacy by Nicholas III. of the Orsini. H. xix. 31 ; Pg. xix. sqq. ; Vill. vii. 54.

1278. Quarrels in Florence between the Adimari on one side, the Donati, Tosinghi, and Pazzi on the other. The Pope sends Cardinal Latino to Florence as peacemaker who effects a reconciliation. Vill. vii. 56. Ottocar king of Bohemia dies. Pg. vii. 100.

1279. Albert the Great dies. P. x. 98. The coiner, Adam of Brescia, burnt alive. H. xxx. 61. The expelled Ghibelines return to Florence.

1281. Pope Nicholas III. dies August, succeeded in the following January by Martin IV. Pg. xxiv. 20. Sordello dies [probably.] Pg. vi. 74. Guy of Montefeltro beats the French at Forlì. H. xxvii. 43.

1282. Sicilian Vespers. P. viii. 73. In Florence the government of the Fourteen is stopped, and the office of Priors introduced in their place. Vill. vii. 59. Laws are passed against the *Grandi*, i.e. the prominent families. The war between the Genoese and Pisans begins. Vill. vii. 84.

1283. Great festivities in Florence. Vill. vii. 89. Quarrel between Charles of Anjou and Peter of Aragon. Ib. id. 86, 87.

1284. Charles, son of Charles of Anjou, taken prisoner. Pg. xx. 79. The Pisans defeated by the Genoese at Meloria in the bloodiest engagement of the Middle Ages. Accession of Philip the Fair. Peter III. of Aragon dies.

1285. Charles of Anjou dies at Foggia, Jan. 7. Martin IV. dies at Perugia, March 24. Pg. xxiv. 22. Honorius IV. succeeds. Vill. vii. 106. The Florentines decide to enlarge the city.

1286. Great scarcity in Florence and all over Italy.

1287. Honorius IV. dies, succeeded by Nicholas IV. The Guelfs driven out of Arezzo and consequent enmity between the Florentines and Aretines. Vill. vii. 115, 120. Two serious fires in Florence. Serfdom is abolished by law.

1288. The Guelfs driven out of Pisa and Count Ugolino imprisoned. Vill. vii. 121. Campaign of the Florentines against Arezzo. Founding of the Hospital at Florence by Simon dei Bardi. Great inundation in Florence.

1289. Death of Count Ugolino. H. xxxiii. Victory of the Florentines over the Ghibelines of Arezzo at Campaldino. H. xx. 1 sqq.; Pg. v. 91 sqq. Siege of Caprona. H. xxi. 94. Charles II. of Anjou returns from imprisonment in Aragon and is anointed King of Sicily by the Pope. The Florentines make an unsuccessful attempt to get possession of the city of Arezzo by treachery. Vill. vii. 138.

1290. Conflagration in Oltrarno in Florence whereby the old family of the Pegolotti are nearly annihilated. The period of office of the Podesta is reduced from a year to six months. The Florentines make a fresh campaign against Arezzo. Together with the Genoese and Lucchese they attack the Pisans and destroy the harbour of Pisa. Vill. vii. 138-140.

1291. The Christians lose Acre, their last station in the Holy Land. H. xxvii. 89; P. ix. 137. Philip the Fair has all Italians in France arrested and holds them to ransom, whereby the Florentine merchants suffer great losses and are in some cases ruined. Vill. vii. 147. Guy of Montefeltro, as captain of the Pisans, captures Pontedera, the most important fortress of the Florentines. These make a fruitless campaign against the Pisans.

1292. Death of Pope Nicholas IV., and interregnum till 1294. Death of William VII., Marquis of Montferrat, and a war in consequence between the Alexandrians and the sons of the Marquis. Pg. vii. 133. An important but unsuccessful campaign of the Florentines against Pisa.

1293. New constitution in Florence. The so-called reform of Giano della Bella. Vill. viii. 1.; P. xvi. 132. Peace between Florence and Pisa. Another fire breaks out in Florence with the destruction of more than thirty houses.

1294. Celestine V. Pope. H. iii. 59; xxvii. 105. Boniface VIII. Pope. D.C., *passim*. Foundation of the Church of Santa Croce at Florence. Giano della Bella expelled from Florence. Carlo Martello, son of Charles II. of Anjou, and titular King of Hungary, visits Florence. P. xviii. 31 sqq. Brunetto Latini dies. H. xv. 23.

1295. Carlo Martello dies. Revolution made by the Florentine aristocracy to overthrow the democratic constitution. It passes without bloodshed and things remain as they were, but it becomes the germ of the subsequent fighting and disorder, for from that time forward the aristocracy were continually devising schemes to destroy the power of the people, while the leaders of the democracy thought how they might depress the aristocrats. Vill. viii. 12. The Guelfs are driven out of Genoa.

1296. Death of Celestine V. Frederick of Aragon acquires the lordship of Sicily and is crowned king in Palermo. P. xix. 130; xx. 63.

1297. Beginning of the quarrel between Boniface VIII. and the Colonna. Enmity between the Pope and Philip the Fair.

1298. Building of the Palace of the Priors, or Government offices, in Florence. War between Venice and Genoa. The Genoese under Lamba d' Oria are victorious in a sea-fight off Curzola. Vill. viii. 24. Great earthquakes in Italy, whereby many buildings are destroyed in Rieti, Spoleto, and Pistoia.

1299. Peace between Genoa and Venice, and between Genoa and Pisa. The building of the third city wall is begun in Florence.

1300. The jubilee in Rome and enormous concourse of pilgrims. According to Villani, who was himself among them, and there came to the decision to write his history,

200,000 pilgrims were in Rome throughout the year every day, not counting those who were arriving and departing. H. xviii. 28; Vill. viii. 36. Quarrels in Pistoia where the parties of the Blacks and Whites came into existence, being afterwards transplanted to Florence. H. xxii. 63. Civil war in Florence. Cardinal Matthew of Acquasparta is sent by Boniface VIII. as peacemaker, the Pope's scheme being to bring the whole of Tuscany into the states of the Church. The Whites oppose it, the Blacks form a conspiracy in the Church of the Holy Trinity. Vill. viii. 41. Boniface summons Charles of Valois to Florence nominally as peacemaker. The heads of both parties are banished.

1301. The Blacks are driven out of Pistoia, the Whites out of Lucca. In Genoa the banished Guelfs return peacefully. Entry of Charles of Valois into Florence followed by civil war and banishment of the Whites.

1302. The first two judgments given against Dante. Treachery of Carlino dei Pazzi on behalf of the Blacks. Vill. viii. 53; H. xxxii. 69. Many conspicuous citizens of the White party who have remained in Florence are executed by Fulcieri da Calboli. Pg. xiv. 58. The Whites and Ghibelines under Scarpetta degli Ordelaffi are defeated at Puliciano in the Mugello. Vill. viii. 59, 60. Fresh attempts at reconciliation made by Cardinal d'Acquasparta without result. Charles of Valois concludes a disgraceful peace with Frederick of Aragon. Vill. viii. 49. The Visconti driven out of Milan.

1303. Boniface VIII. is taken prisoner at Anagni and dies October 12. Pg. xx. 85; Vill. viii. 63. Benedict XI. succeeds. The Florentines' campaign against Pistoia.

1304. Pope Benedict sends Cardinal da Prato to Florence to make peace. His good intentions are thwarted by the heads of the Black party, and on June 4 he departs, laying the city under an interdict. Theatrical representation of the next world held on May 4. The Ponte alla Carraia falls in with great loss of life. Immediately afterwards street fighting and great conflagration in Florence. The Whites and Ghibelines make a fruitless attempt to return by force of arms. Vill. viii. 69-72. Benedict XI. dies, Clement V. elected Pope, and removes the Papal See to Avignon. The Aretines capture the castle of Laterino from the Florentines. The Florentines assume the offensive against the Whites and capture their castles Le Stinche in Valdigrieve and Montecalvi in Val di Pesa.

1305. Pistoia is besieged and captured by the Blacks of Florence in alliance with the Lucchese. Thereupon the Whites are in February of the next year driven out of Bologna. Fra Dolcino in Lombardy. H. xxviii. 55.

1306. Clement V. sends Cardinal Orsini as peacemaker to Florence, but the Blacks who are in power decline to receive him, so he lays the city under a fresh interdict. Thence he goes to Bologna to make peace between the Guelfs and Ghibelines there, but there also is repulsed with contumely by the Guelfs. Successful campaign of the Florentines against the Ubaldini, the supporters of the Whites and Ghibelines. Reform of the democratic constitution in Florence to the disadvantage of the aristocracy.

1307. Suppression of the Templars. Vill. viii. 92; Pg. xx. 91. Extinction of Fra Dolcino and his sect.

1308. Albert of Austria murdered. Pg. vi. 97. Carlo d' Amelia, podesta of Florence, flies in order to avoid a penalty to which he has become liable, taking the city seal with him. Death of Corso Donati. Pg. xxiv. 82. Peace between Florence and Arezzo. The Guelfs return to the latter after twenty-one years' banishment. The Ubaldini make peace with the Florentines. Henry of Luxembourg elected emperor. Vill. viii. 101.

1309. Henry VII. crowned at Aachen on the Epiphany. Charles II., king of Naples, dies, his son Robert takes the crown. P. viii. 76. The Venetians capture Ferrara, and lose it again. The Guelfs are driven out of Arezzo, and war breaks out again between that city and Florence. In Genoa Guelfs and Ghibelines unite to expel the tyrant Ubizzino Spinoli. Defeat of the Venetians by the Papal forces before Ferrara, which is taken from them after a sanguinary battle. Vill. viii. 115.

1310. Henry VII.'s envoys, with Lewis of Savoy at their head, vainly endeavour to induce the Florentines to abandon hostilities against Arezzo. Rise of the Flagellants in Italy. The Guelfs driven out of Venice. Vill. ix. 2; and Spoleto. Henry VII. begins his journey to Rome. At the end of September he starts from Lausanne, reaching Asti on October 10, where he stays two months. The Florentines take measures to resist the emperor.

1311. Henry VII. crowned with the iron crown at Milan on the Epiphany. Vill. ix. 9. He takes Cremona and Vicenza. The Guelfs of Tuscany, under the lead of the Florentines, make a league against the emperor. He takes Brescia after a long siege, and marches to Genoa, where his wife dies. The Florentines refuse to receive the emperor's envoys, whereupon he threatens reprisals. Brescia revolts again.

1312. Disturbance in Florence in consequence of the murder of Pazzino dei Pazzi. Vill. ix. 32. The Cavalcanti are banished on account of it. Cremona revolts against the emperor, also Padua, at the instigation of the Florentines. Henry goes by way of Pisa to be crowned at Rome. Vill. ix. 42. Then he returns to Arezzo and begins the siege of Florence. Ibid. 47.

1313. Henry dies at Buonconvento on August 24, having, according to the belief of the time, taken poison in the consecrated host. The Pisans who had held by the emperor elect Uguccione della Faggiuola as their chief after the office had been declined by Frederick, king of Sicily, the Count of Savoy, and others. The Florentines assign the lordship of their city for five years to Robert, king of Naples. In Genoa a split among the Ghibelines is followed by civil war, conflagration, and pestilence. The Spinoli are finally expelled from the city. Uguccione and the Pisans make war upon Lucca and compel that city to receive back the banished Ghibelines.

1314. Clement V. dies April 20. H. xix. 79 sqq. Uguccione captures Lucca, June 14. King Robert sends his younger brother Peter as his deputy to Florence. He is well received. Vill. ix. 60. Victory of Can Grande della Scala over the Paduans near Vicenza, September 18. In the same month peace is made between Florence and Arezzo. Philip the Fair dies in November by a fall from his horse. P. xix. 120. Lewis of Bavaria elected emperor. Lewis X. of France marries Clemenza daughter of Carlo Martello.

1315. Brilliant success of Uguccione over the Florentines and Guelfs at Monte Catini. Various reforms in Florence. On November 6, Dante and his sons are sentenced by King Robert's deputy to death by beheading.

1316. Dissension among the Guelfs at Florence. Uguccione is driven out of Pisa and Lucca, and takes refuge with Can Grande at Verona. Castruccio Castracani becomes Lord of Lucca. The Count of Battifolle, as Governor at Florence, introduces various reforms. Vill. ix. 77. John XXII. elected Pope.

1317. King Robert persuades the Florentines to make

peace with the Pisans and Lucchese. A new coinage in Florence. King Robert goes to war with King Frederick of Sicily. Revolution in Ferrara resulting in the supremacy of the house of Este. Uguccione makes an unsuccessful attempt to return to Pisa. The Ghibelines are driven out of Genoa. Can Grande at war with Cremona and Padua.

1318. Genoa besieged by the banished Ghibelines and their allies. The Genoese assign the lordship of their city to King Robert. The Ghibelines are defeated and compelled to raise the siege. Revolution in Siena, which is suppressed with the aid of the Florentines. Can Grande is elected head of the Ghibeline league of Lombardy.

1319. Genoa again besieged by the banished Ghibelines. Can Grande captures the suburbs of Padua, and the Ghibelines of Lombardy again get possession of Cremona. Marco Visconti defeats King Robert's army at Alessandria. The Ghibelines take Spoleto and burn the captured Guelfs in prison, 'which was an abominable cruelty.' Vill. ix. 102.

1320. Castruccio Castracani at war with the Florentines. The Genoese Ghibelines beaten at Lerici. Inglorious march of Philip of Valois to Italy. Genoa besieged again. Can Grande defeated before Padua. Death of Uguccione della Faggiuola. Pisa reverts to the Ghibelines.

1321. The Florentines form an alliance with the Marquis Spinetta Malaspina to break the power of Castruccio, but only gain disgrace. Revision of the constitution at Florence. Defeat of the Guelfs in Lombardy. Galeazzo Visconti captures Cremona. Dante dies at Ravenna in September. Vill. ix. 134.

PART I
DANTE IN HIS HOME

CHAPTER I

SOURCES OF INFORMATION AND AIDS TO STUDY

NEARLY forty years ago Carl Witte, the ever-memorable Dante scholar, wrote in his *Dante-Forschungen*, vol. i. p. 72, 'We have had detailed accounts of Dante's life in considerable numbers for the last five hundred years. Yet the data on which we can rely are incredibly few. In order to fill up the large gaps, biographers have been accustomed to allow a free rein to their own fancy or that of their predecessors. We hear much about the intimate friendships of the poet with this or that prince or lord, of frequent missions with which he was entrusted, and other proofs of the honourable confidence which he enjoyed, of profound and salutary counsels which he gave, of universities where he learnt or taught, of courts where he stayed, of castles, convents, and caves in which he composed; in short, of many things excellent and charming in themselves which only lack one thing to complete their value, namely, some corroboration of their truth which it is possible to accept. Then follow pages of extracts from Dante's writings, more or less digested, seasoned with some quite impracticable new explanation of the *Veltro*, the *Donna gentile*, the *Maledetta lupa*, the *DXV*, and so forth, and half an octavo volume, or perhaps the whole of it, is complete. This kind of literature may no doubt be useful to people who in this way make acquaintance for the first time with the points under consideration. But he who has relished half a dozen or so of such "characteristics," "biographies," and the like, may fairly be acquitted of discourtesy if he excuses himself on the plea of loss of appetite when some thick volume by Artaud, or Missirini, or any of the rest of them, is set before him.'

These words are true at the present day and well worth laying to heart. Since they were written the tale of books dealing with the history of Dante's life has been more than trebled, and even Witte in later days was now and again in the position of having to publish reports on works of the kind. Yet we are no whit richer in positive historic knowledge, though we have had plenty of hypotheses and conjectures, for the most part of no value. In nearly all literary languages we possess countless historical romances which pass themselves off as biographies of the poet and claim to be history. Yet one can never repeat sufficiently that, while we have biographic Dante romances to our hearts' content, we possess no history whatever of the poet's life, and there is at present little or no prospect of our ever possessing such. The sources upon which we can depend yield far too scanty a stream. This is indeed the main reason why we possess such innumerable romances on the subject. Boccaccio wrote the first, and up to the day before yesterday we have all been only too faithfully his disciples. We have eked out the incredibly scanty historical matter with incredibly copious combinations, deductions, hypotheses, and assumptions, and therewith have made our romances flourish to such a point that those who do not know the facts might easily fall into the belief that we were in a position to give, if necessary, accurate and trustworthy information about every day of Dante's life from his cradle to his grave. And what, after all, do we actually know that is positive and historically established? Our scientific conscience, if we will only listen to it, will tell us that we have about enough to fill a couple of pages, enough indeed for a short tract, but in no way sufficient for even the most modest volume. It is indeed possible in a general way to understand and enjoy a work of art without having any intimate acquaintance with the development and fortunes of the artist. Even one who knows nothing of Lewes and Düntzer, Hofmeister and Gervinus, may arrive at a complete understanding and enjoyment of the immortal creations of Goethe, Schiller, and Shakespeare. But with Dante the case is otherwise. He is unique among poets before or since in having 'infused his whole self into one great work, and therewith the political and religious life of his people, and compressed therein in a magnificent fashion every side of the feeling, the belief, and the science of his century. Mediaevalism was beginning to break up, but he immerses himself once more in its ideals, and presents them in poetic form as the one and only means of salvation and redemption, being at the same time the first mighty exponent of the civic mind, of the nobility of the soul, of the free spirit which were now taking the place of feudal chivalry and ecclesiasticism. He is wholly subjective, he displays to us the history of his own soul, he himself with his wrath and his love is the centre of his poem, that epic of the inner man in which we have the completion of that which Wolfram von Eschenbach began; but his method of representation has a plastic distinctness which presupposes the eye of the hunter, painter, or natural historian.'[1]

A thorough comprehension of Dante's poem is conse-

[1] Carrières, *Die Kunst in Zusammenhang der Culturentwickelung.*

quently impossible unless we know the poet himself as he lived and struggled, worked, hoped, and endured. But from what source are we to attain this previous knowledge? First of all from his own works. Dante did not indeed write confessions like Augustine, still less like Rousseau, nor reminiscences of his life like Goethe. As in his view of the universe, so in his own individuality he stands always unapproachable among great poets and writers. Not only is he himself the centre of his own great poem, but with his custom of measuring everything by himself he has, in all his writings, the treatise on *Monarchy* perhaps excepted, spoken so often and so much about himself, that even were no other source available, his picture in its broader and even in its individual traits can be reconstructed from his own writings. This reconstruction is, however, involved in considerable difficulty. Poet as he was, and at the same time a child of his epoch, everything—even what affects himself personally—assumes in Dante's hands a poetic and at the same time an allegorical garb, and it is very often difficult, at times almost impossible, to extract the real historical kernel with any certainty from the poetic and allegoric shell. Incredible as it may sound, this is the case even with the letters which have come down to us under the name of Dante. To this must be added that, as we shall see later on, the genuineness of these letters is in all cases problematic and in many something more. Thus Dante's works are and remain our chief sources of information in regard to his biography, and sources, too, from which it is not in every man's power to draw with any vessel that pleases him. It is easy enough to support some historical theory with a quotation from the *Vita Nuova*, the *Convito*, or the *Commedia*, but there is always the question whether what you believe you have found in the passage is really there. Paur has remarked quite correctly that it would be possible simply from Dante's poetical works, and with no aid from other sources, to extract in some measure an ideal history of him which might perhaps fall short in documentary precision, but not the least in inward truth, nor yet in completeness as regards the most important facts. But documentary precision is just the point in which the conscientious historian does not like to fail; and when, as in Dante's poems, so many various interpretations are admissible, this precision is only to be obtained from them in a small percentage of cases.

It may be obtained with the greatest security from such records as are undoubtedly genuine. Dante having been not only a great poet, but also a prominent statesman, such records are fortunately not lacking. For instance, to name only one. We have the testimony of records with regard to the poet's activity in the public service of his country, more especially from the period immediately preceding and following his tenure of the office of prior, June 15 to August 15, 1300, as well as the sentences which were pronounced against him from 1302 onwards. Unfortunately these records have never been collected, and they still have to be hunted up from various writings which are not always easily accessible. Nor indeed are all of them wholly free from doubt as to their genuineness. No sooner was the poet dead than busy gossip took possession of him and called into existence not only a long series of more or less ingenious anecdotes, but even writings which were ascribed to him and documents which claimed to throw a light on events in his career. Hence it becomes the indispensable task of criticism to apply without prejudice, but in a seriously scientific spirit, the strictest tests for the accuracy of every record.

Dante's eyes were hardly closed when he attained a high and steadily-increasing renown. Naturally it became an object to the next generation to learn something about his personality, his life, and his works. People began early to meet this demand for information. The chronicler John Villani, a slightly younger contemporary of the poet, his acquaintance and neighbour for many years, has done for him what he has done for few others, and devoted to him an entire chapter of his history. This is the oldest and also the most trustworthy, we might go so far as to say in an historical sense the only trustworthy, biography of Dante. Yet even this biography is very meagre and not devoid of errors. For instance, he gives, according to most manuscripts and the oldest edition of his chronicle, July 1321 as the month of Dante's death, whereas he undoubtedly died in September. But even if this is the original reading, which is by no means decided, we should have to take into consideration that, in the existing circumstances of Florence, Villani could hardly have accurately ascertained the day on which his great fellow-citizen died in Ravenna. Of a similar nature is the very vague statement that Dante went after his banishment to the university of Bologna, from thence to Paris and into various countries. There is no serious reason to doubt it; the historian knew that his former neighbour had gone to Bologna and to Paris; he would further have known perhaps from Dante's *Convito* that, at all events for a considerable time after his banishment, he had led an unsettled wandering life, but he would not know whither he had actually betaken himself. What he knew positively, that he stated precisely—Bologna and Paris; what he did not know precisely he indicated vaguely with the phrase 'e in più parti del mondo.' This circumstance, far from diminishing the credibility of the old chronicler, shows rather with what precision he went to work in compiling the section of his history which we are considering. Wherever, then, Villani makes a distinct and positive assertion his statements are to be treated as historically accurate until they are proved to be in error by indubitable data from another quarter.

Was it good or ill fortune for Dante that the no less renowned than learned and loquacious author of the *Decameron* was his first actual biographer and for centuries to come the parent of all biographers of Dante? Some four decades after Dante's death (about 1363) John Boccaccio wrote his biography of Dante, or, as he himself modestly calls his work, his 'little treatise in honour of Dante'—the first Dante romance. His aim was not indeed to investigate and establish the historic facts of the biography; it was purely apologetic. He wished to set up a monument in honour of the poet whom he idolised, to deliver a brilliant discourse in his praise, and at the same time in eloquent words to chastise the Florentines for having banished such a citizen from their city, allowed him to die in exile, and as yet taken no thought at least to beg back his mortal remains. A thoroughly honourable and upright man, Boccaccio does not indeed deserve the reproach of having deliberately composed a fictitious biography. But in truth he was a poet and not a student of history; historic criticism was quite out of his line. The declamations, moralisings, and invectives which form the greater part of his work he extracted partly from his own materials and still more from those of others. His invective against women is borrowed from Theophrastus, his digression on poetry from Petrarch. For his professedly historical notices Boccaccio did not deem it necessary to look to original documents; he drew from Villani, and still more from oral tradition. And as legends were already flourishing freely around the figure of Dante, Boccaccio's work could not fail to consist mainly of legends, in some cases doubtful, in others absolutely unhistoric. Moreover, the biographer has set no check on his fancy; on the contrary, he has allowed it to take full command of him. From this source, indeed, he seems exclusively to have drawn his rhetorical talk about Dante's childhood and youth. We must further remark that he trusted to his own recollection, and that this frequently deceived him, as, for example, when he makes the poet be born in the time of Urban IV. instead of that of Clement IV. This work, then, though doubtless well intended and a fine monument of literature, valuable too, indeed indispensable, for the historic study of Dante, has to be used with the greatest caution.

In spite of all his incontestable defects, however, Boccaccio may boast of countless successors. His work being loaded with a good deal of useless and often tedious ballast, people began to abridge it. One of these abridgements has been four times printed, and is now and again quoted in place of the complete work. There have even been learned men who from want of acquaintance with all the facts have expressed and sought to defend the view that the abridgement was Boccaccio's own work. Other similar abridgements are lying yet unprinted in manuscripts. Then followed biographers who issued independent works, but yet drew almost exclusively from Boccaccio. So again in the fourteenth century we have Philip Villani, nephew of the historian, Francesco da Buti, and other editors who prefixed to their commentaries short biographies of the poet. Villani gives only an extract from Boccaccio, making use at the same time of his uncle's chapter on Dante. Buti, Benvenuto Rambaldi and other commentators content themselves with Boccaccio, adding only some few details thereto which they have obviously deduced from passages of the poem. In general it is to be remarked that while in the older commentaries to the *Divine Comedy* one is constantly lighting upon biographical notices, these can only be used with caution, since in the great majority of cases they are derived merely from the writer's own interpretation, whether right or wrong, of the passage before him.

In the fifteenth century, Leonardo Bruni of Arezzo (1369-1444), the Florentine secretary of state, came forward with a new life of Dante, which was admittedly written in opposition to Boccaccio. Accordingly, Bruni now and again expressly contradicts his predecessor, and gives a good deal of new matter to which some value cannot be denied. At one time he was universally honoured as absolutely trustworthy, but in our day he has been charged with writing to maintain a thesis, and most of his new information has been questioned. That he has been guilty of error is not to be denied, but it will be difficult to convict him of having deliberately invented his facts. He wrote, as he himself says, for his own recreation, and therefore may, no doubt, have neglected to investigate thoroughly. Still his work is one of the most important among the old biographies of Dante, and his statements always deserve to be taken into consideration.

The biographers who immediately follow are wholly unimportant. Gianozzo Manetti (1396-1450) draws exclusively from Boccaccio, Villani, and Bruni without adding any information whatever which is not to be found in his predecessors. Domenico di Maestro Bandini of Arezzo copies Villani, mistakes and all. Valueless, too, are the short biographies by Landino, Vellutello, and Daniello, while Giovanni Maria Filelfo does not deserve to be reckoned among the biographers of Dante, for he merely copies Boccaccio and Bruni with the addition of some demonstrable inventions.

About the middle of last century Giuseppe Pelli wrote his charming work, which is even yet by no means obsolete in spite of the many mistakes which it contains. Pelli was the first who looked out for records; which he collected and published and used as the bases of his work. He was followed by the more cautious and critical historian of literature, Tiraboschi, whose work, however, does not form an important contribution to the study of Dante. With him the line of the older biographers comes to an end.

With Carlo Troya of Naples began a new and unfortunate period of historic investigation which may be called the period of fancy. Troya's book, *Il Veltro allegorico di Dante*, 1826, was regarded at its appearance and long afterwards, in spite of the criticisms of Witte and others, as a revelation. With a confidence which must needs startle us, the daily fortunes and experiences of the poet were described exactly as if he had bequeathed his diary to the author. And indeed the diary was extant: it was the *Divine Comedy* which for this purpose was turned into a journal of travel. Upon a foundation of pure hypothesis, assumptions, and combinations a very stately building was erected: another Dante romance! And this romance claimed to be history founded on records. The alleged records were indeed not imparted, but a prospect of their publication was held out. But as they were not in existence they naturally could not be published. Great was the disappointment when thirty years later appeared Troya's book, *Il Veltro allegorico dei Ghibelini*, in which the promised records were to have been brought out. They were not indeed altogether lacking, and to some extent not devoid of importance, but they proved terribly little of what they should have proved.

Meanwhile Count Cesare Balbo, sitting before his own mirror, had produced a brilliant portrait of the poet which till quite recently passed as an original. Balbo's excellently written book, a complete biography with no gaps, for all gaps in the history were beautifully filled up by conjectures, for some decades formed the main source for Dante biographers both in and out of Italy. Even at the present day the most popular and best accounts of Dante's life in Italian, German, English, and French are practically derived from Balbo, historical romances executed with more or less ability of which it is difficult to say whether they have done more good or harm to the study of Dante. To be quite fair all round, I may here point out that my own biography of Dante, published in 1869, belongs to this category.

Balbo was out-done by Missirini. In his case the firm ground of history was completely deserted, and the book is a mere romance passing itself off as a biography. The author, it must be admitted, believed quite confidently in his romance, he was actually credulous enough to imagine that he had discovered the genuine portrait of Beatrice. His ambitious work must be regarded to-day as utterly unserviceable. Fraticelli's work is of more use, so far as it gives in a printed form the documents collected by Pelli, and makes a valuable addition to them. So far as his own exposition goes, Fraticelli walks entirely in the footsteps of Troya and Balbo, in spite of all his claim to historic criticism.

The late Todeschini has the uncontested merit of having been one of the first to substitute historic and critical work for the writing of pleasant romances. He did not write a life of Dante, but his smaller writings, which remained sufficiently long unnoticed, pointed out the necessity of the critical method, and stirred up others to pursue it. Todeschini's footsteps have been followed by Imbriani, Isidoro del Lungo, and Adolfo Bartoli. The life of Dante by the last of these indicates the high-water mark so far of criticism wedded to scepticism. He states indeed expressly that his work is intended to be much more negative than positive; a very modest work, he calls it, meant to indicate which are the few certain facts of Dante's life, which the probable, which the doubtful. Let us add which are the undoubtedly fictitious, and therewith we shall have stated as much as the researcher into the history of Dante's life can at present accomplish. A complete biography of the poet, free from gaps and properly rounded off, cannot be written in the existing state of scientific research.

CHAPTER II

ORIGIN

IN the domain of historic research ignorance with regard to Dante extends farther back than to his birth. To the question, 'Who were the ancestors of the poet?' we can give no answer even approximately satisfactory. If we wished to give a table of descent in the manner of the Bible, it would run as follows:—Dante was the son of Alighiero, which was the son of Bellincione, which was the son of Alighiero, which was the son of Cacciaguida, which was the son ——, and here we are wholly at the end of our knowledge. If we are asked what was the rank of these forefathers, we must answer, 'some say that they were noble, some say that they belong merely of the upper class, others again that they belong to the common people.' Learned men have discussed and debated about it, but have not yet come to an approximately certain result. Those among them who are honest are quite ready to admit that we are still as uncertain as ever on this point.

Of Cacciaguida, the oldest ancestor of Dante whose name has been preserved, the bare existence and no more can be proved from records. The poet himself informs us that Cacciaguida was born in Florence, and baptized there (very probably in 1090 or 1091, but even this date is by no means undoubted. See P. xv. 130; xvi. 37); that he had two brothers, Moronto and Eliseo, that he took his wife from the valley of the Po, probably from Ferrara (but some think Padua or Verona is meant), and that from her, an Aldighieri, the poet's surname had its origin, that he took part in the crusade, that the Emperor Conrad III. gave him the belt of knighthood, and that he lost his life in battle against the infidels. Even though the poet may have erred in his chronology, there is all the less ground to doubt the credibility of his statements that he takes this very opportunity of proving that he knew how to hold his tongue when neither history nor tradition gave him any materials. Upon the request that Cacciaguida would tell him something about his own forefathers, the poet makes him reply:

> This much
> Suffice of my forefathers; who they were
> And whence they hither came more honourable
> It is to pass in silence than to tell.

In this touch we can hardly fail to see an open admission on the poet's part, that he himself knew nothing about his ancestors before Cacciaguida. Objections have indeed been taken to this interpretation, which, however, we can hardly hold for well grounded. The speaker, it has been said, is Cacciaguida, and he must have known who his ancestors were and whence they came. No doubt, but the real speaker is Dante; Cacciaguida holds that place only by poetic fiction: his great-great-grandfather's knowledge was of no use to the poet if he did not partake it. But why then did he put the question if he could not answer it? To bring out the fact that his ancestors lived in the quarter of Porta San Pietro, where, as a rule, patrician families resided. But that the passage contains, as has been supposed, a reproach against Cacciaguida's forefathers, is, if not impossible, in the highest degree unlikely. The passage, in which the poet is obviously intending to glorify his race, was certainly not the place to hint ever so obscurely that his earlier ancestors were people of whom it was best to say nothing.

So far as concerns Cacciaguida's two brothers, it is simple and most reasonable to admit, without any circumlocution, that we know nothing whatever about them. The theory that Eliseo was the founder of the well-known Florentine noble family the Elisei deserves no consideration, seeing that the family in question existed more than a century earlier. In a document of the year 1076 are mentioned the issue of one Moronto de Arco, who stood in relation to the Church of St. Martin as Cacciaguida's descendants did later. Hence an opinion has been formed that this old Moronto de Arco may have been an ancestor of Dante. It has further been supposed, with considerable positiveness, and with an appeal to documents said to be in existence, that *de Arcu* or *de Arcu pietatis* was the special designation of the Elisei. Pursuing this road people have come to the assumption, which has now and again been given out as an historically established fact, that Dante belonged to the family of the Elisei, or at least was of kindred stock to them. Boccaccio has been appealed to in support of this, but who can place any reliance on the testimony of the man who informs us with all seriousness that Dante's family came in the direct line from the family of Frangipani? One regrets the time, the ink, and the paper which have been expended in the treatment of the question whether and to what extent the poet was of the same stock with the ancient noble family of the Elisei. In the first place nothing absolutely certain is known about it; and further, it has been overlooked that all assumptions of the kind are overthrown by the lines quoted above. Had Dante had any knowledge of his descent from or kinship with a house of such old repute as the Elisei he would certainly not have put into the mouth of his ancestor Cacciaguida a statement that it was more seemly to be silent than to speak on the question who his forefathers were and whence they came. This proof is certainly not decisive; only one thing is absolutely indubitable, that we know just nothing for certain about the forefathers or the family connections of Cacciaguida; for even the consideration that the houses of Dante and his forefathers, as well as of the Elisei, were situated in the above-mentioned quarter of the city is clearly not to the point. Neighbourhood has surely little or nothing to do with family connection. Two sons of Cacciaguida are mentioned in documents, Alighiero and Preitenitto. Of the latter we know further that he had a son called Bonareddita, whose name appears in 1215. Alighiero is named in a document of the year 1201, and indicated by the poet himself as a man who for a hundred years and more had had to circle the mount of Purification on the first cornice in order to purge himself of his pride (P. xv. 91). We have no further information about him. So far as is known he had two sons, Bello and Bellincione. The first, who was of the council in the year 1255, was the son of Gieri del Bello, who was stabbed by a Sacchetti, and whom Dante places in Hell (H. xxix. 27). Bellincione had four sons, Gherardo, Brunetto, and Cione, Dante's uncles, who, on the authority of what documents we do not know, have been mentioned as *popolani;* and Alighiero, the father of the poet. Of this last we shall have more to say.

This is briefly all that we know about Dante's forefathers. If it is further asked to what rank they belonged, we shall be yet more perplexed to give an answer. Jacopo della Lana, who wrote his commentary about 1328—not long, that is, after the poet's death—says that he belonged to an ancient and noble family. The nameless author of the so-called *Ottimo Comento*, who wrote ten or twelve years after Dante's death, and according to his own assertion was personally intimate with him, assures us that the forefathers even of Cacciaguida had been noble. What Boccaccio says in his life of Dante has, as we have already observed, no historic value, and there is another reason for holding the contrary. In his lectures on the *Divine Comedy*, which he gave publicly at Florence, and out of which he formed his commentary upon the first part of the *Hell*, Boccaccio asserts that the poet was by descent among 'the nobility of our city.' At that time, some half-century after the poet's death, when doubtless there were still living in Florence persons belonging to the family, it must have been well known in Florence whether the family belonged to the nobility or to the people, and if it was known, Boccaccio must have known it, and if so he would never have ventured to make an erroneous statement in a public lecture. The weight of this testimony is therefore not to be underrated. Further, the younger Villani states that he had it from his forefathers that the poet came of a very noble family. In a document of the year 1299, which, however, as we shall see by and by, is of somewhat doubtful authenticity, Dante is called a nobleman, *nobilem virum Dantem de Aligheriis*. We are therefore in presence of the fact that the view which has universally prevailed since Boccaccio's time, as to Dante's having sprung from a noble family, is no baseless conjecture, but has ancient tradition in its favour.

This tradition is supported by the following facts. In the 10th canto of the *Hell*, where the famous scene with Farinata degli Uberti occurs, the poet makes him ask first of all: Who were thy ancestors?—a question which, in the mouth of the proud chief of the Ghibelines, can only mean that he wishes to know who is standing before him, lest he should haply find himself in conversation with a man of the lower classes. Dante at once gives him full information on the point, whereupon Farinata raises his eyebrows, and says that the poet's forefathers had been terrible foes to him, his ancestors, and all his party. This presupposes, not exactly a noble, but at any rate an eminent and important family.

In the 8th canto of the *Paradise* Dante refers to his intimate relations with Carlo Martello of Naples. Who was Dante then in the year 1294 when the titular king of Hungary visited Florence? Doubtless he had already come to the front as a poet; but would the king have been satisfied to have entered into close relations with the young poet if he could lay claim to no other title? Possible, but not very likely.

Was Dante, then, of noble origin? If so, what was the name of the noble family to which he belonged? No name whatever of any such is known. It is true that even in the case of the most famous families of Italy up till late in the Middle Ages the *casato*, that is, the family name, is often omitted in documents. We may, indeed, say that this happens most commonly, but not always. How comes it, then, that in no single record is the name given of the noble house to which Dante and his forefathers belonged? John Villani gives (v. 39 and vi. 79) long lists of the noble families belonging to the two parties of Guelfs and Ghibelines, but nowhere in these lists is the name of the Alighieri to be found. It is true he does not claim completeness for his lists; but the Alighieri were, as he says in another connection, his neighbours. Is it conceivable that he should have passed them over in silence if they belonged to the nobility, or even indeed to the patrician class? Hardly. The twenty-fourth chapter of the 'Ordinamenti di Giustizia' contains an enactment that no one of the nobility was, under any circumstances, to fill a place in any of the various councils. Yet we find our poet, three years after the passing of these ordinances aimed at the nobility, upon the council of the Hundred, and in the year 1300 among the still more limited body of the priors. It follows from this, one might almost say with absolute certainty, that Dante's contemporaries and fellow-citizens knew nothing of his alleged nobility, and if they knew nothing of it, how was posterity to arrive at this knowledge?

As may be seen, we are here in presence of a riddle; can it be satisfactorily solved? If Dante was noble, the nature of his nobility may and should be inquired into. Of the distinguished noble families of Italy, the greater number both in the Middle Ages, and even to the present day, boasted of a descent from old noble families. It has been supposed that Dante's family might also be noble after this fashion. As we have already seen, Boccaccio makes the poet's family descend from the Roman Frangipani. Leonardo Bruni writes: 'Dante's Florentine forefathers were of a very old family. It appears indeed that he wishes in several places to assert that they sprang from the old Romans who founded Florence. This, is, however, very uncertain, and according to my view only a conjecture.' According to this the poet himself is the source of the story. The passages of which the Aretine historian speaks may be reduced to one, namely H. xv. 61-78, from which most recent interpreters have extracted the meaning that Dante claimed descent from the old Romans. I have indicated in another work how little this interpretation is justified. Moreover, the poet says himself of his forefathers,

P. xvi. 44, 'Who they were and whence they came hither' (to Florence that is); but if they migrated from any place to Florence, they obviously did not belong to the Romans, who, as the story went, founded Florence. Thus it is not true that Dante boasts of his Roman descent, so that there is no question here of this kind of nobility. Nor again can there be any question of the official nobility of Carolingian times, nor the Saxon and Frankish feudal nobility which existed in scattered castles throughout the country. No trace can be found of this, nor has anybody asserted it, that the Alighieri were ever invested with offices which carry hereditary nobility, or that they were even feudal lords of castles.

Another kind of nobility was developed during the Middle Ages in the Italian cities. By means of accumulated wealth individual citizens rose to great importance, and so a patrician order of civic nobility grew up. This nobility had become so very prominent in Dante's time, as he himself testifies, that in the common opinion the essence of nobility consisted of ancestral wealth (Conv. iv. 3). But of this kind of nobility there can in the case of our poet be no question, since not only does history know nothing of ancestral wealth in the Alighieri family, but the debts, very considerable for that period, which the poet and his brother Francesco contracted, are a proof that the ancestral wealth of the Alighieri was not of a kind to tempt them to claim nobility. This view finds a full corroboration in the style one might almost say of suppressed anger with which Dante expresses himself both in the treatise on *Monarchy*, and in the fourth book of the *Convito* with regard to nobility founded on wealth.

There was yet another kind of nobility, namely of those who performed their military service on horseback. This belonged not only to those who were of knightly birth, but also to those who were dubbed knights. This honour was as a rule conferred only on those who were entitled to claim it by noble birth, but still it often happened under the early Hohenstaufen that men belonging to the people were raised to the dignity of knights, so that from the fact of a man having been dubbed knight we can draw no inference as to the position of his family. This kind of nobility, too, was hereditary, but could also become extinct in the descendants. According to a Florentine statute of 1415 it did become extinct, if within the space of twenty years a family had produced no one capable of serving on horseback. Whether this enactment held good in the poet's time is not certain, but it is exceedingly probable, since the statutes of 1415 were based on some of much greater antiquity. If Dante then was of noble origin it could only arise from the fact that some one of his forefathers had attained to the dignity of knighthood more than a century before. This was his belief, and his assertion in P. xv. 139, may claim the value of a document. But for the intelligent reader the immediately following verses at the opening of Canto xvi. contain an admission, or we may say an expression, of regret that the nobility so gained had again become extinct in his family. That he did not technically rank as noble appears with absolute certainty from the fact that he took an official part in public affairs.

CHAPTER III

TIME AND PLACE OF DANTE'S BIRTH

No certificate of Dante's birth or baptism has so far come to light, nor indeed is the discovery of any such to be expected, for Florence no more than any other place in the thirteenth century possessed either church or civil registers. It is interesting and diverting to read in Villani xi. 94 how people contrived, even in somewhat later days, to ascertain the number of children born in a year. The baptizing priest at St. John's Church, where all Florentine children were brought to the font, used to place in a vessel a black or white bean respectively for every boy or girl that he christened. At the end of the year the beans were counted, and in this way people at Florence knew how many boys and girls had been born in the city in the course of the year. It would be difficult to find the black bean which was put in for Dante's baptism, and even were it discovered it would hardly show the year or the day of birth or baptism, so that we are compelled to establish the required date as best we can from other sources.

Let us first question the poet himself. At the very outset of his work, the *Vita Nuova*, he says that when he first saw Beatrice she was near the beginning of her ninth year, and he himself at the end of his. The calculation of the astronomical data which he gives indicates Beatrice's age at that time as eight years and four months. In chapter xxx. of the same work we find the statement that Beatrice died June 9, 1290, and from Purg. xxx. 124, we may gather that at the time of her death she was in her twenty-fourth year. She was therefore born before July 9, 1266, and the poet, who was about a year older, must accordingly have been born in 1265.[1] Whether the *Vita Nuova* is truth and fiction, or only the latter, need not here be considered; we know that the *Divine Comedy* is an allegoric poem, and yet it never occurs to any one to throw any doubt upon the dates there given.

In *Convito* i. 3 the poet says that he had already reached the culminating point of his life when he had to leave Florence. The culminating point of human life is stated by him (ib. iv. 25) to be the thirty-fifth year.

As it was at the beginning of 1302 that he left Florence for good and all, he had passed his thirty-fifth year, and that again agrees with 1265 as the year of his birth. Again, whatever may be the reason for it, he has placed the action of his great poem at Easter time in the jubilee year 1300. At the very first line he says that at that time he was half-way on the road of human life. If he was thirty-five years old in 1300 he must have been born in 1265. In P. xxii. 100, he mentions that at the time of his birth the sun was in the sign of the twins. Astronomical authorities have shown that in 1265 the sun entered that sign on May 18, and left it on June 17; Dante must therefore have been born between those two dates.

[1] I regret to say that I am quite unable to follow this reasoning. If Beatrice was in her twenty-fourth year in June 1290, she clearly cannot have been born more than twenty-four years previously, nor if she was eight years and four months old at a time when Dante was near the end of his ninth year can he have been nearly a year the elder. However, we know the year and month of his birth without these elaborate calculations.

He died at Ravenna, September 14, 1321. His contemporary and former neighbour Villani says that he had reached the age of about fifty-six years. Boccaccio in his commentary relates that an intimate friend of the poet at Ravenna, Ser Piero di Messer Giardino, informed him that the poet on his deathbed stated his own age as fifty-six years and about five months, or more precisely that he had passed his fifty-sixth year by the interval from the last day of May to the actual day of September. The existence of Piero Giardini is proved by documents (see Guerini and Ricci, *Studii e Polemiche Dantesche*, Bologna, 1880), so that there is no reason to doubt the trustworthiness of this statement, which, moreover, agrees accurately with all other knowledge that we have on the point. Tradition again, both among biographers and commentators, has been remarkably consistent to the effect that our poet was born in the spring of 1265, nor in face of this can Landino's mistaken statement which Dolce, Daniello, and others have thoughtlessly followed, assigning Dante's birth to the year 1260, be taken into any more account than the notices which are found in some manuscripts with regard to the length of his life (cf. Witte, *Dante-Forschungen*, ii. 28 sqq.).

That this tradition rests on historical basis is shown by the following considerations. In the first place it agrees with the poet's own statements, and there is no reason to assume either that he did not know his own age or that he stated it incorrectly. Secondly, by Florentine law those citizens only were qualified to vote or be elected who had passed their thirtieth year and belonged to a guild. We have evidence, however, that on July 5, 1296, and the following days Dante gave his vote in the council of the Hundred, so that he must have been born before July 5, 1266. Thirdly, tradition, as is well known, where she has no more certain historical grounds, loves to connect the birth of great men with important natural or historical events. It has, for example, post-dated Galileo's birth a little in order to establish the remarkable coincidence that the great man of science was born at Florence on the same day, and almost at the same hour, in which Michael Angelo died at Rome. There was no lack of important events with which Dante's birth might have been brought in contact. The battle of Benevento, Manfred's death, the unwonted conjunction of the planets which is said to have taken place on March 18, 1267, were all at the service of tradition in this matter; and the fact that she made use of none of them shows that she rested on a secure historic basis, and we believe that we stand on a solid ground of facts when we say that Dante was born between May 18 and June 17, 1265.

There are, however, two apparent difficulties in the way of this. The first may be stated thus: Dante was born in Florence, but his father belonged to the Guelfs, who were banished from Florence from 1260 to 1266; how, then, could the poet have been born at Florence during this period? As to the first point, that Dante was born at Florence, so little doubt exists with regard to it that we can hardly venture to express any hesitation on the point. The poet not only states it quite expressly, but dwells upon it with such an insistence as to arouse our suspicions that he is doing it for a purpose. He brings it forward in the *Convito*, in the book *De Vulgari Eloquentiâ*, and in each portion of his poem, expressly adding that he was baptized in St. John's Church at Florence. One is tempted almost to ask, Why say so much about it? What was the need of bringing the matter up so frequently and insisting so strongly on it if there was no doubt on the subject? Can the matter possibly have been doubtful? Did his opponents assert that he did not see the light of day within the walls of Florence? or was he himself after all not so wholly certain on the point? and did he try to make up for the lack of certainty by asserting it so repeatedly and so impressively? We have absolutely no sure knowledge on the point, we only know that he himself over and over again assures us most positively that he was born at Florence, but the very fashion in which he does it sets us thinking.

In spite of this we are far from wishing in any way to demur to Dante's testimony as to his having been born in Florence. To the first statement, 'Dante was born in Florence,' we give our willing assent. On the other hand we cannot so fully assent to the second statement, that Dante's father was among the Guelfs who were banished from 1260 to 1266. That some of Dante's ancestors were among those banished is established by his own evidence in H. x. 45, but that his father was among them has yet to be proved. It is absurd to suppose that every male person belonging to the party of the Guelfs was banished. We know how matters go in such cases; in every party there are not only leaders and influential energetic men who know what they are aiming at, there are also unimportant people, passive adherents who are not of much use to their own party and harmless to their opponents. Such people naturally pass quite unregarded, even by their victorious adversaries. Suppose that Dante's father belonged to this class of men,—and as we shall presently see, all indications and all probability point to his having done so. From all that we know about him we may safely assume that Farinata and his Ghibelines had much more important business to do than to trouble themselves about a man of the stamp of Alighiero. A man of that kind could stay quiet in Florence.

But even assuming that Dante's father had been among the banished Guelfs, it in no way follows that the poet could not have been born in the city during that period; women were not banished. As we know, Dante's wife was able to remain at peace and undisturbed in Florence after her husband had been not only banished but even condemned himself to be burnt alive, and his and her children to be beheaded. If she had borne a child in the summer of 1302, would there be any reason to doubt that it was born in Florence because its father was at the time in exile? We do not know whether the exiles of 1260 had, during the period of their absence, any fixed place of residence, but in any case the women could go and return as they pleased, and it would appear natural enough to assume that Dante's mother would have made her way to Florence in order to await the birth of her child. The question which has been asked in reply, whether she foresaw before the birth of her son his future greatness, and therefore arranged that he should be born in Florence and not elsewhere, is too childish. There was far from being any need for Dante's mother to be a prophetess, but though we know nothing whatever of the circumstances, they may easily have been such as to make a shelter in Florence seem desirable to her and her husband. Thus we may reply to the objection stated above that it is not probable that Dante's father was among those banished in 1260, and that if he were it in no way excludes the possibility of the poet's having been born at Florence.

The second difficulty is of no importance. It has been said that in 1283 Dante sold certain claims to personal and real property, which points to his having been then of full age, that is of having completed his twentieth year, in which case he must have been born before 1265. But the document which is relied on to prove the transaction has never been accurately proved, and has for a long time been missing. We therefore know neither whether the date 1283 is correct, nor whether the document speaks of a guardian. Further, it is by no means certain whether by Florentine law a minority lasted till the twentieth year. According to the Florentine statutes which were drawn up by Johannes de Montegranaro in 1415, but which were based upon older notes reaching back at least to the thirteenth century, a majority in Florence began with the completion of the eighteenth year, and this definition is repeated in a law of 1565. Thus there would appear to be no sufficient grounds for doubting the old-established date of the author's birth.

[NOTE.—Until the year 1865 it was regarded as an incontrovertible fact that Dante's birth had taken place in 1265. But when the commemoration of his birthday was celebrated, not only in Italy, but in a more modest fashion in Germany, innumerable works appeared dated as on the six-hundredth anniversary of the poet's birth. The only doubt was as to the day, May 14, on which the festival was kept in Italy. Then, however, appeared as a bolt from the blue the work of Giusto Grion, ' That the year of Dante's vision was 1301, and his birthday May 18, 1267.' The book was crammed with paradoxes, and passed unnoticed. Since then several works have appeared throwing doubt upon the accepted date. In 1879 Vittorio Imbriani produced a *réchauffé* of Grion's hypothesis in his work, *When was Dante born? a Study*, illustrated from unpublished documents. Grion's book having passed into oblivion, Imbriani's attracted some attention. The question was argued on the other side by Guerini and the present writer, and finally by Witte in No. 16 of the *Allgemeine Zeitung* for 1880. It may now be regarded as settled for the present in favour of the accepted year 1265.]

CHAPTER IV

INMATES OF DANTE'S HOME

WITH regard to his parents and their other children Dante has preserved the same silence as with regard to his own wife and children. Not a word, not a reference to them in all his works. People have indeed thought to find an allusion to his mother in H. viii. 45, where he relates how Virgil embraced him and said: 'Thou haughty soul, blessed be the womb that bare thee.' It has even been said that in this verse Dante has erected to her a monument of filial piety, but the verse in question is merely a quotation from Luke xi. 27, and the context of the passage in the Bible is not of such a kind as to make its introduction any evidence of filial piety. The fact remains that with regard to all his nearest relations the poet has, from whatsoever motives, preserved complete silence, and we are therefore compelled to look elsewhere if we wish to learn anything about the inmates of his home.

Unluckily we have little enough information on the point. The garrulous Boccaccio squanders a considerable space at the beginning of his biography in relating the wonderful dream of Dante's mother, and at the end the yet more wonderful interpretation of it; but he has little else to say about Dante's parents except that his father, Alighiero the second, will have more reputation through his posterity than through himself, a phrase which was used perhaps not unintentionally. Leonardo Bruni contents himself with the bare statement that Dante lost his father when he was a child. How ignorant even Benvenuto was, to name only the best historian among the old commentators, we may gather from the fact that he confuses Dante's mother with his wife, giving the former the name which belongs to the latter.

Of Dante's father the later biographers assert with the unanimity which probably only results from the fact that one copied another, that he was a jurist or notary. Whence did they get this information? Passerini writes: 'Among the many papers which have gone through my hands in which Dante's father is named he is never designated *Messere*, Latin *dominus*, but this designation was at that time inseparable from the name of a jurist.' That he was anything of the sort is a mere assumption.

Other evidence is not entirely in his favour. Boccaccio's words already quoted obviously imply that Alighiero was an insignificant person. Had the author of the *Decameron* possessed any information favourable to him he would assuredly have been too anxious to exalt his idolised poet in the person of his parents to have suppressed it. We have another piece of evidence, the value of which can speak for itself. Certain sonnets are extant which Dante exchanged with his friend and connection Forese Donati. They were formerly thought to be spurious, but their genuineness has been placed beyond dispute.[1] In one of these sonnets Dante banters Forese to the effect that without asking his mother he could not say whose son he was. Forese gave him as good as he got. He replied in a sonnet, which may be rendered somewhat thus in plain prose[2]: 'So far as

---

[1] See Del Lungo, *Dino Compagni*, vol. ii. p. 618.
[2] For verse translation see Rossetti, *Dante and his Circle*, p. 243.

thou art concerned, it is easy to see that thou art the son of Alighiero for his laziness and paltry cowardice. Through cowardice did he change his colours, and thou hast avenged him so excellently that thou didst run after thy enemies to ask peace of them. Thereby didst thou give us assurance that whoso shall administer to thee a good drubbing thou holdest him for thy friend and brother, and there are people who have already reckoned on this cowardice of thine.' Plain as this sounds we seem hardly at liberty to draw from it any positive conclusion with regard to the character of Alighiero, as some think they may do. In order to preserve consistency one must draw from the sonnet yet more hazardous conclusions with regard to Dante's own character. But if any one is not disposed to do this, it follows that he must hesitate about the other. It would indeed be a risky thing to pass any judgment upon the character, whether of the poet or of his father, on the strength of what is merely the evidence of an overbearing temper like these sonnets which passed between Dante and Forese. We must be, therefore, satisfied to admit that we know nothing positive about Dante's father, though the few hints which we have in regard to him do not seem to speak in his favour.

One thing seems to be undoubted, that Alighiero the second was twice married. First to Lapa daughter of Chiarissimo Cialuffi, a girl it would seem of a plebeian class; secondly to Madonna Bella of whose family we know nothing, for the suggestion that she might perhaps have been a daughter of Durante son of Messer Scolaro degli Abati originates merely from the accident that the poet's full Christian name was also Durante. It is further certain from documentary evidence that Bella, not Lapa, was the poet's mother. Similarly we may regard it as historically sure that Dante had a brother named Francesco and a sister, name unknown, who was married to Leone Poggi, a man of the people. Further questions arise naturally, but when we attempt to answer them we find that we have nothing to go upon save more or less probable conjectures. So far it has been pretty generally assumed that Lapa was Alighiero's first wife, Bella his second; while the question whether Dante's brother and sister were older or younger than himself must remain open. We know for certain that Francesco Alighieri was still living in 1332, but from this of course it does not necessarily follow that he was younger than the poet. From certain indications which however are by no means infallible some people have thought themselves able to conclude not only that Francesco and the sister were younger than Dante, but also that he was Bella's only son while the others were children of Lapa, and he therefore their half-brother only. In that case Bella would have been Alighiero's first wife and Dante must have lost his mother in his childhood, which might account for his never mentioning her. It does indeed appear that Lapa was still living in 1300. If documentary evidence for this can be produced, the fact that Dante lost his mother in his infancy could hardly be doubted, all the less so that, according to Leonardo Bruni's evidence, which everything else that we know supports, he lost his father also while he was a child. But in what year the father died we do not know and can only say with extreme probability that his death took place between 1270 and 1280.

Considering the great, often decisive influence on children's development which the parental home exercises, it would be of great interest to trace this influence in the case of our poet. It is, however, quite impossible to do so since, as may be seen from the previous remarks, our knowledge of Dante's home amounts to little more than nothing.

CHAPTER V

STUDIES

AFTER reading Dante's works we cannot for one moment doubt that he had acquired all the knowledge of his period, and mastered it in an unusual degree. But so soon as we ask when and in what way he had acquired a body of knowledge so copious and so thorough we are again bound to admit that we have no certain information on the point. Villani tells us nothing; Boccaccio and Bruni take refuge in generalities which can lay no claim to historical value, and which on this account we see no need to repeat. The tales that more recent biographies find to relate about Dante's studies in his own home and afterwards in various universities are mere fancy pictures, deserving of no consideration. Only from the information which he himself gives can we safely draw a picture of his studies and their course.

The sum of the knowledge which is included in universal culture was, from the days of the ancient Romans, divided into the seven so-called liberal arts; and these were, in the mediaeval view, distributed into *Trivium* and *Quadrivium*. The studies in which, according to the Romans, every man who would lay claim to ordinary cultivation was bound to be instructed composed the *Trivium*. These were Grammar, that is education in the Latin language; Dialectic, the science of reasoning, which in the Middle Ages passed into verbal disputation and hair-splitting distraction; and Rhetoric, which included prosody. To the *Quadrivium* belonged Arithmetic, Geometry, Music, and Astronomy.[1] Besides the seven liberal arts, science in the more restricted sense was taught at the universities. Dante himself recognises this classification in Conv. ii. 14, where he parallels the heavens of the seven planets to the studies of the *Trivium* and *Quadrivium:* while the sphere of the fixed stars corresponds to Physics and Metaphysics; the *primum mobile* to Ethics, and the fixed or empyrean heaven to Theology. The remarks in the same passage about each individual branch of knowledge are interesting, but not to our purpose here. It is more important to inquire which of them he acquired in his youth; in other words in what schools he learnt up to his twenty-fifth year.

Our only authority for this period is Dante's *Vita Nuova*, written as we shall see between 1292 and 1295. The very fact that Dante was able, before his thirtieth year, to compose such a book is an unmistakable proof that even in his youth, from what source soever, he had attained to a pretty considerable degree of scholarship as we may clearly see if we test this work of his youth by the knowledge which it implies in its author.

In the first place the poet appears to have been already master of three if not even four languages, if we may reckon the Provençal and old French as two separate tongues. His own mother tongue, still young and unformed as it was, is handled by him both in prose and in verse with a mastery hitherto unknown. Of Latin he shows not only a good average knowledge, but we learn that he used this tongue

---

[1] The old couplet serves as a *memoria technica:*
Gramm. loquitur; Dia. vera docet; Rhet. verba colorat;
Mus. canit; Ar. numerat; Geo. mensurat; As. colit astra.

in his annotations and letters, and that he wrote his amatory romance in Italian only in compliance with the wish of his friend Guido Cavalcanti. He shows himself well acquainted with Latin literature, quoting as he does Virgil and Horace, Lucan and Ovid; two quotations from Homer are derived also from Latin writers. The book shows throughout that he had more than a superficial acquaintance with Provençal literature. It further appears from the twenty-fifth chapter that he had already made a thorough study of Provençal and old Italian literature.[1] The laborious scholastic fashion, unfamiliar to our modern taste, in which he dissects his poems and finds distinctions where none exist, shows that he was no novice in the field of so-called dialectic. From the same chapter xxv. it appears that he had occupied himself with rhetoric. Yet again we can see from his penetrating and deep dissection of his own heart, and discrimination between the different powers of the soul, that physiology and psychology were not unfamiliar to him. He evidently had a fair acquaintance with the art of designing, which implies the study of the mathematical sciences. His indications of time, or we may rather say circumlocutions, which demand for their interpretation a pretty good knowledge of the astronomy of the age, offer proof that he had also worked at that science. If we further add that even in this work of his younger days he is gradually breaking the fetters of Provençal and Italian conventionalism, and revealing himself as the creator of the new style, we arrive at the incontestable conclusion that a very respectable measure of learning was even then at his command.

By what means then had he acquired all this in his

[1] See Scherillo, *Alcuni Fonti Provenzali della Vita Nuova di Dante*. Turin, 1889.

boyhood and youth? To this question only one answer can honestly be given; we do not know. That up to this time he had been at no university we shall quickly see. Some have supposed, relying on a passage of the *Divine Comedy*, that Brunetto Latini, the most learned man of his age, had been Dante's tutor. The passage referred to, H. xv. 55-87, which even as early as Leonardo Bruni seems to have been understood in this sense, shows at any rate that Brunetto had exercised a considerable influence on Dante's intellectual development. He had, however, more important things to do than to educate boys, and although the young Dante may have been indebted to him for stimulus and encouragement, there is no reason to suppose that the relation between them was that of teacher and scholar. Brunetto was a learned and far-seeing politician; and, in the passage referred to, his talk is almost exclusively of politics. His influence on Dante was probably much more in a political than in a scientific direction.

Though it may appear a somewhat venturesome statement, Dante was practically self-taught. Yet we do not venture much in saying so. The poet himself supports the accuracy of this view. In chapter iii. of the *Vita Nuova* he testifies that in the art in which to this day he stands forth as an unapproachable master, he had no teacher, but learnt the poetic art for himself. Is it likely that any teacher could have introduced him to Latin, Provençal, and Italian poetry without instructing him, at the same time, in the nature and the laws of this art? Surely not; so that in the science of letters too he was doubtless his own master.

The *Vita Nuova* concludes with a modest confession of the deficiency of his own knowledge. A wondrous vision brings him to the determination to speak no more of his

Beatrice until he is in a position to do it—in a worthier¹ fashion for which he must prepare himself by diligent study. To make this admission even more unmistakable we need only refer to *Convito* ii. 13. The passage is so decisive that it should be quoted in its entirety.

After I had lost the first delight of my soul I remained pierced with so great sorrow that no comfort was of any avail to me. Nevertheless after some time my mind, which was studying how it might be healed, seeing that neither my own consolation nor that of others availed, took measures to return to the method which a disconsolate man adopted in order to console himself. So I betook myself to reading that book of Boëthius which not many know wherein a captive and banished man he found consolation, and hearing further that Tully also had written a book wherein treating of friendship, he had spoken of the consolation of that excellent man Laelius upon the death of his friend Scipio, I set myself to read that. And although it was at first hard to me to enter into their meaning, in the end I entered into it so far as the grammatical law which I had, and some little wit of my own, could carry me. By which same wit I had already seen many things as though in a dream, as may be seen in my *New Life*. And as it befalls that a man goes in search of silver and beyond his expectation finds gold, which some hidden cause presents to him, it may be not without divine ordering, so I who was seeking to console myself found not only a remedy for my tears but also names of authors and sciences and books, the which considering I rightly judged that philosophy, who was the lady of these authors, these sciences, and these books, must be the greatest of all things. And I conceived her fashioned as a noble lady, and I could not conceive her in any act save of mercy, wherefore so willingly did my sense of truth look upon her that I could hardly turn aside from her. And having so conceived her I began to go where she displayed herself most truthfully, namely, in the schools of men of religion and at the discussions of philosophers, so that in a little time, perhaps in thirty months, I began to be aware of her sweetness in such degree that the love of her drove away and destroyed every other thought.

That is the only authentic history of Dante's studies. From this authentic history, if it be read with understanding, much may be deduced. In the first place, more than a year after the death of Beatrice, that is in his own twenty-sixth year, Dante had not read Boëthius's *Consolation of Philosophy*, and had no knowledge whatever of Cicero's *De Amicitia*. Would that have been possible had he up to that time attended any higher-grade school or university? Secondly, he found it at first a matter of some difficulty to understand both these works. Now of what nature were these difficulties? The answer has been given with great confidence that the reference here is not to difficulties of language but of interpretation. This assumption is based on the fear that to assume Dante in his six-and-twentieth year to have possessed a deficient knowledge of Latin would be to disparage unduly the extent of his education. Yet, taken literally, his words appear to imply something of the kind. He obviously speaks not only of the limitation of his grammatical knowledge which might assist him in the interpretation, but also of the store of words which he acquired in the reading of Boëthius and Cicero. Up to this point his Latin vocabulary was extremely modest, as also was his knowledge of Latin grammar. For Boëthius and Cicero certainly do not belong to the more difficult Latin writers. Hence again it seems to us to follow conclusively that Dante had not attended any advanced school, let alone a university. Thirdly, up to his twenty-sixth year, the poet had not studied philosophy. It was then that he first began to do so, and first attended schools. What these schools were is not at present to our purpose. What schools had he then hitherto attended, if up to this time philosophy, taken in its comprehensive mediaeval sense, had remained a region totally unknown to him? Fourthly, he had so little previous training for philosophic study that it took him some two years and a half to acquire the right taste for it. From which again it would seem to follow that he had received in his youth no learned education.

All this finds its confirmation in Dante's words in the opening chapter of the *Convito:*

Blessed are those few that sit at the table where the bread of angels is eaten, and wretched those whose food is in common with the beasts. But whereas each man is by nature a friend to each, and every friend grieves to see him whom he loves in want, those who are fed at so exalted a table cannot be without pity for them whom they see feeding after the manner of beasts and going about eating grass and acorns. And since pity is the mother of kind actions, those who have knowledge ever offer freely of their wealth to those who are in truth poor, and are, as it were, a living fountain, with whose water is refreshed the natural thirst which has been named above. Accordingly I, who sit not at the blessed table, but having fled from the pasture of the common herd, gather at the feet of those who do sit there, of that which falls from them, and know the wretched life of those whom I have left behind me, being moved to pity by the sweetness which I perceive in that which little by little I gather, forgetting not myself, have reserved somewhat for the wretched, the which I have displayed some while already before their eyes, and therein have made them eagerly desirous.

Thus did Dante, even in later years, count himself not among the men of science, but only, to use a modern expression, among the *dilettanti*, and regarded it as his calling not himself to collaborate in the domain of science, but to introduce science to the people; and that in spite of the gigantic learning which, as this very *Convito* shows, was at his disposal. Was this false modesty? Surely not. It is rather the language of the self-taught man who has indeed immense knowledge at his disposal, but yet does not dare to rank himself among the learned by profession. If he says further that he has fled from the pasture of the common herd, and consequently had once belonged to this herd, the question arises when did he fly from it? To this he himself gives the answer. He says (H. ii. 105) that Beatrice had drawn him from the common troop; we saw too that at the end of the *Vita Nuova* he spoke of the diligence with which he was studying in order to become capable of celebrating Beatrice worthily. Thus he must have left the pasture of the common herd after her death, or in his six-and-twentieth year.

But is not this result, which appears clearly to follow from the poet's own expressions, inconsistent with the very considerable knowledge which, as we saw, is indicated in the *Vita Nuova?* We think not. Balancing everything accurately, we must arrive at the conclusion that Dante had received in his youth a good though not a learned education. Attracted from his youth upwards to knowledge, he had learnt much for himself. By his own express declaration he had studied the art of poetry, which implies that he had made himself acquainted with provincial and Italian literature. It was not until after Beatrice's death that he threw himself with such eagerness into the study of science that, according to his own testimony, Conv. iii. 9, he injured his eyes. It was in this way that he acquired his gigantic learning, and as self-taught persons are easily tempted to do, extended his demands upon himself and others to such a point that he had no hesitation in estimating the degree of culture which he had formerly reached as nothing higher than the culture of the common herd.

We need not go into the question whether Dante had learnt Greek, for it is quite otiose. From his works it is quite clear that that language was strange to him. The possibility of his having known the letters and the meaning of some few words is not excluded. The question whether he was familiar with music seems also futile. It has been answered in the affirmative on the strength of some remarks of Boccaccio and Bruni, who, however, only say that the poet took delight in music and singing, and was on friendly terms with the musicians of his time. It does not follow that he was himself a musician and a singer.

Another circumstance, however, offers matter for consideration. In April 1301 it was decided to make certain street improvements in Florence, and Dante was entrusted with the oversight and direction of the necessary works. This looks as if he had some knowledge of building matters, and in fact the architectural completeness with which he has built up the other world in the *Commedia* shows him as a man well acquainted with architecture. His knowledge in this respect may be connected with his knowledge of the art of design. Can he have been in his youth destined for the architect's profession, and subsequently felt no attraction to this calling? As to this we know nothing positive, but here a new field lies open to the fancy of those who have a turn for combinations. But our present task is not to stray into combinations, but simply to establish with as much certainty as possible everything that can be arrived at positively by historic methods with regard to Dante's life; and with regard to his studies we have no positive knowledge save what he has himself imparted, and what we can infer from his works, and this is sufficient.

[NOTE.—In early times we constantly meet with attempts to make Dante out a miraculous child, who from his earliest youth was deeply versed in all branches of knowledge. Boccaccio indeed depicts him as a kind of prematurely aged infant. But his and Bruni's generalities show that they had really no definite information as to Dante's studies, and never even took the trouble to weigh carefully what he himself tells us on the subject. Later writers have followed in their footsteps, in some cases (*e.g.* Missirini), going so far as to describe Dante's university life. The old view that Brunetto Latini was Dante's tutor is now generally given up. A discussion of it will be found in Professor Bartoli's *Life of Dante*, chap. iii.]

CHAPTER VI

MILITARY SCIENCE

THE history of the Italian cities in the latter half of the thirteenth century is for the most part a history of the citizens' struggle against the proud nobility, whose arrogance had become almost intolerable. In all parts this spirit of opposition was stirring among the townsfolk. In Arezzo the popular party at first got the upper hand, but were soon overthrown by a coalition between the Guelf and Ghibeline nobility, their leaders being blinded and thrown into a reservoir. The two sections of the nobles having attained to power, renewed their former quarrel, and the Guelfs were driven out. Betaking themselves to Florence, they found a friendly reception and ready support, which naturally brought about war between the two cities.

At the end of May 1288 the Florentines, with the strength of 2600 horse and 12,000 foot, marched against Arezzo. After gaining some successes, they marched back without coming to a decisive engagement. Their allies, the Sienese, suffered a severe defeat. The consequent exultation of the Aretines led to their own destruction. A second campaign of the Florentines in September 1288 led practically to no result, as the Aretines refused a pitched battle. On May 2 of the following year Charles II. of Anjou passed through Florence on his way back from his captivity in Aragon to his own kingdom. The Florentines showed him much honour, and when after three days' stay he left the city, having ascertained that the Aretines intended to attack him at a farther point of his route, they sent with him an escort of 800 horse and 3000 foot as far as Siena. In return for this Charles left with them an experienced captain, Amaury of Narbonne. At the beginning of June 1289 the Florentines and their allies, 1900 cavalry and 10,000 infantry in all, undertook a further campaign against Arezzo. On St. Barnabas Day 1289 a decisive battle was fought at Campaldino, not far from the Franciscan convent of Certomondo. The Aretines and Ghibelines suffered a defeat from which they never thoroughly recovered (Vill. vii. 131 ; Purg. v. 92, and note of Philalethes). Among the Ghibelines who fell here was Count Buonconte of Montefeltro, whom Dante has commemorated in a striking passage ; Purg. l.c. When the famous captain has named himself, the poet asks him straightway, 'What power or what chance brought thee so far from Campaldino that no man knows thy sepulchre ?' This question gives us the impression of implying that the poet was present at the battle. In another passage he expressly mentions a campaign against the Aretines of which he was an eye-witness, H. xxii. 4. Leonardo Bruni avers that he had seen a letter of Dante's in which the following passage occurred : 'All the ills and misfortunes which have befallen me began with and were caused by my unfortunate election to the Priorate, an office of which, though not worthy of it in abilities, I was not unworthy by reason of my loyalty and my age. For ten years had passed since the fight at Campaldino in which the Ghibeline party was well-nigh annihilated, and at which I was present, being no child in warfare, whereby I had at first great fear and afterwards great joy by reason of the varying fortunes of the fight.' Leonardo Bruni, himself an Aretine and secretary of state at Florence, in his biography, affirms with quite remarkable emphasis the presence of the poet at the fight. His words are: 'In that great and memorable battle which was fought at Campaldino, Dante, then a young man of good repute, bore arms and fought bravely on horseback in the front rank.' And again Dante relates this battle in a letter, and says that he was present and took part in it, describing the operations. Yet again, after giving a short summary of the position of affairs, Bruni says: 'Returning to the matter, I say that Dante fought bravely for his country in this engagement.' He blames Boccaccio sharply for saying nothing about it, and concludes, 'After this battle Dante returned home and devoted himself more sedulously than ever to his studies.'

On the strength of this evidence every biographer without exception has regarded Dante's participation in the fight of Campaldino as an indubitable historic fact. Only in quite recent times has the story been doubted, on grounds which have been found to be of great weight and almost decisive, and which accordingly we cannot pass over.

In the first place we have the absolute silence of Villani. He relates the story of Campaldino at length, he devotes as a solitary exception a longish chapter of his chronicle to the poet, he was Dante's contemporary, neighbour, and admirer, yet he does not utter a single syllable as to Dante's presence at the battle. It is impossible that he should not have known of it, still more impossible that knowing it he should not have mentioned it. It can easily be seen that this objection has been made from the standpoint of later times and admiring posterity. For persons who gaze upon Dante with astonishment it is naturally of the greatest importance to ascertain whether he really bore arms in behalf of his

F

native city and took part in a decisive battle. No one asks about the thousands who were there, they have no interest for later times; but was the one man Dante there? So asks posterity; but who was Dante in the year 1289? A young member of an obscure family which may or may not have been noble, one who, by his own account, had up to that time pursued none of the higher studies, who had certainly borne no high military rank, of whom nothing was known save that he had composed some love poems in Italian. Can it be expected that any one in Florence would have attached any importance to the fact that he took part in the campaign with some 12,000 others, or that people would have looked upon each other with astonishment and whispered: 'Only think! Dante also is with the army!' Surely not. But Villani was his neighbour? Yes, and other neighbours of the historian must have taken part in the campaign, and he has not mentioned them either. History only mentions the names of the commanders and of those who specially distinguished themselves; thousands remain unrecorded. Both alternatives are therefore quite possible, both that Villani either did not know or forgot that his neighbour Dante had been there, and that he remembered the fact, but made no mention of it. He must have known many matters of importance with regard to Dante and not mentioned them. So then if he says nothing about this one circumstance of Dante's life his silence tells us little or nothing.

Just as little can be inferred from the silence of Boccaccio, Philip Villani, and the other commentators. This silence only appears strange owing to the estimate of the poet formed by later ages, coupled with the erroneous assumption that the same existed among his contemporaries. It is quite natural, seeing that no one in Florence in 1289 knew of Dante's future greatness, that no special notice should have been taken of the fact of his having fought at Campaldino. Equally natural would it be that in a few years the matter would be totally forgotten until Leonardo Bruni stumbled upon Dante's letter.

It is, however, exactly the genuineness, nay the very existence of the letter from which Bruno quotes a fragment that is open to serious doubt. In compiling his biography he had a definite intention, namely, to supplement Boccaccio's work by reference to the political aspect of Dante's life. No doubt; but was he necessarily a forger for that reason? He has, moreover, in his somewhat hasty work, fallen into sundry errors. Again, no doubt; but there is a considerable difference between mistake and invention, between error and forgery.—The very special emphasis which by three and fourfold repetition Bruni lays upon this point is said to be striking, and at the same time suspicious. But why not? if the learned humanist, by discovering a hitherto unknown letter, was able to establish a very important fact in the poet's life, his joy at this discovery, and the importance which he assigns to it, are at once natural and intelligible.—But Bruni quotes the passage in Italian, whereas it is certain that a letter of Dante's would have been written in Latin. So it would if he were writing to a scholar; but if his correspondent was a person who was not familiar with Latin, there is no reason why, being as he was a master in the Italian language, to the point of using it to expound the deepest problems of the science of the time, he should have disdained to use it in a letter. Besides Bruni may have translated it, seeing that in the whole of his biography he only quotes one passage in Latin, and that consisting of five words which any Italian could perfectly have understood : ' Popule mee quid feci tibi ? '

In his dialogue upon the three Florentine poets, Bruni makes one of the speakers, Niccoli, say: 'I read lately some letters of Dante which he obviously composed with great care, wrote with his own hand, and sealed with his seal.' Thus the Florentine secretary had looked upon authentic letters of Dante and could hardly have been deceived with a forgery. But, it has been objected by Bartoli, who looked at these letters? Bruni or Niccoli? One might as well ask whether it were Shakespeare or Jaques that said, 'All the world's a stage.'

It is reluctantly that we are compelled to charge Professor Bartoli with having in his criticisms of Bruni's assertions gone to work with even more haste than that with which he taxes the old biographer. What is the object of his wearisomely long exposition concerning the preconceived notions and the deficiencies of Bruni's life? Had not Bruni already written a history of Florence in which, when describing the battle of Campaldino, he remarks, 'Dante writes in a letter that he had been present at this affair, and he mentions in the same place how the enemy had at first the upper hand to such an extent that a panic prevailed among the Florentines, but that they ultimately won the victory with such a slaughter of their opponents that the name of these was nearly wiped out'? Surely there is no preconceived view here, no itch to contradict Boccaccio. This passage has been quite overlooked, otherwise Bruni's authority would have been estimated rather higher. That he forged a letter of Dante's can be as little asserted as that he was himself the victim of a deception. In that case the letter which he saw and perhaps discovered was genuine, and Dante really did take part in the battle of Campaldino.[1]

[1] It may be added that Dr. Moore (*Dante and his Early Biographers*) accepts Bruni's statement with regard to the letter.

But why is Dante himself silent about it? Whether or not he is silent depends upon how we take it. It is not his way to narrate events out of his own life in detail, he contents himself with allusions which usually give the commentator trouble enough. As we have seen, such allusions to Campaldino are not wanting in his great epic; but even had he been quite silent on the point, we could draw no inference therefrom. He did not write an autobiography. His inner life is set forth in his works; with regard to his outward life, he is for the most part silent, only giving occasional hints, and those, as a rule, somewhat obscure.

It remains to test one argument, which we should not have taken seriously if it had not been held up as decisive. One of the leaders of the Ghibelines of Arezzo was Count Buonconte of Montefeltro. If Dante had fought in the foremost ranks of the Guelf army he must necessarily have seen him, and if he had seen him he must have recognised him when he saw him again. But when he meets him in Purgatory, according to the supposed date, eleven years later, he does not know him, and therefore can never have seen him, and therefore was not at Campaldino. This argument is entirely in the air: when thousands are fighting it does not follow that an individual even in the foremost ranks must necessarily see the leaders of the hostile force, but even if Dante did see the count he saw him on horseback and in fighting costume, and might very well have seen him again years afterwards without recognising him, especially in Purgatory, where the souls are naked and bare. Or should we expect the poet to inform us expressly that he said to the count, 'Your excellency must kindly forgive me for not recognising you in civil costume.' Moreover, how does any one know that Dante did not recognise Buonconte in Purgatory? No doubt in Purg. v. 58 he states expressly that, surrounded by a troop of departed spirits, and told to look whether he had ever seen any of them in life, he recognised none. But if the people who pressed upon him were numerous it is quite intelligible that each individual would not come under his eye, and where are we told that he had the Count of Montefeltro under his eye and did not know him? When the count names himself without being required to do so, Dante shows no sign of surprise, but asks him straightway how it happened that no one had knowledge of his fate at Campaldino. That seems to imply acquaintance, and indeed so precise an acquaintance with the individual events of the battle such as could only be possessed by one who had been there.

But, allowing even that Dante really did not recognise Buonconte, this would prove just nothing against his presence at the battle. The system adopted by the poet involves a change in the appearance of the souls in Purgatory of such an extent that he does not recognise them, even in the case of his own most intimate friends.[1] Thus he does not recognise Casella or Belacqua till he hears their voices; nay, in the case of his former intimate and relative, Forese Donati, he says expressly that he would never have recognised him by his face, and only did so on hearing him speak. In presence of these facts, what significance can we attach to his non-recognition of Buonconte?

Balancing all these points then with care, we must accept Dante's presence at Campaldino as a historical fact, at any rate till some one can prove that Leonardo Bruni, the learned humanist and Florentine statesman, has either been deceived in an incredible manner or has consciously lied.

[1] This dictum is not universally true. Dante recognises Belacqua, probably, and Nino di Visconti, certainly, as soon as he sees their faces.

In the fragment of Dante's letter which Bruni has preserved, he says that when he fought at Campaldino he was no child in warfare. The expression corresponds pretty accurately to the Latin *non rudis belli*, and indicates some practice in affairs of war. Dante must therefore have shared in some campaign or another before that battle. It would, however, be lost labour if we were to try to guess which. We have no notice—nay, not a bare indication, to put us on the track.

In August 1289, shortly after the death of the unhappy Count Ugolino de' Gherardeschi, the Florentines, with the confederated Guelfs of Tuscany and the banished Pisans, marched against Pisa; and after eight days' siege the fortress of Caprona capitulated to them. Dante says expressly (H. xxi. 94-96) that he was present at the capitulation; and we might say, what further evidence do we require? But even this authentic testimony of the poet's own has been demurred to. Villani (vii. 132) mentions that the Florentine army did not return from Campaldino till July 24; and as the campaign against Pisa took place in the following August, it has been thought that the interval was too short for Dante to allow himself the fitting amount of repose. Perhaps he thought a week or so was all he needed. But the old biographers and commentators say nothing of it. Is not Dante's own evidence as good as that of all the biographers and commentators put together? Moreover, Benvenuto, the one real historian among the older commentators, actually does say expressly that Dante, being then a youth of twenty-five, took part in the campaign. It is suggested that he merely went as a spectator, out of curiosity; but in that case he would hardly have laid so much stress on his presence, and in any case would have expressed himself differently. What he says is, not only that he saw the men-at-arms come out of Caprona, he also saw their terror, which is just what the existing circumstances recall to his mind. This he could only have read in their countenances; and to do this he must have been in the ranks of the victors, and not merely among curious onlookers. From which it would follow that he actually shared in the campaign.

[NOTE.—The first person to throw doubt upon Dante's presence at Campaldino was Bartoli, op. cit. pp. 81-93; he has been followed by Renier.]

CHAPTER VII

FAMILY LIFE

PRIVATE affairs, one may say; and be easily tempted to pass over this part of the inquiry in silence. We the less need in order to understand his works to know anything about his wedded life and his children that he has himself preserved absolute silence about these matters. Was this accident or intention; who can say? As a modern writer puts it, 'If Dante could say one word to a biographer it would be, "write only the history of my life, but touch not my wife and children." All that is private matters about which the reader need not trouble himself, since I have spoken no word thereof.' But if we are interested in a poet, we do wish to know him also in his private life. We are eager to make acquaintance not only with the genius but with the man. So then in any biography of Dante a chapter about his family life must be included. If, however, we wish to write history and not some kind of romance, the chapter must needs be full of gaps, seeing that about Dante's family life we know as good as nothing. On this point even the garrulous Boccaccio takes refuge in commonplaces and declamation, from which only one thing can be made out with certainty, namely, that for all his pretensions to thorough knowledge, here as elsewhere, he really knew nothing about the matter.

Let us first state so much as rests on documentary evidence, and then pass on to the hypotheses and assumptions that have been based upon it. The first is a short business, and the second, as deserving no profound consideration, can also be quickly done with. Dante's wife was called Gemma, and was a daughter of Manetto of the powerful noble family of the Donati. Her mother, Maria, in a will dated February 17, 1315, left a modest legacy to her daughter, Dante's wife. We have documentary evidence that Gemma was still living 1332, so that she survived her husband, but the year of her death is no better known than that of her birth. Of her character we know as little as of her personal appearance. If she was ever painted, the portrait either has been lost or is no longer recognisable. Boccaccio relates that when Dante fell into misfortune, she with great difficulty saved a small portion of the property as being her dowry, and from the revenues of it obtained a scanty maintenance for herself and her children. If the story is true, and there is no ground to doubt it, it shows only that she was not a vain woman with a taste for finery. To save as much as possible of the property, and to maintain herself and her children as well as might be, was a natural thing to do, and implies nothing one way or the other as to her character for amiability.

She bore her husband several children, but we are in the dark as to the exact number. People have spoken of seven, and even have found themselves able to give their names. Seven, however, is a mystic number, and they might as well have gone as far as nine and so explained Dante's preference for that number. The existence of four children, two sons and daughters, is established by documents, Peter, James, Beatrice, and Antonia. Another daughter named Imperia is also said by Passerini to be mentioned in a document.

Unfortunately, however, this has never been seen by any one else, and in all likelihood will never come to light again. Peter and James, on the other hand, are frequently mentioned, the first in later years settled at Verona, where he held the office of a judge. He is said to have been a poet, and a valuable commentary on the *Commedia* passes under his name, and it is very probable was really compiled by him. His will is dated 1364. His great-granddaughter [1] Ginevra married in 1549 Count Marcantonio Serego, and with her the posterity of the poet came to an end.

Of James there are some grounds for assuming that after Dante's death he lived in Florence, and recovered the confiscated goods of his father. Beatrice lived with her father at Ravenna, and after his death entered a convent. In 1350 a present of ten gold florins was sent to her from Florence by the hand of Boccaccio. All that is known of Antonia so far is that she is mentioned in a document of November 3, 1332. That is all the positive knowledge that we have of Dante's family.

Next for the hypotheses and assumptions. When was Dante married? Various dates have been given by Pelli, Fraticelli, and Balbo, but the truth of the matter is that we know nothing definite. As he went into exile and left his wife at Florence about the end of 1301 or the beginning of 1302, and as she had borne him at least four children, it follows that his marriage cannot have taken place after 1296, nor, on the other hand, is it likely to have been before the death of Beatrice in 1291.

Much ingenuity, much hot argument, much wit and humour, much paper and ink have been expended over the question whether Dante's family life was fortunate or the reverse. Boccaccio has not been able to resist the tempta-

[1] So in the original, but the dates seem to make it hardly possible.

tion to extract from the Latin translation of St. Jerome and embody in his so-called biography, and later in his commentary, the tedious dissertation of Theophrastus against women and marriage. The garrulous author of the *Decameron* concludes, 'I do not indeed affirm, for I do not know, that all this befell Dante. Whether, however, it be true that things of this kind or others were the cause of it, when he had once left his wife, who had been given him to console him in his afflictions, he never would again go where she was nor allow her to come where he was, albeit that he and she were the common parents of several children. Nor let any one suppose that from what I have said I wish to conclude that men should not takes wives, nay I praise it much, but not in every man's case. Let philosophers leave wedlock to rich fools, to lords, and to labouring men, and let them take their pleasure with philosophy, who is a far better bride than any other.' Again, in relating Dante's marriage, Boccaccio asserts that the poet did not select a helpmeet for himself, but that the marriage was arranged by the relations. He forgets, however, to mention who the relations were who could do this; Dante's father was at that time certainly dead, his mother most probably also. There was a stepmother and a younger brother and sister, but Dante was not the man to let a wife whom he did not desire be forced upon him by these relations. Only one of Boccaccio's statements may be correct, namely, that the husband and wife never saw each other again after the beginning of the exile, a circumstance which, though it can perhaps be explained quite naturally, gives one some cause for reflection. But how casually Boccaccio went to work appears from his statement that Dante never would again go where his wife was living, as if it had been open to the banished poet to go to

Florence where, as Boccaccio himself tells us, he had left wife and children.

One might almost think that Boccaccio himself, in later years, regretted the manner in which he had spoken of Dante's marriage and his wife, and had tacitly withdrawn his words. In his commentary, in which he gives us hardly less information about Dante's life than in his biography, we find no syllable of blame for the poet's entry on the married state. He even mentions Dante's wife again in the 33rd Lecture, but has no more reproach for her, only praise and good report. He does indeed again quote Theophrastus's long dissertation against marriage and women, but this time with reference only to the case of Giacopo Rusticucci. This can hardly be an accident; can he have been told in Florence that to speak of Dante's marriage and wife as he had done in the biography was not fitting? It is possible. At any rate in later days Leonardo Bruni expressly and sharply censures him, asserting for his part that after his marriage Dante lived the life of an honourable citizen devoting himself to study. Few words, but significant, since they follow immediately upon his censure of Boccaccio.

People have nevertheless believed themselves justified in assuming that Dante was not fortunate in his marriage. The following reasons are assigned in support of this assumption. First, the authority of Boccaccio, who, if he says nothing, expressly allows his view to be seen plainly enough. But the worthy Boccaccio confesses plainly that he knows nothing about Dante's marriage or the character of his wife. Secondly, the husband and wife, from the time of Dante's exile—that is, in the course of more than twenty years—made no effort to come together, which does not look like mutual attachment. For the first years of the exile the thing is quite intelligible. Gemma, as the mother of children who had not completed their education, could not well go roaming from place to place with her husband. As for the later years, we do not know at all whether the pair saw each other and lived together again. Boccaccio denies it, but what credit does he deserve? If he is to be trusted, all that we can deduce from his words is that Gemma was a good wife but Dante not an affectionate husband. 'He would never suffer her to come where he was:' if he did not suffer it, it implies that she wished it; and from the form of the words it would seem that she repeatedly requested his leave. The only point of any value is that, so far as our information goes, Gemma remained in Florence during the later years of the poet, when he had settled permanently in Ravenna, and had his children, Peter, James, and Beatrice, with him; but as we know nothing about their private relations, it is not permissible to draw any conclusion from the continued separation of the pair with regard to the circumstances of their married life. A third argument against the happiness of Dante's marriage is that he had considerable debts, as though no marriage could be happy without a comfortable income. Would Dante have done better to marry for money? A further point is Dante's complete silence about his wife, which is taken as implying that he did not love her, which, moreover, was naturally her fault. But he is equally silent about his father and mother, brothers, sisters, and children, besides which the etiquette of the time did not allow a poet to sing of his own wife. Again, in P. xiv. 61, the blessed pray for fathers and mothers only, making no mention of wives, from which it would appear that the poet did not wish to see his wife again. But even here mention is made of 'others who were dear to them,' and it is to be remembered that father and mother are the only relations whom every one must necessarily possess. Yet again, in Pg. viii. 76, Dante makes Nino Visconti say that the flame of love does not last long in the woman if sight and touch do not often rekindle it. Even if Dante is here expressing his own experience, there would be nothing to prove that up to the time of his exile Dante had been unlucky in his marriage.

Some, again, suppose the passage, Pg. xxiii. 91 sqq., in which Dante speaks so sharply against the Florentine women, bears reference to his own wife. That this opinion is groundless may be seen from the fact that at the supposed date of the poem Dante was still living with his wife, and it would have been his own duty to see that morals and manners suffered no injury in his house; while if we look to the time when the verse was written, poor Gemma would hardly have been of an age at which she would be likely to fall into the temptation of displaying her charms in the manner indicated. The argument that the perpetual exaltation of Beatrice is inconsistent with a happy married life implies a complete ignorance of the manners of the age, and overlooks the fact that in the *Divine Comedy* she is essentially symbolic, and does not come into competition with any earthly woman. Lastly, a happy marriage would have hindered Dante from other love affairs; but these other love affairs of the poet belong one and all to the domain of fable, and even if they were historic they would tell against himself rather than against Gemma, unless we are to hold that when the husband is unfaithful the blame rests with the wife.

On the other hand, the following arguments have been brought forward in the wife's favour. Boccaccio's words deserve little consideration, since he has to confess that he knew nothing about the character of Dante's wife, and that all his dissertation on the subject is intended merely to justify himself for embodying the invective of Theophrastus in his biography. Moreover, no other of the older writers says a word against her, even those who otherwise copy Boccaccio do not follow him on this point, while, as we have seen, Leonardo Bruni distinctly contradicts him. We cannot, however, tell what positive knowledge they had on the subject. The touching cry of the poet that the first arrow shot from the bow of banishment was the necessity of leaving all that was dearest to him suggests that he was thinking of wife and children, but here again we cannot say that they were among those whom he really loved. A stronger argument is, that all we know of Dante's character excludes the possibility of his having been forced into marriage with a woman he did not love, and yet many a man has married for love and afterwards been disenchanted.

Yet again, Dante's burning desire, which never left him till his latest breath, of returning to Florence, would be inconceivable if he had not at the same time yearned for reunion with his wife and children. Still, a man can love his home without being enamoured of the wife whom he has left there; and his sons at any rate were not in Florence after 1315. Other reasons have been suggested, such as Dante's selection of women like Piccarda and Nella, who were connected with his wife's family, the Donati, and the reticence which he observes with regard to his prime enemy Corso of that house; but these may have been due quite as much to a desire to keep on good terms, in the event of his return, with that powerful clan, as to any tenderness in favour of his wife's relations. The fact that Boccaccio, so far as he has anything definite to record of Dante's wife, says nothing but good of her, is not of itself evidence of her affection for him or even fidelity to him.

To sum up, we have no real evidence whether she was, on the one hand, a good and tender helpmeet or a Xanthippe; nor do we know anything of Dante's own behaviour as husband and father. We may wish to believe the best, but great poets and scholars have not always had the best record in those capacities, as many a wife has learnt. Villani's remarks as to the difficulty which he found in getting on with commonplace and uneducated people may —we cannot tell—have had their application in this matter.

CHAPTER VIII

POLITICAL ACTIVITY

BOCCACCIO, in a passage of elaborate rhetoric, depicts Dante as having been at one time the man of most importance in the state; then, after a vain attempt to reconcile the contending factions, as having made an effort to return to private life. Patriotism and ambition were, however, says the biographer, forces too powerful to be set aside; and the man of ripe years who had been nurtured in the lap of philosophy was constrained (after recognising the impossibility of forming a third party) to join that which seemed to him least opposed to justice; the end of it being that, when the other party got the upper hand, he was compelled to go into exile.

If Dante had lived up to his biographer's ideal he would have remained unmarried and have taken no part in politics: in other words, he would have become a peevish solitary *savant;* and because he was not this, Boccaccio thinks himself justified in blaming him. The picture which he has drawn of the poet's political activity may come pretty near the truth in its general outlines, but it cannot be denied that it is injured by exaggeration and partiality. The long rhetorical exercise contains very little in the way of positive statement, and even that little is very questionable. For instance, it is possible, but by no means probable, that Dante even contemplated a return to private life. Again, though he may have exerted himself to diminish party hatreds, such of his votes as are attested by documentary evidence are not wholly consonant therewith. In short, we can get from Boccaccio no positive knowledge as to Dante's political action.

Nor indeed is much to be learnt on this point from the information given by other early biographers. Villani says:

> This Dante was a respected citizen of Florence, living near St. Peter's Gate, and a neighbour of my own. The ground of his banishment was that in 1301, when Lord Charles of Valois, of the House of France, came to Florence and banished the White party, this Dante was one of the governing body of our city, and belonged to that party though he was a Guelf.

The chronicler says no more about Dante's political doings, whence we may say how little we are justified in drawing conclusions from his silence. Leonardo Bruni again, though he expressly intended to supplement Boccaccio in regard to Dante's political action, is very brief. He writes:

> Dante was much employed by the Republic, and when he had attained the statutory age was nominated Prior, not, as is now usual, by lot, but, as the practice then was, by free election. His colleagues in office were Palmiero degli Altoviti, Neri son of Jacopo degli Alberti, and others; and he held office in 1300.

The Aretine historian passes on at once to his banishment, and we have to rely for further information on what may be gathered from contemporary documents.

At that time no one could take part in the government of the republic unless he belonged to one of the guilds known as *Arti maggiori* and *Arti minori*.[1] Dante is said

---

[1] The greater arts were—notaries, cloth merchants, exchangers, wool merchants, apothecaries, silk mercers, furriers; the lesser—retail clothiers, butchers, shoemakers, builders, blacksmiths.

to have entered that of the apothecaries, but it would be lost labour to inquire why he selected that one. It has been suggested that perhaps some of his ancestors had exercised that calling; or that he had had the idea of adopting it himself; or that he was attracted by the fact that the apothecaries of that date sold books; or that painters belonged to that guild. But all these are bare conjectures devoid of historical matter, and we really know nothing as to the ground of Dante's selection. The fact, however, is beyond all doubt.

We first met with the poet on the scene of public life on June 5, 1296; from which it may be inferred with certainty that he had by that time completed his thirtieth year. On that day he gave his vote in the Council of the Hundred upon a question raised by Peter Forese with regard to the removal of the Hospital of St. John. On December 10 of the same year (and on two subsequent occasions, March 4, 1297 and March 15, 1301) he voted against the granting of subsidies and presents of money to Charles of Anjou, King of Naples. From this it would seem to follow that Dante's friendship with Carlo Martello, titular King of Hungary (Par. viii.), was not inconsistent with hostility to that prince's father; if not indeed, that the friendship itself must be reduced within very moderate limits. Indeed it would seem that the friendship must be read into the passage in question before it can be deduced from it.[1]

Two years later, in May 1299, the poet is said to have been entrusted with a mission to San Gemignano, with a

---

[1] This remark seems a little hasty, in face of Carlo's words: 'Assai m' amasti'; to say nothing of the whole tone of the passage, the dramatic effect of which vanishes if we cannot suppose it really to represent Dante's opinion of the young prince. Compare Raleigh's estimate of Prince Henry.

view to the assembling of a convention by which a new leader of the Tuscan Guelfs was to be chosen. This will be a good point at which to glance briefly at the various missions and embassies on which he is alleged to have been employed. None of his contemporaries says anything about them; nor do we hear of them till the fifteenth century, when a Humanist named Filelfo, who has no good report among biographers of Dante, reckoned up a trifle of fourteen missions with which our poet had been entrusted; four to Rome, two apiece to Naples and Hungary, and the rest to Siena, Perugia, Venice, Genoa, Ferrara, and Paris, making, with that to San Gemignano, a total of fifteen. Of Filelfo the Marquis Gian Giacomo Trivulzio says with absolute justice:

To quote Filelfo as an authority is not less ridiculous than to cite the author of *Don Quixote* as witness to a fact of history. During his life and after his death Gian Maria Filelfo was well known for a rank impostor, and at the present day he deserves no credit.

Apart from this character, a very simple calculation is sufficient to show that these missions belong to the domain of fable. Dante's political activity cannot have lasted more than some six years; from the completion that is of his thirtieth year in May 1295 to his banishment in November 1301. We have documents to show that during these years he was constantly in Florence; so that in the absence of railway communication it is hardly possible that he can have been taking these journeys to Paris and into Hungary.

Nevertheless Filelfo's gasconading long passed for sound history. Pelli, Balbo, Missirini, and all the troupe who copied them, accepted all these embassies as historical facts; while Tiraboschi dismissed them to the place whence they came, and only allowed the two to Naples to pass muster as 'the least improbable.' The usually credulous Fraticelli too in this matter placed himself on the side of the sceptics. It was left for Todeschini with his wonted acumen to put Filelfo's stories to the test of criticism, with the result that the fourteen embassies are now wholly given up, and all the talk about them has at the present day ceased to possess any save a literary interest.

There remains the mission to San Gemignano—we will recur later on to those to Boniface VIII.—which is said to rest on documentary evidence. At all events the learned Father Ildefonso, of San Luigi, has published, in the twelfth volume of his *Delizie dagli eruditi Toscani*, a document referring to it, which has been reprinted by Pelli and Fraticelli. But this is of a very doubtful character. Dante appears in it as *vir pernobilis*, a designation which is given to him in no other contemporary document of any authenticity. This very circumstance might arouse suspicion, as a touch betraying a later date. Only a careful critical testing of the document could settle the question satisfactorily ; but this has long been impossible, for the document was lost. It is curious that so important a document should have been lost after its importance became apparent. No one save Father Ildefonso, who published it, is known to have seen it. We do not know whether he tested it critically, nor what was its date, nor whether it was an original or a copy, nor whether its outward form gave any ground for doubt. On all these points we are bidden to trust a man of the latter half of the last century, and a man too who in less than twenty years produced a series of twenty-five handsome octavo volumes. To believe that he subjected the alleged document to a critical examination and convinced himself of its genuineness is for these times rather too strong an assumption. Too many falsehoods, deliberate or otherwise, have been told about Dante to allow us to be satisfied with the testimony of Father Ildefonso in a matter about which all the older writers without exception are silent. If his fellow-citizens entrusted the poet with a mission, was this a matter of so little importance as not to be worth mentioning? or was the fact unknown or forgotten at Florence? Yet not the slightest allusion to it is found either in Dante's own works, or in Boccaccio, Villani, or Bruni. Not a word for five centuries, when Father Ildefonso da San Luigi was lucky enough to bring to light a document unseen till then, never seen again in the century that has since elapsed, which not only enlightens us as to the embassy, but also gives us for the first time the information that Dante was *vir pernobilis*, a man belonging to the highest nobility. Even Filelfo, who discovered a whole list of embassies, does not mention just the one which in this view the poet really and truly executed.

To this it is replied that the document in question, which was lost since the time of Father Ildefonso, has again been brought to light.[1] That this settles the matter, however (as has been somewhat hastily asserted), seems to us very questionable. Even if the rediscovered paper is of the alleged date—and we say this without casting any doubt on the good faith of Father Ildefonso, only on his critical infallibility—the question still remains whether its authority can override the silence of four centuries. No one would now accept the genuineness of the notorious 'Letter of Brother Ilario,' even if a MS. of it were found dating unquestionably from the first half of the fourteenth century. We must then confess that, with all deference to Milanesi, our historic conscience forbids us to regard Dante's mission to

[1] Gaetano Milanesi in *Rivista Critica della Letteratura Italiana* for January 1885.

San Gemignano as among the established incidents of his life. For the present the question must remain open pending a decisive and final solution. The future will show whether our doubts are well grounded, and we can tranquilly await its verdict.

Meanwhile there is no doubt that Dante discharged the office of prior, that is, a member of the government of Florence. Of this office the tenure only lasted two months; and those who had held were not re-eligible for two years. Thus the number of priors in Florence was considerable; since six were in office at one time, or thirty-six in a year. We mention this in order to reduce to its proper value the importance of the fact that Dante was called to the highest office in the State.

The date at which Dante was prior was beyond doubt 1300. We should remember that according to the style in use in Florence at the period, the year began on March 25. It is agreed on nearly all hands that Dante's months of office were from June 15 to August 15. His colleagues, as given in the list of priors, were: Noffo son of Guido Bonafedi, Neri son of Jacopo del Giudice Alberti, Nello son of Arrighetti, Biondo son of Dante Bilenchi, Ricco Falconetti, and Fazio of Micciole, the 'Gonfalonier.' To test the accuracy of these statements, it may be well to cast a glance at contemporary events.

The most powerful house in the neighbouring State of Pistoia (which had expelled its Ghibelines in 1295) was that of the Cancellieri. In 1300 this was divided against itself; one party, from an ancestress named Bianca, took the surname of 'Whites'; and the other was called in contradistinction, the 'Blacks.' In one of the many squabbles which took place one of the Whites was slightly wounded. The Blacks, for the sake of peace, sent the youthful offender to their antagonists to ask for pardon. The Whites seized him, dragged him into a stable, cut off his right hand on the manger, and sent him back thus mutilated to his friends. This atrocity was the signal for an outbreak. The whole of Pistoia took sides, and bloody fighting ensued. Then the Florentines stepped in, and, in the hope of restoring order, deported the most prominent and influential persons on both sides to Florence. This measure of pacification had anything but salutary results. Pistoia was not quieted; but serious divisions arose in Florence, which hitherto had been tolerably united. Here also every one took sides, and the feud of Blacks and Whites at Florence soon cast those of Pistoia into oblivion. At the head of the Blacks was the ancient and noble house of the Donati, led by the brave, energetic, not to say violent Corso; the leaders of the Whites being the Cerchi, a mercantile family (Par. xvi. 65) not noble but rich and powerful. Their chief was Vieri, a proud man, but lacking energy. To abate the virulence of faction the government invoked the mediation of Pope Boniface VIII. Betrayed, as we shall presently see, by his own bold schemes, he ordered Vieri de' Cerchi before him, and bade him make peace with the Donati and leave the conduct of matters to himself, the Pope. Vieri replied with dignity that he had no intention of fighting with anybody; an evasive answer which drew the wrath of the Pope on himself and his party. The first actual conflict took place; several were wounded, and one of the Whites had his nose cut off. Before evening the whole city was in arms. (Vill. viii. 39.)

Before we go farther we must cast a glance towards Rome. Boniface VIII. cherished the idea of bringing all Tuscany within the states of the Church, and pursued the bold scheme with his wonted reckless energy. 'The Prince of modern Pharisees' (as Dante styles him, H. xxvii. 85) had, so long ago as January 23, 1296, thought fit to launch a bull, couched in terms of childish arrogance and churlish madness, in which he forbade the Florentines, as though his subjects, to revoke the sentence of banishment against Giano della Bella. Early in 1300 three Florentine citizens then residing in Rome—Simoni Gherardi, Noffo Quintavalle, and Cambio di Sesto—were charged with conspiracy against their own city, and after examination held were condemned to heavy fines. Of what nature the conspiracy was we are not informed; but that Boniface VIII. knew something of it appears from his proceedings. Hardly had he got wind of the business when he wrote to the government of Florence, and demanded that the case should be stopped; saying, with some *naïveté*, that it looked as if he was likely to be implicated. As his despatch produced no effect, he applied on April 24, and again on May 15, to the Bishop of Florence, claiming the overlordship of Tuscany, and demanding that proceedings should be taken against those who had revealed the conspiracy and accused the traitors. The Papal Briefs are worth reading in the original.[1] Meanwhile Boniface had, on May 13, addressed a letter to the Elector of Saxony, in which he expressed his intention of bringing Tuscany *again* into the domains of the Church, and subjecting it to her jurisdiction. He bids the Elector use his influence with the Emperor Albert to bring this about, sending with that object the Bishop of Ancona as his plenipotentiary into Germany, with instructions to treat with the Elector, or directly with the Emperor. It is not to our present purpose to proceed farther with this branch of the story. So much is sufficient to indicate the schemes

---

[1] See Guido Levi, *Bonifazio VIII. e le sue relazioni col Comune di Firenze.* (Rome, 1882), Doc. ii. and iv.

of the Pope, the knowledge of which is indispensable for the understanding of the events which ensued at Florence.

As we have said, on the evening of May 1, 1300, all Florence was under arms. The chiefs of the Guelf party, anxious lest the Ghibelines should seize the opportunity to return, invoked the mediation of the Pope. Boniface naturally did not take much asking. In the following month he sent the Cardinal of Ostia, Matthew of Acquasparta, to Florence, with the title of pacificator, but really in the hope of carrying his ambitious schemes into effect. The Cardinal arrived in June, and was honourably received by the Florentines. After resting for a few days, he demanded, assigning sundry good reasons, that the chief power should be put into his hands, as an essential preliminary to the restoration of peace. The Whites, however, who held the reins of government, and were quite alive to the Pope's schemes, fearing, as Villani says, to lose their position, and suspecting trickery, declined to assent. The Cardinal in wrath laid the unhappy city under interdict, and returned to the court of Rome.

Things in Florence went on as before, but no actual collision took place for some months. In December, on the occasion of the funeral of a lady belonging to the Frescobaldi family, a quarrel occurred between the Cerchi and the Donati; all who were escorting the corpse joined in the tumult; every man flew to his house, and the whole city took up arms. The Blacks held a secret meeting in the Church of the Holy Trinity, and bound themselves by oath to send a deputation to Boniface, with the view of inducing him to summon a prince of France to their aid. By some means the plot was revealed; an inquiry was held, and the governing body sentenced Corso Donati to death, with confiscation of his property, while the rest of the leading Blacks were banished. To avoid the charge of partiality they banished at the same time some prominent Whites, including Dante's friend, Guido Cavalcanti. Permission to return was shortly granted to him; but he had contracted an illness at Sarzana, whither he had gone, and died soon afterwards.

It seems, however, that the conspirators had succeeded in sending their deputation to Boniface, or is it possible that they had an understanding with him already? However that may be, Boniface summoned Charles of Valois, the brother of the French king, to Florence, and with a view of inciting him to the enterprise, held out to him prospects of the Imperial throne. The Frenchman came, entered Florence on All Saints' Day 1301; pledged himself on November 5, by oath to make peace in the city; broke his oath straightway, and helped the Black party to gain the supremacy while the Whites were banished (Vill. viii. 49).

Such were briefly the events of 1300 and 1301. The question now arises, Which of these events belonged to the two months of Dante's priorate? The question is interesting, because in such a position the poet must have exercised a powerful influence upon the course of events. We need nothing more than his works to show, that a genius such as he must have been not only one of the most important, but also one of the most prominent and influential members of the government. We have, however, independent and decisive testimony, not Boccaccio's elegant dissertation already quoted, but the evidence of a historian of weight. Leonardo Bruni writes, and that not in his biography of Dante, but in Book IV. of his *History of Florence:* 'Among the priors was at that time the poet Dante, who strongly disapproved the admission of a prince into the city, being of opinion that such a proceeding would bring about the fall of its liberty. He was on this account taxed with belonging to the opposite party, and since he was particularly prominent among his colleagues both in intellect and eloquence, every man attached great importance to his views and to his wishes.' There can be no suspicion with regard to this testimony in such a place.

What, then, were the incidents which occurred during his priorate? If, as is generally assumed, that fell in the period between June 15 and August 15, he must have been one of the priors when the Cardinal of Acquasparta was in Florence. In that case he was one, and surely not the least important, of those who, to use Villani's expression, 'would not listen,' and thereby kindled the wrath of the papal emissary. That would, anyhow, be quite enough to explain the bitterness with which the Court of Rome and its adherents regarded the poet. The only objection is that the older writers take a different view, or at least appear to do so; the question is, whom we are to believe? Villani, neighbour and contemporary, is indeed here somewhat vague. 'Dante was at the head of the government of our city when Charles of Valois came to Florence in 1301.' What does he mean by 'era dei maggiori governatori della nostra città'? Does he mean that Dante was prior at that time, or that, without being actually in office, he exercised the greatest influence in affairs of state? What, again, does he mean by 'Quando Carlo di Valois venne in Fiorenza, l'anno 1301'? Is the meaning that Dante was prior at the time when the Frenchman actually entered Florence? That he certainly was not. Or does the chronicler mean only that the poet was a member of the government when the invitation to the Frenchman was under discussion? Difficult as it is to get a clear notion from his words, they seem undoubtedly to imply that in his belief Dante's priorate did not fall at the date of the Cardinal's mission, but somewhat later; for when Boniface sent the Cardinal to Florence he had not formed any plan of calling in Charles. At that time he was still in hopes to arrive at his aim by an easier road, and thought that Tuscany would fall like a ripe apple into his lap with much less trouble.

Boccaccio's story is as follows: 'While Dante with his party was at the head of the government of the Republic, the party out of power—the Blacks, namely—summoned by the mediation of Pope Boniface, as brother of Philip, king of France, to bring our city into good order. Therefore all the leaders of the party to which he belonged assembled to take counsel, and determined, among other things, to send a deputation to the Pope.' The 'Principi della Setta con la quale esso teneva' must have been the priors; Boccaccio would therefore seem to say that Dante was prior at the time when the conspiracy of the Blacks took place in the Church of the Holy Trinity, that is, in December 1300. We must, however, allow that Boccaccio's words are too indefinite to allow us to draw any safe conclusions from them.

On the other hand, Leonardo Bruni says very distinctly: 'When Dante was prior an assembly of the Black party was held in the Church of the Holy Trinity. What took place there remained a secret. The result was, however, that they prevailed on Boniface VIII., who was then Pope, to summon Charles of Valois of the French royal house to Florence, in order to pacify and reform the city. When the White party got wind of this assembly, their suspicions were aroused to such an extent that they took up arms; then seeing that the city was under arms and thoroughly disquieted, the priors at Dante's advice took steps to strengthen themselves by a popular meeting, and then banished the heads of both parties.' In his history of Florence, Bruni makes a very similar statement. According to him Dante was prior at the time when the conspiracy of the Blacks and the banishment of the party leaders took place —that is to say, not from June 15 to August 15, 1300, but from the following December 15 to February 15. If we consider that Bruni had before him several letters of Dante's, and among them one in which the poet delivers himself with regard to the priorate and his banishment, and that in compiling his history of Florence he had, as Secretary of State, access to the Florentine archives, we cannot form other than a strong opinion as to the weight of his evidence.

Was then Dante prior from December 15 to February 15, 1300 (Florentine style)? According to the information that we have from Villani, Boccaccio, and Bruni, this seems to have been the case. But until we have more evidence we cannot venture to say so decisively. We claim, however, to have shown that the usual assertion that Dante held the office from June 15 to August 15 is not so certainly established as had hitherto been universally supposed; and also to give an incitement to further inquiries which it is to be hoped may in course of time throw more light on the subject.

After the expiration of his priorate the poet held the modest office which we mentioned at the end of chapter v. There is nothing more to be said about this, but in the same year, 1301, we find him on the limited council composed of the presidents of the greater guilds and other 'wise men.' He was also in the larger body to which the lesser guilds were also admitted. Twice at least, namely, in the sittings of April 14 and September 13, he had as *primus sapiens* to give his vote first, which is a proof of the high esteem in which he then stood. As the matters under discussion related only to private business, there is no need to say more about them.

There is, however, another point with regard to which we do not know how far it was connected with his political action, but which must not pass unnoticed. There exist six notes of hand, undoubtedly genuine, from which it appears that between 1293 and 1300 Dante, sometimes alone, and sometimes in conjunction with his brother Francesco, incurred debts on loans amounting in present value to about 37,000 francs. In one of these notes, which is given by Dante himself, Francesco is named as the lender, which has given some reason to conclude that in the other cases Francesco has been only nominally associated with him as debtor. There is nothing very surprising in the fact of one brother lending to another and sharing the other's debts; it shows, at any rate, that the brothers were on good terms. But what did Dante do with these sums, so large for that time, which he could hardly have needed for his domestic expenses? To this question, important as it is in our judgment, we can give only the unsatisfactory answer which recurs so often in inquiries about Dante—we do not know.

His political action had important results for the poet. In the letter of which Leonardo Bruni has preserved a fragment, he himself traces his misfortunes to the time of his priorate. What, then, were his offences during his tenure of office? After relating the assembly in the Church of the Holy Trinity, and the banishment of both parties which followed thereon, Bruni continues: 'This was made a cause of severe reproach against Dante, and for all that he excused himself from the charge of belonging to either party, it was generally believed that he inclined towards the party of the Whites, and was displeased by the resolution taken in the Church of the Holy Trinity to summon Charles of Valois to Florence, viewing this as a source of ill-feeling and much trouble for the city. Jealousies were increased by the fact that that portion of the citizens who had been banished to Sarzana, namely the Whites, very soon returned to Florence, while the Blacks who had gone to Castello della Pieve remained in banishment. To this Dante replies [where? in the letter which Bruni had before him?] that when those at Sarzana were recalled he was no longer in the government and should therefore not be blamed for it. Further, he says that the return of the Whites was owing to the illness and death of Guido Cavalcanti, who sickened of malaria at Sarzana and died of it not long afterwards.' Something further may be said about this; Dante himself ascribes his banishment immediately to the court of Rome, and the anger of that court with him certainly arose not only on account of his conduct with regard to the conspiracy, but quite as much and perhaps even more from the votes which he gave in the various councils. We have already mentioned that he voted three times against the sending of money subsidies to the King of Naples; still more important in this respect must be considered the two votes given by him on June 13, 1301. At the instance of Cardinal Matthew of Acquasparta, the *capitano* brought forward a proposal that day in the Council of the Hundred, that at some undetermined date an auxiliary force of some hundred men should be sent to Boniface VIII. Dante spoke against this, and on his motion the decision was adjourned. Nevertheless the proposal was again brought forward on the same day but with a limiting clause, that this aid should not extend beyond September 1. On this occasion Dante spoke in favour of absolutely rejecting the proposal (*Dantes consuluit quod de servitio faciendo domino papae nihil fiat*). This would have been quite sufficient to kindle the wrath of a man like Boniface VIII.

CHAPTER IX

EXILE

ON All Saints' Day 1301, Charles of Valois entered Florence as peacemaker with an unarmed retinue, and was received by the Florentines with great demonstrations of respect. He rested for a few days from the fatigues of the journey, then demanded that the lordship of the city and the right of guarding it should be made over to him together with the plenary powers necessary to the execution of his task as peacemaker. To this end a great meeting was held on November 5 in the Church of Sta. Maria Novella, which was attended by all the priors and councillors, the *podestà*, the *capitano*, the bishop, and all the 'good men' of Florence. People were enthusiastic for the French prince, they expected every kind of salvation from him, and all his demands were agreed to. He himself made oath that he would keep the peace and see to the repose and welfare of the city. John Villani, then a man of some thirty years old, testifies that he was himself present. The Frenchman, however, at once did the exact contrary of that which he had promised and sworn. He armed his people, and on the same day, whether by accident or by a previous understanding, Corso Donati, who had been banished and condemned to death, entered the city with armed followers, broke into the prisons and let the prisoners free, and turned the priors out of the palace of the government. Charles of Valois looked on and did not stir a finger, the dregs of the populace began forthwith to ply their trade, shops and stores as well as the houses of the Whites were plundered, many of the Whites murdered, and many more wounded. The tumult in the city went on for five days, then came the turn of villages and country houses. Troops of banditti went about unchecked for eight days, robbing, burning, and killing, until in the words of Villani 'a very great number of fine and wealthy estates were devastated and burnt to the ground.' Still Charles, who had bound himself by oath to maintain peace and order, looked on without stirring a finger. Not until city and neighbourhood were devastated did he begin his 'reforms'; which consisted in handing over all the offices from the priorate downwards to the Blacks. While he was thus employed, Cardinal d'Acquasparta came again to Florence, during the course of the same November. Possibly it had dawned upon the Pope that the feeble Charles was not the man to help him in the execution of his audacious plans. The Cardinal sought to restore peace, and succeeded so far as to bring about several marriages between the opposing parties, for instance Cerchi and Adimari on one side, with Donati and Pazzi on the other. It soon appeared, however, that the prelate was more successful as a matchmaker than as a politician. He tried to effect a partition of the offices, but the Blacks opposed. Charles supported them, and the Cardinal could only quit the city once more, leaving as before an interdict behind to remember him by. There were a few more collisions, but the Blacks kept the supremacy, while banishment, confiscation, demolition of their houses, and every sort of criminal penalty, fell to the share of the Whites.

Where then was our poet during this troublous time, and what was he doing? Villani says nothing about it. As will be easily understood, we can take no account of the so-called chronicle of Dino Compagni; be its age what it may, and its author who he may, it is a piece of bookmaking of no value for serious history; we must turn to the old biographers of Dante. Boccaccio says in his life, 'After each of the two parties had several times made trial of its strength with varying losses to one and the other side, and the time had come when the occult counsels of threatening fortune were to be discovered, rumour, which reports true and false alike, having announced that the adversaries of the side taken by Dante were strong in the wonderful astuteness of their councils and in the great multitude of their men-at-arms, terrified so the chief men among Dante's colleagues that it drove out of their minds every counsel, every precaution, and every argument save that of seeking their own safety by flight. In company with whom Dante, being in a moment thrown prostrate from the highest place in the government of his city, saw himself not only cast down to earth, but expelled from that city. Not many days after that expulsion, the populace having in the meantime flown upon the houses of the men expelled and having in mad fashion turned them out and plundered them; as soon as the victors had reformed the city according to their own fancy, all the chief men of their adversaries— and Dante as among not the least of them, but as one of their principal men—were condemned to perpetual exile, and all their real property publicly sold or made over to the conquerors.'

From this exercise in rhetoric very little history can be extracted. So much, however, appears to be deducible from it that Dante in Boccaccio's belief was in Florence at the time of the catastrophe and took flight with the leaders of his party. This is confirmed by what we find in Boccaccio's commentary, Lectures i., xxiii., and xxxiii. Here it is distinctly said on the authority of a nephew of the poet, who was Boccaccio's friend, that Dante was in Florence at the time and fled in company with the Cerchi and other members of the party. The question is whether we can regard Boccaccio as trustworthy. From Leonardo Bruni's account it would seem not. He writes: 'Dante was at this time not in Florence, but in Rome, whither he had shortly before been sent as a delegate to the Pope in order to bring about a good understanding and peace among the citizens.' And again: 'When Dante received the news of his misfortune he left Rome and came with the greatest haste to Siena. Here he received further information, whereupon he decided to join the other exiles.' These are very positive assertions, which carry all the more weight when we think that Bruni had before him one or perhaps more letters in which the poet expressed himself as it would appear with much detail with regard to his banishment. Should we not much sooner believe Bruni, who is not indeed free from error, but is on the whole trustworthy, rather than the fanciful, garrulous, and untrustworthy Boccaccio?

Until quite recently indeed Dante's mission to Rome in the year 1301 passed for a historically assured fact, all the more so that it was testified to by Dino Compagni, who was for a long time, though quite without reason, idolised. It is only some ten years since, from various quarters simultaneously, suspicions were aroused as to the historical character of this alleged embassy. They were so serious that they have not yet been set aside, and it is unlikely that they ever will be. It is our duty to set the most important before the reader's eyes.

In the first place it is questionable whether the Whites sent any deputation in 1301, quite apart from the question whether the poet took part in one. *A priori* it is highly improbable that the Whites should have thought of applying to Boniface. Did they not know enough of him and of his intentions? what then could they seek, what could they expect from him? In point of fact not a single document has so far been found in which any mention is made of the alleged embassy. The contemporary Villani knows nothing whatever of it, at any rate he does not say one syllable about it. His silence is pretty decisive, it is not the mere fact that he makes no mention of Dante's having been absent from Florence on an embassy that is of importance, he has left much unmentioned in Dante's life which he can hardly have failed to know. But what strikes us as inconceivable is that Villani, who relates the events of 1301 pretty exhaustively, and himself took part in them, should have known nothing about an embassy of the Whites to the Pope, or if he did know it, should have been dead silent about it. Surely the matter was important enough to mention.

Those who follow Dino Compagni and Leonardo Bruni speak always of an embassy to Rome. But in 1301 Boniface VIII. was not at Rome, he was holding his court in the city of Alagna or Anagni, in the Campagna. Thither and not to Rome must the delegates of the Pope have gone, but nobody says anything about an embassy to Anagni. Even assuming, however, that the Whites did really send an embassy to the Pope, they would at least have shown sufficient tact to select as delegates men of whom they could hope that they would be *personae gratae* to him. That, however, was just what Dante was not. Apart from his action as prior, his votes given in the various councils can surely not have remained unknown to the court of Rome. His political associates must have lost their heads entirely before they could have thought of sending just this man to the Pope. It would have simply meant rendering any fortunate issue to the embassy utterly hopeless.

In other respects Boccaccio's account is of great weight. Doubtless what he says in his so-called biography is of no great importance, but what he says in his commentary is of all the more value. We must remember that this consists of lectures which he delivered when an old man at Florence before an audience which can hardly have forgotten entirely the events of 1301. The old man expressly refers before this audience to Andrew Poggi, Dante's sister's son—to a man, that is, whom many of his hearers had without doubt personally known; and from this nephew of Dante's Boccaccio avers himself to have heard that Dante was in Florence at the time of the catastrophe, and fled with the members of his party. It would be doing him great injustice even to suspect that he was not speaking the truth, but if he really had it from Andrew Poggi that Dante was at that time not in Rome but in Florence, does not this testimony far outweigh the statement of Bruni? Poggi may have been in the year 1301 a child of tender years, perhaps not even born, but from the picture which Boccaccio draws of him in his commentary he was not the kind of man to invent. It will readily be understood that there was much talk in the family about the banished poet, and the events of 1301. It is also pretty certain that this would have been especially talked about when information reached Florence of the death of the poet, the immortal husband, brother, brother-in-law, uncle, and at that time at all events Boccaccio's informant was no longer a child. What he told he must surely have had from his parents, from Uncle Francis, and from Aunt Gemma, that is from Dante's very nearest relations. Boccaccio's report then brings us back to the poet's own family, and they knew nothing about his embassy in 1301.

But does not Boccaccio himself mention Dante's embassy to Rome? So it appears indeed, but only appears. In his account of the poet's character he writes: 'He had a high opinion of himself, and, according to the reports of his contemporaries, estimated himself at his full value. This appeared, among other occasions, notably on one, when he and his party were at the head of the government; at which time a brother or other relation of Philip, then King of France, by the name of Charles, having been summoned by those who were out of power through Pope Boniface VIII. to reform the state of our city, all the leaders of the party to which Dante belonged assembled in council in order to make provision for that case. Among other things they arranged that an embassy should be sent to the Pope, who was then at Rome, by which the said Pope might be induced either to oppose the coming of Charles, or to persuade him to come in good will towards the ruling party. When it came to the point of debating who was to head this mission, all agreed that it should be Dante. To which request Dante, after a little consideration, said "If I go who remains? and if I remain who goes?" as though he were the only one among them all who was of any use, and the one through whom all the rest were of any use. The expression was heard and recollected.'

This hardly proves that Boccaccio knew of Dante's mission in the year 1301, and regarded it as historical, for in the first place we have to do here with a mere anecdote of no historical value, secondly Boccaccio is plainly speaking of the time when Dante was prior, that is not of the year

1301 ; thirdly Boccaccio says indeed that the Whites took counsel about sending an embassy to Boniface, but does not say that it ever was sent, still less that Dante was one of the members of it. Moreover, both here and in his commentary he mentions Dante's flight from Florence in 1301, so that clearly he knows nothing of any embassy of Dante's in that year.

In the first sentence of banishment, dated January 27, 1302, to which we shall return, it is said that Dante and those condemned with him were to be cited and summoned. How could this be done if he was in Rome? it would have been a flagrant piece of aggression. Moreover, it is said that those who had been summoned and condemned had contumaciously absented themselves, which clearly implies Dante's presence in Florence at the time of the catastrophe. It has been said that the sentence bristles full of false accusations, but even if this be so, which is not proved, its formal accuracy is hardly contestable. It would be absurd to suppose that Cante de' Gabrielli would in a public judgment have violated all the forms of law, and launched accusations against the poet which every child in Florence knew to be untrue.

Let us return to Villani. His silence has been already referred to as strong evidence against the alleged embassy of the Whites to the Pope. He seems, however, to exclude every special point that might imply any participation of the poet. In his chapter on Dante, when mentioning his banishment, he expressly refers to something he has said before. This can only mean the passage viii. 49, where the historian relates how the chiefs of the Whites were summoned after Christmas 1300, but instead of appearing left the city. He certainly does not expressly name the poet, but the later reference makes it conclusive that he meant to include him. At any rate this is certain. According to Villani the heads of the White party were summoned, and, instead of appearing, took to flight; while in a sentence dated the 27th of the following January, it is said that the poet had been summoned according to law, and had contumaciously absented himself. From these two well-established facts it must of necessity follow that Dante belonged to the leaders of the Whites who fled from Florence in January 1302, and that in consequence he never was in Rome in the capacity of ambassador.

Without piling up further evidence, which indeed the reader may collect for himself in the works cited and others, we draw the following conclusion. It is possible, but highly improbable, that the Whites sent a deputation to the Pope in October 1301; possible too, but even more improbable, that Dante was a member of it; but if it did so happen, the poet did not in any case stay long at the Papal court, for he was back in Florence by the end of 1301, and went into exile with his party in January 1302.

The first sentence against Dante is as we have said dated January 27, 1302. Is this Florentine or ordinary style? Some, for instance Balbo, have thought the former, and accordingly supposed that it was issued by ordinary reckoning in 1303. But the newly-appointed *Podestà* Cante de' Gabrielli, who issued the sentence, was from Gubbio; and it is highly probable that he had not got used to the Florentine style. Besides, the fact that his term of office ended June 21, 1302, practically settles the point.

In the document many crimes were recited as having been committed by the poet and those who shared his sentence. They are, jobbery in office (*barattariae*), illegal gains, unfair extortion, corruption, opposition to the Pope and Charles of Valois, disturbance of the peace of Florence, and the Guelf party, incitement to sedition in Pistoia, and causing disturbances there, unjust banishment of Guelfs (the Blacks, that is) 'the faithful allies of the holy Roman Church,' and so forth. After the recital of these grievous offences the document proceeds that the accused shall be summoned, as the law directs, to surrender (within a period which had already elapsed) and defend themselves against the charges before a legal tribunal. They had, however, instead of obeying the summons, contumaciously absented themselves, which in the eye of the law amounted to an admission of their guilt. In order then 'that they might reap what they had richly sown, and receive the just recompense of their deeds,' they were fined 5000 florins apiece, to be paid within three days, and also condemned in damages. If they did not pay the fines, all their goods and chattels were to be destroyed or sequestrated, and become the property of the commonwealth; and even if they paid, they were banished for two years from Tuscany, and condemned to lose *in perpetuo* their civic rights and honours, as 'traitors, forgers, and traffickers in offices.'

Among those of later times who have honoured Dante a cry of indignation has often arisen. Even sober inquirers have believed that the poet was absolutely free from blame, and condemned solely on account of his opposition to Boniface and Charles, and as one of the most influential leaders of the White party. All other charges, they think, are malicious and deliberate calumnies.[1] But is it not almost time to judge of the matter somewhat less *a priori*? Because

---

[1] Professor Bartoli, *Life of Dante*, chap. vii., takes this view very decidedly; and indeed it would seem the only view compatible with what we know of Dante's character, and with Villani's expressions in regard to him; unless, indeed, to the other charges we are to add the grossest hypocrisy. In the text the author must be taken as θέσιν διαφυλάττων.

we admire Dante's genius, we naturally wish to admire in him the ideal man. Unluckily the actual man does not always correspond with the ideal. Nor indeed was Dante an ideal, he was just a man. Say what we please, the form of the sentence is, according to the law and practice of the time, quite correct and indisputable. As to its matter, we have no desire to suspect Dante of having been really guilty of all the transgressions imputed to him in the sentence; but we cannot so easily believe that the whole thing is mere lies and calumny. He must have given some cause for the accusations, or at any rate not have avoided all appearance of evil. We will not call him Saint Dante. We have seen that exactly in the years which immediately preceded his priorate he was seriously in debt; and this makes us reflect. In a position of power and in want of money at the same time, even the noblest and most honest of men are exposed to great temptations. But even if he was able to withstand these, Florence was torn by factions at the time, and the poet had not yet 'formed a party for himself.'[1] We know only too well what is apt to happen in such circumstances. Where every man is a partisan, who can remain impartial? Who does not seek to further the interests of his own party? The honourable man doubtless does it in loyalty and good faith, but the other side sees things in different light, and judges differently. This may have been the case with Dante; unless we are to hold that he was an angel and his opponents sheer fiends.

Naturally he could not pay the 5000 florins. The plundering and devastation of November 1301 can hardly have left his house and property untouched; he had debts as to which we know not when and how he paid them; he was a fugitive, going about, as he says, almost like a beggar;

[1] Is this so certain?

where was he to find the sum? Accordingly, in March a second sentence went forth against him, and fourteen partners in misfortune, running to the effect that whereas they had not paid their fines within the allotted time, they were to be regarded as admitting the charges; and for this cause the sentence of banishment was strengthened by the addition that if ever any of the culprits should fall into the power of the commonwealth, he was to be burnt to death, *igne comburatur sic quod moriatur.* This second sentence also was formally flawless. As we shall see, it did not remain the last.

PART II
DANTE IN EXILE

CHAPTER I

THE COMPANY OF THE WICKED

WE have so far been repeatedly obliged to leave questions open, and express our regret that trustworthy information with regard to our poet's life is wanting. If the reader has cherished any hope that things will be clearer as we proceed, we must tell him with regret that the contrary is the case, and that the darkness grows deeper. The older people take refuge in generalities; and when, as in the case of Leonardo Bruni, they make definite statements, these are of such a kind as to raise well-grounded doubt with regard to their historic accuracy. The poet himself has indeed spoken often, and in touching fashion, about his life in exile; but all that he has said is of too general and indefinite a character to allow us to frame therefrom a faithful picture of the incidents in their sequence. The most important passage no doubt is that of P. xvii., in which he depicts himself as hearing his destiny foretold by his ancestor Cacciaguida. From these lines it has been inferred by many writers, from Boccaccio to quite recent times, that after his flight from Florence the poet repaired directly to the court of the Scaligers at Verona. Boccaccio, however, is clearly in error on one point; for he makes the invitation to have come from Albert della Scala, who had died in 1301. Nor do the lines in question assert that Dante went to Verona at once. Before anything is said 'of the first refuge and first shelter,' mention is made of the inconveniences, not to say sufferings, which befell the poet at the hands of his companions in misfortune; from which two things follow : First, that Dante must have passed a certain time in the 'evil and foolish company' of his fellow-exiles, who, 'all ungrateful, mad, and impious,' became his foes; and secondly, that he had parted from them, and 'formed a party for himself' before he found his first refuge with the Scaligers. We think then that we cannot go wrong if we accept it as a fact established by the writer's own testimony that he passed some time in the society of his fellow-exiles, and did not turn his steps to Verona till painful experience had made him separate from them. As we shall presently see, documentary evidence confirms this; but we must first cast a glance at the doings of Dante's comrades, the banished Whites.

After making what he was pleased to call peace, Charles of Valois left Florence in April 1302, and moved southward in order to conquer the kingdom of Sicily; a task which he did not accomplish. The banished Whites, who had gone some to Pisa, some to Arezzo, and made common cause, as Villani (viii. 49) says, with the Ghibelines and enemies of Florence, left, as may be supposed, no stone unturned in order to gain forcible re-entry into their native city. Fortune, however, did not favour them. Pistoia indeed withstood, in May 1302, an attack from the Guelfs of Florence; but the fortresses of Serravalle and Piantrevigne, in the latter of which 'the best of the recently banished Whites and Ghibelines' were holding out, and waging fierce war against the Vale of Arno (Vill. viii. 53), fell into the hands of the Florentines; and 'many of the best men among the exiles were slain or taken prisoners.' In Florence fresh prosecutions and executions followed, as the result of a belief that a conspiracy had been detected between the banished Whites and those remaining in the city. In March 1303, the Whites and Ghibelines suffered a shameful reverse at Puliciano in the Mugello, 'whereby they were brought very low.'

In October of the same year Boniface VIII., who, having slipped in like a fox, had reigned like a lion, completed the alleged prophecy of his predecessor, Celestin, by dying a dog's death in consequence of the doings at Anagni. His successor, Benedict XI., tried to re-establish peace at Florence. To this end he sent the Cardinal of Prato as his legate into Tuscany. Arriving in Florence on March 10, 1304, he was received with honour. 'This my Lord Nicholas, Cardinal of the district of Prato,' says Villani (viii. 69), 'was a Dominican friar, very learned in the Scriptures, of good natural wit, subtle, sagacious, far-sighted, and practical. He came of a Ghibeline family, and showed himself thereafter a great favourer of them, albeit at first he displayed a good intent to be impartial.' Full powers were given him to conclude peace with the exiles, and to appoint priors, gonfaloniers, and so forth at his pleasure. But as he favoured the commons in preference to the nobles, the latter opposed him in every possible way in order to prevent the return of the Whites and Ghibelines, and secure their own undisturbed possession of the property of those who had been banished. In no way shaken in his purpose, the Cardinal caused twelve commissioners from the exiled Whites to come to Florence, for the purpose of settling peace preliminaries with himself and the leaders of the Blacks. But of this the dominant party in Florence had no idea; and accordingly they sent forged letters to the exiles, purporting to come from the Cardinal, bidding them come at once to Florence under arms. On their approach as near as Trespiano and the Mugello, a great commotion arose in the city; and the deputation from the Whites left it in alarm, and went to Arezzo. The armed force also withdrew to Bologna and other parts of Romagna; and the Cardinal at the same time saw that he must give up his labours in the cause of peace. On June 4, 1304, he left the city, having previously, as we learn from Villani (viii. 69), addressed the Florentines as follows: 'Seeing that ye wish to be at war and under a curse, and will neither hear nor obey the messenger of God's Vicar, nor have peace and quiet among yourselves, abide with the curse of God and of Holy Church.' Six days later a terrible fire took place in Florence, whereby more than 1700 palaces, towers, and houses were destroyed, and many rich families brought to poverty. It was used as a pretext for banishing the Cavalcanti and Gherardini.[1]

On the 20th of the following July the Whites and Ghibelines were so badly beaten at the very gates of Florence that they found themselves compelled to postpone further attempts on the city. Villani, who takes this opportunity of expressly assuring us that he took a personal share in these events, gives the following account of them. The Cardinal joined the Pope at Perugia, and endeavoured to stir him up against the ruling party in Florence. On his advice, Benedict summoned twelve of the principal Blacks, including Corso Donati, to appear before him. They started with a following of over 150 men-at-arms. The

---

[1] They were favourable to the Whites, and unpopular as having held with the Cardinal; and having lost their property in the fire were no longer strong enough to make head against the opposite faction. The incendiary was a cleric, Ser Neri Abati, prior of San Piero Scheraggio, but 'a worldly and dissolute man.'

Cardinal wrote forthwith to Pisa, Bologna, and all Romagna, Arezzo, Pistoia, and all the chief men of the Whites and Ghibelines in those parts to march at once on Florence, capture the city, which in existing circumstances would be easy, and drive out the Blacks. He stated further that he was acting with the knowledge and assent of the Pope. The exiles equipped themselves and their allies straightway, and marched against Florence with a strength of 9000 foot and 1600 horse. The matter was kept so secret that the force had reached Lastra before the Florentines got wind of it. If they had pressed on to Florence at once, they would, the historian thinks, have captured the city with ease. But they halted; and it was not till the following day that the exiles proceeded to Florence, while their allies remained at Lastra. Owing to the many mistakes which they committed as a result of divided leadership, their undertaking failed completely; many were left dead, and the rest fled in disorder. In the following year Pistoia and Bologna were lost to them. The first was recaptured by the Florentines; while in February 1306 the Whites and Ghibelines were banished from Bologna. In May the Florentines captured an important stronghold of the Whites, the castle of Montaccianico in the Mugello.

Did Dante take any share in these operations? That in the period immediately following his exile he made common cause with the others who shared his fate cannot be seriously questioned. There is to some extent documentary evidence for it. We possess an agreement drawn up by a notary by which eighteen Florentines, doubtless banished Whites, and among them "Dantes Aligherii," promised to indemnify Ugolino Ubaldini and his cousins for any damage which had been done to their property in consequence of an attempt upon the castle of Montaccianico.

The document was written by one Ser Johannes di Buto of Ampinana, and drawn up at San Godenzo in the upper Mugello. The date is at present quite obliterated, but June 8th has been read. The Florentine exiles marched thrice into the Mugello, in 1302, 1303, and 1306. There can be no doubt, by comparison with a judgment dated July 21, 1302, of the *Podestà* Gherardino di Gambaro, that the document must belong to that same year. That judgment condemns by default to confiscation of their goods and hanging several Cerchi, Pazzi, Ubertini, and Uberti and others, rebels like themselves, for having in the previous month of June joined with a number of persons banished as Ghibelines of the family of Somaja at San Godenzo, and having with horse and foot fallen upon the castle of Ganghereta, which was held by the Florentine Guelfs. Among the eighteen who are mentioned in the agreement of San Godenzo no less than twelve belong to the four families named in the sentence. It seems therefore impossible to doubt that the meeting which is laid to the charge of the persons condemned on July 21, 1302, was the same as that at which the agreement of San Godenzo was drawn up. It would seem therefore that we have a pretty certain trace of our poet's whereabouts and actions in the summer of 1302. We must, however, again admit that we have no certain knowledge of the causes which brought him into the upper Mugello or his immediately subsequent movements.

Leonardo Bruni's statement is very problematical in spite of his pretensions to accurate information. He writes, 'When Dante heard of his ruin he at once left Rome, where he was staying as ambassador, and came in great haste to Siena. Here he learnt more details about his misfortune, and decided, as he saw no way out of it, to join with the other exiles. His first meeting with them took place in an assembly which was held at Gorgonza. After a good deal of discussion they finally made their headquarters at Arezzo, concentrated themselves there, named as their leader Count Alexander of Romena, and elected twelve counsellors, among whom was Dante. So they went on from hope to hope till the year 1304. They then made the greatest efforts, reinforced by the junction of all the confederates, and in order to force their return into Florence they came with a large army collected not only from Arezzo, but also from Bologna and Pistoia. Arriving suddenly and unexpectedly they at once captured the gate of Florence and took possession of a part of the city. At length, however, they had to withdraw without accomplishing anything. On the failure of these great hopes Dante thought that he had better lose no more of his time, and accordingly left Arezzo and repaired to Verona, where he was honourably received by the Lords of La Scala, and stayed some time with them.' According to this Dante first separated from his partners in misfortune after the defeat of Lastra, and withdrew to Verona. Unfortunately we must call this narrative very doubtful. The untrustworthiness of it has been maintained by Todeschini and Bartoli on grounds which it is very difficult if not impossible to set aside.

Bruni's whole story clearly stands or falls with the election of Count Alexander of Romena to be leader of the exiles. If this falls into the domain of fable it is obvious that the twelve counsellors also were never chosen. Now it is *primâ facie* surprising and extraordinary that no other writer knows anything about the Count of Romena, neither Villani nor, be he genuine or not, Dino Compagni, nor Scipione Ammirato, nor any other of the old Florentine historians and chroniclers. And this evidence from silence is pretty weighty. If the Count of Romena was the leader of the Whites and their allies he must certainly have shared in the defeat of Lastra. And yet Villani does not name him in spite of the exceptional detail with which he relates that event, and his assertion that he himself was present at it. If this contemporary knew nothing of the Count of Romena's position, whence did Bruni, born at Arezzo 150 years later, get his information? Was it from Dante's letters? There are no doubt two letters existing in Dante's name which do at least appear to confirm Bruni's account. We can, however, with a perfectly clear conscience set aside these two letters without further consideration. The reader will find our reasons later on when we come to speak of Dante's letters.

The best of the whole story is that Leonardo Bruni himself in his history of Florence not only knows nothing of the election of the Count of Romena to be leader of the Whites, but tells a story absolutely inconsistent with it. After explaining the reasons for the failure of the attempt of July 1304, he proceeds: 'The mistakes which have been related are often liable to happen in war when there is no single commander but a good many officers, and when soldiers do not follow the colours in regular order, but march every man at his own good pleasure in a crowd composed of different elements. This was just the case here, for there were many officers of equal authority, and the army consisted of novices collected out of the lands of many lords.' Are we then to believe Bruni the historian, or Bruni the biographer of Dante?

Besides this Count Alexander of Romena, leader of the Whites in the years 1302 to 1304, is absolutely undiscoverable. He must be the same man who was selected at Florence in the year 1285 as general against the Pisans, and in 1291 marshal to the Counts of Romagna. But this man belonged to a Guelf family, and himself held Guelf views. He would hardly have taken the command-in-chief of a force which proposed to overthrow the power of the Guelfs in Florence, and indeed we have no evidence from documents that Alexander of Romena, of the family of the Conti Guidi, was ever in Tuscany after 1300. Again, if any Alexander of Romena had been the general of the Whites we should find his name among those who were condemned and exiled, which again is not the case. As Todeschini says, 'We possess long registers containing an endless list of persons from the city and neighbourhood of Florence who were condemned to exile and other penalties in consequence of the revolution brought about by the treachery of Charles of Valois which placed the power in the hands of the Blacks. But we shall search those registers in vain for the name of the alleged commander of the banished party. Nor need we suppose that any special regard would have been paid to him as a foreign noble. The Counts of Romena were regarded as subjects and vassals of the Florentine republic belonging to the division of Porta del Duomo, and accordingly Count Aghinolfo and his son Ruggieri were in 1313 condemned as rebels and traitors for taking sides with Henry VII.'

To this we may add that according to Villani viii. 60 the commander of the Whites in 1302 was Scarpetta degli Ordilaffi, of Forti ; and that Leonardo Bruni proves himself in this very passage quite untrustworthy, since he represents the poet as being in Rome at the time of the catastrophe, whereas he was in Florence. It is thus difficult to escape from the objections we have brought forward, nor will any appeal to the writings which we have mentioned as professing to emanate from the poet hold water, since they are exceedingly suspicious, and even if they are genuine, prove nothing. It has been customary to revolve at ease in the following circle: the genuineness of the letters has been proved by means of Bruni's account, and the accuracy of the account by means of the letters. As matters stand at present no decisive judgment is possible. There may be some truth at the bottom of Bruni's narrative, but this truth is so mixed with fiction that the two can no longer be separated. We cannot unconditionally reject the statement that the Whites chose Count Alexander of Romena as their general, and assigned him twelve counsellors, Dante being among them; but it is highly improbable.

After the deed dated at San Godenzo, then all traces of Dante are again lost. We know, however, for certain, from his own words, that after a time he separated from his companions in exile, and as we now say retired into a corner. With regard to his companions in misfortune he expressed himself with a bitterness that can only have been caused by a serious breach in their relations. The words which he puts in the mouth of his ancestor Cacciaguida, P. xvii. 61-69, are well known, and he could hardly have uttered more severe invective. More grievous, more oppressive, more painful than exile itself was to be the companionship of men whom he charges with ingratitude, folly, impiety, and brutality. With regard to this hard judgment we must not forget that it gives us in any case only one side of the question. It is the judgment of a man by his own admission proud; of one who was accustomed to regard everything in its relation to himself, and who either had been seriously offended or believed himself to be so. Reasonable men cannot attach much importance to such judgment. The Whites may have committed many mistakes, but they were far from being such an abandoned brutish rabble as Dante thinks fit to depict them. His complaint of their ingratitude is to us unintelligible, since we do not know and cannot conjecture what reason they had for being specially grateful to him. It would seem as if the allusion here were to some advice given by him and disregarded by them. That would have been quite sufficient for a man like Dante who, from all that we know of him, was not a man to tolerate opposition. In the entire absence of information from other sources we are driven to mere conjecture, but probably we shall not go far wrong if we assume that Dante's inability to impress the Whites and Ghibelines with his view of the situation and plans for the future, and his annoyance at seeing his counsels rejected, were the chief causes of the breach between him and the rest of his party.

How serious the breach was and how deeply it must have wounded him is clear from his own words, especially when we consider the date at which they were written. The *Paradise* was undoubtedly composed in the later years of his life, so that we see how little time had availed to heal the wound; it was still open after so many years and so many new experiences. In our judgment this can only be explained by the supposition that the poet lived in the conviction that his life would have shaped itself otherwise, that he would soon have returned to Florence, and as before have been at the head of the government if only his views had been accepted. This would account for the terrible bitterness shown even in his later years. For a man like Dante it would have been inconceivable that his counsels could be anything but infallible, and that the ways and means suggested by him might have failed to lead towards the desired goal. Few people have been so convinced as he was of their own infallibility.

With regard to the date of the breach the poet's words

give us two hints. He says that shortly after its occurrence the evil company and not he would have their 'foreheads red for it,' and presently that after separating from this company he would find his first refuge with the great Lombard. If, as is probable, the 'red foreheads' contain an allusion to the defeat of the Whites and their allies in July 1304, the separation had taken place before that time. It is, however, uncertain whether the words refer to just this defeat, which was not the only one suffered by the Whites and their allies. To fix approximately, then, the date of the breach between the poet and the Whites, we must inquire when he turned his steps towards Verona. But this question involves the further inquiry, who was the great Lombard who received the poet at Verona? That it was not Gianfrancesco, or, as he is commonly called, Can Grande, appears with absolute certainty from the poet's own words, P. xvii. 76. Who, then, was the great Lombard?

When Albert della Scala died in 1301 he left four sons—Bartholomew, Alboin, Can Grande, and the Abbot of San Zeno. It was obviously not the last, nor, for the reason given, Can Grande. We must choose, then, between Bartholomew and Alboin. With regard to Alboin, Dante speaks contemptuously in Conv. iv. 16. 'There are indeed,' he says, 'some fools who think that by this word *noble* is implied merely the being spoken of and known by many people, and they say that it comes from a verb meaning to know, namely *gnosco*. But this is most false, for if it were so, things which are most spoken of and best known in their kind would be the most noble in their kind. Thus the obelisk at St. Peter's would be the most noble stone in the world, and Asdente, the shoemaker of Parma, would be more noble than any of his fellow-citizens, and

Alboin della Scala would be more noble than Guido da Castello of Reggio ; but each of these statements is most false.' Dante would surely have never spoken thus of the great Lombard who received him so hospitably. It has, indeed, been argued that the words of the *Convito* do not actually involve any blame, but when Dante takes Alboin as an example of a man who is much talked of and yet is not really noble, and puts him beside the cobbler Asdente, this may not perhaps be blame but is certainly contempt. The theory that the *Convito* was written before Dante's sojourn with the great Lombard does not deserve consideration, for if the work had been already published Dante could hardly have gone to Alboin, and if not, he would surely have altered the passage. We shall see besides that the *Convito* was not written till towards 1308.

The great Lombard, then, can be no other than Bartholomew della Scala, and this is the view of all the old and most of the new commentators. Now he died March 7, 1304. The poet must then have been with him not much later than the beginning of 1303, since the passage in the *Paradise* obviously assumes a fairly long acquaintance. As to the hypothesis of two journeys to Verona, two separations from his fellow-exiles, and the like, they do not deserve the trouble of noticing them. They are mere theories in the air, which owe their existence only to an effort to set at rest as well as possible all difficulties in the way of preconceived opinions. If Dante was at the court of Bartholomew della Scala, he must have left it immediately upon the death of that prince, perhaps at the instance of Bartholomew's successor, Alboin, which would sufficiently explain the attack upon him in the *Convito*. Here, however, we stand on the ground of probabilities, not of securely established facts. We do not know with absolute certainty either when Dante separated from his fellow-exiles or who was the great Lombard who received him so courteously and sheltered him so hospitably. But all probability points to the view that Dante had left the Whites by the beginning of 1303, that he then repaired to Verona, and remained there till the death of Bartholomew della Scala in 1304.

CHAPTER II

STUDENT OR TEACHER?

'WHEN exiled from Florence he repaired to the schools at Bologna, afterwards to Paris and other parts of the world.' This is all that Dante's contemporary and neighbour, Villani, has to tell us about his life after his banishment, if we except what he says about his literary activity. The few words are, however, significant, for they contain the testimony of a fellow-citizen and personal acquaintance, who says distinctly that Dante after his banishment visited the universities of Bologna and Paris. No doubt Villani at Florence could hardly get accurate information about every step taken by the exile. He is, however, too honest to say more than he knows positively. He knows, indeed, that the poet led an unsettled life, and accordingly he is contented with the general remark that he went into many parts of the world. We have no right to assume that this includes Oxford, but the historian knew one thing, to him the most important, namely that Dante went to Bologna and to Paris.

According to Boccaccio, Dante visited Bologna twice—once in his youth and again after his banishment. It is, however, not quite clear whether in the first passage he is really speaking of a youthful sojourn of the poet in Bologna. He names that city in close connection with Paris, in the words 'Dante first studied at home, thence he went to Bologna, and when he was drawing near old age to Paris,' but when he went to Bologna is not stated. He expresses himself, however, more distinctly when he is speaking of the poet's short stay in Bologna after his exile, and then of his journey to Paris. In his commentary again he repeats that Dante went to Paris, and every time he has something of interest to say about his doings there. Indeed he mentions the journey to Paris a fourth time in the Latin poem which he sent to Petrarch with a manuscript of the *Divine Comedy*.

This evidence is the more weighty that we have really no reason to doubt its trustworthiness. Other evidence is of less weight. Philip Villani, Gianozzo Manetti, Benvenuto of Imola, and the rest of them have obviously drawn from Boccaccio, and the statements made by John of Serravalle, Bishop of Rimini, in his commentary composed during the Council of Constanz, probably sprang from the same source.

Documents on the subject are indeed not forthcoming, so that some doubts must always remain, but even the latest inquirers allow that the poet's journeys to Bologna and Paris, and longer or shorter residence in those places, must be reckoned among the historical facts of his life. On the other hand, the statement made by Boccaccio in his Latin poem and by John of Serravalle that Dante undertook a journey into England, and notably to Oxford, must, until we have further evidence, be relegated to the domain of fable. Even starting from Paris, a journey to Oxford was not so easily accomplished in the fourteenth century as in the nineteenth. It cost time and money, and even if Dante had the time at his disposal it is hard to divine whence he would get the money for the journey. The Bishop indeed informs us that in Paris Dante found himself in need of money, and indeed, as he makes him return from thence to Florence, he seems to assume that the visit to Paris took place before the exile. If he was then short of money, he must have been much more so after that period. The expression in Boccaccio's poem may be taken for what it is worth as a touch of poet's rhetoric, and indeed Boccaccio may be said to have retracted it later on by his silence in his biography and commentary. In these he leaves the *extremos Britannos* alone, and has nothing to say about the poet's visit to him.

The other grounds upon which people have tried to base a belief in Dante's visit to Paris are worth little. There are no doubt in his poem many references to French affairs and to places in France, but his epic is not a journal. Are we to assume that he also visited Flanders, Germany, Russia, Libya, Ethiopia, Egypt, and all the countries which he mentions? It has been said that he mentions Siger of Brabant and knows that he lectured in Paris in the Rue du Fouarre, but Siger died before 1300, and that not in Paris but at Orvieto.[1] But we really do not want these confirmations; and till no other document is found to contradict it Villani's evidence must hold good, and Boccaccio must have known what he was talking about or he would hardly have recurred so frequently and in so many different works to Dante's sojourn at Paris.

In the next division of our work we will go into the question of the date at which Dante visited Bologna and Paris. We have here to consider another question which, important as it is to our knowledge of Dante, has never yet been seriously faced by any biographer. If Dante betook himself to Bologna and Paris and visited the universities at

[1] Par. x. 136-8. But there is much uncertainty about him.

that time so famous during the period of his exile, with what object did he do so? or what did he seek there? and whence did he obtain the necessary means of subsistence banished as he was and robbed of his property, unable, too, no doubt, to meet the debts which he had incurred at home? Of any patrons whom he may have had at Bologna, Padua, or Paris, history knows nothing. That any other patrons had magnanimously supplied him with means beforehand we can, in view of his complaints both in the *Convito* and the *Paradise*, hardly suppose. Dante's journeys were scarcely pleasure tours. What then did he do? how did he earn his living in Bologna, in Padua (we shall see presently why we speak of Padua), and in Paris?

So far as we are aware it has occurred to nobody to propound the second of these questions. None of his biographers have told us upon what they suppose him to have lived. They have spent a disproportionate amount of time and space on discussing imaginary foolish love affairs on the poet's part, as though they supposed that he had subsisted on these. But in the world of reality people are wont to need, for their livelihood, clothing and shelter. Dante can hardly have eloped from Florence with a chest full of money, and the question cannot be evaded among those of the highest importance towards a knowledge of his life.

It was natural to pass over the question of how he lived, since the question of what he did was never propounded. People frequented the university for the sake of study, and it is accordingly assumed that Dante went to Bologna and Paris to pursue his studies there. It is curious, however, that a man who had already written the *New Life*, the book on *The Vulgar Tongue*, the treatise on *Monarchy*, the *Banquet*, and even according to those who believe the story of Frate Ilario, the first part of his great epic, should thereafter have gone to study at Paris. One would hardly have conceived such an idea possible if it did not stand printed in innumerable books. Dante at Padua and Paris must have been a student turned of forty, and a student, moreover, of whom we cannot say how he found the money to pay for his courses of lectures, seeing that his monthly remittance from Florence can hardly have come regularly. The only possible supposition is that he earned his bread by begging in the streets or some similar lawful method.

Who was Dante at that time both as man and as scholar? As man we know of him that he was one who may be described without fear of contradiction as proud, in the highest degree self-conscious, impressed with one might almost say a morbid feeling of independence. Yet he was not one of so ideal a nature as to be in any way incapable of reckoning with the very practical facts of everyday life. He felt keenly enough the weight and pain of poverty; strangers' bread tasted very salt to him; and the way up and down a stranger's stairs was to him hard enough. A man of such character still in the full power of his life is hardly likely to have been content for any length of time with living on the magnanimity or help or support, let us say plainly on the alms, of others. Dante no doubt did what any honourable man could do, that is, considered by what ways and means he might lead his life in independence. What ways then stood open to him? To go to the university and study there was hardly necessary for a man of forty who had been studying hard for the last fifteen years. No doubt even the greatest scholar has always something to learn, and if Dante had been a man of completely independent resources we might easily conceive of his visiting Bologna and Paris with the sole aim of deepening and widening his knowledge. But in his circumstances this could only be a secondary object. If he, one of the most prominent scholars of his time, betook himself in his mature years to universities, we may be sure that, in addition to learning, his object was to secure an independent and honourable position in life by instructing. In other words he went to Bologna and Paris not as student but as teacher.

Is not this, however, the mere creation of fancy? We think not. No doubt we possess no documents on this point, and we can certainly not hope that any university record will ever come to light in which we may find Dante Alighieri entered as a regular professor. That is not our meaning. We only say that according to all the evidence we have Dante practised as a teacher at Bologna and at Paris. Here again the Bishop of Rimini comes to our help. He says: 'He was a bachelor in the university of Paris and lectured there on the Sentences for a Master's degree. He lectured on the Bible, he disputed with all the doctors as the custom is, and kept all the acts which have to be kept for the Doctorate of Divinity.' Who can suppose that the Bishop evolved these statements from his own fancy? It is true that he makes the poet return from Paris to Florence which in any case is wrong, but there is a considerable difference between blunders in chronology and pure invention. John of Serravalle's position in the Church must have made it easy for him to obtain information in Paris with regard to Dante's doings there. We are therefore at liberty to think that his report at least represents the tradition still surviving at Paris in his time.

Boccaccio in his biography affirms that at Ravenna Dante trained sundry scholars in poetry and specially in the vulgar tongue. Untrustworthy as Boccaccio may be, he must have had accurate information about the poet's life in Ravenna. In this matter the censures of hypercriticism can be triumphantly repelled with the aid of facts established by documents. Boccaccio has no doubt fallen into many errors and has no doubt also invented now and again in the interests of rhetoric, but with regard to the poet's life at Ravenna he must have guarded himself against invention for the simple reason that personal recollections must still have been in full vigour. If Dante in the latest years of his life trained many scholars, some of them at least must still have been living about forty years later, when Boccaccio was writing. Even if none of these were still there, at any rate there must have been plenty of old people at Ravenna who could remember the poet's life and work among them. That Dante taught at Ravenna then may be indicated as an established fact of history, and if so it is hardly likely that his career as a teacher first began in the evening of his life at Ravenna. If he was actively teaching at the age of fifty he must surely have been doing it at forty whether in Bologna, in Paris, or it may be at Padua. Indeed his own writings composed in those years, especially his book *De Vulgari Eloquentiâ*, seemed to establish this. The last-named work is in principle a text-book on the poetic art, and may well have formed the basis of lectures on that art or have been a summary of some such. The *Convito* too is couched throughout in a didactic tone, and does not in any way seem to have been written from the mere impulse of authorship. As is well known, both works are incomplete. We do not indeed know the reason for this, but if they owed their inception merely to the impulse for writing, the fact would be all the more unintelligible that Dante lived many years longer and had plenty of time to finish them. On the other hand if both works proceeded from the poet's practice of teaching which from whatever cause was suddenly and for a long time interrupted, it is easy to conceive that both works might for that very reason have remained incomplete. When the poet resumed the task of teaching in later times at Ravenna he would have been too much occupied with his great poem to be able to think of continuing and completing the works which he had begun at an earlier period.

We will not, however, lose ourselves in conjectures, we only wished to point out that Dante must have visited the universities not to study but to teach.

CHAPTER III

DANTE'S WANDERINGS

'AFTER it pleased the citizens of the fairest and most famous daughter of Rome, that is Florence, to cast me forth from her sweetest bosom wherein I was born and fostered until the culminating point of my life, and wherein with her good-will I desire from the bottom of my heart to repose my weary spirit and finish the time which is allotted to me, I have gone as a pilgrim, almost a beggar, through nearly all places to which this language extends, displaying against my own will the stroke of fortune which in most cases is wont to be unjustly charged to him who is stricken. Of a truth I have been borne like a hulk without sails and without helm to various ports and harbours and shores by that dry wind which woful breathes poverty forth, and I have appeared vile in the eyes of many who had perchance through some report imagined me in another form, in the sight of whom not only did my person grow vile but all my works were held of less account, both those which I had done and those which still were to do.'

So wrote Dante (Conv. i. 3), probably about the year 1308. If we had of his only that elegiac idyll in which he depicts his life as an exile in the 17th canto of the *Paradise* we should form some such picture as the following. When banished from Florence he first passed some time with his fellow-exiles, but their unreason, coarseness, and ingratitude wounded him so deeply that he found himself obliged to separate from them and thenceforth to remain aloof from partisan life. So he went to Verona, was received there in the most honourable and friendly way by the 'Great Lombard,' found there Can Grande, who was, if possible, more favourably disposed towards him, and passed at the court of the Scaligers several years of agreeable freedom from care. If any one is inclined to criticise this picture, he may refer to the poet's own words, and convince himself that they scarcely admit of any other interpretation.

Unhappily, however, history is not poetry, and real life has very little correspondence with poetic pictures. Where he speaks in plain prose the poet, as we have just seen, depicts his life in exile in more gloomy colours as the life of a needy and weary wanderer. The question is whether we can retrace his steps or any of them.

From the fact that he himself calls the court of the Scaligers his first refuge and his first shelter, we may, no doubt, rightly conclude that he went thither immediately after his separation from his comrades. In the 'Great Lombard,' as it was pointed out, we can only recognise Bartholomew della Scala, who died in March 1304. The contemptuous terms which Dante uses in the *Convito* about his successor Alboin make us suppose that Alboin gave him cause by unfriendly treatment to leave the court at Verona and turn his steps elsewhere. Further, we learn from Villani, a witness of absolute trustworthiness so long as contemporary documents do not contradict him, and also from the less trustworthy Boccaccio, that after his banishment Dante went to the schools in Bologna. Next comes the question when this stay at Bologna can have taken place. That the poet went thither before his split from the Whites is too improbable for any one to suppose, while that he went to Verona immediately after the quarrel his own words seem to leave no doubt. His stay at Bologna then cannot have been previous to 1304, nor again can it have been after March 1, 1306, the day on which a riot took place at Bologna when the Guelfs rose against the Ghibeline government, and as Villani (viii. 83) says, 'drove out of the city and its territory the heads of the White party and all the Ghibelines and the Florentine exiles, banishing them as rebels, and ordering that no White or Ghibeline should show his face in Bologna or its territory under pain of losing his goods or his life.' From that time forward Bologna remained Guelf, and it can be easily understood that after such occurrences as these Dante could hardly have thought of settling in Bologna. If then, as is most probable, he did not go there till after the death of Bartholomew Scala, his stay there cannot have been long, as indeed Boccaccio expressly observes.

Among those who were banished from Bologna were sundry professors and teachers in the university. All these went to Padua, and there set up their chairs and resumed their occupation of teaching. Naturally a large number of students followed them, some perhaps voluntarily, others no doubt banished with their masters. That Dante was among these academic exiles can neither be affirmed nor denied, since all documents, all information worth considering, are lacking on the point. Till recently indeed it was thought that we had one quite secure piece of evidence which left no doubt with regard to Dante's stay at Padua in 1306. In a document of August 27 in that year, which has been several times printed, appears among other witnesses Dantino, formerly son of the late Alighiero of Florence, now residing at Padua in the street of St. Lawrence. The genuineness of the document has never been doubted, but the diminutive *Dantino* has long been a difficulty, and it has been thought that our poet could not be intended by it. It has been suggested that the Dantino of the document was not the poet himself but a son, and if a son of his was living in Padua in 1306, it was concluded that he himself may have been so. But this hypothesis was overthrown by the fact that we know nothing of any son of the poet who was named after him, while even allowing the existence of such a one, he could not under any circumstances have been in 1306 of sufficient age to be a witness. Lastly, no son of his would in his lifetime have been called 'son of the *late* Alighiero.' The riddle has been solved much better and quite satisfactorily by Andrea Gloria. From contemporary documents he shows that it was at that time the universal custom in Padua to give all names in the diminutive form, and sometimes even in a double diminutive. For instance, *Enrico* appears as *Enrighetto*, and further as *Enrighettino*. In the very document under discussion we find besides *Dantino*, *Giacopino*, *Manfredino*, and *Ugolino*, and other diminutives. This seemed to settle the matter, and it was accepted as incontestable that *Dantino quondam Allegierii de Florentiâ* could be no other than our poet, and since the words 'et nunc stat Paduae in contracta Sancti Lorentii' obviously could not refer to a mere passing sojourn, and it was further unlikely that a stranger who was casually present would have been called in as witness for an important agreement (the sum in question was 1075 *lire*, which were not repaid till September 10, 1328), it was universally assumed that Dante had at that time his fixed residence in Padua. The question, however, at once arose how he made his living there, since history knows nothing of any patron who may have taken him up and sheltered him in

Padua. It was very natural to assume that he had migrated from Bologna to Padua with the professors and students, and had continued to teach in the latter city. Even if this only remained a conjecture it could, assuming the fact of the stay at Padua, pass as a fortunate one.

But the fact of Dante's stay at Padua, which was so long believed to rest on good evidence, has now been seriously questioned. The Dantino of the deed of August 27, 1306, is thought to be not our poet at all, but a quite different person who long survived him. Yet the identity of the descriptions is very striking. Then was there besides Dante, son of the late Alighiero of Florence, also a Dantino, son of the same who was dwelling in Padua in 1306?

Here again, then, where till recently it was thought we were on firm historical ground, we find ourselves driven back into the dark wood of the uncertain and unknown. For the present we cannot any longer presume with certainty that Dante was in Padua at all, much less speak of his stay there in 1306 as an incontestable historical fact. It is certain that by October of that year he was not in Padua, since by a document brought to light by Lord Vernon, upon the genuineness of which no doubt has so far been cast, we find that on October 6th he was with the Marquises Malaspina in Lunigiana engaged in the task of framing a treaty of peace between the Marquises Franceschino, Moroello, and Corradino of one part, and the Archbishop Antonio of Luni on the other, a task which he accomplished successfully. That he was received in most friendly manner by the Malaspina he has himself testified. Unluckily we are not able to say exactly who these Malaspina, Dante's entertainers, were, since investigation on the subject has led to no certain result, nor do we know how long the poet stayed there. The tale told by Boccaccio in the thirty-third lecture of his commentary about the discovery of the first seven cantos of the poem, implies that it was of some length. When the cantos were discovered the poet's friends and relations at Florence made inquiries as to his whereabouts. They ascertained that he was staying with the Marquis Moroello Malaspina—which of the three contemporaries of that name does not appear—and sent what they had found not to the poet himself but to his host. He, according to the story, read it, showed it to the poet, and besought him to complete the work he had begun, to which the poet agreed. These various events could not have happened in a day nor in a month. It may be said that Boccaccio's tale is incredible, but let us be clear on that point. That the first seven cantos in the shape in which we have them were not composed before the exile, and therefore could not have been found in Florence, admits of no doubt, nor was Boccaccio unaware of this, since in his commentary he plainly expresses his suspicion. Yet that Boccaccio did not invent the story may be inferred with absolute certainty from what he says in his commentary. He names as his authorities Dante's nephews, the good-natured but uncultivated Andrew Poggi, and the intelligent Dino Perini. Both, says Boccaccio, told him exactly the same story with scarcely any variation. The only contradiction between them was that each asserted himself to have been the finder of the cantos in question. Boccaccio like an honourable and kindly man adds that, he does not know which of the two he should believe. The case therefore stands thus. Two Florentines tell exactly the same story, only contradicting each other so far as that each claims to have played the chief part in the little drama. This certainly does not look as if both had invented the story, and apart from the contents of the papers it may well be true.

But suppose it were a legend which arose, it is hard to see how or with what purpose. Legends are apt to have some connection with actual fact. How could a legend arise regarding the inquiry as to the poet's whereabouts, the ascertaining that he was with Marquis Malaspina, the despatch thither of the discovered papers, if nobody in Florence knew anything about a long sojourn of Dante with Malaspina? Boccaccio's story, therefore, at the very last represents a Florentine tradition of a lengthy sojourn with Malaspina, a tradition which is supported by documentary evidence and by the passage already referred to from the *Divine Comedy*, Pg. viii. 114-139.

Whither did the wanderer betake himself when he left Lunigiana? It is perhaps best to say plainly that we do not know. People have said that he was in Forli in 1308, and there was employed as secretary by Scarpetta degli Ordelaffi. For this they appealed to the evidence of Flavio Biondo, a writer of the fifteenth century. He professes to have seen letters dictated by Dante, in which the person dictating is strangely enough himself frequently mentioned. Who can say whether any, and if so what, of this is true?

A second visit to Lunigiana has been alleged, but this has no other support save that foolish document which has been so notorious under the name of the 'Letter of Frate Ilario,' as to which it would be absurd to waste any more words.[1] We may assume that he returned to Padua to resume his teaching there, but this hypothesis again has nothing to support it, and owes its existence merely to the wish of displaying a complete picture of the poet's life and of filling up any existing gaps. Let us leave all hypotheses, suggestions, conjectures, anecdotes, and fables, and say honestly that serious history must admit itself to be quite

[1] See Bartoli, v. 189.

incapable of filling any gaps in the account of Dante's life from 1306 to 1309.

We have seen that there was no good ground for doubting the historical truth of the journey to Paris reported by so many writers, but when did this journey take place? We must in any case reject the opinion of the Bishop of Rimini that the poet had visited the University of Paris before his exile. He holds that Dante failed to take his doctor's degree through want of funds. This may very well have been the case after his exile, but not before, for at that time he must have had, if not money, at all events credit among his countrymen who were bankers in Paris sufficient to raise the necessary sum. The usual view is that Dante went to Paris about 1308. This would at all events explain the fact that it is exactly that time at which all traces of the great exile are lacking in Italy. We can also appeal in support of this to Boccaccio, who says that Dante was in Paris at the moment when the report of Henry of Luxemburg's election reached him and brought him back to Italy. The matter is, however, by no means without doubt. Vellutillo indeed reports, though from what source we do not know, that not until Henry was dead did the poet visit various districts of France and Germany. Quite recently Cipolla has maintained the view that Dante stayed in Paris approximately from 1316 to 1318. That is possible but not likely. A man of fifty would hardly have thought of such a journey. Cipolla indeed admits the possibility of his having been in Paris once before, but that he should have taken two journeys thither is also possible, but still less likely.

So we come back, alas, to the old story of our ignorance. The most probable assumption would seem to be that the poet went to Paris in 1308, and returned to Italy at the news of Henry's march upon Rome, but this assumption again is not accurate history.

It is remarkable that Leonardo Bruni knows nothing of Bologna, or Padua, or Paris, or, it may be, chooses to know nothing, and yet, if we may believe his own assertion, he had already read Boccaccio with care, and read him again immediately before beginning his own work. In spite of this he neither agrees with him nor contradicts him; he merely says nothing. *His* Dante, after the defeat of the Whites on 20th July 1304, goes to Verona and stays there, 'and he was very humble, for he sought to obtain the favour of readmission to Florence by good works and good conduct at the voluntary summons of those who govern the city. And to this end he took much trouble, and wrote frequently not only to individual members of the Government, but also to the people. Among other letters he wrote one very long, which begins with the words, "Oh, my people! what have I done to thee!" While he was living in this hope of returning home by free grace the election of Henry of Luxemburg as Emperor took place.'

CHAPTER IV

LOFTY HOPES

IT would not have required personal misfortune to open the eyes of a man like Dante to the disorders under which his fatherland in both the wider and narrower sense was torn in pieces. Indeed he could only have escaped seeing them by deliberate closing of his eyes, and he was certainly not the man for that. Italy lay under his gaze split into parties. In each city were at least two parties standing in a hostile position opposite each other, fighting each other, plundering and banishing according as fortune declared now for one side, now for the other. What was the stimulus to all these parties? Simply as with partisans in all ages,—selfishness, rivalry, and ambition. It is not true, however often it may be asserted, that party spirit has anything to do with principle. Principles are vaunted merely as a bait for the masses; the true partisan cannot conceive existence without a following of the credulous populace which is accustomed to let itself be fed with hollow phrases, and to take sides blindly. What were Guelfs and Ghibelines fighting for in Dante's days? Was it about principles like the opposition between Empire and Papacy, or State-rights and the demands of the Church? About such things they asked few questions. Their contest was over personal, dynastic, or family interests. A girl was jilted by her bridegroom in Florence, and there was sufficient ground for a feud which for a century and more brought untold disasters upon the city. The two parties called themselves Guelfs and Ghibelines, as if the principles of these two factions concerned the lady of the Amidei and young Buondelmonte. In Pistoia a family quarrel was sufficient to set the whole place in uproar, and to transplant the parties of Whites and Blacks to Florence. Florence and Pistoia were only examples of what went on all over Italy. We need merely read the impressive sketch which Dante himself gives of the 'enslaved Italy' of his days, and his lamentations that no single state is in enjoyment of peace, and that in one and the same city fellow-citizens are at each other's throats.

Whence was the remedy to arise? We can see from everything he says that Dante expected the healing of Italy to come from none but an Emperor. If, as has been often assumed, his treatise on monarchy dates from the latter years of the thirteenth century, he had already begun to build his hopes on an Emperor while he was still living in his own city and taking a share in its government. After his exile it is quite certain that he could only expect the reformation to come from an Emperor, and the Emperor who stayed in Germany, and left Italy to herself, was no true Emperor in his eyes. It was for him a matter requiring no argument that a true Emperor had no more important, no more pressing duty than to come to Italy and restore order there. Accordingly Rudolf of Habsburg, Adolf of Nassau, and Albert of Austria, are for him no true Emperors. They had never thought to make their imperial rights of as much avail in Italy as in Germany. He calls Frederick II. the last Emperor of the Romans, and justifies his expression with the remark, 'the last, I mean with reference to the

L

present time, irrespective of the fact that Rudolf and Adolf and Albert have been since elected.' Hence also the terribly bitter apostrophe in Purg. vi., which, by a poetical fiction, is addressed to the 'German Albert,' but in reality no doubt was intended to reach Louis of Bavaria, wherein he invokes God's terrible judgments upon the head of the Emperor for having left Italy to grow savage and untamed, and in her neglected state to appeal to the Emperor.

> Come and behold thy Rome, how she laments
> Widowed and desolate, calling night and day :
> My Caesar, why dost thou not mate with me?

But the German Emperors had more reasonable work to do than to travel into a country where they had so often found their ruin, in order to establish problematic rights resting on tradition. The shades of Barbarossa and all the Hohenstaufen rose from their graves, pointing a warning finger to their successors to check them from crossing the Alps. The Habsburgs—calm, practical, and politically quick-witted—took the warning to heart. They cast no greedy looks towards Italy, so hard to conquer, and harder still to hold, and only considered how to found their Empire on a firm base in Germany. Had not the imperial crown passed to an unpractical idealist there would have been little more thought of German Emperors marching to Rome even had a hundred poets beckoned them to their weeping capital.

As we know, however, just at this time the crown was placed upon the head of an idealist. Owing to the activity of the Archbishops of Mainz and Trier, Henry, Count of Luxemburg, was crowned Emperor at Aachen on 9th January 1309, and in him a hero of romance was seated on the throne of the Caesars. The Cardinal of Ostia described him as the best man in Germany, noble and chivalrous, of a religious nature, and destined to great things. In fact, however, he was a thoroughly unpractical idealist, quite incapable of reckoning with existing conditions and with actual facts. Brought up at the French court, and an enthusiast for French culture, he thought only of external brilliancy, and conceived himself capable of conjuring up again times that were gone by for ever. His ideal was the old universal monarchy of Rome, which he deemed himself called to re-establish, while he thought little enough about the affairs of Germany. It was natural that immediately after his coronation he should decide upon a journey to Rome. There was perhaps no great objection to this, but the notion that his mere presence would suffice to bring back respect for the monarchy in Italy, and his belief that he could dispense with all the means which prudence and foresight counselled, showed his unpractical mind. In the year 1310 he came to Lausanne, stayed there some time receiving deputations from Italy, crossed the Alps in September, and on 10th October reached Asti, where he stayed more than two months. On Christmas Eve he arrived at Milan, where, on the following Epiphany, he received the Iron Crown at the hands of the Archbishop. In Lombardy his affairs at first prospered. 'Nearly all the Lombard cities, with their lords,' says Villani, 'came to Milan to assure him of their devotion, and to bring him large sums of money, while he sent governors to all the cities with the exception of Bologna and Padua, which had allied themselves with the Florentines against him.' In April 1311 he took Vicenza and Cremona, and then marched upon Brescia, but only captured it after a long siege and heavy losses, on 16th September. He then started for Genoa, whence he sent commissioners to Florence, who were ignominiously repulsed. The Florentines took very little notice of the suit which he brought against them on this account, but rather made preparations for defence. Meanwhile he lost his wife at Genoa in November, a lady who, as Villani says, was 'esteemed saintly.' A revolution at Brescia was suppressed at once by Can Grande, but Parma, Reggio, and Cremona, at the instigation of the Florentines, rose against the Emperor, and in February 1312 Padua followed suit. Henry behaved in presence of these risings like the unpractical man that he was. Instead of taking steps for their suppression he thought of nothing but his coronation at Rome, as though that would be sufficient to bring all Italy to his side. From his conduct we can only suppose that he really had some dream of the kind. From Genoa he moved on to Pisa, stayed there till April, and then went on to Rome. He entered the city on 7th May, and there, not without some preliminary fighting, he reached in June, or according to Villani, August, his goal, the imperial coronation. Then at length he marched against Florence, the focus of insurrection, and besieged the city. He abstained from a direct attack, always hoping that it would surrender to him now that, having been crowned at Rome, he was the lawful heir of the Roman emperors. He fell ill and returned by San Casciano and Poggibonzi to Pisa, where he occupied himself with drawing up indictments against the Florentines and King Robert of Naples. He was engaged in preparing for a campaign against Robert when his death at Buonconvento on 24th August 1313 put a sudden end to all his planning and dreaming.

It is of course not to our purpose here to relate the history of Henry VII.'s journey to Rome, we merely wish to call attention to the more important points, since our poet was to some extent connected with it. The idealist Emperor must have been in a high degree sympathetic to the idealist poet.

We do not know where he was when he received the first news that Henry had undertaken a journey into Italy. From his letter to the Emperor, of which there is no valid cause to doubt the genuineness, and to which we must again return, it appears that the poet had presented himself to him in person. 'I,' he says, 'who write on my own behalf as on that of others, have seen thy great goodness and heard thy great clemency as becomes the imperial majesty, when my hands touched thy feet and my lips discharged their debt. Then did my spirit rejoice in thee, and in silence I said within myself, "Behold the Lamb of God! behold Him who takes away the sin of the world!"'

When did Dante see the Emperor? The letter is dated April 16, 1311, and from its terms we may infer with certainty that the meeting had taken place some time before; but whether at Lausanne, where the Emperor, as we have seen, received deputations from Italy, or at Turin, or at Asti, or at Milan, we have no means of ascertaining, for even the old writers seem not to know. According to Boccaccio, Dante was in Paris and first heard of the expedition when the Emperor was already besieging Brescia, whereupon he returned to Italy with many enemies of the Florentines. This is in any case incorrect: it is possible that Dante returned from Paris on hearing of the Emperor's expedition, but it is clear from the letter we have mentioned that this return must have happened before the summer or autumn of 1311, which was the period of the siege of Brescia. Not only the date but the contents of the letter are against this. If Dante was really in Paris at the time, and there is no reason to distrust Boccaccio on this point, he must have returned at least as early as 1310, for when he wrote his letter to the Emperor he was in Tuscany, and had already waited on the monarch.

As to all this period of our poet's life Leonardo Bruni reports merely as follows : 'While he was living in the hope of returning to Florence with a free pardon, Henry of Luxemburg was elected Emperor. In consequence of this election and of Henry's expedition to Rome, which had excited all Italy with the expectation of great changes, Dante could no longer hold to his purpose of calmly awaiting his pardon. He rose up proudly, full of wrath against the authorities of Florence, styled them reckless and profligate, and threatened them with condign punishment by means of the might of the Emperor, in presence of which, as he said, they would surely find no deliverance. Yet the love of his fatherland restrained him so far that, when the Emperor marched against Florence and pitched his camp before her gates, he himself, as he writes, would not be present, although he had encouraged the Emperor to come.' We can easily believe the historian's statement that Dante did not bear arms against Florence, for he was then getting on for fifty years old. Bruni, however, appeals to the poet's own letters. Of the one in which he is recorded to have said that he would take no part in the campaign we know nothing, but the others which Bruni had before his eyes are not unknown to us.

John Villani reports that Dante during his exile 'wrote three noble epistles. One he addressed to the government of Florence, and charged them with banishing him for no good cause. The second he addressed to the Emperor Henry, who was then besieging Brescia, and reproached him in well-nigh prophetic terms for lingering there so long. The third he addressed to the Italian cardinals when they were in conclave after the death of Pope Clement, charging them to be unanimous in electing an Italian Pope. These epistles are all Latin in a lofty style, rich in notable thoughts and authorities, and were highly prized by wise men who understood affairs.'

These three letters are preserved to us, assuming that they are those which the chronicler had before him and not forgeries of later date based upon his report. With regard to the third there are some doubts, not wholly unfounded; the other two pass universally for authentic. Besides these there is another not mentioned by Villani, which so far has not been contested, but for the genuineness of which we are not disposed to vouch. If genuine it be, it must be the first in order, although it bears no date. It is generally called 'The letter to the princes and lords of Italy'; its address is as follows: 'For each and every of the Kings and Senators of the parent-city as well as to the Dukes, Marquises, Counts, and Peoples, Dante, son of Alighiero of Florence, a humble Italian and an undeserving exile prays peace.' The letter itself is a song of joy from a heart filled with delight at the rising of dawn. If it is really Dante's it must have been written when the first news of Henry's expedition to Rome reached him. We can see from it, always assuming its genuineness, how high Dante must have pitched his expectations; but we can see no less what an idealist he was. The letter has naturally been admired and renowned as anything written by Dante must be, but Robert of Naples, Frederick of Sicily, the Senators of Rome, and all the other persons addressed, supposing them ever to have seen the letter, must surely have smiled at it. From the frontier of Tuscany, 'by the sources of Arno,' so wrote the poet on March 31, 1311, 'to the wicked Florentines at home'; it was an invective in the style of a prophet announcing somewhat prematurely the success of the Imperial arms.

When Dante wrote the letter he was, the date makes it

impossible to doubt, staying in Tuscany; but as to his place of abode we have no more certain information than that it was in the upper valley of the Arno. It has indeed been thought that the poet was under the protection of the Counts Guidi at the Castle of Porciano, a conjecture which seems to be demolished by the disrespectful fashion in which Dante (Purg. xiv. 43) expresses himself with regard to the lords of Porciano. Equally without foundation is the other hypothesis that Dante was staying at Poppi with Count Guido Salvatico. It is even said that he was acting secretary to the Countess. It is a thankless task to go any farther into these conjectures, for the upshot always is that we know nothing for certain about Dante's sojourn in the valley of the Arno.

That he was not merely passing through seems pretty clear, since he addressed his letter to Henry from the same place more than a fortnight later. It appears further from his second letter that the poet was not the only one of the exiles there at the time, and was not acting only in his own name. The 'most holy and triumphant' Henry VII. is in that letter summoned by 'Dante Alighieri, an innocent exile, and all the Tuscans who love the peace of their country,' to attack Florence without delay and cast her to the ground. This and the two preceding letters have been on all hands highly extolled, and set forth as an elevated example of noble thought and lofty eloquence. In order to estimate them aright, we transfer ourselves on thought to the time when they were written. This Biblical style, this audacious exegesis, this introduction of mythology and poetry, and appeal to them as unquestioned history, was thoroughly in the spirit of the age to which Dante, for all his eminent gifts, wholly belonged. Yet even judged from the point of view of that age, every one will not find it easy to agree with all the praise that has been lavished on these letters. There is no need to criticise in this place; we cannot, however, refrain from asking one question—What would a sovereign say at the present day to such a letter, and how would a modern state judge, and if necessary behave towards a citizen who would use such language with regard to it as is used in these letters?

The letters were not of the slightest use to the poet. Henry did not listen to his voice; he wasted much time before Brescia, and saw his forces materially weakened. When he at length started for Tuscany his star was already paling, and even Dante might have reduced his soaring hopes and expectations to a more modest measure. The death-bed at Buonconvento gave a tragic reply to all the incitements and threats of prophetic inspiration. For their part the Florentines had, by the end of April 1311, recalled all the banished Guelfs in order to strengthen themselves against Henry, and thus, by the so-called reform of Baldo d' Aguglione, had granted an amnesty to most of the banished Whites on 2nd September. Dante, however, was, with others, expressly excluded from this, so that, while he was fully counting on a speedy triumphant return to his native city, the gates of it were being closed afresh upon him.

After the writing of his letter to Henry VII. we wholly lose all traces of our poet for some time. In the present state of historical inquiry we are compelled to answer the question where he spent the time from 1311 to 1314 with a confession of complete ignorance.

CHAPTER V

UNDECEIVED

OUR poet never ceased to yearn for his native city and to long for return. In moments of quiet meditation he may perhaps have said to himself that there was no longer any chance of his wish being fulfilled, and that even his steadily advancing fame as a poet would never unlock to him the gates of Florence. All biographers are agreed that, after Henry's death, every hope of return was irrevocably cut away for him. Thus Boccaccio writes: 'On account of the death of Henry VII. all his adherents lost hope, Dante especially. Abandoning all thoughts of return he crossed the Apennines into Romagna, where the day which was to put an end to all his labours awaited him.' So Leonardo Bruni. After the Emperor Henry's death every hope was lost for Dante. He had himself blocked the road to pardon by his invectives against the government of the Republic, and there was no longer any power whereon he could base his hope. He therefore abandoned all hope, and passed the rest of his life in poverty under the protection of various lords in Lombardy, Tuscany, and Romagna, repairing at last to Ravenna, where his life came to an end.

We can obtain little material enough from these generalities for the history of the poet's life after the unfortunate issue of the journey to Rome. Both the old biographers are, however, agreed that after Henry's death no more hope remained to Dante of a return by peaceful methods. In fact, as we shall shortly see, the Florentines were so far from any idea of recalling their great fellow-citizen that they hurled at him a fresh sentence of condemnation and of death, sharpened with heavy accusations. We must first, however, glance rapidly at the course of historical events.

When the news of Henry's death reached Florence and the allied cities of Siena and Lucca, there were great rejoicings, as though all dangers had now been lived down. Pisa, however, the Emperor's faithful Ghibeline city, was in no small perplexity. An attack from the Tuscan Guelfs was inevitably to be expected. In vain did the Pisans offer the lordship of their city to Frederick, king of Sicily, then to the Count of Savoy, then to Henry of Flanders; all three declined the honour. 'Finally,' says Villani (ix. 54), 'as they could not secure any other commander, they chose Uguccione della Faggiuola of Massa Tribara, who had been imperial vicar in Genoa. He came to Pisa and took over the lordship, and with the aid of the German cavalry who had remained, did great things in Tuscany. The Florentines for their part had, while the Emperor was yet living, given the lordship of their state to King Robert of Naples, whose first vicar, the Provençal James of Cantelm, entered Florence in June 1313. Lucca, Pistoia, and Prato followed the example of Florence, and put themselves under the protection of Robert. So the two parties stood facing each other in Tuscany, both ready for the conflict.'

Uguccione did not wait for an attack from the Guelfs. Before the end of 1313 he marched against Lucca, severely defeated the Guelfs, took the city on June 14, 1314, and gave it up to plunder for eight days. With unusual good fortune he extended his conquests, and after being victorious everywhere in Tuscany he besieged in the following year the strongly-garrisoned fortress of Montecatini in Valdinievole. The Florentines marched, on August 6, to the relief of the place under the command of Robert's brother, Philip of Tarentum, with a powerful force. On the 29th August a decisive battle took place. The Florentines were completely beaten with heavy loss, and Montecatini and Monte Sommano surrendered to the conqueror. Uguccione, however, reaped only ingratitude; Lucca and Pisa simultaneously rose against him in the following April, and, hurled from his position of command, he fled to Can Grande at Verona.

Where was Dante at this time? To this question no certain answer can be given, and we have to fall back on indications. Even from such of these as we have we can draw no conclusions with any approximate certainty. An old tradition reports that after Henry's death the poet, undeceived and wholly discouraged, retired to the monastery of Santa Croce di Fonte Avellana, and there stayed a long time sunk in deep meditation. This quiet and solitary sojourn of the poet in the above-mentioned monastery has been rendered immortal by an inscription which marks the very cell which he is said to have occupied. But the inscription dates only from 1557, and we cannot now say whether it is based on any historical fact. No doubt some fact is generally at the bottom of a tradition, but how many cities and spots of Italy boast of having sheltered the poet for a longer or shorter period? These boasts are in all cases based upon descriptions in the *Divine Comedy*, from which it has been concluded, with or without reason, that the poet must have composed them on the spot. Such a piece of local description may have been the original authority for our poet's stay at the monastery of Avellana. It is true the description in Par. xxi. gives an unprejudiced person quite the impression of having been written by a man who had himself been there. But even if we allow that Dante had actually visited the monastery and its neighbourhood, we have gained little so long as we do not know when the visit took place. It may have been after his banishment, but it may just as well have been before it, so that we are driven to the admission that, even granting Dante's stay at Avellana, we know nothing about either its date or its duration.

Another passage, viz. Purg. xxiv. 43 sqq., seems to permit of a somewhat more certain inference. Dante there makes another poet, Bonagiunta degli Urbiciani of Lucca, prophesy: 'A woman is born, and wears not yet the wimple, who shall make my city please thee, blame it who will.' If Lucca in later times pleased our poet, he must surely have been there. Further, if the city pleased him for a lady's sake, he must have stayed for some time there; for one does not in a couple of days fall in love with a lady, and, for her sake, with the place in which she lives. Now, according to the poetical fiction to which he adheres throughout the poem the words must be regarded as having been uttered in 1300. At that time 'the woman' was a young girl, as the words expressly imply; so that Dante's stay at Lucca took place after 1300. Now from that date to 1314 that city was in alliance with the Black Guelfs, who were in power at Florence, and so again after the revolution of 1316; so that we may fix with some approach to certainty the period between 1314 and 1316 as that which included Dante's stay at Lucca.

At any rate Dante was at that time not so much discouraged as one might suppose; for he clearly still felt a call to take his share in public affairs. After the death of the avaricious and profligate Pope Clement V., Dante seized his pen and wrote to the Italian cardinals assembled in conclave at Carpentras, urging them by the election of an Italian Pope to bring about the restoration of the Holy See to Rome. This we know to be a fact on the evidence of John Villani, who knew of the letter and makes special mention of it. But have we got the letter? Such a letter no doubt exists, but it may be questioned whether it is genuine, or fabricated on the strength of Villani's statement. If it be really Dante's, it forms a striking proof that his courage and his energy were in no way weakened. If he wrote in those terms, new hopes must have arisen in his heart; and they can have been based on nothing but the victorious progress of the Ghibelines in Tuscany under Uguccione, and in Lombardy under Can Grande.[1] We cannot point to any effect produced by the letter, even supposing that it reached its address. After an election, long interrupted and stormy, John XXII. was chosen Pope, and remained at Avignon, a dependant of the French king and an arrogant opponent of the German Emperor, whom he affected to treat as his vassal. Thus the poet was again bitterly undeceived.

In Florence meanwhile he fell into fresh disgrace. Whether this was owing to the language, excusable perhaps but hardly to be passed over, which he used with regard to the Florentines in his letter to Henry, we cannot say. It may have been that his fellow-citizens suspected him of giving advice to Uguccione. But whatever their reasons may have been, after their defeat at Montecatini they launched a fresh sentence against several of the former exiles, including our poet, and (for the first time) his sons. King Robert's Vicar, Ranieri di Zaccaria of Orvieto, on

---

[1] Cf. the explanation of the DXV of Purg. xxxiii. 43, adopted by the present translator in his edition of the *Purgatory*, p. 428 (2nd ed.).

November 6, 1315, condemned among others Dante and his sons as Ghibelines and rebels, as well as for divers other crimes, to death by beheading, in the event of their ever falling into the hands of the Florentines.

What reasons could they have had in Florence for this severe procedure in respect of the poet's sons? They were then youths of twenty or so, and it seems natural to assume, though it is but an assumption, that they had borne arms under Uguccione against the Guelfs. But here again we are in darkness; we have the sentence, but know not the grounds for it. Just as little are we able to discover any traces of the great exile until we find him again at Ravenna. Various persons endowed with the faculty of imagining and combining, have done their best to supply the deficiency, and save us from having to confess our ignorance. It has been suggested that Dante was at Ravenna with Guido Novello as early as 1313 or 1314, and was sent by him on a mission to Venice. This assumption, based on a foolish document calling itself a letter of Dante's, forgets among other things the fact that Guido could not have sent an ambassador to Venice in any of these years, seeing that he was not lord of Ravenna, but had just become *Podestà* of Cesena. Other views are that Dante stayed for some time at Genoa, at Pisa, at Gubbio, at Udine, and sundry other places; all which is quite possible, but gives us nothing definite to go upon. One story gives him credit for a miracle at Gubbio; namely that he taught French (which he might have done) and Greek, which he certainly did not know. On the other hand it has been assumed, and indeed since the time of Troya announced as a fact, that after Uguccione's expulsion from Pisa and Lucca, Dante repaired, perhaps in his company, to Verona; and there stayed for an indefinite number of years at Can Grande's court, until some not well-ascertained unpleasantness drove him to exchange Verona for Ravenna. Here again, however, we know nothing positively, and the appeal to Par. xvii. 88 proves little, since the receipt of benefits does not necessarily imply a stay with the benefactor, while the letter to Can Grande, if it be genuine, seems distinctly to exclude any long sojourn of the author at the court of the person addressed. On the strength of a rhetorical exercise of later date, which was innocently accepted as a letter of Dante's, a beautiful and touching chapter has been composed in which it was related how in 1316 Florence opened her gates once more to the great poet, but upon conditions so humiliating that his proud soul rejected with contempt the offered pardon, and preferred rather to go on eating the bitter bread of exile than to return by a way unworthy of him.[1] But history must confess that from the death of Henry VII. to his settlement at Ravenna Dante's life is a blank.

[1] The reference is to the 'Letter to a Florentine friend,' No. X. in Fraticelli's edition. It should be said that Boccaccio knew of the letter, for he quotes a phrase from it; that Witte accepted it as genuine; and that Bartoli, who is by no means easy to satisfy, appears to do the same.

CHAPTER VI

THE LAST REFUGE

As was said at the end of the last chapter, we lose all trace of the great exile from the death of Henry VII., until we find him at Ravenna; and in the present state of our information it is lost labour to try to discover where he stayed in the intervening period. If it could be proved that Dante paid a second visit to Verona, and stayed for any time at Can Grande's court, we must assume that this took place between 1313 and 1316. But there is no historical evidence for the second stay at Verona of which the biographers speak, although the tradition which affirms it deserves respect. It is indeed supported to some extent by the often-quoted passage (Par. xvii. 88) in which the poet receives from Cacciaguida the advice to hold by Can Grande and his benefits; but not to such an extent as to exclude all doubt. As has been already pointed out, one can place one's hopes on a benefactor, without being in his close company. Still the words do imply that Dante received favour from Can Grande, and it is more probable that they were received in Verona than in some remote spot. So far then, the passage corroborated the tradition.

In the letter of dedication to Can Grande, we find it stated that the fame of the prince had moved the poet to go to Verona and see for himself, and that he there learnt how far the actual fact surpassed the rumour. This would be decisive evidence, were the genuineness of the letter beyond dispute. But there is another difficulty. The words of the letter clearly imply that Dante had never seen the prince until he was drawn by the fame of him to Verona. But from the *Paradise* it appears undoubtedly that he had seen Can Grande some years previously, when he found his first shelter with his father Bartolommeo.[1]

According to the once famous, subsequently notorious treatise *De aquâ et terrâ*, Dante was at Verona early in 1320, but the genuineness of the treatise is now given up and no argument can be based on it.

It is commonly assumed that about the end of 1316 or the beginning of 1317 Dante went to Verona with Uguccione della Faggiuola, when the latter being driven out of Pisa and Lucca fled to Can Grande, but this assumption is based solely on the conjecture that Dante stayed at Lucca till Uguccione was driven from that city, while all that we definitely know about the matter is that his stay there must have taken place some years later than 1300. Here then again we are in uncertainty, and find no sure traces of the poet until close upon the end of his life. The fact that he spent his last days at Ravenna is certain beyond doubt, but as to the date of his arrival in that place authorities differ. Villani's account is, 'On September 14th, 1321, died at Ravenna in Romagna, Dante Alighieri of Florence, having returned from a mission to Venice in the service of the lord of Polenta with whom he was staying.' Here as will be seen the statement of time is quite vague although the form of the expression seems to point to a long stay.

[1] Is it necessary to point out that Dante may quite well have seen Can Grande when a boy of eleven or twelve, and yet have known nothing except by rumour of the magnificence of his adult years?

Boccaccio, who may have been well informed about Dante's life at Ravenna, says: 'Upon Henry's death all who had held with him lost all hope, especially Dante, who abandoning all idea of return, crossed the Apennines into Romagna, where the day which was to put an end to all his toils awaited him. At Ravenna, a city in Romagna of ancient renown, the lord at that time was a noble knight, by name Guido Novello of Polenta, who being a man of cultivation valued very highly all eminent persons, and more especially those who were distinguished for learning. When it came to his ears that Dante, whose worth he had long known by report, had lost all hope and was staying in Romagna, he formed the resolution to take him up and show him honour. Nor did he wait to be besought by him but rather considered magnanimously how much it shames worthy men to be beggars, and met him with pressing invitations, beseeching Dante as a special favour for the very thing which he knew that Dante might have begged of him, namely that he should come to him and be his guest. Wherefore since the wills of both agreed, of him who asked and of him who was asked, and moreover the liberality of the noble knight pleased Dante well, while he on his part was constrained by necessity, he went without awaiting a second invitation to Ravenna, where the lord of the city received him with much honour and raised his fallen hopes with friendly speech, giving him abundantly that which he needed and keeping him for several years even to the end of his life. Dante, who, whatever he might wish, had abandoned all hope of ever returning to Florence, lived for several years in Ravenna under the protection of its gracious lord; and there by his teaching trained many scholars in poetry, especially Italian poetry.' Two points have to be specially considered with regard to our question. In the first place,

Boccaccio says distinctly that Guido Novello was already lord of Ravenna when he invited Dante to come to him, but he did not succeed to the lordship until after the death of his uncle Lamberto on June 22, 1316. According to Boccaccio's story then Dante must have settled at Ravenna in the autumn of 1316 at the earliest. Secondly Boccaccio twice says that Dante stayed several years at Ravenna. According to Boccaccio then we must assume that Dante settled at Ravenna towards the end of 1316 or in the course of 1317. The only evidence for an earlier date is the alleged letter to Guido of Polenta, quite the most foolish among the many forgeries in which Dante literature abounds.

Leonardo Bruni, Vellutello, and others are too indefinite for us to form any conclusions from their words in regard to the question under discussion. The *Anonimo fiorentino*, edited by Fanfani, says on the contrary that Dante spent at Ravenna the greater part of the time of his exile, a statement which is clearly taken from Boccaccio. But what we get from Boccaccio report is confirmed by other facts. Dante's sons also, whether with him or after him, went to Ravenna, where Peter held two benefices. He with other holders of benefices was behind-hand in paying the taxes due upon them, whereupon a suit was brought against him, and he was cast in a judgment, dated January 4, 1321. From the terms of the judgment it appears beyond doubt that Peter, the son of Dante, had held the benefices several years at the date of his condemnation, whence it follows that Dante cannot have gone to Ravenna much later than 1317. Again the poetic epistles exchanged between Dante and Giovanni del Virgilio, if they are genuine, show conclusively that in 1319 Dante had already been some time at Ravenna. In 1318 the plague raged in Romagna, particularly in Ravenna, and Guido Novello would hardly have thought of inviting the poet to the city when it was suffering under this scourge, still less would the poet have thought of settling there. This again fixes his arrival at a date not later than 1317. Here we seem to be on firm historical ground, though there is always the possibility that he may have gone there at the end of 1316 or the beginning of 1318.

We would not of course say that the poet may not have left Ravenna and its neighbourhood temporarily; in the course of fifteen years he had become accustomed to a wandering life, and when a man has once been used to travelling he does not remain four years and more on end at home, and we have indeed positive testimony to a pretty long excursion on Dante's part. That singular and unfortunate person Cecco d' Ascoli relates in his curious poem the *Acerba* that Dante wrote to him in a letter, 'I am returning to Ravenna and shall not leave it again.' If these words are genuine, which there seems no reason to doubt, it follows that Dante had left his abode at Ravenna for a certain time. Thus an expedition to Verona comes again into the domain of possibility. Professor Bartoli replies to this, 'In the fourteenth century it was a long journey from Ravenna to Verona, and Dante was no longer young and was not rich. Is he likely to have made a journey in order to spend his autumn holidays in Verona?' But this is forming too narrow a conception of the way in which people travelled before the days of railways. We have known a man who in his sixty-third year travelled on foot from the south-east of Switzerland to Rochefort and back, a somewhat longer journey than from Ravenna to Verona, in order to pay a fortnight's visit to his son. The men of the Middle Ages, like those who in the present day live in remote mountain regions, had very different notions of travelling from us who live at the centres of traffic. Whether Dante went on foot or on wheels or on horseback, it is certain that neither the length of the way nor his limited means would have kept him back from travelling to Verona if he had wanted to go there. Besides Can Grande may have invited him and provided him with means for his journey.

To explain Professor Bartoli's sarcasm about autumn holidays, it must be said that he does not hold the view (for which the present writer has long contended) that Dante maintained himself in exile by teaching, but that he lived on the alms of his patrons. We have, however, no evidence to discredit Boccaccio's testimony that Dante trained scholars at Ravenna, and even without this testimony we should have expected something of the kind.

Of Dante's life at Ravenna an idyllic picture has been drawn by some recent writers, of which we can only say that there is no historical basis for it. The words of P. xvii., which was probably written at Ravenna, do not point to a life of comfort and ease, and beside them the playful tone of the Latin Eclogues does not count for much. Still Dante had his sons, Peter and James, with him, and the former was the holder of two benefices. He was not in holy orders, but in the practice of the time this was no objection. His daughter Beatrice is also said to have been with him at Ravenna. Her existence, however, has been seriously called in question, and that on grounds deserving respect, though perhaps hardly sufficient to prove the document quoted by Pelli a forgery. At any rate we can say in a general way that Dante lived with his children at Ravenna. Antonia, who survived her father, seems to have remained at Florence; and it is a striking circumstance that Dante's wife remained there also in preference to joining her husband and children at Ravenna.

We have already mentioned that Villani makes the poet's death take place after his return from a mission to Venice in the service of Guido Novello. It follows from this that Dante's patron was capable of estimating his deserts and making his talents of use in the service of the state. No doubt the reality of this mission has been contested on the plausible ground that no documents have been found referring in any way to it. History does, however, tell us that in that very summer of 1321 a breach existed between Ravenna and Venice, and that diplomatic communications took place; and from a document of October 20, 1321, it appears with absolute certainty that Guido Novello had been sending envoys to Venice, and it is but natural that an experienced statesman like Dante should have been among them.

It was customary in those days to travel from Ravenna to Venice by road when speed was essential. The city of the lagoons could be reached in this way easily in three days, whereas the way by sea was dangerous and usually took longer. It was in the nature of things that Dante and his companions should take the way by land. From Venice people went by boat to Chioggia, and by the end of the first day reached Loreo by road, thence two days more over marshy ground sufficed to reach Ravenna. In that district during the autumn marsh fever rages, and it was there that in 1849 Anita Garibaldi died. Philip Villani tells us that Dante also took fever there, and in this case there is no reason to doubt his statement. On September 14, 1321, he died. Even in death the mortal remains of the great exile failed to find the rest for which he had so yearned in life. 'At Ravenna,' says Villani, 'he was buried before the door of the great church with high honour robed as a poet and a great philosopher.' According to Boccaccio the news of his decease put all Ravenna in mourning, and Guido Novello took steps to have a worthy funeral. The noble cavalier caused Dante's body to be adorned on his deathbed with the insignia of a poet, and to be borne to the grave by the noblest citizens of Ravenna. He was solemnly laid in a stone sarcophagus in the Lady Chapel of the Franciscan church of San Piero Maggiore. Then the procession returned to his dwelling, where Guido Novello in person delivered the funeral oration and exalted the merits of the departed. He cherished the intention of erecting a worthy monument to the poet, and many living poets hastened to send in epitaphs. But the plan could not be carried out, for in the following year Guido was treacherously deposed and driven from Ravenna. So Dante's sarcophagus remained for more than thirty years without any adornment, and perhaps a simple name only announced whose remains rested there. Not till 1353, on the occasion of a restoration, were two inscriptions added, which we may give in full. The one composed by Dante's scholar and friend, Menghino Mezzano, is as follows:

> Inclita fama cujus universum penetrat orbem
> Dantes Aligherius florentinâ natus in urbe
> Conditor eloquii lumenque decusque latini
> Vulnere saevae necis stratus ad sidera tendens
> Dominicis annis ter septem mille trecentis
> Septembris idibus includitur aula superna.

The other, which has been erroneously ascribed to Dante himself, but is really due to Bernardo Canaccio, also a friend and scholar of the poet, reads thus:

> Jura monarchiae superos Phlegetonta lacusque
> Lustrando cecini voluerunt fata quousque;

> Sed quia pars cessit melioribus hospita castris
> Actoremque suum petiit felicior astris
> Hic claudor Dantes patriis extorris ab oris
> Quem genuit parvi Florentia mater amoris.

For a hundred years after this the poet's tomb remained practically altogether neglected, and towards the end of the fifteenth century had fallen into a ruinous condition. In 1483 the then governor of Ravenna, Bernardo Bembo, father of the famous Cardinal Peter Bembo, had it thoroughly rebuilt and beautified. The same was done in 1692 by the cardinal legate Domenico Corsi, and again in 1780 by the cardinal legate Luigi Valenti Gonzaga. The last restoration and renovation took place in 1865, on which occasion Dante's bones were discovered and exhibited.

These bones no less than the tomb itself have a long and somewhat complicated history. A man of Cahors, the cardinal legate Bertrand du Poyet, who exercised almost a sovereign rule in Romagna in 1329, caused Dante's book, *De Monarchiâ*, to be publicly burnt as heretical. 'He made great efforts,' says Boccaccio, 'to the eternal disgrace of his memory to do the same with the author's bones. Had it not been for the opposition of a valiant and noble Florentine cavalier, by name Pino della Tosa, who happened to be then at Bologna where the matter was discussed, and with him Messer Ostagio da Polenta, both of them having much credit with the aforesaid cardinal.'

This tale has indeed been stigmatised as fabulous, and it would be almost as well if it were so, but it is only too easy to prove that in this matter the good Boccaccio was well informed and related no fables but genuine though melancholy facts. As Hettinger points out, the feeling on the papal side had been terribly embittered by the proceedings of Lewis the Bavarian and his partisans. Nor was Boccaccio the first to relate the lamentable history. Bartolo a Saxo-Ferrato who died in 1357, and cannot therefore have borrowed from the work of Boccaccio, not written till 1363, relates that Dante went near to be condemned as a heretic after his death on account of his *De Monarchiâ*.[1]

But even when this storm had happily passed over, there was as yet no rest for Dante's bones. Florence found out somewhat too late whom she had driven forth, and would gladly have given a resting-place to the bones of the man whom in life she had banished and persecuted. On December 22, 1396, the Florentines determined to put up a monument to Dante, with Petrarch, Boccaccio, and others, in Santa Maria del Fiore. To this end his bones were to be requested, and if necessary purchased back, from Ravenna. No documents exist bearing on the negotiations, but it is certain that the Florentines did not obtain their end. In 1429 the government of Florence approached Ostasio da Polenta with a fresh request for the return of the sacred bones, but it was again refused. Even the power of the Pope was insufficient to obtain for the Florentines the achievement of their object. Leo X., Florentine as he was and lord of Ravenna as well, in 1515 gave his fellow-citizens permission to transport Dante's bones to Florence. Negotiations were protracted, but at last the desired goal was reached. The last request on the part of the Medicean Academy at Florence, dated October 20, 1519, produced its effect. One day, or it may have been one night, the messengers from Florence, with the Papal governor of Romagna and other persons, approached the sarcophagus of the great poet with the view of at length taking possession of his bones. They opened the sarcophagus; it was empty, or contained nothing save a few fragments of bone and withered bay leaves.

[1] Witte, *Dante-Forschungen*, first series, p. 472.

When and how were Dante's bones removed from his original grave? Much has been conjectured, much written thereupon. It is most probable, almost certain indeed, that they were quietly taken away between 1515 and 1519, as the result of Leo's demand for their transport to Florence. The pious thieves were doubtless the Franciscans, who from the interior of their cloister were easily able to reach the tomb through a hole made in the wall, and thus saved the sacred bones for the city of Ravenna. That this was the case was verified by ocular evidence on April 14, 1890.

When the Florentines found the tomb empty in 1520 they must certainly have seen the hole that had been made, and divined who had abstracted the treasure, but what were they to do? The matter was referred to Clement VII., but he had other business on hand than to trouble himself about a skeleton, and so no legal inquiry into the theft was ever made. There was, however, no secret about it. There are documents in abundance of the seventeenth, eighteenth, and nineteenth centuries which show that the facts about the rifling of the sarcophagus were not unknown. It is, however, entertaining to see the expressions that were used in order so far as possible to hush up the matter. When in 1780 Cardinal Valenti Gonzaga restored Dante's monument he had the sarcophagus opened in presence of the civic officials, and what was found? "What was necessary," says the contemporary Cami lo Spreti. But his words are too precious not to be given here, and given in their original form:

Vi si rinvenne ciò ch' era necessario per non dubitare, e alle memorie ch' esso rinchiudeva altre pure ne aggiunse per far conoscere ai posteri l' indubitata verità senza contrasto che Ravenna soltanto gloriavasi di possedere le ceneri di un sì gran poeta.

Simultaneously a Franciscan friar, Father Tommaso

Marradi, who then was sacristan, left the following much more straightforward notice: 'Dante's sarcophagus was opened and nothing whatever was found in it. It was then sealed up again with the Cardinal's seal; the whole thing was kept secret, and no one was any the wiser.' That means that only a few of the initiated knew the real state of affairs; the multitude continued in the belief that Dante's bones were still in the sarcophagus. Only the initiated confided to his confidant the truth in strict confidence. For instance, Philippo Mordani relates that on July 1, 1841, Dionigi Strocchi said to him: 'As we are here alone, I will tell you something; you must know that Dante's sarcophagus is empty—the bones are no longer therein. Your archbishop, Monsignore Codronchi, told me; but don't you let a word out—it must remain secret.'

Those who best knew the secret were the Franciscans of Ravenna. On June 3, 1677, Father Antonio Santi made a 'fresh inspection' of Dante's bones, which showed that since 1520 they had been 'inspected' once or oftener. He placed them in a wooden chest, on the inside of which he wrote with ink, 'Dante's bones inspected afresh June 3, 1677.' What he did with the chest for the next three months or so is unknown. On the lid he wrote later on, 'Dante's bones placed here by me, Pater Antonio Santi, in 1677 on the 18th of October.' Where he then concealed the chest is not known; it certainly was not in the place where it was found in 1865. We see, then, that for some centuries Dante's bones never got repose. They may, perhaps, have been inspected again by the Franciscans at the beginning of the eighteenth century, but nothing certain is known of any inspection after 1677. There are very plausible grounds for supposing that it was only during the French Revolution, or more probably not till 1810, when the Franciscans were suppressed, that the chest was moved to the place where it was discovered in 1865.

All these things, which now are established by documents, were totally forgotten in 1864, when the Dante Jubilee, so magnificently planned and so bare of results, was first set on foot; even the information given only twenty-three years before by Cardinal Codronchi to Dionigi Strocchi was overlooked. It was believed that Dante's bones still lay in the original sarcophagus. Once again, on May 4, 1864, did Florence beg to have them back and Ravenna refuse the request, this time on the ground that as Italy was now happily united, Dante's bones could remain at Ravenna without its being regarded as a perpetuation of his exile. It would have been pleasant had Ravenna agreed and the scene of 1520 been repeated, but it is pleasant enough to think that when the request and refusal were made no man knew where Dante's bones actually were hidden.

It was an event for Ravenna, for Italy, one may say for the whole educated world, when on May 27, 1865, a stonemason, Pio Feletti, having occasion to break away a piece of wall, discovered Pater Santi's chest with its consecrated contents. Our descendants will hardly be able to conceive the excitement into which we were thrown by this discovery. Everything was forgotten for it; all thought only of hastening with all speed to Ravenna to see Dante's bones. These were golden days for the local innkeepers! Pamphlets, essays, articles poured in; criticism did not only swim in a sea of enthusiasm—it was drowned in it.

There is no need to occupy ourselves here with all the talk of the Jubilee. Dante's bones had been found again. They, the chest, the wall, and much else have been preserved since 1865 at Ravenna, and the older criticism is, we may trust, drowned past hope of resuscitation.

PART III

DANTE'S SPIRITUAL LIFE

CHAPTER I

BEATRICE

No man, says the poet expressly in the first chapter of the *Vita Nuova*, can read in the book of his memory much before his ninth year, meaning thereby that he himself had preserved only very few recollections of his childhood before that age. This fact is somewhat remarkable. Did he remember nothing of his life with father, mother, brothers, companions? The expression has been explained as meaning that we do not remember anything clearly from our earliest childhood; but the earliest childhood hardly lasts till the end of the ninth year, and people's clear recollections usually go back before that age. The fact is simply that Dante does not wish to speak of his childish recollections. It may be that he had nothing cheerful to report at that period of his life, and therefore said nothing about it. Since we are not in a position to lift the veil which he has spread over his earliest years, every attempt directed to that end must be considered love's labour lost.

The history of his soul begins with his first meeting with Beatrice, through which, as the very title of his youthful work imports, a new life arose in him. Of this first meeting Boccaccio has composed a highly-coloured and idyllic picture which we regard merely as a product of the novelist's luxuriant fancy, and to which we attach no value. We feel bound, however, not to withhold it from our readers.

At the season when the sweetness of heaven reclothes the earth with its adornments and makes her smile all over with the various flowers mingled with the green leaves, it was the custom in our city for the men and the ladies together in their districts to hold a feast each with his separate company. On account of which it befell that among the others Folco Portinari, a man well honoured at that time among the citizens, had assembled his neighbours at his own house on the first of May to keep the feast, among whom was the aforesaid Alighiero, in company with whom, according to the custom by which little boys accompany their fathers to places of festivity, was Dante, not having yet completed his ninth year. It befell that, mingling there with others of his own age, of whom there were many, both boys and girls, in the house of the giver of the feast, after the first course had been served he betook himself to the best of his youthful ability to sporting in boyish fashion with the others. Among the crowd of children was a daughter of the aforesaid Folco, whose name was Bice, although Dante always called her by her original name Beatrice. She was about eight years old, comely and beautiful in accordance with her age, lady-like and pleasant in her actions, with demeanour and with words more serious and quiet than the fewness of her years demanded. Besides this the features of her countenance were very delicate and finely cut, and, besides her beauty, full of such a kindly dignity that she was held by many little short of an angel. She then, such as I depict her, or perhaps far more beautiful, appeared at this feast, not, I think, for the first time, but for the first time with power to kindle love before the eyes of our Dante, who, albeit he was a boy, received the fair image of her into his heart, with such affection that from that day forward so long as he lived he never departed from it.

We will let this idyll rest on its own merits and question the poet himself about the love of his youth, who on his own testimony became his guide to God and to virtue. He was a boy of nine, she a girl of eight, when he first beheld her.

He saw her 'clad in a rich garment of a noble blood-red colour, modest and well mannered, girt and adorned as befitted her childish age.' From that day forward he glowed with love towards her, a thing not so extraordinary and marvellous as has been now and again supposed. There is no need to explain this early love by referring to the influence of a southern climate or the premature ripening of Italians. A boy and girl love is no unheard-of thing, and if every one chose to write his own 'new life' we should get many similar histories.

After that first meeting he often sought an opportunity of seeing her again, and 'found her of such noble and praiseworthy deportment that truly of her might be said that word of the poet Homer, "She seems not the daughter of mortal man, but of God."' His love was of so ideal a character that it allowed no sensual thought to have a place in his mind even when he was no longer a child. In a young Italian of sixteen to eighteen years this is far more remarkable than precocious love. He knew this well himself, and for this reason he skips a period of nine years, 'since to dwell upon the passions and actions of so early youth seems like telling an idle tale.' Further, up to this time Dante's love had remained an unexpressed silent adoration; he had not spoken a word to its object nor ever heard her voice, from which we may conclude with certainty that she had never been his playmate, and that he had never come into contact with her even in her father's house. The charm of silent gazing was all that he had reached. It was not until the youth of eighteen met the maiden of seventeen that she made him happy with a word of greeting, and this was the first time that her words sounded in his ear. Thereupon he had a wondrous vision, in consequence of which he composed a sonnet, which after the fashion of the time he sent to the most famous poets to question them of its meaning. Vision and sonnet are simply a new version of the legend common at that time of the devoured heart, a circumstance which should remind us that in the *New Life* we have a poetical work of art and not a historical representation of objective facts.

To the sonnet many replies of various character were returned, among them one by Guido Cavalcanti, who on the strength of it became Dante's 'first friend.' After this he languishes in a longing sweet but unappeasable. Friends and acquaintances vainly try to draw from him the secret of his inner life; he guards it most jealously, and on this account conducts himself for a period of months, even years, as though another lady were the object of his passion. When after some time she leaves the city and goes to a distance, he addresses to her some poetic entreaties to return, by way of preserving his secret. He does the same on the occasion of the death of another lady, a friend of the unacknowledged mistress. Then again he makes believe to be enamoured of another young lady, this time more successfully than he intended. The matter becomes a subject of gossip in the city, to such a point 'that many people talked of it beyond the bounds of courtesy, so that more than once it was a hard burden to me. And by reason of this excess of talk, which methought abominably slandered me, she who was the bane of all vices and queen of the virtues meeting me in a certain place denied me her most gracious salute' (V. N. § 10). No doubt she either guessed his secret, and suspected that the pretence was turning to earnest; or not knowing it, she may have wished to avoid all appearance of being acquainted with a young man who was getting himself so much talked about. The refusal of the greeting grieves him deeply, and he now

decides to abandon all pretences, but without betraying his
secret. After this an inward conflict takes possession of
him whether he would not do better once for all to abandon
all thoughts of love. His love, however, is too deep; it
emerges victorious from the conflict. On the occasion of
a meeting in large company he loses his senses in the
presence of the beloved one; he is laughed at and mocked,
and, as often happens in this world, Beatrice also, it may
be only in appearance and not from the heart, joins in the
mockery. Again the inward conflict is renewed. 'Why
do I love her if I cannot bear to be near her? and what
would happen if she were to address me and I had to
answer her?' However, love again gets the upper hand.
'I would say that so soon as I imagine her wonderful
beauty, there at once comes upon me a desire of seeing her,
which is of such power that it slays and destroys in my
memory everything that can arise against her, and thus my
past sufferings cannot draw me back from seeking the sight
of her' (V. N. § 15). He believes that he has abandoned
all further wishes. His only guerdon shall be the benediction
of her greeting and the right to chant her praises. No un-
common delusions of a mind in which passionate love has
power. During this period he writes the famous ode in
which the first germs of the *Divine Comedy* appear (V. N.
§ 19), in which it is said that Heaven itself yearns to possess
his beloved, and the angels pray God to associate her with
them, while He in His mercy bids them have patience.

> Oh, my elect, now suffer ye in peace,
>   That while it pleaseth me your hope abide,
> There where is one who dreads the loss of her.
>   And who shall say in hell to the foredoomed,
> 'I have beheld the hope of those in bliss.'[1]

---

[1] C. E. Norton's translation.

After this the forebodings of death begin and are only too soon fulfilled. First her father dies, 'then,' says the poet, 'alas! she too, the only one, must die,' and she does die, according to his statement, on June 9, 1290, aged twenty-four years and two months. In his benumbing grief he writes his letter to the great men of the city, which, however, was never sent. Then he bewails her for a long time, writes mourning poems to her both in his own name and, by request, in the name of her brother. On the first anniversary of her death his thoughts were wholly occupied with her, and since she from a mortal had become an angel of God he sets to work to draw an angel on a tablet. But not long afterwards life reclaims its rights.

That is briefly the history of his youthful love, as the poet himself relates it. But is it history? is not the story of the *Vita Nuova* much rather fiction?

History in the modern sense Dante's youthful work certainly is not. It goes forward from vision to vision, from dream to dream. Seven visions are mentioned in all, the last of which is not related. Some writers have been so innocent as to ask in all seriousness whether Dante really had these visions, which is very much like asking whether he really and in the body travelled through the three kingdoms of the next world. That he certainly did not. He cast into the form of a vision what he had to say to contemporaries and posterity. Similarly he never really saw the visions of the *Vita Nuova*; he was of too healthy a nature to be a dreamer of dreams, but he chose to cast the history of his inner life into this form.

Is, then, what is related in the *Vita Nuova* poetry, allegory, picturesque representation of an abstract thought, rather than actual truth? What, then, is actual truth? Must it necessarily repose upon documents and incontestable evidence? Are there not inward and spiritual truths, and is it not free to him who wishes to set forth such truths to choose as he pleases the form in which he will set them forth?

The answer to this will be, that not only the visions and poems, but everything in the *New Life* is an allegorical, poetical wrapping-up of purely psychologic events. Well at any rate Guido Cavalcanti, who appears in the book, is no allegory but a very real person, and it might not be so easy, we will not say to prove, but even to make it probable, that any of the people mentioned in the *Vita Nuova* are merely allegory.

The conflict thus turns really on the sole figure of Beatrice. Was she a maiden of flesh and blood, or is she merely an allegory, a symbol, an idea, an abstraction?

This question will undoubtedly give pause to any one who has read the *Vita Nuova*, and considers that Dante wrote the book when he was about twenty-seven years old. Is it likely that a young man of that age who, according to his own statement, knew nothing as yet of the higher studies, would have composed such a work, to all appearance a plain and unvarnished history of his youthful love, if there was really nothing of the kind to relate. The Dante of the *Vita Nuova* was a long way from being the poet of the *Divina Commedia*, a point which must not be forgotten in any discussion on this subject.

That the Beatrice of the later work is really an allegorical personification is too evident to need pointing out. But when Dante went to work upon his great poem, Beatrice, however real she may once have been, had long been in the grave, and when he wrote the *Vita Nuova*, he had already planned a work to the glorification of the love of his youth, but surely not such a work as the *Divine Comedy* became. In view of the period of almost two decades which separated the conclusion of the former work and the first putting into shape of the second, it will be well to leave the Beatrice of the *Divina Commedia* on one side when we are considering the question with regard to the Beatrice of the *Vita Nuova*.

For four centuries no biographer and no commentator, with the exception of the worthy Giovan Maria Filelfo, whom our modern allegorists will hardly care to recognise as their spiritual father, doubted the physical reality of Beatrice; for if some commentators did occupy themselves with the purely allegorical meaning of the Beatrice of the *Divine Comedy*, that does not imply any denial of her having once had a corporeal existence. Their work of exposition involved the fixing of their eyes only on the allegorical meaning as a person in the great drama. Not till the second decade of the last century did Filelfo find a follower. This was the reverend canon Anton Maria Biscioni, who made himself ridiculous at that time with his suggestion that Beatrice was only an abstraction in the *Vita Nuova* also. A still more worthy follower did Filelfo find in Gabriele Rossetti to whom Dante's Beatrice was neither more nor less than a personification of the Holy Roman Empire. Then came the ingenious Francesco Perez, and proved to us, with an expenditure both of acuteness and erudition, that Beatrice was the symbol of the active intelligence. None of these systems had much fortune, and it was necessary to think of something else. Adolfo Bartoli, the learned and meritorious historian of literature, advanced the hypothesis that Beatrice was not a real but the ideal woman. The professor must settle with his students how a boy of nine years old was to fall in love not with a girl but with the ideal woman. Nevertheless, this system has been fortunate enough to persuade an inquirer of such importance as Professor Ridolfo Renier of Turin to retract a former work in which he contended for the reality of Beatrice, and allow himself to be converted not merely to the ideal theory but to preach it with all the zeal of a convert. The latest defender of this view up to the present time has been Father Gietmann of the Society of Jesus. He, with acuteness equal to that of Perez and still greater erudition, maintains that Beatrice is the symbol of the Church, whereby he is compelled, contrary to all the old biographers and commentators and to the poet's express testimony, to date the writing of the *Vita Nuova* as late as 1314. Being a German, however, he was too honourable to contest unconditionally the personal reality of Beatrice; he was willing in the end to allow it, but he felt himself compelled to show that she whom Dante glorifies in his writings was not the earthly woman, but simply and solely the ideal Church. Did Dante then in his ninth year fall in love with the Church? Did the Church first honour him with a greeting when he was eighteen? Did he pretend that the object of his love was some other than the Church, and did the Church on this account refuse him her greeting and mock him?

In other works we have undertaken the thankless task of going into the arguments of the symbolists and idealists, and putting their tenableness to the test. Even if we had space here to go into the question again, we could hardly decide to do so; what indeed would be the use? It will be quite enough to question Dante himself as to whether his Beatrice is a being of flesh and blood or only an abstract ideal.

At the very beginning of the *Vita Nuova*, Beatrice appears with the traits of a human individual. The poet states definitely her age, describes what she wore, and even gives the hour at which he first saw her. She was at the beginning, he at the end of their ninth year. Her first greeting was nine years later, and at the ninth hour of the day. To a child of the Middle Age it was as natural as it seems strange to us moderns to consider the symbolism of numbers, and draw conclusions therefrom. The number nine is constantly being brought forward until we at last reach the conclusion that Beatrice herself is a nine, a miracle of the Trinity in Unity. All these are the exaggerations of a passionate love which conceives itself as beholding in the beloved object a manifestation of the Divine, and in this Dante is by no means solitary.

We might almost suppose the poet to have had a foreboding that posterity would be tempted to change his beloved into a mere abstraction, and to have wished to anticipate it. He summarises his whole love-story during a period of nine years, and sketches it in few but significant words. He often sought an opportunity of seeing the beloved one, saw her, preserved her image in his heart, but did not allow himself to be carried away by passion, rather to be ruled by the faithful counsels of reason. What sense could these words have if Beatrice were not an earthly maiden? The passion of youth is opposed to the faithful counsels of reason. This suits only the position of a real lover, while it is difficult to see how an opposition could be established between reason and passion if only a symbol or an ideal was in question. So again the remark that he 'will say nothing more about it since it seems fabulous that at such an age passion could have full sway' can only suit the natural relations of love between opposite sexes.

As the narrative proceeds, Beatrice displays further human traits. She walks through the streets of the city in company with two older ladies; she sits in church during divine service; she has a friend who dies in the flower of her youth; when gossip about Dante is circulated, she refuses him her greeting, whether from maiden modesty or from a touch of jealousy, and, as we may read between the lines, is subsequently reconciled to him; she is with other fair ladies at a wedding, and takes part—perhaps only half-heartedly—in the banter which is directed to the shamefacedness of her adorer; she loses her father, and is inconsolable at his loss; she dies herself on a stated day and at a stated age; she has a brother who begs the poet to write on her death. Surely all these are the acts of a real personage, and in no way capable of application to a symbol, an abstract ideal.

In the copious diction of idolising love, Dante relates how 'she was in so great favour among men that when she passed along people ran to behold her; whereof great joy came upon me. And when she drew near to any, such reverence came into his heart, that he dared not lift his eyes, nor return her salute; and hereof many who have felt it can bear me witness to whoso would not believe it.' Is not this the real human woman? When did Theology, or the Empire, or the Feminine Ideal, or the Church ever pass people in the street; or who ever ran to see an abstraction? Was there in those days such reverence in Florence, a city where freethinkers abounded, for Theology or Church? Or did the Guelfic state stand in such awe of the Imperial dignity? Men would have taken less heed of Dante's ideal woman than of the real woman who corresponded little enough with that ideal; women would hardly have hurried to see the ideal which they would believe they could see better in their own mirrors. Nor could the host of witnesses to whom Dante appeals testify much to the effect upon themselves of beholding an ideal of the poet's fancy, whatever might be the case in regard to a living woman.

Take again the pretended passion for another, invented in order that his true passion should not become public. What reason have the symbolists to suggest for his desiring so anxiously to conceal an enthusiasm for Theology, the Empire, and so forth? If, however, Beatrice was a real woman, the whole thing falls into common experience.

In the famous ode, 'Ladies, who have intelligence of love,' it is said that the presence of Beatrice is the only thing lacking to the happiness of the blessed in heaven. That is perhaps an exaggerated deifying of the beloved object; but love-poetry can show exaggeration in plenty. But what can symbolism make of it? Heaven cannot stand in want of Theology, Church, Empire; and as for the Feminine Ideal, both for the Christian Church and for the Poet, that Ideal is already present there in the person of the Virgin Mother.

In short, throughout the *Vita Nuova* up to the final conclusion, where the hope is expressed of meeting Beatrice again in eternal glory, everything points to a living object of Dante's love, and no abstraction, symbol, or ideal.

In the *Convito* Dante allegorises, if anything, too much. The 'noble lady' whose lineaments in the *Vita Nuova* are thoroughly human, appears there in the allegoric explanation of the first ode as the symbol of philosophy. Beatrice, on the other hand, remains a woman and nothing else, and no trace is found of any allegorical meaning to her. Should we not have had some indication, some raising of the veil, if the Beatrice of the *Vita Nuova* had been only an abstraction? All the more so that Dante, in composing the *Convito*, admittedly aimed at screening himself from the accusation of having in his youth abandoned himself more than was fitting to the love of the senses. How is this to be explained if Beatrice was no really existing woman? Even if the readers of the *Convito* did not know the *Vita Nuova*, they must have thought of her as such.

Again in the *Commedia*, where no doubt as we have said Beatrice has become a symbol of high things, the traits of actual humanity are not wanting in her. She speaks there of her death as she was on the threshold of the second period of her life, and of her passage from the life of the flesh to that of pure spirit. She speaks of the fair limbs wherein she was enclosed, and which are now scattered as dust upon the earth; she even speaks of her flesh which was buried. Is it possible that this Beatrice who speaks of her mortal body, of her flesh, and of her burial, be only an abstraction?

We might go on for long with these instances, but there are limits, and what has been said must surely be enough. We think we have shown that according to Dante's own representation whenever he speaks of Beatrice, it is an absolutely necessary assumption that she was a real being of flesh and blood. But if she was an attractive maiden of Florence what more do we know about her? To this question we might answer simply that we know nothing, and science would have to be content with this answer. But unfortunately Boccaccio has made it difficult to do this. He knows well enough who she was, she was Dante's neighbour, the fair daughter of Folco Portinari. If this statement occurred only in the biography we could easily pass it over, but he repeats it in the commentary and appeals to a person worthy of credit from whom he had the story. According to him Dante's Beatrice was the daughter of Folco and afterwards the wife of an otherwise obscure gentleman named Simone dei Bardi. That Folco had a daughter named Beatrice who married Simone dei Bardi appears from his will dated January 15, 1288, and there was no need whatever of any of the proofs that have lately been brought forward to show that Beatrice Portinari really lived and was a youthful acquaintance of the poet's. But why does the student of Dante need to ask about Folco Portinari, his daughter and his son-in-law? only in so far as that daughter was the person of whom the poet sang and whom he deified, and on one side people have said 'so she was,' while on the other side it has been easy enough to show that the object of Dante's affection cannot have been a married woman. The objection that we must not transfer the ideas of the nineteenth century to the fourteenth is of little avail. No doubt we know all about the troubadours and their moral code, but we know Dante still better, and know that in matters of morality his views were even stricter than those of the nineteenth century. It would indeed betray a serious lack of accurate thought if we did not grant to the idealists and symbolists of the present day that so far as regards Beatrice Portinari, the married wife of Simone dei Bardi, they are no doubt in the right.

It is not ten years since, contradicting the tradition which goes back as far as Boccaccio or perhaps as far as Dante's own son Peter, we first contested the identity of Dante's love with Beatrice Portinari.[1] At first the attitude adopted towards our deductions was one either of somewhat sceptical agreement or of a suggestion that we were merely making concessions to the idealists. Now, however, we no longer stand alone. The most eminent Dante scholars of Italy have quite independently of us given up the identity in question, and it can hardly be doubted that before long it

[1] In the original *Frau Beatrice Bardi-Portinari.*

will be completely abandoned. This assurance does not, however, relieve us from the duty of laying briefly before our readers the grounds which point to the impossibility of recognising Beatrice Portinari in the object of Dante's youthful love.

Let us begin with the name. That Folco Portinari's daughter who married Simone dei Bardi was called Beatrice, we are not prepared to deny; but the fact only concerns us in so far as it suggests an origin for the myth. Dante's love was certainly not called Beatrice. The poet no doubt calls her so; but poets of all ages and of all countries have been in the habit of calling their ladies, not by their baptismal names, but by other names of their own selection. Thus if Beatrice had been the real name of the love of Dante's youth, that he should call her by it would have been an exception to the rule. Indeed he indicates as much himself. No doubt there is still controversy as to the meaning[1] of the words at the opening of the *Vita Nuova*, 'la quale fu chiamata da molti Beatrice, i quali non sapeano che si chiamare'; but no controversy could have arisen but for the assumption that Beatrice was really her name. All artificialities set aside, the words mean, 'Who was called Beatrice by many who did not know how to call her,' that is, did not know her real name. But whatever be the meaning of the sentence, there can be no doubt of the poet's statement that *many* called her Beatrice. But if it was her real name, why not all?[2] And if those who 'non sapeano che si chiamare' called her Beatrice, what did they call her, who 'sapeano che si chiamare'? Clearly the poet wants to make it plain at the outset that Beatrice was not his lady's baptismal name.

[1] And, it may be added, the reading.
[2] We cannot refrain from rejoining—If it was not, why any?

This is corroborated by another fact. The poet relates at length the trouble which he took to prevent the secret of his love from escaping. How then could he have brought himself both in the lifetime of his lady and immediately after her death to trumpet forth his secret? Only by admitting such irrational conduct can we escape from admitting that *Beatrice* was only a fictitious and assumed name, and that the name which she bore in real life may have been any but this.

Folco Portinari was a neighbour of Dante's parents, their houses some fifty paces apart. One would expect that the children being of about the same age would have seen each other frequently. Yet Dante says expressly that he never saw Beatrice till the end of his ninth year. Boccaccio feels this difficulty and gets out of it by remarking, 'I do not think it can really have been the first time, but for the first time after she was capable of kindling the flame of love.' Boccaccio may of course believe if he pleases that a child of eight years old is capable of kindling such a flame, but we prefer to take Dante's words in their literal sense, inferring from them that the girl whom Dante saw cannot have been his neighbour Beatrice Portinari.

With still greater preciseness he further assures us that he heard the voice of his Beatrice for the first time when as a maiden of about eighteen years she first saluted him. Therewith Boccaccio's whole idyll appears to collapse, unless we are to assume either that Beatrice was dumb or Dante deaf until that date.

It must be admitted further that she was still unmarried when she refused her greeting to the poet, for it could not concern a married woman if he did pay his court to a maiden. One must further allow that neither in the *Vita Nuova* nor elsewhere in Dante's writings is any indication to be found that his Beatrice was married. No doubt some have wished to see a suggestion of this in V. N. § 14. But up to the present no proof has been produced that maidens were not allowed to join the wedding. On the other hand we have in § 41 a very distinct intimation that Beatrice died unmarried. To every unprejudiced mind the sentence 'Where this most noble lady was born, lived, and died,' implies that she had never left her parent's house.[1]

Folco Portinari's will, dated January 15, 1288, in which his daughter is described as wife of Master Simone dei Bardi, would seem to show that she is older than the lady of Dante's love, for the latter would at that time have been only in the twenty-first year of her life.[2] If, moreover, she had been a married woman, Dante's remark in § 29 that among other reasons for not speaking of the departure of his Beatrice he could not do it without praising himself, would seem out of place. The inspiration which he derived from her would in that case have been a ground for self-reproach rather than self-praise.

Folco Portinari died December 31, 1289, Dante's Beatrice some five or six months later. Her death is related in § 29, her father's in § 22; now if her father had been Folco, all that is recorded in the intervening sections must have taken place in the five months of mourning. We should be curious to know if any one is hardy enough to defend such a theory.[3]

---

[1] Will it be believed that the antecedent to *where* is 'the city,' and that the words quoted are merely Dante's way of indicating the city of Florence?

[2] The calculation is hard to follow, but why should she not have been married by that age?

[3] Considering that the sections in question relate almost exclusively to Dante's own musings, one would have supposed that five months had been quite sufficient time to allow for the action of them.

On the news of Beatrice's death Dante takes up his pen in order to write a letter of lamentation to the most eminent men of the city. The letter can scarcely have been finished, it is almost impossible that it can have been sent, but that the thought of it can have arisen in his soul is significant. Unless he were beside himself he can never have dreamt of writing a letter about the death of Simone dei Bardi's wife and publishing it throughout Florence, perhaps even beyond.

The nearest relation of the lady, her brother as has been universally assumed, entreats him to write a poem on her death. This would be conceivable if she died unmarried, always supposing that this nearest relation had been admitted to the secret of his love. But how the nearest relation of another man's deceased wife could have asked her adorer for a poem, conceive who may! The invitation would probably have taken another form.

Again, according to his own story, Dante mourned the death of his Beatrice for a long time, and that not in privacy but, as from his description it is impossible to doubt, in the full sight of all men. Was he more likely to have done this for another man's wife or for one who would have been his if death had not torn her away. Further, the episode of the 'noble lady' (V. N. §§ 36-40) remains on the hypothesis that Dante's Beatrice was a married woman, an unsolved riddle. What would be the meaning of all his self-accusations if all that he had to reproach himself with was disloyalty to another man's wife, and even the composition and publication of the *Vita Nuova* would be incomprehensible and in no way creditable to the poet's taste if we are really to assume that his Beatrice was a married woman. The rejoinder which has been made to objections based on the fact of the marriage of Beatrice Portinari by appeal to the manners of the time we may dismiss as trivial. We know all about the manners of the time and the poetry of the Troubadours. In the present case we have to do not only with love poems but also with a work which, though deeply imbued with mysticism, is written in prose. In the case of Dante we cannot recognise as possible the continued hymning of a married woman; but when it comes to collecting the hymns shortly after her death, furnishing them with a commentary which forms a love story in plain prose, and publishing the whole thing, it is more than any troubadour ever did. Even Boccaccio saw the improbability, and tried to escape with a statement that in his riper years Dante was ashamed of his *Vita Nuova*. He might have had reason for being so if the object of his love, the heroine of his work, had been the wife of Bardi. But his own words (Conv. i. 1 ; Purg. xxx. 115) show pretty plainly that he felt no such shame.

Among the grounds which induced him to compose the *Convito*, Dante mentions a care for his own good name. 'I fear,' he says, 'the disgrace of having followed a passion such as he who reads the aforesaid odes can conceive to have had the lordship over me, which disgrace comes entirely to an end by what I am saying at present about myself. For it shows that not passion but the love of virtue was the moving cause.' The odes referred to are those which he addressed to the comforter who appeared to him after Beatrice's death. Is it possible that Dante should have feared to come into disgrace if people had believed that after the death of a married woman he was in love with a maiden and yet feared no disgrace on the assumption that he had for years been enamoured of another man's wife. If any one can reconcile himself to such an assumption it would be better to avoid all scientific inquiry and be content with tradition. But if we are to test the matter critically the fashion in which Dante expressed himself in the *Convito* in regard to his love affair should be decisive. To his love for his Beatrice he allows its full and complete value, it is only the second love that is not to be taken literally but is rather a spiritual love for philosophy. Since, then, he is in no way anxious lest his first love should be made a reproach to him, it was clearly no illicit passion.

The magnificent vision at the end of the *Purgatory* points in the same direction. The reproofs which the poet puts into the mouth of Beatrice have no doubt a highly symbolical meaning, but so far as their form goes they are just such reproaches as a woman would address to a man whom she loves, and who has proved himself untrue to her. What right would Bardi's wife have to utter such? Surely no reader could ever have imagined that Beatrice was a married woman had it not been for tradition. In that case, too, we should have been spared the symbolical and idealistic systems. All honour to Filelfo, Biscioni, and their followers; they have noticed that Dante's Beatrice could certainly not have been Bardi's wife.

But how did the tradition itself arise? It certainly goes farther back than Boccaccio; he found it already in existence. For the 'credible person' to whom he appeals is assuredly no invention of his own. The testimony of this 'credible person' is, however, rendered somewhat suspicious by the fact that he or she was one of Madonna Bardi's nearest relations. Forty or fifty years after the poet's death, when he had already attained a high fame, there must have been a strong temptation first to conjecture, then to say, and lastly to believe, that the Beatrice whom he had glorified and rendered immortal was no other than the narrator's mother, grandmother, sister, aunt, as the case may be. Yet we would not say either that Boccaccio's 'credible person' was the first to set the tradition on foot. The person may have found it in existence, so that the question as to its origin is not yet solved.

The following solution has recently been suggested. On Dante's own showing he was talked about in connection with two ladies whom he pretended to love with a view of concealing his secret. One of these may well have been the Bardi-Portinari lady, and the gossip which he relates may afterwards have been made up into the tradition. The assumption involved in this acute and clever hypothesis is that in the first twenty years of the fourteenth century people in Florence should have troubled themselves to ascertain who was the fair lady who had aroused the enthusiasm of a fellow-citizen known to them as having been exiled and frequently condemned to death. Being unable to share this assumption, we must venture to attempt another solution.

Even before the *Vita Nuova* was completed there may well have been some curiosity to know who was the object of the author's passion; there are indeed indications to this effect in the work itself. But he was quite able to guard his secret. Then he entered himself on family life, and took part in public affairs in the government of the state. During these years people would hardly have inquired any further with whom the statesman and father of a family had been in love in his young days. Then came his exile, and the question was even less likely to be asked. Thus the whole love story must have fallen into oblivion; even though in 1290 guesses might have been made at it. But now the poet published his *Convito*, and then the *Commedia*, which quickly sprang into renown. Then was kindled a lively interest in the question of the identity of the lady whom he so glorified. But if the secret had been so closely kept all these years, who would now be able to discover it? Conjecture was driven to fix itself on the name Beatrice. It was assumed that this was her real name; inquiries were made as to possible acquaintances or contemporaries so named, and one was found in his near neighbourhood. 'Beatrice Portinari, of course,' said every one; 'it would be no other.' And perhaps after this fashion the tradition grew up.

Perhaps also in quite a different fashion. Who at the present day can ascertain the truth with any security? Just as the people of old could only conjecture as to the true Beatrice, so can we only conjecture with regard to the origin of the tradition regarding her.

But that the love of Dante's youth was wholly chaste and ideal, that there was no touch of anything illicit or immoral about it, appears with certainty from its fruits. From his first meeting with its object he dates his New Life, his regeneration. The senses no doubt are active in the years of youth, but can be controlled by the reason. Let us hear what he has to say himself. 'When she approached me from any quarter through my hope of her wondrous greeting I had no enemy left. Rather a flame of charity came over me which made me pardon whosoever had offended me, and if one had then asked me concerning anything, my only answer would have been *love*, with a countenance clad in humility.' His beloved is for him the destroyer of all evil and queen of all virtue. The influence of her beauty is such that he strives to clothe himself with noble thoughts, love, and faith. When human weakness almost overpowers him, it is her image that awakens him and recalls him when he has already gone astray. Her image gives him new strength when he is on the point of letting his courage fail or is growing weary and shrinking from danger. For her sake he turned his back on the common herd and fled from their pastures; she became his guide to Heaven, even to God Himself, and when he thought on her he beheld the realm of the blessed to which he was able partly to raise himself, partly felt himself raised. When in later years he looked back upon this period of his life it seemed to him like a lost Paradise, then did the beautiful countenance keep him upright, then did the eyes of his beloved in all the beauty of youth lead him on the straight road. Then did he learn from his yearning for her to love God, the highest good beyond which no man may aim. This then was a period of innocent life in which the highest virtues—faith, hope, love, bloomed and flourished in the heart of the young poet as in the garden of God.

And then some one comes and teaches us, appealing to the troubadours and to the manners of the Middle Ages, with their homage paid to ladies, that Dante's beloved, who became his guide to virtue and to God, the guardian angel of his life, was in reality another man's wedded wife.

CHAPTER II

ON THE WRONG ROAD

THE poet witnesses with no flowers of speech that not long after Beatrice's death he left the right way. Our task now is to inquire of what nature was the wrong way that he took, and this we can only do by citing his own expressions.

With the death of his Beatrice his inner life underwent a shock which soon shattered the inner harmony of his soul. From the first we miss anything like tranquil resignation to a higher will, complaints only are heard. The city appears to him lonely, deserted, or stripped of all that is worthy and honourable; no less desert is his own life. His great grief shatters his soul, and he longs for one thing only—death. In his mourning he avoids and is avoided by the world, he passes his days in solitude and grief, buried in thoughts of the departed one.

Some half-century after the poet's death we come across a tradition that Dante in his youth entered the Franciscan order and wore the dress of it for a time, but left it before the end of his novitiate. This is the story told by the commentator Francesco da Buti, who was born only three years after Dante's death, and he relates it as a genuine and undoubted fact, or rather he never does relate the fact, he simply alludes to it as something well known to his hearers, of which they only need to be reminded. Landino also mentions it, but only as a thing which 'some say.' Father Antonio Tognocchi, without more ado, reckons Dante among the writers belonging to the Franciscan order. The Franciscans have never ceased to count him among their members, and, as we have seen, he found his grave with them. In his own works we find two allusions. He relates, in Conv. ii. 13, that after the death of Beatrice he frequented the schools of the religious, meaning no doubt the convent schools. In Inf. xvi. 106 he speaks of a cord with which he was girt. This cord cannot be the leather girdle which was worn at that time; it can only be that which was borne by the followers of St. Francis.

This tradition cannot, however, rank as a fact established by documents. The poet's own allusions are too faint and indecisive,' and indeed there has been much controversy as to their meaning. But meanwhile there are no valid grounds for regarding the tradition as unfounded, and many commentators, from Tiraboschi and Balbo to Witte and Hettinger, have admitted its historic quality. For our part we will confine ourselves to saying simply that though not certain it is probable that Dante once intended to devote himself to a cloistered life, and took the first steps towards it.

When did he form this intention? Buti says in his boyhood, an expression which is too vague to allow us to draw any certain conclusions from it. Dante's own indications, if they refer to this at all, point to the time immediately following Beatrice's death, and the passage quoted from the *Inferno* forbids us to bring it later than the year 1300. But he can hardly have thought of entering a cloister when he was a married man with a family; the only possible assumption that remains is that this plan was in immediate consequence of the impression made upon him by the death of Beatrice.

If we had to do with an ascertained historical fact instead of with a somewhat doubtful tradition it would be natural to ask if it was not in his later years, it may be after his disillusion in consequence of Henry VII.'s death, when he found himself in a state of discouragement and despondency, that he regretted having given up his plan and left monastic life. Then the reproaches which he makes against himself in the latter cantos of the *Purgatory* would have a very definite and hitherto unsuspected significance, a significance which would be all the more appropriate when we consider that in the great vision with which the *Purgatory* concludes Beatrice is actually a symbol either of the authority of the Church or of the Church itself, or of theology. It would be worth while to investigate in all possible ways such documentary evidence as we have in order once for all to ascertain whether it is a fact that Dante once had a serious purpose of renouncing the world and withdrawing into a cloister. Up till now the matter has been too lightly passed over, as though it were a side issue of quite subordinate importance; there has been no suspicion that a final solution of the problem would be of decisive importance in explaining the leading passages of the poem.

With regard to Dante's life during the first year after the death of Beatrice we have practically no information. For more than that period he remained faithful to her memory, mourned for her, and delivered his soul in elegies. On the anniversary of her death, while thinking that she has become an angel, he sets to work to design an angel. Then some time elapses, and then the following episode, which we will let him tell in his own words, takes place:

> Thereafter for some time, whenas I was in a place which brought the past to my memory, I remained for a long time in thought and in sad meditation in such wise that it made me

appear outwardly an object of terrible despondency. Wherefore I, taking heed of the trouble that I was in, lifted my eyes to see if any beheld me. Therewith I saw a noble lady, young and very fair, who was looking at me from a window in appearance so pitifully that all pity seemed to be assembled in her. Wherefore seeing that when poor wretches behold compassion of themselves in another almost as though they had pity for themselves they are more quickly moved to tears, I felt a desire to weep beginning in my own eyes, and therefore fearing to display my weakness, I departed from before the eyes of that noble lady and said within myself, 'Of a surety a most noble love must dwell with this pitiful lady.' . . . After that it befell that wherever that lady saw me she became of a pitiful visage and of a pale colour as with love, whence many times I was reminded of my own most noble lady who showed herself before me of a like hue ; and surely many times when I was unable to weep and unburden myself of my sadness I went to see this pitiful lady, as it seemed that with her very look she drew the tears forth from my eyes. . . . Through the sight of this lady I came to such a pass that my eyes began to take too great delight in seeing her. Wherefore I was often angry with myself and held myself for very vile. Often too I would revile the vanity of my eyes and say to them in my thought, 'Verily ye were wont to make him weep who saw your woful condition, and now it seems that you wish to forget that for the sake of this lady who looks upon you and looks upon you only in so far as she grieves for that glorious lady for whom you are wont to weep. Do what ye will, accursed eyes, for I will often call her to your mind, seeing that ye ought never to have checked your tears until ye were dead.' And when I had thus spoken within myself to my eyes, sighs great and full of anguish assailed me, and to the end that this struggle which I had with myself might not remain known only by the wretch who felt it, I purposed to write a sonnet. . . . Thus then the sight of this lady brought me into so new a condition that many times I thought of her as a person who pleased me over much, and I considered thus of her: 'This is a noble lady, fair, young, and wise, and she has appeared, it may be by the will of Love, to the end that my life may have rest.' And many times I thought yet more amorously so that my heart assented to her, that is to her conversation. And when it had so consented I reconsidered myself as though moved by reason, and said within myself, 'What thought is this, pray, that will console me so basely, and lets me think as it were of nothing else?' Then another thought would rise and say, 'Now that thou hast been in so great tribulation of love, why wilt thou not withdraw thyself from so great bitterness? Thou seest that this is an inspiration that brings before us the desires of love and starts from a quarter so noble as are the eyes of that lady who has shown herself so pitiful towards thee.' Wherefore, having thus debated many times within myself, I wished to say yet a few words thereof, and seeing that in the battle of my thoughts those which spoke on her behalf had the upper hand it seemed to me that it was meet to speak to her, and I wrote the sonnet which begins:

> A noble thought which speaks to me of you.

Against this adversary of reason there arose one day at about the hour of nones a vivid fancy in me, for I seemed to see that glorious Beatrice in the crimson raiment wherein she had first appeared to my eyes, and she seemed to me youthful, of an age like to that in which I first saw her. Then I began to think of her, and as I was calling her to mind according to the order of the time past, my heart began wofully to repent of the desire which it had so cowardly allowed to take possession of it for certain days against the constancy of my reason. And when this evil desire had been chased away my thoughts returned wholly to their most noble Beatrice, and I say that from that time forth I began to think of her with all my shamefast heart in such wise that my sighs often declared it. So that at their issuing forth they seemed all to say that which was being pronounced in my heart, the name that is of that most noble lady and how she departed from us. And many times it befell that some thought had in it so much grief that I forgot all about it in the place where I was. Through this rekindling of sighs my suspended weeping was rekindled in such fashion that my eyes seemed to be two things that desired only to weep. And often it befell that through the long continuance of my weeping a purple colour was formed around them such as is wont to appear through some torment that one receives, whence it appears that they were justly requited for their vanity. So that from that time forward they could not look upon any person who gazed on them so as to be drawn into a like intention. Wherefore I, wishing that such evil desire and vain temptation might be destroyed so that the rhymes which I had before written might not cause any doubt, purposed to make a sonnet in which I might embody the meaning of this reason.'

Therewith, as the *Vita Nuova* sets forth, the whole episode of this second love was at an end. Thenceforth the poet's thoughts remained true to his Beatrice, until a wondrous vision made him decide to speak no more of her for the present until he could do it in a more worthy fashion, for which he prepared himself with diligent study.

So that if it shall be the pleasure of Him to whom all things live that my life shall endure for some years longer, I hope to say of her that which has never been said of any woman, and then may it please Him, who is the Lord of graciousness, that my soul may go to behold the glory of its lady, that is of that blessed Beatrice who gloriously looks upon the face of Him *qui est per omnia saecula benedictus.*

With these words ends the work of the poet's youth, the *Vita Nuova.*

If this had been the only account which we possessed, no one would ever have thought of going into fanciful interpretations. It would have been assumed universally and without contradiction that rather more than a year after the death of Beatrice the poet found it necessary to resist the growth of a new *penchant* for an attractive young lady which he had allowed, though not without inward struggles, to gain a mastery over him; and that in consequence of a dream he had torn himself free, beaten down the new fancy, and returned with contrition to his faithful memory of the departed. The reproofs in the vision at the end of the *Purgatory* would as a matter of course have been taken as referring to this episode, and regarded as a repetition of the frank and honest avowals of the *Vita Nuova*. But the matter is not so simple; and this time it is the author himself who has rendered it much worse and more complicated for us to unravel. The 'noble lady' who is spoken of in the *Vita Nuova* appears again in the *Convito*, written many years later, and appears there in a totally different shape. In the opening chapter of the later work Dante no doubt expressly declares: 'If in the present work, which is called *The Banquet*, the treatment appears more manly than in the *New Life*, I do not wish in any way to derogate from that thereby, but rather to confirm that with this, since I see that as it was reasonable that that should be fervid and passionate, it behoves that this should be temperate and manly.' It appears from this that the man would confirm what the youth had written, and that the *Convito* was not intended to correct the statements of the *Vita Nuova*, but rather to expound them. We are all the less likely to find a contradiction between the two works that the author in composing the second not only had the first present to his mind, but also expressly refers to it with a distinct declaration that he had nothing to retract, to improve, or to modify; and that the only difference which will be perceived is in the form which his statement takes, since the language and treatment which suit one age of life are different from those which suit another, seeing that certain manners are appropriate and praiseworthy in the one, which in the other are unseemly and blamable.

But, strange to say, immediately after this declaration we catch the author in a contradiction of the most flagrant kind. In the *Vita Nuova* his inclination towards the 'noble lady' was contrary to reason, a shameful desire, an evil longing, against which he struggled earnestly, and for which he felt deep contrition. Yet now he turns round and purposes to show that the moving cause was not passion but virtue. How are we to reconcile this?

It will be profitable to begin by quoting the passage Conv. ii. 2, in which Dante speaks about his second love.

To begin then I say that the star of Venus had revolved twice in that her circle which makes her appear as evening and morning star according to the two divers periods, since the departure of that blessed Beatrice who lives in heaven with the angels and on earth with my soul, when that noble lady of whom I made mention at the end of the *New Life* appeared before my eyes, accompanied in the first instance by Love, and took up a place in my mind; and, as I have related in the book in question, rather through her nobility than of my own choice it came to pass that I fell into sympathy with her, for she showed herself to be affected by such pity over my widowed life that the spirits of my eyes became in a very high degree her friends, and having become so they rendered me such inwardly that my will was content to wed that image. But whereas love does not all at once come to the birth and grow up to perfection, but requires a certain time and nourishment from thoughts, especially in the case where there are contrary thoughts which hinder it, there was need before that this new love was perfect—of much conflict between the thought which nourished it and that which was contrary to it—the which was still holding the fortress of my mind on behalf of that glorious Beatrice, for the one was continually being reinforced from the front on the side of my sight, and the other from the rear on the side of my memory. But the reinforcement from the front increased every day, which the other could not do, in opposition to that which in some measure hindered me from taking to flight. For it appeared to me so marvellous, and moreover so hard to suffer, that I could not withstand it—and as it were crying out to excuse myself against the contrary plea—whereby I seemed to myself to be lacking in fortitude. I directed my voice towards that quarter whence proceeded the victory of my new thought, which as being a power from heaven, was most full of virtue, and I began to write:

> Ye whose intelligence the third Heaven moves.

Between this description and that of the *Vita Nuova* there is no lack of discrepancies. An attempt has even been made to detect a chronological discrepancy which, however, does not really exist. The date at which he first beheld the 'noble lady' is indicated by the statement that since Beatrice's death Venus had twice completed her course. Now the revolution of Venus takes about 225 days, but at that time it was generally assumed that it occupied nearly a year, and in this respect Dante was not in advance of his time. He tells us here then that his first meeting with the 'noble lady' took place some two years after Beatrice's death. In the *New Life* he says, after mentioning the anniversary of Beatrice's death, that he first beheld the 'noble lady' some time after that, an expression which may very fairly be taken to indicate a year.

On the other hand, according to the *Vita Nuova*, his inclination for the 'noble lady' lasted only certain days, and was then set aside through his remembrance of the departed Beatrice, while, according to the *Convito*, this new inclination ultimately got the mastery. Further, the *Vita Nuova* condemns the new desire as base and evil, the *Convito* glorifies it as a virtuous and heavenly flame. Can we suppose that these discrepancies escaped the poet when he expressly declares that in the *Convito* he wished only to strengthen and confirm what he had set in the *Vita Nuova*?

We must not, however, overlook the points of agreement. In both places we learn that the poet had to undergo an inward struggle. In both places he tells us that it was mainly the sympathy of the 'noble lady' which caused him to turn to her; in both places the gradual development of this affection is expressly brought forward in contradistinction to the first, which flamed up at once at the first sight of the beloved object.

But how about the undeniable discrepancies? Here we must make a small digression. There are some well-known and not exactly edifying sonnets which Dante once on a time exchanged with his friend and relative Forese Donati. In these sonnets Dante attacked not only his friend but also his friend's wife in such a fashion that decency forbids their repetition, but in Pg. xxiii. 85 this same wife is represented as the most pious and most chaste, nay as the only chaste wife, in Florence. Supposing some one had reproached the poet with contradicting himself, would he have allowed himself to be influenced by the reproach? We think not. It is far more likely that he would have answered that the sonnets were a product of a youthful spirit of mischief, while in the epic justice towards his friend's wife was allowed to prevail. There we have amends made to Forese's wife, so in the *Convito* we have amends to the 'noble lady.'

On the point of severe inward struggles experienced by the poet we saw that the *Vita Nuova* and the *Convito* agree, the latter work supplying omissions in the former. When the earlier work was written the struggle was not yet at an end. He hoped indeed that he had for the time stifled the new passion, but as he points out himself in the *Convito*, the new had the support of actual sight, the old that of memory only. Even after the conclusion of the *Vita Nuova* the former made itself felt; it was only gradually that the poet came to see another aspect of things. The end of the struggle is related only in the *Convito*, in the *Vita Nuova* we hear merely of an armistice, and the end was in the following fashion: 'It came to pass that I agreed to be hers.' Having come to this conclusion he naturally perceives that his inclination to her was not unreasonable and base, but a heavenly flame. In order that the reader may so understand him he has made from the

P

first the definite declaration that the *Convito* is in no sense derogatory to the *Vita Nuova*, but is to serve rather as its completion and confirmation.

Thus the second love, after a long and hard struggle, became perfected, and the struggle ended with his consent to surrender himself to the 'noble lady.' About this there can be no quibbling, for he says it quite expressly; but Boccaccio also has information to give about a struggle of the affections after Beatrice's death. According to him also the struggle ended with Dante's consenting to be hers, seeing that he married her.

Is it, then, to be understood that the *donna gentile* was Dante's wife, Gemma Donati? This is a supposition that can hardly become a certainty. But are we so sure of this? Does not the poet say distinctly that he finally gave his assent to the new love? His indications, too, carry us at least to the year 1293, probably even later, and was not that just the date at which he married Gemma Donati? We can scarcely believe that after agreeing to belong to the 'noble lady,' he should then have committed an act of double disloyalty by straightway marrying another.

We have not, then, to deal with a mere conjecture, but simply with the understanding of Dante's express words, and we should be curious to see how else they can be understood without doing violence to his simple and clear statement.

But it will be said Dante has expressly declared that the sympathetic lady is only an abstraction and denotes philosophy; and no doubt he writes in *Convito* ii. 16: 'And so at the end of the second treatise I say and affirm that the lady of whom I was enamoured after my first love was that fairest daughter of the Lord of the whole world, to whom Pythagoras assigned the name of Philosophy.' Was he, then, enamoured of the 'noble lady'? In the *Vita Nuova* he does not say that; he speaks only of a certain satisfaction which he found in the sight of her, but which he fought down, and after a few days suppressed. It is a long way from that to being in love.

Only unwillingly and under compulsion we must say that it is trivial superficiality to appeal to the above-cited passages of the *Convito* in order to prove that the 'noble lady' of the *Vita Nuova* is only a symbol of philosophy. Not a syllable of this is to be found in the *Vita Nuova*, but rather the contrary. Would Dante have applied the term *young* to philosophy who had existed for thousands of years? Where is the window out of which she looked? Did philosophy sympathise with the poet in the loss of his love? Did philosophy grow pale at the sight of him? Did Dante reproach himself so bitterly for taking pleasure in philosophy? Was it a mean thing to think of philosophy? Was his budding love for philosophy an opponent of reason? Such a philosophy is, in truth, as attractive as her disciple who so thinks of her.

Yes, indeed, it has been said the 'noble lady' of the *New Life* is obviously a real woman of flesh and blood, and Dante's inclination towards her is a natural one. But later on, when he came to write the *Convito*, he read into the *New Life* an allegory which was originally foreign to it. This is surely untrue. The *Convito* has up to the present time been read and commented on; its readings have been fought over without any proper study of it. The second division of the work, which alone concerns us here, consists of the ode, 'Voi che intendendo il terzo ciel movete,' and the commentary thereon. The latter again falls into two parts, the literal explanation, chapters i.-xii., and the allegorical, xiii.-xvi. In the first part there is not a word about philosophy; it is all about the woman. It is not till the second part that, in the allegorical explanation of the ode, this woman appears as a symbol of philosophy. From this it follows, as a matter of course, that in Dante's meaning the 'noble lady' was a real woman, whom he used as a symbol of philosophy.

That this was his actual meaning appears to demonstration from the first chapter of the second division, where we read: 'Writings can be understood and are to be explained mainly in four various interpretations; the first is the literal, and this is that in which the words are taken closely according to their proper meaning; the second is the allegorical,' and soon . . . 'This may be seen in the psalm of the prophet, which says that when the people of Israel came out of Egypt Judaea became holy and free. For although this is literally true and correct the spiritual meaning is none the less true, namely, that the soul, after she has put off her sins, becomes holy and free under her own control.' Thus, although it is literally true and correct that after Beatrice's death Dante loved another woman, it is equally true in a spiritual sense that his soul, seeking consolation in her grief, turned to philosophy, and gradually became enamoured of her. This seems to follow with absolute necessity from Dante's own expressions.

Moreover, the chronological data contain a hint that the literal and allegorical sense do not coincide. From the concordant indications of the *Convito* and the *Vita Nuova* the second love begins in the second year after Beatrice's death, but according to the allegorical meaning his love for philosophy would seem to have begun a good deal later. Beatrice had been dead for a longer time when he sought consolation in Boëthius and Cicero, and it was still some thirty months after this date when he began to feel the sweetness of philosophy to such a degree 'that his love for her chased away and destroyed every other thought.' We must then with the poet himself distinguish two separate loves—his natural love of the senses for the 'noble lady,' and his symbolical love of the intellect for philosophy, and these two are not the same.

There is another circumstance, by comparing which with what has gone before we may arrive with certainty at our conclusion. Just as in his literal meaning Dante speaks of a woman, so he speaks of the nine moving heavens, without giving us any ground to suppose that he means anything but a living woman and the natural heavens. And just as in his allegorical explanation he surprises us with the statement that by the 'noble lady' he understands philosophy, Conv. ii. 14, he surprises us by explaining: 'I say that by heaven I mean science, and by the heavens the sciences.' Similarly, in the literal sense, the motors of the heavens are the angels; in the allegorical sense, they are teachers of the sciences, 'like Boëthius and Tully, who by the sweetness of their discourse set me in the way.' Were the heavens and the angels mere abstractions and no realities for Dante? What sort of exegesis would it be to say, The heavens and the angels are real things, turned to allegorical use by the poet, but the noble lady is purely allegorical? Where has Dante said, or implied, anything of the sort? We can obviously only conclude that the allegorical lady is also a real lady, no less than the allegorical heavens and angels are also real beings.

If, then, the 'noble lady' of the *Vita Nuova* was afterwards the poet's wife, it is difficult to see how the reproach that he had withdrawn from his Beatrice and given himself to others, that he had gone on the wrong road while following false images of happiness, could have been cast upon his second love. From the fact that the element of love plays so considerable a part in Dante's lyric poetry, amours of all kinds have been freely assigned to him, and the energetic man has been pictured as a sensual person, nay, even as a profligate. The question has been talked about till it is positively wearisome, and it is really high time to declare Dante's supposed amours outside the pale of discussion. As to the reproaches which he puts in Beatrice's mouth in the great vision at the end of the *Purgatory*, I can only refer to what I have said in my commentary on that passage and elsewhere. Again the so-called evidence of older writers such as Boccaccio and others may be at once dismissed. No reasonable man troubles himself about the evidence which they give of Dante's having been a traitor or a miser, and it is hard to see why they should be believed in the case of the one charge of sensuality. The foolish writing which passes for a letter from the poet to the Marquis Malaspina is one which any serious admirer would be ashamed to adduce as proof. In brief, it is high time to reject altogether from the study of Dante all the protracted and tedious gossip about the poet's amours, and to take as little heed of it as of the marvellous dream of his mother, which Boccaccio thought so important—of the woman who called him *Messer Asso*, of the bones at his feet in the dining-hall at Verona, of the Veronese women who noticed on his face the traces of his journey through Hell, and all the other anecdotes which are worth just as much or as little as the love tales.

The often-repeated assertion that the poet charges himself with profligacy is as untrue as it is childish. The man who mourns for his deceased love a whole year, and then has to go through a long struggle before he can make up his mind to a second passion, is not the man to fall in love with the first pretty face. A man who expresses himself as Dante has done in the *Convito* surely does not after that say anything about his amours, even in the case of his having really surrendered himself to such. He is said to have had an intrigue with a lady in the city of Lucca, but all that we find is a prophecy that a young lady will persuade him to find pleasure in that city, and surely this could not have been the result of any venal attachment. Nay, but it has been replied, he does not speak of this lady as *donna* but as *femmina*, which is significant. But he uses the same word of our mother Eve, of Camilla, Lavinia, Lucretia, Marcia, and even the Holy Virgin. Still more unfortunate is the appeal to his conversation in *Purgatory* xxiii. with Forese Donati, for there he merely expresses his sorrow for the old relations between himself and his friend, and recalls the insults which he had uttered in his sonnets against Forese's wife.

We must beg the reader to pardon us for having said so much about this foolish gossip. We have done it with a feeling of repugnance; but since whole sheets of the biographies of Dante up to the present time have been full of it, it has been impossible to avoid briefly dismissing it to the place where it belongs.

But Dante speaks of a wrong road upon which he turned his steps; of his grievous fall; of the false pleasure of present objects which turned his steps aside; of perishable things which enticed him away; of temporal vanities which weighed his wings downwards; of a school which he had followed, and whose law was a whole heaven apart from God's law; of a dark wood in which he strayed; and of the hindrances which were in his way when he had emerged from it, and wished to ascend the sunlit hill. What does he mean thereby?

CHAPTER III

GOING ASTRAY

THERE is a well-known remark of Goethe's to the effect that 'the secret of the world's history is contained in the fight between Christianity and human wisdom.' But, since the world's history is older than Christianity, the great man must have meant dogmatic religion generally. This has from all time been in conflict, not merely with human wisdom, but with human reason. It does not even concern itself with matters of which reason takes cognisance, but with emotion and its needs. Its efforts are directed to showing the course of the world in another and fairer shape than that in which they will appear to the natural eye of the observer. The lofty visions begotten of the heart's yearning presages, it proclaims as a higher view of things, and makes weal and woe depend upon a man's acceptance of them as realities, or recognition of them for what they really are. For the most part it expressly requires man to abstain from logically thinking out his conclusions, and expects him to yield his reason a submissive prisoner to faith. The absurd must be received in childlike simplicity as indubitably the higher truth, as expressed in the famous phrase, *Credo, quia impossibile.*

Alexander von Humboldt penned in his youth the following words, which he cited in his old age: 'Every dogmatic religion presents three distinct elements; an ethical system, the same in all and always very pure; a dream of creation; and a mythus, or small historical romance; and the greatest importance is attached to the last of the three.' And, indeed, it is upon the last that the greatest amount of labour is expended; and the myth becomes ever more mythic, the romance ever more romantic. Upon this is based the superstructure, compounded of the abortions of fancy and stray fragments borrowed from science, especially philosophy, which man in his modesty hesitates not to call theology, or the science of divine things. The essence of the work of fancy is the negation of all the data of actual existence, which, as being transitory, cannot be truly real. A persistent evolution in Nature is banished in favour of free interference by the Deity; as though it were feared that Deity might disappear altogether if not allowed arbitrary freedom unrestrained by law. The laws of the visible world cannot be unalterable, but must be capable of interruption, and actually interrupted, by a higher power. But this science cannot allow without abolishing herself. Directly she attains to the consciousness of herself, she becomes aware of the great gulf which lies between herself and faith. Faith and knowledge, religion and science, can never dwell side by side in peace. In science, on the one hand, is innate the impulse to destroy all illusions, poetical, comforting, beautiful though they be; on the other, faith will never submit to be a result of a more or less amiable fancy, but claims to be, not merely knowledge, but the highest knowledge, to which all others must be subordinate and subject. Conflicts are thus unavoidable; but as faith is by nature intolerant and persecuting, and shrinks from no use of force, knowledge, as has often happened, finds herself compelled, wherever the physical power is in the hands of faith, to hold her peace, and at least in outward appearance accept a subordinate position and do obeisance. Naturally peace lasts only so long as faith is able to compel respect, or, at all events, external obedience; and the conflict when it comes is all the fiercer.

In men of keen intelligence and deep emotion, whose souls are divided between the demands of the intellect and the desires of the heart, the strife often rages inwardly. No man of normal organisation finds it easy without a long struggle to give up the lofty dreams of the heart in which he has been nurtured. Indeed it often happens that the man surrenders himself to self-deceit. Thus the great mediaeval thinkers, though extolling the power of reason, fancied that their speculations were at one with faith. Even when conflicts arose, the freest thinkers deemed themselves able to assert that they stood wholly on the ground of faith. The opposition existed, but no one would recognise it or even see it.

In Dante's time, however, there was no concealment of the opposition.

> The whole thirteenth century (says Reuter, *Geschichte der Aufklärung im Mittelalter*) was in commotion from the strain and conflict between science and faith. This turmoil did not remain theoretical only, nor did it stand alone. A great social crisis declared itself, with new notions. The period in question which, in regard to its historical results and its brilliant achievements in science and art, may be called perhaps the classical period of the mediaeval Church, was at the same time the period of a revolution which shook men's ideas to their base. It was attempted to check this revolution by force of legislation, by the development of new forms of social life. The efforts towards an anti-Catholic reform aroused or strengthened men's thoughts in the same direction on Catholic lines, while religious heresy was followed by rationalism. The negative emancipation which, during the twelfth

century, had been restricted to esoteric societies, became in the thirteenth an undisguised ally of culture, which lived to see its day of conquest in the history of the world.

In Florence the opposition had reached such a point, even by the beginning of the twelfth century, that, as we learn from Villani (iv. 30), street-fighting was going on between the followers of the old faith and those who had adopted materialistic views. Some sort of improvement, the historian adds, was brought about by the establishment of the mendicant orders. But the improvement consisted solely in the fact that materialism, or 'Epicureanism,' as it was then and in Dante's time called, was compelled to hide its head. It was by no means rooted out, and continued to flourish in secret. There were plenty of people in Dante's *Hell* who denied the immortality of the soul. It was popularly said of Dante's friend, the philosopher Guido Cavalcanti, that the sole aim of his researches was to find a scientific basis for atheism. We find St. Bernard of Clairvaux lamenting that even in his day a childlike faith was derided, the mysteries of Christianity cavilled at, the Fathers mocked, and nothing believed which could not stand the test of the investigation of reason. Mendicant orders, persecution, the Inquisition itself could not eradicate the tendency to rationalism. Petrarch laments the fact in just such language as is now used at Methodist prayer-meetings and clerical gatherings.

All this is only to show how erroneous and ignorant is the assertion so often made that to talk of an opposition in Dante's day between Christian faith and philosophic speculation is to impart modern notions into that period; as though there were then no conflicts between faith and science, theology and philosophy, tradition and inquiry, heart and reason. History tells us that they existed, and that not sporadically, but no less than in our time a matter of everyday life.

Now did Dante pass through any conflicts of the kind? Was there in his life a period when he went astray from the Christian faith, allowed doubt to enter his soul, did homage to the rationalistic tendency? This question has been answered in the affirmative no less distinctly than in the negative; and we cannot avoid going into it, for the very reason that upon its solution depend the interpretation and significance of his great work.

In the first place there can be no doubt that the poet has designated a period of his life as one of error. He begins his great poem with a straightforward admission of this. Before the thirty-fifth year of his life he was so overcome with a sleep of the spirit that without knowing how, he went astray in a wood, dark and grisly. In 1300, the year of Jubilee, he awoke, and on coming to a sense of his situation, he struggled to escape from darkness to light. He weighs every word, so that there is clearly a deeper meaning in the emphasis which he lays upon the darkness of the wood and the light which streams around the hill; and that he means to indicate that his life in the earlier period was darkness, and the light that life for which he strove when awakened. But on the road by which he is laboriously trying to reach the light he finds the way stopped, and himself ultimately scared back by the three beasts—leopard, lion, and wolf; and Virgil's shade teaches him that he must take another route, since the bright summit cannot be reached by that upon which he is going. Later on, in the reproaches which he puts into the mouth of Beatrice, we have his admission that he turned his steps in the way of error. The connection of this latter passage with the opening canto is obvious, and the only question is whether under the 'false way' we must understand his entry into the dark wood, or the way which he took at first to reach the illumined hill. Our answer must be decisive for the latter. There is nowhere any mention of a way, right or wrong, into the wood. He enters it unconsciously, in sleep. To stray from the right road and to take a wrong one are two very different things. Beatrice further reproaches him with having followed false images of good, which promise and do not perform. But in the wood he had followed no images of good fortune, and so soon as he awoke he strove to escape from the wood. It was when, after awakening, he sought to climb the hillside that he followed those images. Finally Beatrice speaks of his deep fall, which is clearly a reference to the *rovinar in basso luogo* of Inf. i. 61. Thus we have to distinguish the straying in the dark wood and the taking of a wrong road when, being awakened, he sought to escape from the wood.

Dante himself explains the wood by a phrase in Conv. iv. 24, where he speaks of 'this life's wood of error,' the hurry of worldly life into which the youth enters. It was in this, he would say, that before the year 1300 he himself had gone astray. Those were precisely the years in which he not only set up a home of his own, but was occupied with affairs of state, was raising money—for what purpose we know not, and was exchanging with Forese Donati those sonnets which say so much to one who can read them with understanding. The poet himself hints at this when he identifies the life he had led in the company of his friend with his wandering in the dark wood. We are not in a position to state more definitely wherein this worldly life consisted. We have no sure points of which to lay hold, and all that has been said on the subject is bare conjecture. On awaking from this sleep, that is out of this life of lethargy, in his struggle for emancipation he took the wrong road. What was that wrong road? Beatrice sums up her reproaches in 'he withdrew himself from me and gave himself up to others,' which she modifies presently by saying that she became less pleasant and less clear to him. For himself his guilt consists in having become estranged from his Beatrice. To a superficial interpretation it is very obvious to see in these reproaches a reminder of the noble lady of the *Vita Nuova*, and to find in the reproaches of Beatrice a reference to that episode. But then it is forgotten that in the great concluding vision of the *Purgatory* Beatrice is symbolical; that the short and bitterly-regretted attraction towards the 'noble lady' could not subsequently be made a reproach to the poet. Besides, he absolutely excludes this reference when he makes Beatrice say that all her efforts to recall him through visions and other means had been in vain; while, according to the *Vita Nuova*, the first vision had been sufficient to call him back from his inclination towards the 'noble lady.'

If we wish to discover what it was with which the poet in his later years charged himself, and wherein he beheld a departure from the ideal of his youth, we must devote our researches to what he says in the *Convito* about his spiritual progress. The principal passage, that in which he records how he began in the second year after Beatrice's death to read Boëthius and Cicero, and thirty months afterwards became enthusiastic for philosophy, has been already quoted. But let us hear how he expresses it elsewhere. In ii. 16 he tells us how—

> Boëthius and Tully led [me] with the sweetness of their words upon the way of love—that is, upon the study of this most noble lady, philosophy, who truly is a worshipful lady adorned with dignity, admirable in knowledge, the glory of

freedom. Her eyes are her demonstrations, which, when directed upon the eyes of the intellect, enamour the soul set free in all her relations. Oh! lineaments of ineffable sweetness, suddenly taking the human mind captive, which are displayed in the eyes of philosophy when she discourses with her paramours. Verily in you is salvation, by the which he who looks upon you becomes blessed and saved from the death of ignorance and from all vices, if he fears not the labour of study and the struggle of doubt which rise up manifold from the first of this lady's glances, and then, as she continues her light, fall like morning clouds before the face of the sun, and the intellect which has become familiar with her remains free and full of certitude, like the air when it is purged and illumined by the beams of noon. . . . Mighty was the hour when the first manifestation of this lady, which was the cause of my becoming instantly enamoured of her, entered into the eyes of my intellect. . . . And so I say and affirm that the lady of whom I became enamoured after my first love was that fairest and most honourable daughter of the emperor of the universe, to whom Pythagoras gave the name of Philosophy.

In the first chapter of the next book he proceeds:

My second love took its origin from the pitiful countenance of a lady, which love thereafter finding my life ready to receive its flame, kindled like fire from a little spark to a great blaze, so that not only when I was waking, but when I was sleeping, a light from her made its way into my brain. Nor can I say, nor could it be understood, how great was the desire of seeing her which love inspired in me. And not only of her was I thus desirous, but also of all those persons who were in any way connected with her either by acquaintance or by kinship. How many were the nights when the eyes of other persons were reposing closed in sleep, and mine were gazing fixedly upon the place where my love dwelt; and even as a conflagration when increased will show itself outwardly since it is impossible for it to stay hidden, so did a will come upon me to speak of love which I could in no way contain. And albeit I had little power over my purpose, either by the will of love or by my own readiness, I drew so near to it many times that I deliberated, and saw that in speaking of love no discourse was fairer or more profitable than that in which the beloved person was commemorated. . . . I thought, I say, that I might be blamed by many behind my back for inconstancy when they heard that I had changed from my first love. Wherefore for the removing of this reproach there was no better means than to say who that lady was who had wrought the change in me, since by reason of her manifest excellence a consideration of her virtue may be had, and by the understanding of her great power it may be conceived that all stability of the mind can be turned aside to her, and therefore I shall not be judged fickle and unstable.

From these and many other passages in the last two books of the *Convito*, it is quite obvious (1) that after Beatrice's death Dante sought for consolation in studying philosophy with the help of Boëthius and Cicero, and gradually believed that he had really found it; (2) that by degrees he became in the highest degree an enthusiast for philosophy, even to the point of fanaticism; (3) that this passage from his ideal love to Beatrice to his enthusiasm for philosophy was by no means easy to him, but rather led him through bitter inward struggles; (4) that enthusiasm for philosophy, though it forced the old love into the background, was unable entirely to extinguish it in the poet's soul; (5) that at the time when he wrote the *Convito*, Dante looked upon his old life of love as upon a level which he had surpassed; and (6), that his enthusiasm was even at that time somewhat cooled since he had not found in philosophy that soothing effect for which he had hoped, or, in other words, that he already could tell of disillusions experienced. We do not think that any one will feel tempted to find fault with these statements since we can claim to have drawn them with the strictest scientific conscientiousness from the poet's words. Now, however, the question arises, What are the mutual relations of Beatrice and philosophy?

Repeated attempts have been made to identify them, and people have tried to find everywhere in *Vita Nuova*, *Convito*, and *Commedia* one and the same allegoric figure of Beatrice under various poetical conceptions and shapes. Nor have people been deterred by Dante's declaration in *Convito* ii. 9 that he would speak no more of that 'living Beatrice now in bliss.' The words were explained as meaning that he would speak no more of Beatrice the mortal woman, but only of the allegoric Beatrice the symbol of wisdom; as though Dante had not expressly declared that he would speak no more of the *blessed* Beatrice, as though he did not at the end of the *Purgatory* make Beatrice address to him bitter reproaches for having abandoned himself after her death to a second love. Only those who have a thesis to defend can fail to recognise that there is a connection as close as can possibly be conceived between the declaration in the *Convito* and the reproaches of Beatrice in the *Purgatory*. When Dante feels himself drawn from his first love by the strength of the second, and when his soul unites itself to philosophy so as to become one with it, is he not withdrawing from Beatrice and surrendering himself to another? When his love for philosophy chases away and shatters every other thought, does not Beatrice become less pleasing and less dear to him? When he thinks to find in the demonstrations of philosophy full contentment in every position of his life, but is left in the lurch by her, and receives no satisfying answer to his inquiries, is he not pursuing false images of good which fulfil none of their promises? The parallels might be continued further. The only one which we do not find is any parallel in the *Convito* to the reproach of having taken the wrong road (Purg. xxx. 130). Naturally when he wrote that work he still thought that he was on the right road.

The only charge which is brought against the poet in the concluding vision of the *Purgatory* is that of unfaithfulness to Beatrice, but this unfaithfulness is expressly identified with the following of a certain school. This cuts away all possibility of seeking in the domain of morals the ground of the charges which the poet brings against himself. When he asked Beatrice why she so speaks, that her speech is incomprehensible to him, she answers, 'That thou mayest know that school which thou hast followed and mayest see how little its doctrine is able to follow my words.' But it may be objected that there is nothing said there about a false school. Certainly the school which Dante followed is not expressly called false, but she will have him arrive at an insight into the nature of that school, and speaks in depreciation of it, and calls it a human way which is as far from the divine way as earth from heaven. It cannot then have been a true school, and surely between true and false there is no middle term. How again does Dante receive the reproach? Beatrice's words that he has followed a *certain* school are accepted by him as equivalent to a reproach of having estranged himself at some time from her, and he simply answers, 'I do not remember that I ever did estrange myself from you.' Her reply, 'Thou rememberest it no more since thou hast drunk of Lethe,' shows that she allows this interpretation to pass as correct.

If anything in the field of Dante research is settled, we may without hesitation announce as such the statement that in his later years the poet regarded the enthusiasm for philosophy, to which he has given eloquent expression in the *Convito*, as an estrangement from his Beatrice, the ideal who was guiding him to God, and as such regretted and condemned it.

What then was the character of this limitless, enthusiastic

surrender to philosophy, and what consequences followed from it for the poet ? On this question we cannot avoid noticing the system based on that of Dionisi, which was constructed in the full spirit of an artist, and maintained for half a century, by Karl Witte, up to now the unsurpassed master of Dante research. Looking to the great importance which has been given to it, and recognition which it has gained from supporters and opponents, we feel bound to give it in his own words :

From his childish years a flame of pure love was kindled in the poet. We find even at the present day noble spirits in whom love takes a similar form. To the heart which still, unconfused by the strokes of destiny, lives full of the joy of childhood, the whole Heaven is laid open in the person of its beatific Beatrice. Her beauty, her goodness, all her perfections are to him only proofs of God's unending love, and even a corporal attraction does not lead to seductive desire but to a devout joy in the beauty which God has revealed in His creature. Here is no unsatisfied longing, no jealousy, no complaint. The beloved one herself is merely the most wonderful and the most precious of the flowers which blow in God's wide garden, before which we stand in tranquil pleasure enjoying their scent with no temptation to break off the rose. Her voice is but the most resonant among those of the thousand nightingales to which we listen without any wish to catch and encage them. The lovely flowers, the solemn wood with its inhabitants' song of praise, speak of the nobleness of nature, of the goodness of its Creator, and in unmingled blessedness exalt the spirit of him who feels the charm. But far deeper and more animated is this joyful piety when it is not the unknown language of plants and animals, but the fulness of a beloved spirit, itself surrendered in pure devotion to God which declares the praise of the Lord to us. Such a love we need not call an allegory of piety, it is the very contemplation of God upon earth, and to this love Dante's *Vita Nuova* is dedicated.

But when we come to regard more closely this same nature which joyously smiled upon us, we recognise a poisonous germ in it. That glad life which drew us forth to the praises of its Creator, could only come into and maintain itself in existence by means of revolting cruelty. Scarcely can one creature live without causing the death of hundreds, and all these victims bring us to nothing else than to an endless and useless repetition of the old vicious circle.

Dante had grown up to manhood when the Beatrice who had accustomed his eyes to look up to Heaven with joy and thankfulness as the object of the love which he dreamt that he had wrested, through the pure piety which hallowed her, from earthly mortality, was torn from him by the iron caprice of death. There may exist privileged dispositions who even in such terrible moments have the power to maintain a cheerful resignation to the will of God. Our poet, however, was as little capable as are many others even at the present day to direct, now that he was alone and without a guide, the eye which his beloved had formerly led upwards to the point from which he felt that ruin rather than a boon had been sent to him. His faith in God's love and goodness was shaken to its foundations and was no longer capable of silencing questions as to the secret reasons for such apparent cruelty.

It is indeed pardonable if at such moments confidence and resignation, however firm they may formerly have seemed, break down ; and if those very persons who had with the keenest joy appreciated the happiness which is now destroyed, are now inclined in their madness to rail most loudly against Him who has changed His benefits into chastisements. All the more praiseworthy must we deem the others who with our poet strive to beat down the cry of despair by strenuous research after the solution of the gloomy riddle, even though this groping may lead them away from the paths of religion in which in their sorrow they think that no more consolation is to be found, and into the arms of an arrogant and overweening philosophy.

This, the sole activity of which the shattered spirit is at the outset capable, leads gradually to others, and speculation in all directions appears to the broken heart a consoling friend. In the allegorising fashion of his time Dante pictures this as a graceful maiden in whose glances he thinks to find a reflection of Beatrice's love and an expression of heavenly pity. Many a disconsolate man has before this made the discovery that strenuous activity on behalf of others, or for the common good, has been able to tranquillise him for a long time, and when the spirit has once acquired a bent in this direction, it has at last come to the point of feeling that it has found here its vocation. Not otherwise did it fare with our poet after the death of Beatrice. The study of abstract philosophy first attracts him, then he turns to moral reflections, he fathoms the nature of justice, courage, nobility. He develops his theories about the ordering of the state, about the significance of the great events of his time, and devotes his life to bringing about what he holds to be right. Into this period of his life falls his participation in the government of his city, and also the development of his views about language and poetry.

But if there were troublous moments in which to his shattered mood Christianity itself seemed a comfortless tradition, still less can he have found an enduring satisfaction in vague groping about his own spirit. It takes but a short wandering to reach in all directions the limits of our capability for hopelessness; and of the original consolation there remains at length nothing but the exhaustion of a barren conflict.

This fruitless struggle, this unrequited love, this tormenting situation brought about by a hope ever nourished in vain, of seeing after redoubled efforts its longings satisfied by philosophy, is depicted in the *Convivio Amoroso*. Restless and joyless is this love since the peace of a childlike unexacting resignation has faded from the poet's heart. If he demands vehemently and ever vainly new favours from his beloved he deems that she turns with a hard heart from him until he recognises at last, loudly complaining all the time, that love even though unrequited is its own highest reward.

The enthusiasm for right and truth which this love kindled in the poet's breast was not able to keep him clear of participation in the conflicts of his time, from which contemporaries can never wholly withdraw themselves. Earthly anxieties and growing passions threatened to draw him into their vortex, and once accustomed to live in the passing moment, his impressionable heart is not likely to close itself against new attractions of mortal beauty. If at the same time philosophy unveils to him the second countenance of her Janus head, that namely which is directed beyond the limits of this earth, in order to point him away from earthly enticements, and from the busy arena of life to the steep paths of contemplation, yet the beaming eyes of his guide have not the power to light him to the goal, which can only be reached by the aid of divine revelation.

Seduced long ago from his childlike Christian faith by the pride of unfettered speculation, Dante sees the way of truth transformed to him by the evil passions whose antitheses are the three virtues which we call exclusively Christian. Instead of hoping for the coming of God's kingdom, he depends on the present time and its enjoyments, his heart is entangled in selfishness. Instead of believing in the divine revelation and surrendering himself to it only, he is stupefied by spiritual pride, and persuaded that his own reason is sufficient to fathom the depths of eternity. Finally instead of love his breast is filled with hatred against his brethren who think differently from him or are mistaken, he is full of party spirit and desire of persecuting. And so he sees himself driven back as by wild beasts from the slopes of the mountain upon whose summits shines the sun of truth into a life of darkness and storm.

Then God's grace kindles the beam of religion again in his breast, he sees how fruitless, how sinful even were the researches of the over bold reason into matters which to it must remain ever unfathomable. He regrets ever having given in to the error of assigning too great importance to the transitory interests of earth, and the old faith, the old love towards his glorified Beatrice awaken in new fulness. On the day on which the Saviour redeemed mankind upon the cross, in the year when the Church was seeking by means of the Jubilee to bring Christians to Heaven on a new road, then did Dante also receive the inward assurance of redemption. But his newly-awakened faith is no longer the almost unconscious faith of a joyous childlike spirit, it is the result of year-long wanderings and doubts now impenetrably armed against outward storms and inward waverings, and firmly fixed on a basis of deep scientific thought. When his love for the living Beatrice was once inseparably bound up with the faith which looks up in gratitude to God, she in her heavenly exaltation became a bright symbol of theology, the enlightened and enlightening queen of sciences.

Now, however, the guilt of his ancient errors weighs upon his soul, and according to the teaching of his Church he cannot enter into the full glory of God otherwise than by open confession of the sin which he had committed in parting from God, followed by contrition of the heart, and appropriate penance in order to wipe out from his soul the spots by which its original purity was defaced.

At this point begins the *Divina Commedia* and this concludes the great poem whose earlier portions are the *Vita Nuova* and the *Convito*. It is the universal eternally true epic of our spiritual life, it is the history of the childlike simplicity, the inward falling away, and the gracious call with which God, who alone is light, truth, and life, brings us back to Himself. As represented it is the inward experience of a poet who died more than five hundred years ago, and yet it is the way by which all Christians, except a few elect, must go in order to arrive at salvation. And so the poet stands for the whole human race fallen and called to redemption, upon whom a thousand different sins weigh, but to whom Christ reaches a thousand arms in order to draw them from the brink of the precipice to His breast.

That these deductions contain much that is true is undeniable. The development of the poet's mind in the form of a trilogy, as it has been undesignedly represented by him with poetical embellishment in his three works *Vita Nuova*, *Convito*, and *Commedia*, can in future be regarded as an established fact. Nor can any objection of importance be made to the description of the first period as one of innocence, childlike faith, and a life of happiness in God, or of the third as the period of penitential return to the old faith and the old love. It is the actual character of the second period that is still in dispute. That the ground of the poet's self-accusation in the concluding vision of the *Purgatory* must be something connected with the Christian faith can be doubted only by those who will not admit that Beatrice, as she there appears, is a symbol standing in the very closest connection with that faith. Being as we are the children of the nineteenth, and grandchildren of the eighteenth centuries, we have become so used at the mention of sins against Christian faith as distinguished from those against Christian morals to think of doubt, indifferentism, infidelity, irreligion, and so forth, that it is only too natural to us to suspect something of the same sort in the mediaeval poet. But that Dante was ever hostile, or even indifferent towards the Christian faith, is a thing of which we find not the slightest trace in his writings. But is there no indication, nay, even distinct evidence, that there was a period at which religious doubt found its way into his soul when over-estimating the powers of his own reason he rated too cheaply the childlike faith of the Christian?

This question can only be answered in the affirmative with scientific certainty if it were possible to offer any evidence that Dante doubted the truth of any definite article of the Christian faith. Attempts have been more than once made to offer this proof, but it will not be asserted that they have been successful. All the points that have been brought forward involve either questions of subordinate importance which were not definitely settled even for the most thoroughgoing theologian of the Middle Ages, or such as have no connection with the maxims of Christian dogma, as for instance the question to which he gives different answers in the *Convito* and in the *Paradise* as to the reasons of the markings on the moon. From his change of opinion in regard to such questions we are not entitled to draw any conclusions about his attitude towards Christian dogma. Just as little can we do so from his change of opinion in regard to questions which are connected with the Christian faith. It is true he modified at a later time his former view with regard to the position of certain angelic orders in the three heavenly hierarchies, but religious doubt would surely have concerned itself rather with the existence of the angelic orders than with their position in the hierarchies. From the fact that in the *Convito* Dante appeals expressly to the teaching of the Church, it follows that he regarded that as of supreme authority. It is true that in the *Convito* and in the *De Monarchiâ* he often quotes not only Aristotle but also his commentators, including Averroes. But that proves in any case the extent of his learning rather than any religious doubt. Even the schoolmen, whose faith is above suspicion, quote the same Arabic authorities even more frequently.

Some surprise has been caused by Dante's practice of glorifying in his great poem men whose religious faith was not undoubted. To quote Witte again (*Dante-Forschungen*, i. p. 172), 'Abbot Joachim of Flora, whose teaching was the mainstay of Amalric of Bena and his scholars, served as the basis of the eternal gospel, the symbolic secret book of the Fraticelli, who were hostile to the Church, has his place in the sun beside Francis and Dominic, Thomas and Bonaventura. In the same sphere we meet also Siger of Brabant, whose very hazardous work *Impossibilia* caused so great a shock to the Church.' But if in the last division of his poem Dante had glorified men whom he knew to be hostile to the faith, it would no doubt have created a strong prejudice against his own orthodoxy, but would at the same time have implied necessarily that in the later years of his life he stood himself at the same point of estrangement from the faith, and this would obviously upset Witte's whole system. It is to be said, however, that in Dante's time, and even later, Joachim of Flora passed for a man of thorough piety and prophetic gifts, and he could hardly have foreseen in him the father of the Pantheistic sects of Amalric of Bena and David of Dinànt. Siger, too, is quite outside of consideration. Three different persons o this name have been identified, and the one mentioned by Dante appears to have been a scholar and colleague of St. Thomas Aquinas. Moreover, though the *Impossibilia* is replete with sophisms, it contains no attack on the faith.

'But,' says Witte again, 'even in the *Commedia* Dante seems by no means to reject evidences of divine truths drawn from reason in preference to revelation. In presence of the Apostle Peter, when speaking of the foundation of his faith in a personal God exterior to the world, he appeals in the first place to physical and metaphysical proofs.' But the conclusion from this is simple, that even in the later years of his life the poet not only saw in the appeal to such proofs, and so in the use of reason as a means of inquiry into religious dogmas, no departure from the right road of faith, but rather recognised therein the right road, since immediately thereupon he represents himself as being complimented on his faith in a truly heavenly fashion by Peter the apostle of faith.

The chief stress is laid upon a passage in the *Convito* (iv. 1), which deals with the question whether matter emanated from the divine intelligence, and was already in existence before the creation. It is as follows: 'And whereas this my lady (namely philosophy) had in some measure changed her loving mien towards me, especially in those places where I considered and inquired whether the first matter of the elements existed in the intelligence of God, for which reason I refrained a little from seeking her glance, I betook myself in her absence to considering human weakness in respect to the error aforesaid' (namely, the nature of nobility). Here we find our poet in a state of doubt in respect to the gropings of reason. If the question for him had been whether matter was eternal, as Aristotle taught, or had been created out of nothing, we could then have come to the conclusion that 'if Dante in this conflict of two opinions, of which one was undoubtedly orthodox, was unable to come to any decision, then we should have to say that, at this stage of his development, the teaching of the Church, and that of Averroes, were regarded by him as two authorities of equal weight, and thus that from his then point of view he could, like the pure philosophers of the schools, have explained the same judgment as theologically and philosophically true' (Witte).

Only how could Dante be in any doubt on the question of the eternity or creation of matter after having just before declared distinctly for creation? He had written: 'in conclusion, I say for the highest praise of wisdom, that she is the mother and principle of all things that exist, for I say that with God the world began, and especially the movement of the heaven which brought all things to birth, and from which all movement begins and goes forth, and my words mean that she was in the thought of God when He created the world. Hence it follows that she it was who created it, and therefore Solomon says in the Proverbs, speaking in the person of wisdom, "When He prepared the Heaven I was there."' Did he then, after expressing himself thus, wish to surprise his reader with the confession that he was in doubt upon the point whether matter was eternal or created? That is impossible. It was a different question upon which philosophy gave him no satisfactory answer. To quote Hettinger:

> The ancients formulated the question thus: 'Utrum materia facta sit ad rationem sive ad exemplar aliquod.' The difficulty lies just in the point that matter does not possess a form, but only the potentiality of assuming a form. But of that which is without form no idea can exist, since the

idea is only the image of the form of the thing in the intelligence. It appears, then, that God had not from eternity in His spirit cognition of matter. The difficulty is increased by the consideration that the *materia prima* is purely material, and that therefore its primary image must be purely material, while the divine nature is spiritual. As a further consequence we are led to the thought that this formless matter cannot have been created by God, since all that God created was created according to His eternal ideas as 'causae exemplares et prototypae.' If all existence begins in the world of divine ideas, Dante, as a beginner in philosophy, must necessarily have felt the difficulty that he could not venture to assume for the *materia prima* any idea in the divine intellect. He found a basis, as he immediately afterwards puts it, of his own accord in the fact that everything is compounded out of matter undefined, without properties, purely potential; and form through which the thing becomes what it is, which, entering into matter, and combining itself with it in existence, constitutes the thing as such, and forms the principle of its actuality. But that such matter must be assumed as the subject of the various definitions, and the abiding substratum under all changes of generation and corruption he had learnt from Aristotle and Augustine. There arose for him an apparent antinomy out of these two equally true propositions: Only the definite and rational is an object of the divine idea, and: Matter is indefinite, purely potential, which only receives its rationality and intelligibility through form.

Now, if the poet could not arrive at perfect clearness in regard to questions so difficult as this, it would be too hazardous to draw therefrom conclusions in regard to his religious views and convictions. Perfectly orthodox scholastics and mystics were often in doubt on this point.

The argument above stated is therefore wholly untenable. There is no single dogma of the orthodox faith as then held of which we can show that Dante at any time, or in any of his writings, either contested the truth or even felt any doubt. On the contrary, it can be shown without any trouble that even in the *Convito*, wherever he has occasion to speak of an article of the faith, he does so not only with respect, but as a thoroughly believing Christian. At every step he appeals to Holy Scripture as the highest authority; and he expresses, recognises, the infallibility of the Catholic Church in one place (Conv. ii. 4), where, if his profession were not made from the heart, he might easily have held his peace. Miracles, which at all times have provoked doubt, and which, we know on Dante's own evidence, were doubted in his day, are to him the main foundation of faith; and the 'many who doubted of them are regarded by him as obstinate and deluded' (*Ib.* id. 7). While his friend Guido Cavalcanti was meditating a scientific basis for atheism, our poet found in God the highest and ultimate blessedness to which man can attain. While the dogma of the Trinity was to the mediaeval freethinkers an object for importunate inquiry, Dante speaks of it with the childlike faith of a saint. As to the immortality of the human soul he speaks in not only an orthodox, but an elevating, even edifying fashion, and the denial of it is to him the most stupid, vulgar, and corrupting brutishness. In short we may read the *Convito* from end to end without finding the smallest ground for concluding that when he wrote that work Dante was in any way estranged from the faith. On the contrary we may safely affirm that this work, wherein the poet's conflict with his doubts is said to be reflected, reads like an edifying book, in which the straitest sect of orthodoxy will find nothing to shock it.

The same may be said of the *De Monarchiâ*, which also belongs to the alleged period of religious doubt. One fancies that in this one hears at times rather a fanatical priest than a sceptic. In the *Convito* we meet with passages like: 'O most foolish and vilest of brutes that feed in the guise of men, who presume to speak against our faith, and with your spinning and delving would know that which God has ordained with so great foresight. Cursed be ye, and your presumption, and whosoever believes in you.' And in the *De Monarchiâ* : 'Faith itself will be shaken, if the authority of the Divine Scriptures totters. . . . If this is caused intentionally, those who go thus astray must be treated like tyrants, who do not follow the laws for the common advantage, but try to wrest them to their own. Oh ! crime above all crime, even in dreams to misuse the purpose of the eternal Spirit ! for the sin is not against Moses, or David, or Job, or Matthew, or Paul, but against the Holy Ghost who speaks in them.' The man who wrote this was no sceptic, still less an infidel.

We must then reject as incorrect, or at any rate as grossly exaggerated, the statement that at a certain period of his life, Dante, instead of believing in Divine revelation and surrendering to it, was befooled and misled by spiritual pride into thinking that his own reason was sufficient to fathom the depths of infinity. But still more decidedly must the other views be rejected, according to which Dante was a hopeless egotist, a partisan filled with hatred, ill-will, and the love of persecution. If in the *De Monarchiâ* he has indicated as the aim of human life the attainment of eternal blessedness, it shows that he hoped for God's kingdom to come. And how joyous and genuinely Christian is the hope of this expressed in the *Convito* where he describes the soul's entry into the haven of eternal peace ! In his great poem he testifies by his own mouth that the Church militant has no son more endowed with the gift of hope ; nor is there the slightest trace of any time when his hope failed ; just as little trace is there of any hatred or ill-will towards his brethren who differ from him or who have been misled. At the outset of *De Monarchiâ*, *Convito*, *De*

Vulgari Eloquentiâ, he expressly declares that his impulse to write was given by his love to his neighbour. Nay, let us hear his own words :

After I had become the paramour of this lady above named, I began to love or hate according as she loved or hated. Thus I loved those who followed after truth, and hated the followers of error and falsehood, even as she does. But whereas everything is of itself to be loved, and none to be hated save by reason of the accession of wickedness to it, it is reasonable and honourable to hate not the things but the wickedness that is in the things, and to find means to separate from them. And if any person has this intention, my most excellent lady has it above all, namely to eliminate the evil in things which is the cause of hatred ; since in her is all reason, and in her is honour as in its source. Following her in doing as in feeling to the best of my power, I loathed and despised the error of the folk, not so as to disgrace and revile the erring, but the errors ; the which by reproving them, I thought to make displeasing, and when they displeased, to remove them from those who on their account were hated by me. (Conv. iv. 1.)

Was this man's heart full of hatred, party-spirit, ill-will towards his erring brethren ? Surely the judgment of every reader with regard to the suggested picture of a life without faith, hope, or love, must be that it is a bit of rhetorical fancy devoid of all historical basis.

To the modern man it may seem strange, well-nigh inconceivable, if we express our view that the fault with which Dante reproaches himself was not scepticism, not infidelity, not religious indifference, not any lack of faith, hope, or love, but simply that he had neglected divine science, and thrown himself with exclusive enthusiasm into the arms of that which the world offers. So far the poet's own admissions and intimations bring us of necessity, but not a step farther ; that philosophy made of him a sceptic or an infidel is an assumption for which his works afford no support whatever, and which can owe its rise only to the fact that according to modern views the confessions of the great epic require us to look for something more than the mere preference of secular to divine science. The Middle Ages thought otherwise—to them a neglect of theology and of matters of the faith counted as a sin, and not one of the lightest. And it is of this sin that Dante confesses himself guilty, both in the great vision at the end of the *Purgatory*, and in the first canto of the poem, when he mentions his fruitless efforts to reach the sunlit hill; while in his wandering in the dark wood we should rather seek an allusion to a life turned aside to worldly cares.

CHAPTER IV

ANOTHER AND YET THE SAME

WHEN Dante wrote the *Convito*, which was, as we shall see, about 1308, he was still at the philosophical standpoint, and fanatically enthusiastic about it.[1] About the same time he wrote the book *De Vulgari Eloquentiâ* in which he seems to stand at the same point. The same appears from the letters which he had then written, and in which, at any rate in that to the Florentines, he uses language very unlike that of Christian love. When his neighbour Villani charges him with the arrogance of a learned man, he may be drawing from experiences of his own during the last decade of the thirteenth century; but perhaps the chronicler is basing his reproach upon the letters which he knew and mentions.

However that may be, the three periods of Dante's spiritual development are so clearly visible in his works that it would be mere dilettantism to deny them. As to the duration of the first period no doubt can prevail; it embraces the years of boyhood and youth till the death of Beatrice. On the other hand, the boundary between the

---

[1] How then, we may ask, can he have confessed his errors to Beatrice, and repented of them in 1300? Clearly the sins for which he expresses his contrition in the *Purgatory* must have belonged to a period of his life previous to the supposed date of the vision.

second and third periods cannot be determined with equal certainty. In the introductory canto of the *Commedia* the jubilee year 1300 is named as the date at which Dante awoke and tried to escape from the dark wood. In that year then the poet must have undergone a revulsion; but we dare not assume that he fully renounced the life and bustle of the world so soon as this, for he was at the time a member of the government, and until his banishment took an active part in public affairs. But if, as the latter cantos of the *Purgatory* place beyond doubt, he recognised in his later years that his devotion to philosophy had been an error, this recognition must have come to him after he had written the *Convito*. We must otherwise arrive at the monstrous conclusion that Dante chanted his song to the glory of Philosophy after he had recognised and lamented as a sin his too passionate love for her.

As with mankind so with the individual, spiritual development proceeds gradually, in most cases imperceptibly. No doubt various phases, steps, periods can be distinguished, but it is seldom possible to assign with any certainty the moment at which one ceases and another arises. Still it often happens that some important external event, whether joyful, or, as more often occurs, sorrowful, marks a turning-point in the inner life. You look for such an event in Dante's life; the death of the Emperor Henry VII., on whom he built so great hopes, at once presents itself. His grief, his disillusion must have been overpowering, well adapted to transform his whole existence. We maintain accordingly that the deaths of Beatrice and Henry VII. mark the two turning-points in the poet's spiritual life. At the same time we do not mean to say that the revulsions were suddenly complete. Probably the second no less than the first came gradually to completeness. It must not, however, escape notice that the assumption that Henry's death marked the limit of the second period, is only a hypothesis, based on the fact that the letters belonging to the time of the march to Rome show us the poet at the same standpoint as does the *Convito*.

In his poem Dante's penance is completed in harmony with the teaching of all the schoolmen after Thomas Aquinas in regard to the sacrament of that name. We find all the stages necessary to penance,—contrition, confession, satisfaction. This could not be otherwise in a mediaeval poem whose hero is not merely an individual, but man in general, collective humanity represented in an individual. In reality Dante's penance can hardly have been completed upon the scholastic lines. In it there must have been question merely of a psychologic progress, a serious return upon himself, silent regret and straightforward purpose to tread other paths, and energetic carrying of it into effect. These mental processes are in the poem, notably in the final vision of the *Purgatory*, applied to mankind at large, and set forth in accordance with the teaching of the Church. It can therefore hardly be called a critical method of procedure to press individual expression too closely, and speak of 'crushing grief' or 'heart-breaking scenes.' From beginning to end of his poem Dante expresses a consciousness not only of his intellectual and scientific endowments, but also of his moral merit. Even before he has made his peace with Beatrice he knows himself to be a 'good soul' not destined to hell; while if the almost universal interpretation of Inf. vi. 73 is correct, he indicates himself as one of the two righteous men who then were living at Florence. If he accuses himself in unmistakable fashion of pride, it cannot be doubted that he was proud of his own worth. His own consciousness must have told him that such a man had no great reason to be especially contrite, or to do penance in a heart-breaking sort. We must accordingly assume that the powerful disillusion which he experienced when Henry died, the irrefragable necessity of abandoning every hope till then cherished, whether of an honourable recall to Florence or of playing any part on the public stage of the world, gave the poet cause for a self-inspection, the result of which was, on the one hand, regret for his pursuit of temporal things and his idolatrous devotion to worldly wisdom, and on the other, a determination at once to begin striving after the eternal, and devoting himself with no reservation to divine wisdom. Afterwards when in his great epic he depicted this psychologic progress in poetical terms, he decided to depict it on the lines of the Church's teaching, and drew the portrait of an ecclesiastically correct penance and conversion.

According to abstract theory, which is indeed older than Christianity, a man changes wholly when, as the result of a serious return upon himself, he abandons his former standpoint and places himself at another. As a matter of fact he remains the same as he was. The character, once formed, never alters; at the most it undergoes some modification. A man does not become another man when he passes from the dominion of one principle to that of another; least of all when, as in the present case, the question is not of two principles but of two shades of what is really the same. According to abstract theory we should in the third period have to do with a different Dante from the Dante of the second; in reality in each of the three we have to do with the same poet, the same scholar, the same man. A progress there is; but as the transitions are slight and hardly perceptible, so also is the difference between the man at one stage and the other in no way conspicuous.

We may say rather it is so small that many inquirers have been unable to perceive it, and therefore have simply denied the existence of any 'trilogy' in the poet's development; which would not have been possible if the poet of the *Commedia* had been another man than the writer of the *Convito*. Further, as has been expressly noted by Witte, even in the *Commedia* Dante has been unable to dissemble his predilection for philosophy, and for the research of truth by process of reason. This mental change consisted simply in the fact that, after a long neglect, he returned to divine science, and confided himself again to its guidance.

But did not a far more serious alteration take place in him? did he not from a humble, faithful child of the Church become her terribly severe judge? It is true that in his epic he is zealous against the abuses which had crept into the Church, and therewith he in no wise spares the bearer of her highest authority. In his earlier writings, as might be expected, nothing of the kind is found. When he wrote the *Vita Nuova* he was still too young to set himself up as a judge, and the *Convito*, from its whole arrangement, offered him no opportunity of testifying against abuses in the Church. We cannot speak of any change in this respect until we can succeed in proving that the poet had formerly condoned or showed himself indifferent to abuses of the kind which he brands in the *Commedia;* and this is impossible. There is then here no question of a conversion, only of a natural progressive development.

This seems to be the place to touch briefly on another question which should be banished as an utter anachronism from the study of Dante. Was Dante an honest faithful Catholic? Was he with his whole heart devoted to the Church, or did he take up a position of antagonism? With the dreams of those who would stamp him as a member of a secret society, an Albigensian, a freemason, a socialist, or the like, there is at the present day no use in troubling ourselves. There is more importance in the question whether in his inmost soul he was not at variance with the Church of Rome and her system, a conscious or unconscious reformer. This has often been supposed, especially by Protestant theologians, and people have not hesitated to reckon Dante among the pre-Reformers, that is among those who in early times expressed and defended the fundamental ideas of the reforming movement of the sixteenth century. The list of those who have held this view is opened by Matthias Flacius, the notorious Lutheran fanatic, who in his *Catalogus testium veritatis* (1556) appeals to our poet as a witness against the Church of Rome. He devotes indeed but a few lines to him, but these are enough to show that he knew very little of him, and that little only at second hand. He mentions the *De Monarchiâ*, adds that in the *De Vulgari Eloquentiâ* the poet reproves the Popes and their teachers, and quotes in proof of this two expressions which certainly seem to be taken from the *Commedia*. Finally, he says that in the *Convito* Dante puts the married state on a level with celibacy, of which it is needless to say not a trace is to be found in that work. The appeal to Dante as a witness against the Church of Rome has all the less weight that among the hundred and forty witnesses catalogued by Flacius are sixteen Popes, who may be supposed to have been good Papists.

Just thirty years later there was issued, it is said by Johannes Schwarz of Munich, a work in Italian, called *Avviso piacevole*. The author of this was a Frenchman of rank, François Perot de Mézières, in which an attempt was made to get Italy to accept the Reformation on the strength of Dante's poem. Cardinal Bellarmine thought the little work important enough to be systematically controverted. At the same time Du Plessis-Mornay in his *Mysterium Iniquitatis seu Historia Papatus* brought forward our poet as an adequate champion for the Reformation against the Papacy. The Dominicans entered the lists against him with great zeal in defence of Dante's Catholicity. Then the fight rested for two hundred years. Dante was far too serious and far too profound for the freethinkers of the eighteenth century to adopt him as a prophet and apostle of freethought. Voltaire, being unable to understand the poet and his great work, was content to poke fun at them. 'The Italians,' he says, 'call him divine; but it is a hidden divinity. Few understand his oracles. He has commentators; perhaps a further reason why he is not understood. His fame will always remain, because he is not read. Some score of passages are known by heart; that is enough to save the trouble of testing the rest.' And of the *Commedia*, ' It has been supposed that this farrago is a fine epic poem, but it is only an extraordinary poem.' Naturally, after this, French freethought left Dante alone, which we can only call fortunate, since we should otherwise have a whole literature on the question whether Dante was a forerunner or an opponent of the '*philosophes.*'

In the present century the question was first taken up by a Catholic, Ugo Foscolo; a name honoured by students of Dante. He laboured to deduce that Dante had not only foretold the Reformation, but had indicated himself as the heaven-sent reformer. The Neapolitan Gabriele Rossetti made a daring attempt to establish from Dante's writings a secret widely-ramifying conspiracy against the Roman Church. Following in Rossetti's steps, and indeed far outrunning him, Ernest Aroux tried to prove that Dante was a disguised heretic, a revolutionary and a socialist, an adherent of the Albigenses, a secret friend to the Templars, an infidel and an adorer of classical antiquity, a pantheist, a Protestant before the days of Protestantism, and a master of secret symbolic language. These dreams, which have found opponents in Italy, France, England, and Germany, may be regarded as done with, and have to-day only the value of historical curiosities. But it is still under discussion whether Protestantism is not right in claiming the singer of the next world as its ally. The Lutheran theologian, Karl Graul, delighted in our poet as 'one of the first of those precious witnesses of the truth who have successively arisen to combat the errors of Rome'; and he consoles himself for the thought that Dante does not stand exactly on Luther's ground, with the other thought that 'if only in a presentiment he would have looked over to Germany, and come with joy to our side, had he but been permitted to see accomplished in our Luther, in a higher sense than he could have understood, his prophecy concerning the hound who was to slay the she wolf; without which the *Commedia* is for the most part a riddle without solution, a prophecy without fulfilment, a building incomplete, like the cathedral of Cologne'! More than a hundred years earlier Valentin Ernst Löscher, the last important defender of the orthodox Lutheranism of the sixteenth century, had said, referring to the famous passage of the DXV, 'Dante prophesied that in 1515 one should come, sent by God, to do judgment on the harlot, and on the giant who sinned with her!' The addition of $M = 1000$ was necessary to bring out the desired date. Others were pleased to find in VELTRO an anagram of LVTERO. A learned archaeologist of Berlin, Ferdinand Piper, states that Dante's evangelical character is so predominant, his testimony so clear, and his voice so mighty, that he must be recognised

with grateful honour as one of the forerunners of the
Reformation. With this many Lutheran theologians agree.
On the other hand Ebrard of Erlangen : 'Dante has hurled
the red-hot shot of his verse with boldness and the bitterness
of a wrathful nature, not only against the sins and crimes of
individual occupants of the Roman see, but against the
very idea of this overlordship of Rome; but only from the
moral standpoint, and in antagonism rather to her political
than to her ecclesiastical supremacy. He stands wholly
upon the ground of mediaeval dogma. His conception of
Hell, Purgatory, and Heaven is poetically grand, but
dogmatically rigid; quite according to the laws of Rome,
wholly unevangelical. He puts the heretic in the fiery
torments just as much as the inquisitor. He assigns the
degrees of guilt according to Aristotelian and scholastic
models, not according to the heart's attitude towards
salvation. The strange medley of Pagan and Christian
elements may have been only the form in which he chose
to express his ideas, but the ideas are only those of a
manful Ghibeline morality, both public and private, and in
no way those of an evangelical Christian.' Similarly Herzog :
'Dante's *Commedia* is a homily against the transgressions
of the age, especially those of the Papacy, and a prophetic
announcement, giving hope of a fundamental reformation
both of head and of members, and more particularly fore-
telling the fall of Rome for assuming to itself both swords.
Yet this unsurpassed masterpiece of mediaeval poetry in no
way abandons the imperfections which lie at the base of
Roman Catholicism. Christianity and Paganism are blended
in it. On these foundations the true Reformation could
never stand.'

Much more might be quoted of the same kind, if we let
all the reverend gentlemen who have written upon Dante

have their say. That would, however, be lost labour, if only because a certain superficiality is to be met with throughout their writings. No sure conclusion can be reached from a few detached passages. Dante is not a writer upon whom every worthy person can form an opinion on the ground of a superficial perusal of some of his writings. He must be studied thoroughly, profoundly, with that honest love which sinks itself in its object, conceives it only in its own medium, flies across centuries, awakes on the farther side, and abandons all foregone conclusions of its own. If we question Dante's conception of the world in its entirety, we shall find that only the crudest dilettantism could doubt of its strict Catholicity. If, as it has been assumed he would have done, he had rejoiced to see the day of the sixteenth-century Reformation, he would have had to abandon his whole system and become another man. For his system is rooted in the mediaeval Catholic conception of things, and stands or falls with it. His dogma is strict Catholic; we may safely affirm indeed that Aquinas had no more faithful disciple. Every kind of schism, of division in the Church, is hateful in his eyes; and there can be little doubt that Dante would have placed the sixteenth-century reformers, all and sundry, in Hell. He strove for a reform, if you will, in head and members; but it was a moral, not a doctrinal reform. The doctrine of the mediaeval Church is to him inviolable. Heaven and earth may pass away, but it, the eternal truth, will never pass. Nowhere in his works, least of all in his great epic, can any declension from Catholic dogma be discovered. And if he utters his condemnation of the abuses that have crept in, or of the unworthy bearers of authority in the Church, he does it from a holy and pure zeal for religion and Church, not from any irreligious or antagonistic impulse. It is zeal for God's house which eats him up; a thoroughly pure zeal, free from every thought of self-seeking or schism; a holy zeal which seeks only the honour of God, the good of the Church, and the welfare of society organised in Christendom. This pure and holy zeal, so rare in our time, sore stricken as it is with indifference, has been misunderstood; and men debate over Dante's attitude towards confessions which the Christian Church of those days still held as mere embryos in her womb. Pierre Bayle thought that Dante had afforded material enough for both the views of those who like to hold that he was a good Roman Catholic and those who detect the contrary in him. That is quite correct, in so far as Dante was a faithful, enlightened, and thoughtful Christian. Catholic and Protestant alike can find in him what is true Christianity. As for special peculiarities in doctrine, Catholicism can always find some such in Dante; while, on the other hand, Protestantism can only find a protest, quite proper in the mouth of a serious and pious Christian of that day, against the crying abuses and corruption of the hierarchy.

Throughout his whole life Dante was a pious believing Christian. In the first stage of his spiritual development his faith was childlike, of the kind that accepts upon authority the traditional Christianity of its Church, and feels itself blessed in the contemplation of the divine which is mirrored in a pure being. In the second stage he was a Christian who, without denying the pious faith of his youth, has strayed somewhat from it, and who, distracted by the claims of worldly cares, of temporal affairs, and perhaps pleasures, no less than by scientific studies, thinks mostly about other things than questions of faith and problems of eternal salvation. In the third stage, a Christian, who, bitterly deceived in his hopes and expectations by the world, turns again to the one thing needful; and with the senses and thoughts of a trained man of mature mind, immerses himself in the consideration of the eternal. In all stages a genuine Christian, and a faithful son of the Church in which he was born and brought up, he may be conceived of as in a constant state of development and progress, and therefore another man in his second stage, and yet another in his third; but always true to himself, always consistent, always developing on normal lines; and therefore always the same.

CHAPTER V

ATTITUDE TOWARDS POLITICAL PARTIES

THE extent to which the Italy of the thirteenth and fourteenth centuries suffered from party conflicts is a matter of universal knowledge. This party spirit had in Dante's time become all the more noxious that it concerned itself no longer with principles, but only with the interests of parties, and still more with those of individual families and potentates. The old party names served only selfish ends; the old parties split up further among themselves, and smaller local parties were formed. The Guelfs split into White and Black; the Ghibelines into Green and Dry. How little political principles had to do with these divisions is sufficiently shown in the history of Florence. The division of the city into Guelfs and Ghibelines came about through a young noble's breach of his troth towards a maiden of distinguished family. The division into Whites and Blacks arose from a family feud which was transplanted from Pistoia to Florence. Dante had good grounds for his emphatic condemnation of both parties.

But setting aside these abuses, it cannot be denied that two great conflicting principles were at stake; the old strife between empire and papacy, State and Church, had not been finally fought out. Rather the controversy had been acutely brought forward in the struggle between Boniface VIII. and Philip the Fair, and the policy of the

Roman hierarchy had found its fullest development in the bull *Unam Sanctam* of November 18, 1302. So again, when the Emperor Henry had fallen in the midst of victory, the bulls of that very Clement V. who had shown himself so complaisant to the King of France announced that the Pope was the Emperor's lord, and that during the vacancy in the throne the management of the empire in Italy was in his hands. The battle continued after Dante's death. During the struggle of Lewis the Bavarian with the French popes there was even more literary discussion as to the rights of State and Church than there had been in the time of Frederick II.

With regard to Dante we may confidently assert that he was neither Guelf nor Ghibeline in the sense in which these catchwords were used by his contemporaries for their petty aims. If, however, we are to believe his first biographer Boccaccio, things would bear another aspect. He says:

> Dante's forefathers were, as Guelfs, twice driven from their home by Ghibelines, and he under the title of Guelf held the reins of the Republic in Florence; whence being expelled, as has been shown, not by the Ghibelines but by the Guelfs, and seeing that he could not return, he so changed his mind that no one was a fiercer Ghibeline and more opposed to the Guelfs than he. And that of which I feel most shame, for the sake of his memory, is what is a most notorious fact, that in Romagna every woman, every little child, when speaking to him about parties and condemning the Ghibelines, should have moved him to such madness that he would have gone so far as to throw stones at them if they had not held their peace, and with this animosity he lived till his death. And of a truth I am ashamed that it should be my duty to blot the fame of so great a man with any fault; but I am in some measure constrained to do so by the order of narrative which I have adopted, seeing that if I shall be silent about matters which are less than praiseworthy in him, I shall take away much credit from the praiseworthy things that I have already set forth.

Boccaccio might in truth have dispensed with his shame; he need only have obtained more accurate information and adhered more strictly to the truth. The foregone conclusion with which he wrote appears indeed here quite clearly. He felt himself bound to recount what was discreditable to his hero in order that he might more easily obtain acceptance for all that he has related to his credit. At the same time it cannot be said that Dante's Ghibeline fanaticism is merely an invention of his biographer. In that case he would not have appealed to the fact that the matter was notorious in Romagna; he was not so impudent as that. Credulous he was and in a high degree uncritical. He took his matter indiscriminately wherever he found it, working it up and embellishing it after his own fashion. But he cannot without great injustice be charged with consciously relating what was untrue. Even where he lays to the poet's charge greed and avarice, and even suspects him strongly of graver crimes, he is acting in good faith, for he supposes that this is implied in the passages of the sacred poem upon which he is commenting. He has, we may suppose, actually heard tell in Romagna that Dante was in his later years a very decided Ghibeline, and has repeated this with embellishments in his own style. The women, and the children, and the stones, and the rage, and the animosity are probably only the offspring of his fancy. But the offspring would probably never have come into the world had not Dante's Ghibeline opinions been a fact. How otherwise could the story of his Ghibeline fanaticism have arisen?

This may serve to prove how ungrounded is the frequently repeated assertion that Dante was a Guelf throughout his life. Even if this assertion were not negatived out of the poet's own writings throughout which the Ghibeline system is defended, Boccaccio's report would be sufficient to prove it erroneous. For even if one would accuse Boccaccio of going to no other source than his own fancy one must consider that he would not have depicted Dante as a fanatical Ghibeline if he had been a Guelf. It was surely not forgotten in Boccaccio's time at Ravenna and about Romagna what Dante Alighieri had been in his political tendencies.

Boccaccio is again so far right that Dante belonged to a Guelf family, and himself in his early days reverenced the Guelf system, not only from family tradition but from personal conviction. His family connection with that party is too well known and too generally undisputed to make it necessary to say more on the point. That he was also a Guelf from conviction appears from his own statement at the beginning of the second book of the *De Monarchiâ*. He there says :

> As when we cannot attain to a view of the cause, we wonder at an unfamiliar effect ; so when we know the cause, we look with a certain contempt on those who remain in wonder. I myself once wondered that the Roman people should have become without any resistance the foremost of the world; when, looking at it superficially, I deemed that it had gained that place by force of arms alone, and with no right. But after I had let the eyes of my mind penetrate to the heart of things, and recognised by most effective signs that the Divine providence had brought this to pass, my wonder ceased, and a certain derisive contempt takes its place ; when I learn that the nations are raging against the pre-eminence of the Roman people ; when I see the people imagining vain things, as I myself was wont to do ; when, above all, I lament that kings and princes are taking counsel together in this one thing, that they may oppose the Lord and His anointed, the Roman Emperor.

The anointed is beyond question the Roman Emperor. To what nationality he belonged was no concern of Dante's.

As Emperor he was a Roman; the imperial dignity made him one, even if he were not one by birth. For a cosmopolitan idealist like Dante the Roman Emperor, so long as he was lawfully elected, need not even be an Italian. The people who speak vain things, the kings and princes who are united in this one thing, to oppose the Emperor, are the republics, cities, kings, princes, and lesser lords of Italy. But it was exactly these who then formed the Guelf party. Thus in the passage quoted our poet declares that he had once belonged to that party, and that from personal conviction, though it was based only on a superficial consideration of things. He had no objection to the study of history; Roman history at all events was, as his own word shows, not strange to him. From these studies he arrived at the view that military power was the sole basis of Rome's supremacy. But as he studied more deeply he altered his view, and came by degrees to the conviction that the Roman Empire was ordained and willed by God, and therefore existed of divine right.

But if it is thus shown to be an historical fact that a revolution took place in Dante's thought, this does not justify us in accusing him, with Boccaccio, of turning his coat from personal motives. We cannot indeed speak as to the latter point, since we have no certain data for deciding whether the change was accomplished before or after his banishment. But we may believe the poet unconditionally when he tells us that his studies and his meditations had led him to another view of things. In that case, however, we have merely to do with a natural progress in knowledge, not with any change of system; nor has the question, which of the two views is historically and philosophically the more correct, anything to do with the matter. It is enough if he himself lived in the belief that he had found the truth, and did not shut himself up against advance in knowledge.

Nor can any certain conclusion as to the state of Dante's political tenets at that time be drawn from the fact that immediately before his exile he took part in the Guelfic government of the Florentine republic. Even if at that time his opinions had been wholly Ghibeline, it would not have stopped him from joining the governing body. Florence was not at that time hostile to any imperial rights, as she was later in the time of Henry of Luxemburg; indeed, as Dante regarded the position of affairs, the imperial throne was then vacant. Frederick II. was (as he says, Conv. iv. 3) for him the last Roman Emperor. Rudolf of Habsburg, Adolf of Nassau, Albert, albeit they had been subsequently elected, were no real Emperors; since they supposed themselves to have better work to do than to meddle with the affairs of Italy. Such being his opinion, there was no motive to withhold him from taking part in the very moderate Guelf government of Florence. That the Whites belonged originally to the Guelfs cannot be denied; but after they were banished the Ghibelines became their natural allies and the Emperor their hope; from which it may well have come to pass that most of them became Ghibelines even in theory. In Villani the banished Whites are always coupled with the Ghibelines; and we can hardly suppose that they were conscious of any opposition in their respective political opinions. That Dante attached himself to the Whites is no sort of evidence that he was then faithful to the Guelfic traditions of his family. As matters then stood, he could call himself a White holding decided Ghibeline views. The opposition which he offered to the wild theocratic plans of Pope Boniface VIII. leaves no doubt at any rate that he was at that time by no means a strict Guelf.

If, as we have his own assurance, his political change came about in consequence of a widening and deepening of his studies, it seems natural to assume that this took place during the year when he sought in diligent study consolation for the loss of Beatrice. This assumption would become an established fact if we could be sure that the *De Monarchiâ*, that eloquent and learned apology for the Ghibeline system, was composed before his exile. But the date at which that work was composed is too uncertain to allow us to draw any conclusions from it. It is an established fact that Dante was born and brought up as a Guelf, but that in his scientific works no less than in his great poem he shows himself a decided advocate of Ghibeline views. Another difficulty in the way of fixing the date of his change is, that all such inward changes, when brought about by study and meditation, are accomplished so gradually that one is seldom in a position to state the year of them, let alone the month and day.

In his later years Dante took credit for having turned his back on all the political parties of his time and having formed a party for himself. But on what grounds did he separate from his fellow-exiles? According to his own statement the reason was the hostility which he had to undergo from those who shared his fortunes. As to the actual nature of this hostility we have no further information. But a more important question for us here is as to the real reasons which caused the dissension. The poet himself has attributed them to the ingratitude, unreason, and profligacy of his companions, and there may be much truth in it. But we can hardly venture to form our judgment on a mere *ex parte* statement. From all we know of him out of his own writings and by the testimony of his contemporaries, tolerance passing under given conditions into noble self-suppression was not among our poet's virtues. Everywhere he appears as a man of thoroughly autocratic, masterful, impatient character: that he was not particularly considerate is more than sufficiently evident from his great poem. If his counsels were disregarded by his companions, a man of his stamp was quite capable of accusing them of base ingratitude. If he met with vigorous opposition, can we wonder at his flinging out reproaches of malice, folly, unreason, impiety? His bitter expressions in *Paradise* (Canto xvii.) seem to point to something of the kind, and as we are in the dark about the actual position of events it is hard to decide on which side the rights and the wrongs lay.

From a theoretic standpoint, however, one may imagine that the greater proportion of right was on Dante's side. Thorough-going idealist as he was, he may not have been the man to reckon so accurately with the faults before him. His affair was mainly with principles and fundamental laws, which otherwise were at that time sadly at a discount. He held that God is the origin and source of all earthly authority, but in the political world of Italy as it then was he would not find many to share his views. Ideally, no doubt, Guelfs and Ghibelines would agree therein. According to the former the papal authority sprang immediately from God, but all other authority, not excepting that of the Emperor, only mediately through the intervention of the Pope. With the Ghibelines, on the other hand, the principle held good that temporal power as well as spiritual sprang immediately from God, for which reason the Roman Emperor was not subordinate to the Pope, but co-ordinate, and therefore independent of him in all worldly matters. We should, however, be much mistaken were we to suppose that the division of parties in Italy turned upon these two principles. The Guelfs indeed allowed the maxim that the papal authority sprang immediately from God to hold good in theory so long as it did not thwart them in practice. But as soon as that happened they had no hesitation in associating themselves with those of whom Dante speaks who started from the principle that all power owed its origin to force of arms and to good fortune, but the papal power, in addition, to trickery and cunningly calculated deceit. But if there are upon earth no other rights than those of the stronger and the more cunning, then one must set strength against strength, cunning against cunning, and must let the final victory rest with the side where strength and cunning are superior and upon which fortune smiles. All who took part in the endless party struggles in Italy acted practically on this principle. Respect for authority, as for a higher divine ordinance, was undermined alike on one side and on the other. It is thus intelligible that a man like Dante could not go far with such associates, and his separation from his party, no less than his progress in political views and opinions, can only redound to his honour.

CHAPTER VI

DANTE'S PERSONALITY

Of Dante's outward appearance his earliest biographer, Boccaccio, draws the following picture:

> Our poet was of moderate stature, and after he had reached mature years went somewhat bowed, and his gait was dignified and unassuming. He was always clad in good clothes, of a style befitting his mature age. His face was long, his nose aquiline, his eyes large rather than small, his jaw large, and the lower lip somewhat in advance of the upper. His complexion was swarthy, his hair and beard thick, black, and crisp; and in face he was ever melancholy and thoughtful. Whence it came to pass one day in Verona, the fame of his works having already been spread abroad, and especially of the division of the *Commedia* which he intitules *Hell*, and being known to many, both men and women, that as he passed before a gateway where many women were sitting, one of them said in a low voice to the others, but not so low as not to be plainly heard by himself and by one that was with him: 'See the man who goes to Hell and comes back when he pleases, and brings up news of those who are down there.' To whom one of the others answered in simple fashion: 'Of a truth thou sayest right: seest thou not how his beard is crisped and his colour darkened by the heat and the smoke down there?' Which words he overhearing behind his back, and knowing that they came from a pure belief on the women's part, was pleased; and as though content that they should be of such opinion, passed on, smiling a little. In his behaviour both at home and abroad he was composed and orderly, and

in all matters more courteous and urbane than any other man. In food and drink he was most temperate; both in taking it at regular hours, and also in not taking it beyond the limit of what was necessary; nor was he at all fastidious about one thing more than another. He would praise delicate food, but for the most part feed on coarse; blaming those exceedingly who spend much of their thought in having choice things, and causing them to be prepared with extreme care; affirming that such did not eat to live, but rather lived to eat. No man was more attentive than he, whether to his studies or to any other matter that keenly interested him;[1] so much so that his family and his wife often complained of it, until they had got used to his habits, and troubled themselves about it no more. He seldom spoke if not called upon, and when he did it was with well-considered words and tones suitable to the subject; yet when occasion demanded he was most eloquent and ready, with prompt and excellent choice of words. . . .

He loved to be solitary and apart from mankind, that his meditations might not be interrupted; and if anything struck him that gave him much pleasure when he was in the company of others, if any question were addressed to him, he would not answer the questioner until such time as he had confirmed or refuted the imagined point; which often befell him when he was at table, or on a journey with companions. He was most assiduous in his studies during such time as he betook himself to them; so that no news which he might hear could take him from them. And according to a story told by credible persons with reference to this absorption in anything that pleased him, being once on a time in Siena, and finding himself by chance in an apothecary's shop, and having had put into his hands a book which before had been promised him, and which was very famous among men of ability, but had never been seen by him; and having as it chanced no facility for taking it elsewhere, he flung himself prone on the bench which was outside the shop, and placing the book in front of him began to look at it with eagerness. And albeit that in the same street, close by him and before his eyes, an assault of arms got up by some noble youths on the occasion of some festival of the Sienese, was taking place,

---

[1] Cf. the opening lines of Purg. iv.

and therewith loud shouts from the spectators (as it is the fashion in such cases to express applause both with various instruments and with the voice), and many other things going on which might have attracted any one to look, such as dances of fair ladies and many sports of well-graced and gay youths, no one saw him move from the spot nor once raise his eyes from his book; but whereas he had taken up his position about noon, it was past vespers, and he had looked through the whole and got a general understanding of it before he rose up; affirming afterwards to certain who asked him how he had been able to refrain from looking at so fine a festival as had been taking place before him, that he had perceived nothing of it. Whereby in addition to their first wonder, those who asked the question not unduly felt a second.

It is quite clear that the author of the *Decameron* is here drawing a picture after his fashion; the colours for the picture he takes from his own fancy, the design on the other hand may be drawn from nature. Boccaccio was indeed still a child when he was brought before the great poet, but the poet made a deep impression on the child, and childish— impressions are not so easily wiped out. Besides, Boccaccio when at Ravenna had much intercourse with the poet's intimates, who must have known his personal appearance, and had no motive for depicting it otherwise than it really was. The picture of Dante's person which Boccaccio has drawn has all the more claim to pass as genuine that it does not strike us as being in any way flattered.

As regards his exterior, Dante was, in any case, no imposing figure. His own indications leave us in no doubt thereon. He regrets, indeed, that he appeared insignificant in the eyes of many men who had imagined him quite otherwise (Conv. i. 3). This complaint, together with the subsequent inquiry why personal knowledge is apt to reduce existing admiration to a more modest measure, speaks plainly enough to those who will understand it. Wherever he went in Italy, it was known that he was an exile whose goods had been confiscated. No one, therefore, could conceive him as a *grand seigneur*, who would make his entry with outward magnificence. If, then, he appeared to many otherwise than they had conceived him, their disillusion can only have had reference to his personal appearance. We might, indeed, assume that they have conceived him as wiser, more learned, of wider experience than really was the case : but of this there can be no question here. It is, on the other hand, very intelligible that the appearance of a man short rather than tall, and somewhat stooping, as Boccaccio depicts him, may have produced a certain disappointment.

We are quite extraordinarily rich in portraits of the poet. If all that are extant be reckoned, we arrive not only at hundreds but at thousands. Yet none the less, or perhaps for that very reason, we cannot claim that we know his features. Considering the great discrepancies among them it is quite clear that the large majority owe their existence only to fancy. Whether there be among them one or more genuine, it is hard to decide. Vasari asserts that Giotto painted the portrait of our poet in the chapel belonging to the palace of the Florentine *podestà*. Great was then the joy when, in 1840, a fresco portrait of Dante was discovered at Florence in the palace of the Bargello. It was announced at once, as an undoubted fact, that this was the very portrait painted by Giotto, and mentioned by Vasari.

Giuseppe Giusti wrote a poem to celebrate the great discovery as it deserved, and the picture has been reproduced uncounted times in and out of Italy. Unfortunately, there are grave suspicions about its genuineness. That the portraits which were discovered were those seen by Vasari, and by him taken for works of Giotto, can indeed hardly be doubted, but whether they really are by Giotto is quite another question. In February 1332 the palace was terribly damaged by a fire in which no fresco painting can have survived, and yet no traces of the fire were observed at the time of the discovery. Giotto, however, quite certainly did no more work in the palace of the Bargello after the fire; indeed, he died in 1336, and the restoration of the palace was not finished till 1345. Moreover, the picture in question was at the time of its discovery so injured that, even if it was genuine, we should not gain much from it towards a knowledge of the poet's features. Most of the reproductions which we see of it are almost worthless since the picture has been arbitrarily restored. Not less questionable is the portrait which exists in the Riccardian MS. 1040, which, in recent times, has been declared to be the only genuine. Of the many others it is better to say nothing. It is possible that among the number some one is the comparatively genuine likeness of the poet. But science is not at present in a position to offer any certainty on the point.

Dante is doubtless the most powerful of all poets in thought and purpose; but, on the other hand, by no means the most attractive. Endowed by nature with pre-eminent talents he honestly put them out to usury, and allowed none of them to lie idle. He was well aware of his own merit, and it is surely with no false modesty that he confesses himself guilty of pride. His straightforwardness, his incorruptible love of truth, know no respect for any one; he is as severe against others as he is against himself. If we would express the essence of his character comprehensively, we may say, perhaps, that his nature was out-and-out idealist; perhaps too much so for this world; and, accordingly, he was little understood by his contemporaries. The rough side of his nature is also closely connected with his idealism.

We may also, perhaps, add that the ill fortune which overtook him was caused and brought about by his ideal conception of the relations of the world and life. Dante was no man for compromise, he had no mind and no patience for half measures and undecided standpoints. His decisiveness often approaches close to the borders of obstinacy. He was surely more feared than loved, and, as we know him from his own writings, he can hardly have been a pleasant or entertaining companion. Doubtless he constantly sought, in all honesty, the highest good of his fellow-men, and strove accordingly to bring about reforms in politics, society, morals, and religion, and to point out to men the road to temporal and eternal happiness. But he was therewith too zealous to be able to put himself amiably at another man's point of view, in order to win over those who differed from him. Subjective in the highest degree, he was much inclined to see in whatever appeared to him error an aberration rather of the will than of the intellect. His contemporary and neighbour, Villani, has undoubtedly drawn his character accurately, when he says, 'By reason of his learning he was somewhat overbearing, reserved, and sensitive; and, as is apt to be the way with philosophers, he did not rightly understand how to get on with uneducated people.'

Boccaccio praises his extraordinary ability, his faithful memory, and his penetrating acuteness, qualities which are apparent from all his writings. Further, Boccaccio is able to assert that he was very desirous of honour and splendour, more perhaps than was in accordance with his exalted virtue. That he was susceptible to honours is certain, but we should hardly otherwise have any evidence that he loved splendour.

Legend and anecdote very early took possession of our poet. They begin with the unborn child, whose future greatness his mother beholds in a wondrous dream, and extend to the departed poet's ghost which appears in a dream to his son, in order to preserve the last cantos of his poem from disappearance. Most of these anecdotes show him as extraordinarily ready and witty in repartee, but we miss throughout any touch of amiability, nor are we able to discover it in his writings. Yet, in spite of the mass of anecdotes, we cannot, as Bartoli says, speak of any real Dante-legend. The Middle Age was already in act to die, and the Renaissance was not the soil in which legend could flourish.

PART IV
DANTE'S SMALLER WORKS

CHAPTER I

LYRIC POEMS

In ancient times those who wrote poems of love wrote not in the vulgar tongue, but rather certain poets in the Latin tongue. I mean among us, although, perchance, the same may have been among others, and although likewise, as among the Greeks, they were not writers of spoken language, but men of letters, treated of these things. And, indeed, it is not a great number of years since poetry began to be made in the vulgar tongue, the writing of rhymes in spoken language corresponding to the writing in mètre of Latin verse by a certain analogy. And I say that it is but a little while, because if we examine the language of *Oco*, and the language of *Si*, we shall not find in those tongues any written thing of an earlier date than the last 150 years. Also, the reason why certain of a very mean sort obtained at the first some famous poets is that, before them, no man had written verses in the language of *Si*, and of these the first was moved to the writing of such verses, by the wish to make himself understood of a certain lady unto whom Latin poetry was difficult. This thing is against such as rime concerning other matters than love, that mode of speech having been first used for the expression of love alone.[1]

As is well known, the literary poetry of Provence (and it is of this alone that Dante is thinking, for popular poetry had existed much longer than 150 years) is older than that of Italy, and was indeed its parent. William I., Count of Poitiers (1071-1127), was either unknown to Dante, or not

[1] *Vita Nuova*, chap. xxv.—Rossetti's Translation.

reckoned by him among literary poets, since his poems, though with an obvious effort after literary style, bear in a high degree the stamp of simplicity, and cannot be fully discriminated from the mere popular poetry. In other respects, Dante's indication of time is pretty accurate, a proof that he was familiar with Provençal poetry when he wrote the *Vita Nuova*. Indeed, it is not open to doubt that, at the beginning of his poetic career, he was under the influence of the Provençals.

The poetry of Provence spread from its home to the neighbouring countries, and thus to Italy. From the last decade of the twelfth century onwards, we find Peire Vidal, Guillem Figueira, and many other troubadours, singing their poems, and seeking love adventures at the small Italian courts. The spread of the troubadours' poetry excited the rivalry of the natives, and thus we find a number of Italian troubadours, among whom Sordello and Albert, Marquis of Malaspina, are the most famous singing in the Provençal tongue. But Provençal poetry never had the power of becoming popular in Italy. With few exceptions, it remained confined to courts and castles, while the old Italian poetry began to resound in streets and market-places. Sicily was its cradle, at least both Dante and Petrarch testify to the fact that the cultivated poetry of Italy came from Sicily. Dante writes in Vulg. Eloq. i. 12:

> The Sicilian vulgar tongue seems to have earned itself a fame before all others, seeing that all the poetry which Italians write is called Sicilian; and, moreover, that we find many of the teachers of that country to have composed important poetry. But this renown of the Trinacrian land, if we regard lightly the mark at which it aims, seems to have remained only as a reproach to the princes of Italy, who, not like heroes, but like common folk, are led by pride.
> If, indeed, those illustrious heroes, Frederick the Emperor,

and Manfred, his well-begotten son, displaying the nobleness and uprightness of their training, so long as their fortune remained, pursued ends worthy of men disdaining the actions of brutes; wherefore being noble in heart, and endowed with graces, they endeavoured to stick close to the majesty of princes so great as they were in such wise that whatever the most eminent of the Latins brought forth in their time came to light first in the court of such great monarchs. And since Sicily was their royal throne, it came to pass that whatever our predecessors produced in the vulgar tongue is called Sicilian, a custom which we retain, and our posterity will not be able to change.

Nevertheless we should err if, as former historians of literature have done, we were to begin the history of Italian poetry with the Sicilian school. Independently of this, dialectic poetry self-evolved up to a certain point was developed in central and especially in northern Italy, though even this could not separate itself entirely from the influence of the Sicilian school. But one may fairly say that the courtly poetry of Italy was developed and brought to perfection in Frederick's and Manfred's court at Palermo. Since this poetry had no soul it could not be long-lived; soulless it was since the writers of it worked to a model instead of expressing their own feelings transfigured in poetry. They did not question their own heart, they only imitated the Provençals. The Love whom they sing is no real tangible woman, she is an empty abstraction who has next to nothing of the actual woman in her. The nature too which they sing is not that which is all around them but that which they find in the books and in the poems which serve them as models. This poetry forms a transition stage, necessary in order to bring about a reform through which Italian poetry begins to travel on the right road.

The reform begins with Guido Guinicelli of Bologna whom Dante celebrates in Purg. xxvi. as his father in the poetic art. His work was continued and completed by the Tuscan poets of the 'sweet new style,' among whom the most important are Lapo Gianni, Dino Frescobaldi, Guido Orlandi, Gianni Alfani, and Dante's friends, Cino of Pistoia and Guido Cavalcanti.

Dante began his poetic career by treading in the footsteps of his predecessors and elder contemporaries. So far as we know, lyric poems were the first work with which he occupied himself. The first sonnet of the *Vita Nuova* is the earliest monument which remains to us of his poetic creation. Any former attempts have been lost, perhaps Dante himself destroyed them. It is obvious that when he sent that first sonnet to the most famous poets of his time he was not a beginner in versification, and this is confirmed by his statement that at that time he had already found out for himself the art of speaking in rhyme, which necessarily assumed some previous practice. It is perhaps to those youthful years that certain poems belong which have come down to us under Dante's name, but are rejected by critics as spurious, chiefly on the ground that both in form and matter they differ entirely from the poet's undoubtedly genuine works and appear unworthy of him. How easy it is to deceive one's self in this matter we may see exemplified in the history of the sonnets exchanged between Dante and Forese Donati. It is no long time since these sonnets were universally rejected as spurious, as being no less bad in their versification than vulgar in their contents (Witte, *Dante-Forschungen*, i. p. 443), and assigned to the fifteenth century; but they are found to be mentioned by the 'Anonimo fiorentino' and elsewhere, so that now not only are they just as generally accepted for genuine productions of our poet, but also important conclusions as to Dante's development are built upon them. Nor is the possibility excluded that there are other productions which at present seem to us too mean and trifling to be ascribed to the great poet, but which in course of time with further inquiry and discovery will be recognised as belonging to him. At any rate it is not yet possible to fix with any certainty the boundary where our poet's genuine lyric works end and those erroneously ascribed to him begin. So far the first sonnet of the *Vita Nuova* must reckon as the earliest among those which we know to be undoubtedly genuine.

When he composed this his knowledge was still small and he was not yet free from the conventional prejudices of his time. When he wrote the *Vita Nuova* he was of opinion that the only subject of which a poet could treat in the vernacular was the love of the sexes. In later years, when he had materially widened the circle of his knowledge by dint of the assiduous studies of which he makes mention in the *Convito*, he had no further hesitation in singing on themes quite other and more exalted than earthly love. This fact gives us a certain criterion by which we can approximately fix the date at which particular poems were composed. At all events we can at least infer from it that all his philosophic poems must have been produced after the conclusion of the *Vita Nuova*. Further, since the poet when he began to write the *Convito* about the year 1308 speaks of fourteen philosophic odes which he had already published and now proposes to provide with a commentary, we may infer that the cycle of poems belonging to the *Convito* came into existence during the last five years of the thirteenth century and the first five of the fourteenth. Perhaps all of them date from after his exile, a view for which we may cite the testimony of Villani. 'While he was living in exile he composed about twenty excellent odes on amatory and philosophic subjects.' This testimony is all the more worthy of consideration that we know of barely twenty odes whose genuineness is undoubted.

A further and certain datum by which we can approximately fix the time at which Dante's poems appeared is the death of Beatrice in June 1290. All the poems in which the poet celebrates her belong naturally to the period before this date, those in which he bewails her loss to that following it. Most of these poems are contained in the *Vita Nuova* and are there explained, but some few others have reached us independently. Of the poems which compose the cycle of the *Vita Nuova* we can say with certainty that they came into existence between 1283 and 1291. In the earliest Dante appears still as an imitator of the troubadours and of the old Italian poets. The very first sonnet deals with a matter at that time so well known and so often handled, and displays in its form so little originality, as to give no indication of the height to which the young poet was to soar, nor is it surprising that Dante of Majano replied so discourteously to it. After this he gradually frees himself from the fetters. Even with the first ode of the *Vita Nuova*—

Donne che avete intelletto d' amore

he began to strike quite a new note. Undisturbed by usage and conventional rules he followed the lead of his enthusiasm and wrote down what his own feeling dictated. It is no blame to him if he began where all other poets of his time began, but that he rose so swift and so high is his imperishable fame.

Another series of lyric poems belongs to the cycle of the *Convito*. Fourteen odes were intended to form the basis of that work and to be explained therein both in their literal and their allegorical sense. But unhappily the work remained incomplete, and out of the fourteen only three were interpreted. Attempts have been made with much spirit and surprising acuteness to detect which were the eleven other odes that the poet intended to discuss, for only ignorant dilettantism can doubt that he had selected and decided upon them all beforehand. The means of detection are found in thoughts which are expressed in certain odes, and which according to Dante's own indications should have been further developed in the *Convito*. Obviously this test is not entirely trustworthy, as is shown by the fact that in any case only three odes can be detected by this method. Another argument seems to us of much more weight. Fourteen odes and one *sestina*, the genuineness of which can hardly be doubted, are found in the earliest and best manuscripts as a connected whole. Hence it is easy to suppose that these are just the fourteen odes which Dante himself regarded as a completed cycle and intended to collect in one work provided with a complete commentary. So far as we know, nothing worth consideration has been alleged against this very significant test, while the first must be allowed to have many deficiencies.

The odes which Dante intended in the *Convito* to provide with a complete commentary seem to have been the following:

1. Voi che intendendo il terzo ciel movete.
2. Amor che nella mente mi ragiona.
3. Le dolci rime d' amor, ch' io solia.

(Of these three the commentaries exist in the *Convito*; and Dante refers to them in other works.)

4. Io sento sì d' Amor la gran possanza.

(The poet's younger contemporary, the author of the so-called *Ottimo Comento*, testifies to the genuineness of this.)

5. E' m' incresce di me sì malamente.
6. Così nel mio parlar voglio esser aspro.
7. Amor, tu vedi ben che questa donna. (Vulg. El. ii. 13.)
8. Io son venuto al punto della rota.
9. Amor, dacchè convien pur ch' io mi doglia.
10. La dispietata mente che pur mira.
11. Amor che muovi tua virtù dal cielo. (Vulg. El. ii. 5, 11.)
12. Poscia che Amor del tutto m' ha lasciato. (Vulg. El. ii. 12.)
13. Tre donne intorno al cor mi son venute. (Quoted by Leonardo Bruni.)
14. Doglia mi reca nello core ardire. (Vulg. El. ii. 2.)

This does not exhaust the list of lyric poems written by Dante or ascribed to him. For an account of those contained in the older collections Witte's introduction to his excellent commentary may be consulted. The translation due to him and Kannegiesser contains besides the penitential psalms and the eclogues, of which more hereafter, twenty-six odes, twelve ballads, eighty sonnets, and three epigrams. It is obvious that all these cannot be accepted as the genuine offspring of Dante's muse. Fraticelli's useful and widely-known collection gives as undoubtedly true, twenty odes, three sestines, ten ballads, forty-four sonnets, and one stanza; as doubtful, one ode, two ballads, and five sonnets; as decidedly spurious, fourteen odes, three madrigals, two ballads, and thirty-five sonnets. Giuliani, Torri, Serafini, and others hold each his own views; in any case a fair number of poems are undoubted. Whether we shall ever succeed in settling exactly how many of Dante's lyric pieces have come down to us the future only can show.

That besides the poems which belong to the cycles of the

Vita Nuova and the *Convito*, Dante wrote others which have come down to us, it is hardly necessary to observe. Quite recently it has been thought that a new group had been discovered; much paper and ink has been expended over this, not to mention a good deal of unnecessary excitement. In certain odes of undoubted genuineness the term *pietra* occurs both in and out of rhyme with such striking frequency that we cannot fail to recognise an intention on the poet's part. It has been supposed accordingly that these form a special group, and the designation of *Canzoni pietrose* has been devised for them. They are the following four:

'Così nel mio parlar voglio esser aspro.'
'Amor, tu vedi ben che questa donna.'
'Io son venuto al punto della rota.'
'Al poco giorno dal gran cerchio d' ombra.'

In the frequently-repeated term *pietra* there is thought to lie, as in the *Selvaggia* of Cino da Pistoia and in the *Lauro* of Petrarch, a plain allusion to the name of one of the many objects of our poet's fickle affections. As to who she was, opinions, as might be expected, differ. At one time it is said to be the lady Pietra Scrovigni of Padua, at another time Gentucca of Lucca or the notorious goitered lady of the Casentino, or the pitiful beauty of the *Vita Nuova*. It has even been discovered that the lady in question was no other than Pietra, wife of Donato Brunacci, Dante's sister-in-law. It would be waste of time and trouble to concern ourselves any more with fancies of this kind. As we have seen, the first three of these four odes belong to the cycle of the *Convito*, and were to have been included and expanded therein, and therewith all the airy hypothesis so loudly trumpeted of the particular group of the *canzoni pietrose* falls to pieces.

Dante's lyric poems had already earned him great renown before he had even begun his *magnum opus*, nay, as appears from H. i. 87, even before his exile. Nor can we doubt that the fair style which won him honour is identical with the sweet new style of Purg. xxiv. 57. His very first sonnet, moving though it does on traditional lines, gave him an advantageous reputation as a poet, and earned him the friendship of Guido Cavalcanti. As he himself relates in *Vita Nuova* iii., many replied to this sonnet in very various senses. We possess only the replies by Guido Cavalcanti, Cino of Pistoia, and Dante of Majano, but that many others were sent appears from Dante's own statement, for he would not have spoken of many had they been but three. Also the fact that he undertook to write an exceedingly full commentary upon a selection from his odes, and quotes three of them with obvious satisfaction in his great poem, shows how widely known and how popular they must have been in the days before his exile. The oldest opinion of them which has reached us is that of Villani, who speaks of the odes of Dante, which were known to him, as most excellent. Boccaccio finds Dante's odes and sonnets marvellously beautiful, Leonardo Bruni praises the odes, but seems to have had no great taste for the sonnets. Salvini on the other hand held that the sonnet

> Tanto gentile e tanto onesta pare

was the best out of the million of sonnets which threatened to swamp the Italian Parnassus. Only the pedantic Salviati felt himself bound to blame Dante's lyric poems, the later even more than the earlier. At the present day all connoisseurs are agreed that if Dante had written nothing but the lyric poems, he would be in the first rank of Italian poets.

CHAPTER II

THE *VITA NUOVA*

NOT long after the death of Beatrice, Dante formed the resolution to erect a literary monument to her. With this object he collected the greater number of the poems which he had composed during her life and since her death, sifted them, arranged them chronologically, and fitted them out with an historical commentary, and with elaborate divisions after the scholastic method of that day. From this work arose the *Vita Nuova*, so far as we know the earliest, and, next to the *Commedia*, the most attractive and interesting of our poet's writings; forming an indispensable introduction to his great epic and a key to its interpretation.

In the very first lines of the little book the poet indicates by the Latin words *Incipit Vita Nova*, the title by which he wished his work to be known, and he repeats it in its Italian form both in the *Convito* (i. 1), and in his great Epic (Purg. xxx. 115). By this name he would imply that the love for Beatrice, which gave to his whole being a definite direction towards higher things, was to him the beginning of a new existence, so that *Vita Nova* may be taken as equivalent to παλιγγενεσία, or 'new birth.' Indeed, he testifies expressly that Beatrice had been to him a destroyer of all vices and the queen of virtues, and that for her sake he had turned his back on the common herd. Every page indeed of the work gives evidence of the ennobling influence under which the young poet had passed after his first meeting with the love of his youth. If certain Dante students on the other hand have supposed that *Vita Nova* means simply 'young life,' relying upon the fact that in old Italian writers *nuovo* and *novello* are found in the meaning of 'young' or 'youthful,' they must overlook the fact that Dante did not use the Italian expression *nuova* but the Latin *nova*, which no Latin writer ever used in the sense of 'young.'[1] Further, it also escapes their notice that the life of youth does not begin at the end of the ninth year of life, the point at which the *Vita Nuova* starts, and that the narrative of the book reaches at most to a year or two after the poet's twenty-fifth year, at which, according to his view (Conv. iv. 24), the period of adolescence ends.

The genuineness of the little book is beyond all doubt. The poet has recognised it as his, and the testimony of the earliest biographers and commentators—Villani, for instance, and Boccaccio—is to the same purpose; the latter says that the book is even, for unlearned people, very beautiful and attractive.

The contents of the work have been detailed in the first two chapters of the last section, where it was observed that after the fashion of Boëthius's *Consolation of Philosophy*, from which the idea of it must have been intentionally taken, it consists of a selection of poems (twenty-five sonnets, one ballad, four odes, and the first strophe of an unfinished one) with a prose text introducing and explaining them. The poems were composed at considerable intervals;

---

[1] This argument will hardly apply to the use of the Italian word in Purg. xxx. 115.

the first sonnet, as Dante expressly tells us, in his eighteenth year, that is in 1283, the last not before 1291 or 1292. The question therefore as to the date at which this first of our poet's writings was composed applies only to the prose text. This cannot have been written before the death of Beatrice in June 1290; we can, however, date it somewhat more precisely. Chapter xxxv. makes mention of the first anniversary of her death, and at that time, namely June 1291, his glorified youthful love held still exclusive possession of his heart. It was not till some time later, at the very earliest in the autumn of 1291, that he for the first time beheld the compassionate lady at a window. The following chapters embrace a longer period, in any case, of several months, which brings us far into the year 1292. We say this in spite of the fact that only 'some days' are spoken of in chapter xl., for the poet nowhere says that the entire episode of the 'noble lady' lasted only some days, but that this period measured his longing for her. But again, the events depicted in chapters xl., xliii. must be measured by months, so that the book cannot well have been finished before 1293, and the view of Fauriel, Fraticelli, and others, that it was written in 1291, is shown to be erroneous. Nor can the opinion of Bianchi, Giuliani, etc., that it came into existence in 1292, be correct. Dante says, no doubt, that he wrote the *Vita Nuova* at the beginning of his period of youth which, as we have seen, according to his theory, begins with the twenty-fifth year, with which Boccaccio's statement agrees. But the expression 'at the beginning of my youthful age,' cannot be taken so literally as Boccaccio has done. A man advanced in years, who considers that the age of youth begins with the twenty-sixth year of life, may very well say that he did anything at the beginning of his youthful age, when he did it at the age of twenty-seven or twenty-eight.[1] On the other hand, Dante's own words exclude as erroneous the opinion of those who think that the *Vita Nuova*, as it has reached us, was not completed before 1300.

In support of this latter view they appeal to chapter xli., which has been held to contain an allusion to the year of jubilee. He relates how it came to pass that pilgrims were going through a street in the middle of the city in which that gracious lady was born, lived, and died in order to see that holy countenance which Christ left to us as a portrait of His sacred features. This, it is said, refers to the exhibition of the Sudarium at St. Peter's on the feast of St. Veronica. But the Sudarium was displayed to the faithful not only in the jubilee year, but three times every year, in the middle of January, in Holy Week, and on the day of the Assumption. We may indeed safely suppose that if Dante had meant to speak of the jubilee year, he would have expressed himself quite differently, and not have spoken merely of many people. Many people went every year to see the Veronica, but in the year 1300, not merely many people, but as Villani says, a great portion of all the Christians then living, both men and women, from distant and various lands, undertook the pilgrimage. Moreover, in 1300, the sight of the image was only a secondary object, the main object was to obtain the plenary indulgence which Boniface VIII. had announced for the first time since the establishment of the Christian Church by his bull of April 22nd, 1300. It cannot be then of the jubilee year that Dante speaks but of the much smaller

[1] The author appears here to have fallen into confusion between *adolescenzia* and *gioventute*. In Dante's view, the first of these ends and the latter begins at twenty-five, and his words (Conv. i. 1), with regard to the *Vita Nuova* are, 'in quella dinanzi all' entrata di mia gioventute parlai.'

pilgrimages that occurred every year, and those who wish to understand the passage of that year must, to be consistent, place the composition of the *Vita Nuova* after 1300; for the expression 'at that time' could not well be used of the year actually current, but must denote a year which had already gone by. But after 1300 Dante certainly had other matters in hand than the writing of the *Vita Nuova*.

In this work visions play an important part. From the devoured heart at the beginning of the narrative to the 'wondrous vision' at the conclusion, the subject of which is not stated, everything moves, as one may say, in the sphere of visions and dreams. It were superfluous to inquire whether Dante really had all these. A sickly nature might have done so, but Dante's nature was thoroughly sober, his mind sound to the core. He assuredly never had a vision in his life, but following the example of Boëthius, has chosen this form in which to clothe his thoughts. It is a form which appears strange to us moderns, but was familiar to mediaeval times. The *Vita Nuova* is thus a work of art in which fact and fiction are so cunningly interwoven that it is no longer possible for us with anything like a secure hand to separate the threads and trace the boundary between truth and invention. On a foundation of his inward experiences Dante has raised a building—ideal, poetic, partly allegoric. The kernel of the narrative is historic, the shell is the free creation of the poetic spirit.

We are thus far from agreeing with those who hold that the *Vita Nuova* is from a historical point of view, if not equally valueless, at least totally useless for both the inner and the outer side of the poet's history. Rather it is like the *Divina Commedia*, of incalculable value for our knowledge of the poet. Or are we to say that Dante's great epic is historically worthless, because from beginning to end it is cast into the form of a vision? If the *Vita Nuova* were, as Bartoli thinks, 'a book from which nothing can be gained towards the history of Dante's life,' would not the *Commedia* be so in a still higher degree? We thus regard it as superfluous to test critically what the founder of the idealistic system, whom we have quoted, and his disciples, have written on the subject. We are convinced that we have to deal there with errors which, no doubt, are to-day widely spread, but will disappear as quickly as did the dreams of Rossetti and his few adherents.

No doubt the *Vita Nuova* no less than the *Commedia* offers difficulties which are never likely to be entirely solved. For instance, the very first sonnet is said to have been written in Dante's eighteenth year, that is in 1283. Among the sonnets written in reply to it is one by Cino Sinibaldi of Pistoia. The genuineness of the reply can hardly be doubted, but in 1283 Cino was only thirteen. But in those days a poet would not have sent a sonnet about by telegraph or even by post, so that some time may have elapsed before the other poets of the time became acquainted with the sonnet which Dante wrote at the age of eighteen. Nor, again, would they have been in any very great hurry to honour with a reply a person who was totally unknown to them. The answers would probably have dropped in after longer or shorter intervals, Cino's perhaps not for some years.

This example may remind one that one may often make difficulties and riddles at will if we insist on importing modern relations into the Middle Age. Lessing, for example, addressed two epigrams to the wise Solomon, but the wise Solomon had been some thousands of years in the grave, and yet Lessing's epigrams are undoubtedly genuine. Is this an insoluble riddle?

On the other hand, there is a difficulty in the *Vita Nuova* which there is no need to import into it. We mean the presentiments of death which begin to crop up from the very commencement. In regard to this we need not consider the prose portion. This was not written till after Beatrice's death, and the writer, who was not composing precise history, might very well transfer his later feelings to an earlier date. But the presentiments appear also in the poems which were certainly contemporaneous with the events which form their motives. Did Dante really foresee the death of his Beatrice? If so, she must have been a sickly being, which is inconsistent with Dante's whole portraiture of her. (Incidentally we may remark that all the allegorists and idealists have been for very good reasons careful to avoid raising this question.) . Nay, the very way in which he relates her death gives us reason to suppose that she died quite suddenly and unexpectedly. How then are we to explain the early presentiments? No doubt by assuming that the poems included in the *Vita Nuova* were retouched to correspond with the purpose of the book when Dante was putting it together. There would be nothing strange in this, the poems may well have been generally known before 1294; but after their final form was fixed the earlier editions would naturally have disappeared. No one can believe that the ode of chapter xix., as it now appears, was composed any long time before 1290.

Dante's *Vita Nuova* is not, therefore, as people have deemed it their duty to call it, a frank history of his youthful love, but rather a poetical work of art. To produce such a work was the poet's chief, if not his only, aim; he wished to become better known as a poet. It is the work of an extraordinarily talented youth, who feels that he is called to play a prominent part on the poetic stage. It forms, no doubt, with the *Convito* and the *Commedia* a magnificent trilogy, an organic whole. But the trilogy grew up unconsciously. When Dante completed the *Vita Nuova* he had surely no notion of writing the *Convito*. Of the *Commedia* he doubtless had an idea, but the plan was not yet settled.

He had, so to say, written his work at one draft, without dividing it further than the mingling of prose and verse naturally involved. It was not till our century that the division into paragraphs was introduced, primarily for the greater convenience of quotation. As a whole it falls obviously into two parts after the fashion of Petrarch's poems, before and after the death of Beatrice; all other subdivisions are more or less arbitrary, as appears not only from the fact that every student subdivides it differently, but from the necessity in which the greatest of students, Karl Witte, found himself of subdividing it variously at various times. All these dismemberments seem to us of use only for the purposes of a commentary.

Boccaccio is able to inform us that, in his later years, Dante was much ashamed of having written this book, and Benvenuto copies him faithfully. The source of this statement may be Dante's own words in *Convito*, 1-2: 'I fear the discredit of having pursued so great a passion as he who reads the aforesaid odes may conceive to have had the mastery of me.' But Dante is here speaking only of his love poems; of the *Vita Nuova* he says, on the other hand, in the preceding chapter, 'If, in the present work, which is called *The Banquet*, and which I wish to be so, matters are treated in a more manly fashion than in the *New Life*, I do not intend thereby to derogate in any way from that, but rather to aid that, by means of this.' A man who can so write of his own work is not ashamed of it, and if there is really, in Purg. xxx. 115, an allusion to the title of Dante's youthful work, we have a proof that Dante was in no way ashamed of it. This, however, is unnecessary, the *Vita Nuova* has nothing in common with the *Decameron*, but Boccaccio is not the last who, in order to paint a picture of Dante, has placed himself before a mirror.

CHAPTER III

THE *CONVITO*

THE 'sweet new style' of his poems had earned for the poet among his fellow-citizens, even before the year 1300, the fame of eminent talents. When, at the end of 1301, he had to share the fortune of the defeated Whites, being in addition accused with official solemnity of a commonplace offence, and condemned first to banishment and then to death, many voices in Florence must have been raised in his favour in spite of all party tumults and passions. The thoughts to which Boccaccio afterwards gave so eloquent expression undoubtedly were already there in the germ. Dante might have belonged to the Whites, and played no unimportant part on their side, but he was none the less a poet of importance, who for the sake alike of his poetic achievements, his talents, and his learning, deserved to be treated with quite different consideration from an ordinary partisan. He at least was a son whom Florence should not have thrust from her lap, for his expulsion will never be to the honour of the republic, but to her everlasting shame. If thoughts like these were openly expressed, the obvious course for the poet's enemies would be to belittle his poetic fame and to throw discredit upon his name of poet. He had no doubt written many verses which, taken in a formal and word-for-word sense, were distinctly to his advantage. But if their contents were more closely scrutinised, his character must appear in a suspicious light. He showed himself there in his unbounded sensuality as a fool in love, who, moreover, knew nothing of true and deep love, since, in his fickle fashion, he paid his court one day to one maiden and the next to another. That such reproaches were made against Dante cannot be doubted; they were often enough repeated after his death in every sort of tone by biographers and commentators on the strength of his own verses. One really cannot say whether it is more wearisome or amusing to read the list of the many fair ladies whom, if we are to believe certain old biographers and commentators, Dante wooed with incredible fickleness. That this foolish accusation had already been raised at the beginning of the fourteenth century, if not earlier, appears with certainty from the words with which Dante himself states in *Convito* i. 2 the occasion and aim of that work.

I am moved by fear of disgrace and I am moved by the desire of giving information which no other can truly give. I fear the discredit of having pursued so great a passion as he who reads the aforesaid odes may conceive to have had the mastery of me; a disgrace which, by this present speaking of myself, is entirely brought to an end. For this shows that not passion but virtue was the cause which moved me. I intend also to show the true meaning of those odes which no one can see if I do not relate it, since it is hidden under the figure of an allegory, and this will not only cause a good delight to hear, but will be a subtle method of teaching both how to speak in this way and to understand what others have written of this kind.

If, then, the poet expressly declares that he feared shame, an attempt must already have been made to put this shame upon him, and he himself indicates the source from which people drew for that purpose. It was not from recollections of his former life and conduct, not the gossip of Florence, but simply and solely his love poems.

Who knows? perhaps the thought of composing a work of the kind had been suggested to him by friends in Florence. At an early point of it he expresses the wish of his heart, that he could return to his own city. Is it possible that even by that time attempts had been made on the part of his friends to get the sentence of banishment revoked? In that case it would be easy to suppose that his enemies, who might be ashamed to revive the old charges of corruption and jobbery, would make use of his poems to blacken his character by displaying him as a man of sensual and fickle character, and if anything to this effect came to his ears what would be more natural than that he should put a stop to it once for all by a work in the nature of an Apologia?

For the *Convito* is indeed of the nature of an Apologia. From many passages of it we may see how near it was to his heart to clear himself from the suggested reproaches. Take, for instance, the solemn, but for that very reason significant, assurance that philosophy had been the object of his second love, or again the fact that he cannot omit to return later on to the apologetic aim of the work which he had already brought sharply forward in the introduction. He writes (iii. 1): 'I thought that I should haply be reprehended by many that came after me for fickleness of mind when they heard that I had changed from my first love. Wherefore, to take away this reproach there was no better means than to say who that lady was that had changed me, seeing that through her manifest excellence a judgment of her virtue might be formed, and that by the study of her boundless virtue it might be deemed that all stability of mind was, compared with her, changeable, and that therefore they should not judge me fickle and unstable.'

Besides the apologetic aim, however, he had another in view, and equally early in the work he expounds this with emphasis (i. 1).

Oh blessed are those few who sit at that table where the bread of the angels is eaten, and wretched they who share their food with the beasts! But whereas every man is by nature friendly to every man, and every man grieves for the lack of him whom he loves, they who sit at so exalted a table are not without pity towards those whom they see going about eating grass and acorns after the fashion of the feeding of beasts. And seeing that pity is the mother of kindness, those who know always hold forth freely of their riches to those who are truly poor, and are, as it were, a living fount, with the water of which the natural thirst above named is refreshed. And therefore I, who do not sit at the blessed table, but who, having fled from the pastures of the common herd, gather up at the feet of those who do sit there somewhat of that which falls from them, and know the wretched life of those whom I have left behind me, through the sweetness which I perceive in what I gather up little by little, and being moved to pity, while not forgetting myself, have reserved somewhat for the wretched ones which long ago I displayed before their eyes, and therein have made them more desirous of it. Wherefore, wishing now to cater for them, I intend to make a general banquet of that which I have shown them, and of such bread as is fitting for a repast of that fashion, without which it would not be possible for them to eat at this banquet. . . . The food of this banquet will be arranged in fourteen manners, that is, fourteen odes, whose matter is love no less than virtue; the which without the present bread used to have a shadow of certain obscurity, so that to many their beauty was more attractive than their goodness; but this bread, namely, the present exposition, will be the light which shall make every tint of their meaning apparent.

According to this Dante had a twofold inducement to undertake the work, and pursued a twofold aim in it. The inducement was on the one hand sympathy with his fellow-men, and on the other the danger of the disgrace to which he believed himself exposed. The corresponding aim is on the one hand to teach the unlearned, on the other to justify himself. But he would know little of the human heart who would deny that the apologetic is the main aim, the didactic only subsidiary. Even where he is instructing, Dante has an apologetic aim fully in view. He would offer a proof that in the years of his youth he had done something else than rave about maidens and compose love songs to them, that he had studied other things than the poetry of troubadours and the old Italian bards. Thence comes all that monstrous expenditure of space upon philosophy, astronomy, physics, and politics, which is undoubtedly the chief reason why the book has never been and never can be nearly so popular as the *Vita Nuova* and the *Commedia*. Dante had a conscious purpose in displaying himself in the doctor's robes in order that people might learn to have a better knowledge and appreciation of him than they had been able to form on the strength of his early poems.

But is this self-justification absolutely truthful and trustworthy? Some things awake suspicion, especially the contradictions to the simple narrative of the *Vita Nuova*, which no art can set aside. Is it conceivable that the base desire of *Vita Nuova* xl.•can have changed all at once into the new thought which was full of virtue, like the virtue of Heaven, of Conv. ii. 2; or that the thoroughly human, natural, pitiful lady of the earlier work should in a surprising fashion become Philosophy? It cannot be sufficiently proclaimed that Dante nowhere says expressly that this lady was no real human being but a pure abstraction. He protests, no doubt, that she was philosophy, but he protests it only in the allegorical portion of his explanation, while in the literal explanation he speaks constantly of 'a lady.' Only with regard to the actual and original nature of the object of his second love he leaves the readers of the *Convito* so far in doubt that even at the present day they are still disagreeing and disputing about it. Even if he has not in the *Convito* expressly excluded the corporeal reality of the pitiful lady, his references to her are still of such a kind that if we did not possess the *Vita Nuova* it would perhaps not have occurred to any one to seek behind the object of his homage something more real and tangible than the personification of philosophy. But behind Dante as he depicts himself in the *Convito*, behind the youth and the man whose passion is for science and science only, wholly given up to his studies, and with no heart, or ear, or eye, or thought but for his books, who would look for the author of the sonnets exchanged with Forese Donati or the penitent of the vision which concludes the *Purgatory?* We may say without hesitation that in the *Convito* Dante speaks with regard to himself the plain truth but not the whole truth. He passes in silence over more than one thing which lay behind him, and the fact that this was done intentionally leaves no room to doubt that he was interested in, so far as was possible, covering with oblivion certain incidents of his life. Dante Alighieri in real life was certainly not the student devoted to books that he here depicts himself. He has here exhibited only one side of his nature; when he wrote the *Convito* he was still astray in the dark wood. In his great epic he has depicted himself as a whole very differently, indeed in a somewhat more human guise.

The title of the work is obviously borrowed from Plato's *Symposium*. Whether in Italian it should be called *Convito* or *Convivio* is in truth a somewhat otiose question, although much has been written on the point. *Convito* is modern,[1] *Convivio*, the old Italian spelling, in any case that employed by Dante.[2]

In form the work consists, apart from the introduction which reckons as the first treatise, of a commentary on three of the poet's odes. That he cared less for explaining these odes than for writing his own Apologia, and giving evidence of his exhaustive learning, is obvious; and the commentary is accordingly a kind of encyclopaedia of all the knowledge of the time, and would be still more so if it had not remained incomplete. The commentary on each ode has two divisions, the literal explanation and the allegorical, and the second of these is for the author the important matter; it is here that he succeeds in displaying his whole learning. Valuable as it is for the student, and not for the Dante student only, from the literary point of view it is the reverse of entertaining, mainly from the very fact that it is written in the form of a commentary and in such a way that one is often apt to forget in the commentary the text of the odes commented on. One word of the ode gives an excuse for treating repeatedly and in various connections every conceivable subject. Nature and human life, existence in all its manifold forms, questions of philology, metaphysics, politics, theology, astronomy, heaven and earth, God and man, body and soul, virtue and vice, time and eternity, come under discussion and are often discussed in a thorough manner. The single thread that holds together this farfetched and multiplex matter in one organic whole is found in the odes to which it is a commentary, or rather in the individual sentences and words of the odes. Yet Dante

---

[1] It is the form used in the text of the first edition, though the title was *Convivio*.
[2] See Witte, *Dante-Forschungen*, ii. 574.

nowhere appears so marvellous as in the fact that the work is not in the remotest degree a piece of mosaic. We saw, when speaking of the lyric poems, that the sequence of the fourteen odes which were to be commented on was distinctly settled beforehand, whence it follows that the work was set out upon a distinct and carefully elaborated plan. But no doubt in proportion as Dante worked the development of the plan acquired ever larger dimensions, so that if it had not remained incomplete the *Convito* would have been a work in a very fair number of volumes. As we have it it consists of four treatises, the first comprising thirteen chapters, the second sixteen, the third fifteen, the fourth thirty, but it must not be supposed that the third is any shorter than the second. The work grew like an avalanche, as appears from the fact that in Fraticelli's edition with notes the first treatise occupies forty-nine pages, the second sixty-four, the third seventy-two, the fourth one hundred and thirty-six. We can conceive what the other eleven would have been if their contents had increased in this proportion.

For a work laid out on these broad lines Dante, with accurate tact, selected the Italian language. For this reason it was formerly supposed that the *Convito* was the first example of scientific Italian prose. This opinion, however, can be no longer maintained. Prose works in Italian, and among them works purporting at least to be scientific, are not wanting even in times before Dante. Many such have been already brought to light, others will doubtless in course of time become known. It is, however, true that the *Convito* indicates a step forward in Italian prose hardly less than that which Italian poetry makes in Dante's lyric poems, while in this respect also it soars high above everything then in existence.

To give a short summary of the contents of a work like the *Convito* is in truth an impossibility. We have already pointed out that an endless series of questions on the most diverse subjects are discussed in the most varied confusion. The most important are the scattered fragments which treat of Dante's own experiences; but in estimating these, as has been remarked, due care must be exercised. We will therefore content ourselves here with calling attention to some part of the introductory treatise. The line of thought, put as shortly as possible, is the following :—

The thirst for knowledge is innate in all men, since knowledge is the last and highest perfection of the soul; few, however, alas! attain to this perfection, whether on account of bodily infirmity or from the tyranny of baser passions, or from the cares and associations of their outward life. Very few, therefore, are elected to the blessed position of feasting on the bread of knowledge. These look down with pity upon the many who are living like the brutes. So, too, do I, although I do not sit at the table of the blessed but only gather up crumbs. One must impart to the best of one's ability; and I, having imparted somewhat already, have aroused in many the thirst which in this work I shall endeavour to quench, a duty which is all the more pointed out to me by the fact that my poems have not been rightly understood. In doing this I cannot avoid speaking of myself and my own circumstances, for I must wash myself clean from a grievous charge which the reader of my poems may easily bring against me, namely, that I am a person of easy and frivolous disposition. I will put a stop to that by my commentary on fourteen of my odes. The commentary will, no doubt, appear now and again hard to understand. I have intentionally arranged it so. Since my exile from Florence I have appeared to very many a person of less consequence than they had previously imagined me. I deem it expedient, therefore, in the present work to pay attention to a more exalted and dignified style, in order that the work may acquire greater importance. Then why not write in Latin? For three reasons: First, because the odes on which I am about to comment are in Italian, and a Latin commentary would not be appropriate; Secondly, because I wish to be understood of many, and only scholars understand Latin; Thirdly, because I love my mother tongue and have full confidence in its future. . . .

The chapters, indeed, which treat of the Italian language, when we consider the date at which they were written, are of great interest and deserve to be read and pondered even at the present day.

Dante's contemporary, and sometime neighbour, Villani, writes: 'He began a commentary on fourteen of the aforesaid odes in the vulgar tongue which, by reason of his death, was not completed save only in respect of three odes; which, from what we see, would have turned out a noble, beautiful, acute, and comprehensive work, seeing that it presents itself to us adorned with lofty language and with noble discourses, philosophical and astronomical.' Boccaccio says, 'He composed also a commentary in prose and in the speech of the Florentine people upon three of his odes; when he began it he had the intention of commenting on them all, but later, whether it was that time failed him or that he changed his purpose, his exposition was carried no further. This very beautiful and useful work was called by him *The Banquet!*' Leonardo Bruni does not mention this work, while Manetti thoughtlessly ascribes it to Dante's youth, a view which, with some modifications, has found adherents in our century.

In any inquiry as to the date of composition of the

Convito, we must distinguish between the time when the poems came into existence and that at which the prose commentary was written. The former are naturally of older date and no doubt were written at various times, the first perhaps, as has been conjectured, in 1295, while we may gather with certainty from Purg. ii. 112 and P. viii. 37, that the second and third odes existed before 1300.

As to the date at which the work proper was composed—the introduction, that is, and the commentaries to the three odes, we may extract from it the following data. (1) In i. 1, Dante says he is writing after his youth has gone by. Now, according to his theory the age of youth lasts from the twenty-fifth to the forty-fifth year, which brings us in his case to the middle of 1310. (2) In i. 3, he uses the following words about his life in exile: 'From the time when the citizens of Florence, that fairest and most renowned daughter of Rome, thought fit to thrust me from her kind bosom, I have wandered as a pilgrim and as a beggar through almost all the regions over which this tongue extends, and against my will I have displayed the wounds inflicted by fortune,' words which cannot have been written till some years after 1302. (3) In iv. 14, he refers to Gherardo da Cammino as deceased, saying that his memory as a noble man would last for ever. Now Gherardo died March 26, 1307. (4) When he wrote the *Convito* he had not yet heard of Henry VII.'s journey to Rome, which was decided upon in September 1309. He says (iv. 3), 'Frederick of Swabia, the last Emperor of the Romans, I say the last with respect to the present time, albeit that Rudolf, Adolf, and Albert have since that been elected.' He would never have written thus had he known of the decision taken in September 1309 at Spires, while previous to this, even though Henry had been elected, he might have seen no occasion to mention him either for praise or blame. (5) The *Convito* presupposes that Charles II. of Naples, who died May 5, 1309, was still living, since he addresses him personally in iv. 6. Even with the means of communication of those times it could not have been many months before Dante got the news of the king's death; the passage in question can therefore have been written at latest in the summer of 1309.

From these dates we may infer with certainty that the book was written between 1307 and 1309. We may remark, however, that in their daily life men do not always follow out with exact precision the theories which they have made their own. Even if Dante was writing in his forty-fourth year he might very well say that his youth was already passed. After having fixed the date by such a simple method, it seems superfluous to go farther into the differing views of Fraticelli and others. Those who are interested in the matter may consult their writings.

As to the place in which Dante wrote the work we know nothing positively. Perhaps, as has been conjectured, he was with the Malaspina family in Lunigiana, perhaps with Count Guido Salvatico in the upper valley of the Arno, perhaps in Paris. A very learned treatise might be written in support of this last view, but after all said and done an honest inquirer would have to admit that we are thrown back on conjecture and have no certain knowledge on the subject.

Just as little do we know of the poet's reasons for leaving his work unfinished. As a pure hypothesis we would offer the following suggestion. Dante was engaged upon the *Convito* when he received the news of Henry's decision to go to Rome; he thought then that in the altered circumstances he would have no further need of an Apologia and dropped the work all the more readily that political affairs claimed his whole attention, and at such a time he might naturally have no great disposition to occupy himself with a learned work. He was personally deeply interested in the success of the imperial arms, for if Florence fell into the Emperor's hands Dante could have returned triumphantly into his own city, and might again have found himself at the head of the government. As we shall see presently, it is extremely probable that at this very time he was occupied in working at his book on the relations of Church and State, so that one may easily conceive him to have laid the *Convito* on one side. But after Henry's failure he would have had no object in taking any further trouble about his Apologia. Henceforth the gates of Florence were for ever shut upon him, and his enemies, as the sentence of November 1315 shows, had far wider charges to bring against him than sensual passion and fickleness in love. Moreover, an important change had come to pass within himself, instead of writing any more in his own defence he now began to write the serious accusations of himself which are contained in the *Divina Commedia*.

CHAPTER IV

DE VULGARI ELOQUENTIÂ

It was a new and daring undertaking on Dante's part to set about writing a work upon a language which as a written language was still so young, and which was treated by the learned world of the day with some contempt, as having neither dignity nor capacity sufficient to be employed in serious scientific work. No doubt it had been spoken for centuries even at a time when Latin was the ruling language. In ancient Rome we may be quite sure that the lower classes did not speak the language of Cicero, even though they may have been still farther from—as some people have supposed—speaking Italian. The popular language of Italy in the early Middle Ages indicates a very gradual and imperceptibly effected transition from Latin to Italian. From the fourth to the ninth century of the Christian era we know very little of this popular language, and if we were to know more of it philology would be in no small perplexity how to name it. Latin it was no longer, but it was not yet Italian. Latin was in a state of incipient dissolution, Italian was slowly and imperceptibly coming to the birth. Which was to be the speech of the country in the future it would have been hard to predict even in the twelfth century. The new tongue had indeed begun to take rank as a written language at that date, but not as the language of science. In Dante's time and even later it was universally considered by men of learning and cultivation in Italy that science and literature could employ only the language of ancient Rome. According to an old and by no means to be despised tradition Dante himself hesitated in the first instance as to which language he should employ in his great epic. His very greatness is shown in the fact that he foresaw the future, and with a sure tact departed from the deeply-rooted prejudices of the learned clique and composed his *chef-d'œuvre* in the language of the people. Who would at the present day write a 'Divina Comoedia' in Latin? who now reads Petrarch's *Africa*, a work of which the author's estimate was in inverse ratio to that of posterity?

In the *Convito* Dante found himself obliged to justify himself at the outset with no less energy than thoroughness by having written not in Latin but in Italian. When composing the chapter in question, he doubtless for the first time conceived the idea of devoting a special work to the subject. That the idea quickly developed we may gather from his own words, Conv. i. 5 :

The common speech is modelled according to the fancy of the moment, and undergoes changes; whence we see in the cities of Italy, if we will look carefully fifty years back, that many words have grown obsolete, and have come to birth, and have varied, so that if a short time produces such changes, a longer time produces many more. So I say that if those who departed from this life a thousand years ago were to return to their cities, they would think that these were occupied by a strange people through the difference of the language from what they spoke. Concerning this I shall speak more fully elsewhere in a book which, God willing, I intend to compose upon the Vulgar Tongue.

From these words, as would appear, we may infer with certainty that when he was writing them in 1308 or 1309 the work in question was already planned but not yet carried into execution. Yet some think that the book is older than the *Convito* in which it is announced as one to be composed hereafter. Witte, for example, says that when a man has calculated a work at five books and has finished less than two he can but say he purposes, if God permits, to produce such a work. Yet we in modern times are wont in such cases to express ourselves differently; we speak of books that have been begun and have made some progress as 'to be published shortly.' Witte himself has more than once spoken thus, though, alas! the promised works have never appeared. The same remark applies to Fraticelli, who repeats Witte's view. D'Ovidio thinks that the passage quoted simply implies that Dante was withholding the part of his work which he had already finished but had not yet abandoned the intention of completing and publishing it. On the same principle the expression 'Dio concedente' might imply that the poet was getting a little disgusted with the work. But this exegesis is shattered beyond recovery by a very significant contradiction between the two works. We read in *Convito* i. 5, 'That language is the more beautiful in which the words correspond most precisely to their meaning, and this they do more in Latin than in the vulgar tongue, because the vulgar tongue at its best follows custom while Latin follows rule. We must therefore admit that Latin has more beauty, more power, and more nobleness.' Compare with this Vulg. El. i. 1: 'The vulgar tongue we call that to which infants are accustomed by those about them when they first begin to distinguish words, or, to put it more briefly, that which we acquire without rules by imitating our nurses. Besides this we have a second language . . . of these two the vulgar tongue is the more noble both because it is that first used

x

by mankind, and then because the whole world possesses it, albeit it is split up into various terms and words, and lastly because it is natural to us, while the other rather comes into existence artificially, and our intention is to treat of the more noble.' According to the first passage Latin is the more noble, according to the second popular speech. How are we to explain this contradiction?

In this way, it has been said, Dante has used the word *nobile* in very different senses in the two passages. In the *Convito* it means 'perfect' or 'of high quality'; in the *De Vulgari Eloquentiâ* 'well-known' or 'widely spread.' But it would be strange if an author, discussing the same subject, were to use the same expression in quite different senses, without a syllable to call the reader's attention to the difference. It is, however, only necessary to read *Convito* iv. 16 to be convinced that the meaning of high quality is the only one which Dante admits for *nobile*, and that he will have nothing to say to any derivation from *gnoscere*, 'to know.'

This explanation being untenable, an attempt has been made to find another. In the *Convito*, it is suggested, Dante sought to justify himself for handling philosophic subjects in the Italian language, and this he does by saying that it was not from any disrespect for Latin that he wrote in Italian, but the contrary, since the odes upon which he was commenting were Italian, and it would therefore not be seemly to use the more noble language for his commentary. In *De Vulgari Eloquentiâ*, on the other hand, he was addressing himself to scholars who held Italian in low esteem, and it was in opposition to them that he maintained that it was the nobler tongue. This simply means that Dante held opposite views according to the object which he had in view and the people whom he was addressing at the moment. This, however, was not Dante's way.

No, the matter must be regarded quite otherwise and more simply. We may admit that in the passage quoted from the *Convito* Dante, as his words imply, first expresses his intention of writing in course of time about the vulgar tongue, and that accordingly *De Vulgari Eloquentiâ* was written after the first treatise of the *Convito*, and so we shall have the matter plain without its being necessary to employ any artifice. The expression used in *De Vulgari Eloquentiâ* betokens a progress in the development in the author's ideas. In his time it was universally assumed, and so far had never been contested, that by comparison with the Roman popular languages Latin was the more beautiful, the more powerful, and the more noble. This universal opinion naturally had its influence on Dante. That he shared it in his earlier years is apparent from that passage of the *Vita Nuova* where he says that only love poems ought to be written in the language of the people; but that he afterwards changed his opinion appears from the fact that he himself composed poems on subjects quite other than earthly love. If anybody had on this account reproached him for having himself incurred the blame to which he had given expression in the *Vita Nuova*, he would have answered something as follows: No doubt I thought so in those days, but my views on that point have changed and become clearer. In the passage quoted from the *Convito* he is still defending the traditional common opinion, but even in the very first treatise of the *Convito* the newer and more mature view begins to have its weight. From what he says in the eleventh, twelfth, and thirteenth chapters in the way of praise for the vulgar tongue and of his own deep love for it, to the notion that the vulgar tongue is more noble than Latin, is but a short step. This step is taken in the *De Vulgari Eloquentiâ*, whence it follows that this was written later than the *Convito*, or at all events later than the first treatise of it.

We reach the same result through another consideration. In *De Vulgari Eloquentiâ* Dante shows himself thoroughly conversant with all possible Italian dialects, and displays such comprehensive knowledge of dialectic forms as is for that time simply astonishing. When did he acquire this knowledge? Certainly not in Florence before his banishment. He mentions this incident repeatedly in the book, but such knowledge could not have been gained in a short period. It presupposes undoubtedly all the wanderings spoken of in the *Convito*. A book like this about the vulgar tongue could not be written until its author had travelled over nearly all the regions to which the Italian tongue extends.

The evidence of older writers, were it needed, is all in the same direction. The statement of Villani and Boccaccio that the book was written shortly before his death may be pure conjecture, but even this conjecture implies a knowledge on their part that its composition was subsequent to that of the *Convito*.

The intention to write the book was, as we have seen, distinctly expressed in the *Convito*, that is to say, not later than 1309. The object in view was similar to that of the former work. He says:

Finding that no one before us has ever treated of the teaching of the vulgar tongue, and seeing that that tongue is thoroughly necessary to all, since not only men, but also women and children, strive after it so far as nature allows, and wishing in some measure to throw light into the reasoning of those who walk about like blind men through the streets thinking for the most part that behind is before; by the inspiration of the Divine word we will endeavour to be of some service to the speech of the common folk, drawing for such a cup not only the water of our own wit, but mingling better things which we can take or borrow from others, so that we may thereafter pour forth the most sweet hydromel.

Thus he will teach while treating of a matter of great importance, but hitherto left untouched. And while he writes for the instruction of others, he once more writes his own Apologia. He gives a fresh proof of his comprehensive studies, of the breadth and depth of his attainments, of the height of his genius. In the *Convito* he justified himself by revealing the deeper allegoric and moral sense of his odes; in *De Vulgari Eloquentiâ* he justifies himself by showing that his lyric poems did not proceed from sensual passion, but were works of art shaped by a man who was thoroughly conversant with the poetic art. This being the scope of the work, it may be inferred that it was written not long after the *Convito*, perhaps indeed Dante worked at both simultaneously.

In our judgment, accordingly, all those arguments fail with which people have thought to prove that *De Vulgari Eloquentiâ* was written before the *Convito*. One of these arguments only deserves short consideration. It is said that in i. 12 John I. of Monferrat, Azzo VIII. of Este, and Charles II. of Naples are introduced as still alive, but they died respectively in 1305, 1308, and 1309; thus the first book at least cannot have been written later than 1305. To this we have to remark, in the first place, that when an early writer mentions any person as dead we may conclude with certainty that the passage cannot have been written before the death of the person referred to. The converse is, however, by no means true, even though it be proved that the writer had information of the person's decease. Even at the present day the conclusion cannot always be drawn, how much less in the Middle Ages.[1] In reference to smaller princes, years might pass before the news of their death reached any individual scholar. The mention of a person as still living shows at most that the writer supposed him still to be alive when he wrote the passage in question, but in the present case there is no need even of this supposition when we read the passage in question with its context. The author is praising the good old times in contrast to the present, and calling attention to the way in which the Italian princes had degenerated since the days of Frederick II. and Manfred. For this purpose there was no need to name princes who were living at the moment; it was sufficient for his purpose to mention any who were contemporary, and the selection need not be decided by the fact of their being alive or dead, but simply by their appropriateness as examples of the assumed deterioration. Thus with regard to the question of the date of the work we can infer no more from this passage than from that in ii. 6, in which some words in praise of Azzo VIII. are quoted.

Although Dante himself mentions that he had this work in view, and it was known and spoken of by Villani, Boccaccio, Leonardo Bruni, and others, it was so completely lost sight of that when in 1529 Gian Georgio Trissino published his Italian translation of it, learned men at Florence contested its genuineness and doubted the existence of the Latin original. Nor were their doubts silenced when Corbinelli published the Latin text at Paris in 1577. On the contrary, suspicions were expressed that this might have been fabricated by Trissino. Even in our own century Filippo Scolari impugned its genuineness, and did not abandon his opinion even when three manuscripts

---

[1] See, for example, *Prolegomeni*, part ii. chap. ii. sec. 4.

of the work undoubtedly earlier than Trissino were brought to light. One of these certainly, another very probably, belonged to the fourteenth century, and this old Latin text is beyond all doubt the work of which Dante, Villani, and Boccaccio speak. Nor can any internal evidence against its genuineness be discovered. Inconsistencies with Dante's other works have been spoken of, but these are for the most part only apparent, and in any case they prove very little, since there is no lack of such between his undoubted writings. Accordingly, since Scolari all doubts have been silenced, and at the present day the genuineness of the work is held to be incontestable.

It has been known under two titles, *De Vulgari Eloquentiâ* and *De Vulgari Eloquio*. In Dante's own writings we find only the first, and Boccaccio knows it only under this, while in Villani the reading is uncertain. It agrees, too, with the contents of the book, which, had it been completed, would have been a treatise on poetry. But since in the first book so much is said about speeches and dialects, that part of it which we have might pass for a work on philology, and consequently the second title was for a long time the more commonly used. Fraticelli keeps it even in his latest edition. Giuliani, on the other hand, returned to the original form, which, as being that chosen by Dante himself, must be regarded as the only authentic title.

Like the *Convito*, this was to have been a comprehensive work; only two books, however, were written of it, the second not being even complete, for it breaks off in the middle of a sentence in the inquiry with which the 14th chapter opens. After the fashion of that time, Dante starts his investigation from the beginning of the world. Man, alone, of all created beings, was endowed with the gift of speech, for he alone had occasion to express to others his mental conceptions. Angels, the good as well as the fallen, have no need of speech for this purpose, while the brutes have no mental conceptions to impart. For man, however, the intercourse of speech was necessary, so that language was given to him simultaneously with his creation. The first word which man spoke was the word which means God, namely *Eli*, whether in interrogation or in response; man must therefore have spoken first in Paradise, and to his Creator. But what was the original language of which man made use? Each man thinks that it was his own mother tongue.

But we, who have the world for our fatherland, as fish have the sea, although we drank of Arno before our teeth were grown, and loved Florence, so that for the sake of our love to her we are suffering exile unjustly, must sustain the shoulders of our judgment by reason rather than by feeling. And although for our pleasure, or for the rest of our senses, there be on the earth no sweeter place than Florence, yet when we turn over the volumes of poets and other writers in which the world is described wholly, or in its parts, and when we come to reason within ourselves, we conceive that there must be many situations in the world, and habitations thereof, between either pole and the circle of the Equator, and regions and cities more noble and more delightful than Tuscany and Florence, whereof I am by origin a citizen; and that many nations and peoples employ a more charming and a more useful language than the men of Italy.

By favour of this cosmopolitanism, it is assumed that Hebrew was a language which the lips of the first speaker formed. This language endured until the building of the Tower of Babel, in consequence of which it was lost to all other nations, and remained only with Shem's descendants the Hebrews. In later times three different peoples wandered from Asia to Europe, and brought with them three different languages—German, Greek, and Latin. From each of these three languages (German, for example) in course of time many dialects sprang. Dante will, however, pass over the other two, and confine himself to Latin, 'for whatever reason tells us about one will probably be found also in the others. Now the language of which we propose to treat is threefold, for some say *oc*, others *si*, and others *oil*; and that it was one before the confusion began is clear from the fact that we agree in many forms of expression.' But each of these three languages undergoes endless changes, so that not only the inhabitants of the same country, but, what is yet more strange, the dwellers in one and the same city speak different dialects. The reason of this is that after the confusion of tongues all languages, with the exception of Hebrew, were given up to the arbitrary will of men, and man is the most inconstant and changeable of created things, so that language can neither be enduring nor persistent, but, like everything else which belongs to us, such as manners and customs, must alter according to distance in time and place. Hence comes the necessity of grammar, that is a written language. 'Now this grammar is nothing else than a certain unalterable identity of speech in different times and places. This having been regulated by the common consent of many people does not appear to be subject to the will of individuals, and consequently cannot be variable. They invented it then in order that we might either not at all, or very slightly, by reason of variation in language, or its fluctuation by the will of individuals, meddle with the rules laid down by or actions of people of former time, or those whom a difference of place causes to be different from us.'

Which of the three Romance tongues, that of *oc* the Provençal, that of *oil* the French, and that of *si* the Italian, deserves the first place? Dante does not venture to decide, but he thinks that he may claim a certain pre-eminence for Italian.

Each of the divisions is supported by wide evidence, thus the language of *oil* alleges for itself that, on account of its more easy and agreeable common speech, whatever has been handed down or invented in ordinary prose belongs to it—namely, books made up of the doings of the Trojans and Romans, and those very charming romances about King Arthur, and many other works of history and instruction. The second, that of *oc*, argues that vernacular writers were the first to use it for poetry as being a more perfect and sweeter speech, as, for instance, Peter of Auvergne, and other more ancient teachers. The third, which is that of the Italians, calls witness for its pre-eminence in two privileges—the first, that those who have composed the sweetest and most subtle poetry in the vernacular were of its family and household, like Cino of Pistoia and his friend.[1] Secondly, because they seem to rely more upon a common grammar, which, to those who look upon the matter reasonably, appears a most weighty argument. Let us, however, setting aside any decision in this matter, and confining our treatise to the Italian vernacular, endeavour to speak of the received variations in it, and to compare them with one another. We say, therefore, first, that Italy is divided into right and left parts, and to any inquiry as to the dividing line we answer briefly that it is the ridge of the Apennines. . . . The right side discharges its waters into the Tuscan sea, the left into the Adriatic; the regions on the right are Apulia (in part), Rome, the duchy of Spoleto, Tuscany, and the Genoese March; on the left part of Apulia, the March of Ancona, Romagna, Lombardy, the March of Treviso and Venice. Friuli and Istria must belong to the left side of Italy; the islands of the Tyrrhene Sea, Sicily, and Sardinia to the right. Now on each of the two sides the languages vary. . . . Italy, therefore, seems to be divided into not less than fourteen vernaculars, which, again, have variations within themselves. . . . So that, if we would calculate all the various vernaculars of Italy, primary, secondary, and subordinate, we shall

---

[1] The *friend* is understood to be Dante himself.

chance to come in this little corner of the world, not merely to the thousandth variation, but even a good deal beyond.

We need hardly remark that Dante confuses speech and dialect, as he immediately afterwards confuses both these with style.

When there is such a multitude of dialects, how are we to proceed in order to write beautiful and correct Italian? Are we to select one of the number and make use of it? Certainly not; for all, without exception, have very perceptible defects. To prove this, he passes in review the various Italian dialects. His judgments are, in all cases, sharply condemnatory. 'The speech of the Romans is not a popular language, but rather a hateful jargon, which is not to be wondered at, since they appear foul above all others from the deformity of their manners and customs.' The Sicilian dialect seems to be pre-eminently entitled to fame, since whatever poetry Italians have written is called Sicilian, and many of the native poets have sung in earnest. But the language of the middle class there has no advantage, and that of the upper class is in no way distinguished from that which deserves most praise. The Apulian's language is horribly barbarous, and so on through all the other dialects; Bologna alone finds some grace, but the Bolognese pronunciation is not what we call courtly and noble. In every dialect there is something good, but in none everything. The beautiful and noble Italian language which we seek is that which forms part of the universal Italian citizenship, and seems to belong nowhere, and is that by which the vulgar tongues of all the Italian states may be measured, weighed, and compared. After he has shortly explained why this language is called the exalted language of court and judicature, he continues:

This vulgar tongue, we say, is that which is to be called the Latin vulgar tongue. For as it is possible to discover a vulgar tongue which is proper to Cremona, so we may find one which is proper to Lombardy, and in the same manner one which is proper to the whole left side of Italy, and in the same way one which belongs to the whole of Italy, and as we speak of the Cremonese, and the Lombard, and the third which belongs to half Italy, so that which belongs to all Italy may be called the Latin vulgar tongue. For this is what those illustrious teachers have used who have written poetry in the vulgar tongue in Italy, men of Sicily, Apulia, Tuscany, Romagna, Lombardy, and either March. And whereas our intention, as we promised at the beginning of this work, is to hand down teaching concerning the use of the vulgar tongue, we will begin from that, as from the most excellent, and will treat in the next following books of those whom we think to have used it worthily, and how, when, where, and towards whom it should be employed. Having thrown light upon which, we will do the same by the inferior vernaculars, gradually coming down to that which is proper to one single family (i. 19).

With this ends the first book, which, like the first treatise of the *Convito*, was obviously intended to form the introduction to the whole work.

The second book opens with the inquiry, Who ought to use the cultivated vernacular? As the introductory words seem to imply, this was written not immediately after the first, but somewhat later and after a longer or shorter interruption. 'Not all writers and versifiers,' says Dante, 'ought to use the nobler language, but those only who are distinguished by capacity and scientific knowledge, and not any chance subject but only the best things ought to be treated of in this nobler Italian. What then are the best things?'

In order to perceive this we must know that according to the threefold division of man's spirit, namely, the vegetative, animal, and reasonable, he walks on a threefold path, for he seeks what is useful which he has in common with the plants, that which is pleasurable in common with the brutes, that which is honourable in which he stands by himself or is allied with the angelic nature. Whatever we do it appears that we do through one of these three, and since in each one of them some things are of more, some of most importance, according to this those that are of most importance seem most to be treated of and consequently the most important vernacular. But we have to discuss which are the most important, and first in regard to utility, in which, if we consider carefully the intent of all who seek after utility, we shall see that it is nothing else than self-preservation; secondly, with regard to that which is pleasurable in which we say that that is most highly pleasurable which causes pleasure by reason of the object of desire being the most precious, but this is love. Thirdly, with regard to what is honourable, and here no man doubts that it is virtue; wherefore these three things, namely, self-preservation, love, and virtue, seem to be the great subjects which are most to be treated of, and accordingly those things which bear in the highest degree reference to them, namely, valour in arms, the kindling of love, and the right guidance of the will (ii. 2).

But has not Dante himself in his great epic handled other subjects than arms, love, and virtue? Certainly, and therein again the restless progress of this unwearied thinking and creative spirit again displays itself. When he wrote the *Vita Nuova* he thought that love was the only subject for vernacular poetry. Now arms and virtue have been added, and later in the *Commedia* no subject is too high or too deep for him. Heaven and earth, God and man, time and eternity are all sung in the language of the people. We must suppose then that when he wrote *De Vulgari Eloquentiâ* the plan of his great poem was far from being what it afterwards became in execution.

Among the various forms of poetry into which he now proceeds to inquire, namely the ode, the ballad, the sonnet, and the other irregular forms, he indicates the ode as the most important, and begins accordingly to treat of it, promising to explain the method of the ballad and the sonnet in the fourth book of his work, 'when we shall treat of the middle class of the vernacular.' What now follows is a fragment of an Art of Poetry in which the metre of the ode is considered. Those who composed verses in the vernacular are called poets rightly since 'the poetic art is nothing else than an oratorical composition thrown into metre.' They are, however, to be distinguished from the Greek and Roman poets 'since the latter composed at greater length and with art governed by rules, but the former more casually.' According to this the old poets must be the model and example for the modern, both with regard to the careful selection of matter and the method and treatment of the same. 'For tragedy we choose a higher style, for comedy a lower; by elegy we understand the style of those in misfortune. If a man thinks to handle his matter tragically he must choose the purest vernacular and compose an ode; if comically the middle or lower vernacular will be selected. The distinction between these will be shown in the fourth book of this work, but if the matter is to be treated in elegiac fashion then only the lower vernacular need be brought into employment.' But to compose an ode according to the rules of art costs much time and labour, since it can never be brought about without a strain on the spiritual power, diligence in the art, and a ready command of knowledge. Of the various kinds of verse only those of eleven, seven, and three syllables are fitted for the ode, and among these the hendecasyllable is to be preferred. Of the two forms of construction, the regular and the irregular, the second is absolutely excluded in the composition of an ode and so forth. Great care must also be employed in the selection of individual words (ii. 7). After the preliminary questions have been thus decided comes the question what the ode is, what its different variations, what are its main divisions, the stanza, that is, which again undergoes various changes. In the middle of the inquiry about the stanza, nay, in the middle of a sentence, the work breaks off; whether it were that the writer was suddenly interrupted in some manner unknown to us and was subsequently unable to resume his work, or that some pages of the original manuscript were lost and have not since been found.

From the fact that Dante now and again refers to the fourth book it has been concluded that the work was to consist of four books, but obviously the reference proves only that the number was planned not to be less. It may, as Witte thought, have been five or more; in any case the view that Dante was not himself clear how much his work was to comprise may be dismissed, for the reference to the fourth book shows that he was working upon a fixed plan.

From the rules and laws laid down in this work for the art of poetry it has in recent times been supposed that we might obtain a certain criterion for a final decision as to the genuineness or spuriousness of the odes ascribed to Dante. This view, however, forgets that we have nothing to show whether the poet accepted these rules at the beginning of his poetic career, and without this the criterion is of no service.

CHAPTER V

DE MONARCHIÂ

DANTE wrote in Latin two important works, that which we have just been discussing, upon the vernacular tongue, and the strictly scientific political treatise to which he gave the title *De Monarchiâ*. This consists of three books; the first treats of the necessity of monarchy, in the second the question is discussed how far the Roman people were justified in assuming the functions of monarchy or the imperial power; in the third to what extent the function of the monarchy, that is the empire, depends immediately upon God. The division into chapters is not due to the author, but was introduced in later times.

He begins by remarking that the man whom God has endowed with the desire of inquiry and the love of truth feels himself compelled to instruct others. Thus he who is familiar with political science is in duty bound to use his experience and knowledge for the profit of the state. Considering this, and in order to avoid the blame of having buried his talent, he feels himself induced to examine and throw light upon a question that has not yet been fittingly set out, that is the all-important question of universal lordship or monarchy. In taking up this inquiry he hopes both to be useful to others and to earn fame for himself.

The undertaking is indeed very difficult, but he hopes for the divine assistance.

What then is in its idea and its essence the temporal monarchy? It is a solitary supremacy exalted above all to which the measurement of time can be applied. Then arise at once three questions: first, whether monarchy was necessary for the prosperity of the world; secondly, whether it could justly appropriate the Roman folk to itself; thirdly and lastly, whether its authority springs immediately from God or mediately through any representative of God. The first question may be answered without hesitation in the affirmative, the ultimate end of man and of humanity is to develop all its capacities and set them in activity for the common good. But this end can only be reached when universal peace prevails on the earth, and peace among men can only be brought about and maintained when one man is lord and leader, just as in the individual all the mental and physical powers should be ruled by the one power of the understanding or the individual household by one head. That which is fitting and necessary for the individual is also for the whole, and as the individual cannot subsist and thrive unless led and ruled by one will, so the whole cannot exist and thrive unless one is governor. Heaven ought to be mirrored upon earth, and in Heaven there is only one God and Lord. Men being of heavenly origin ought to strive to become as like Heaven as possible; and since the Heaven is guided in all its parts by a single movement, namely, the prime motive force, and by a single mover, God; so also humanity, if it will be like Heaven, must be guided by a single prince as the one mover and by a single law as the one movement. And where there can be the possibility of a law-suit there must be one judiciary power. If there be a number of independent princes, who can in a final instance settle disputes? There must therefore be a monarch who, standing over all and independent of all, can give the ultimate decision in every dispute. Thus monarchy corresponds to a real want of humanity, for this world is best off when justice rules in it, and this is only possible when there is a single monarch, since justice is often wrecked upon human cupidity, so that this must first be eliminated. But cupidity is then only impossible when there can be nothing to wish for, and this is the case with the monarch; wherefore he alone among mortals can most clearly exercise justice. The human race further for its happiness stands in need of freedom, which is the greatest boon that God has bestowed on it; but it is freest under a monarch. Under him it is best off; whence it follows that monarchy is necessary for the good of the world. Further, he who is best adapted for ruling is able best to dispose others, but the monarch alone it is who is best adapted for ruling, since he can have no occasion, or at all events the least occasion of all men for cupidity, the one thing which destroys judgment and hinders justice. Again, what can be done by one person is done better by one than by several. All superfluity is displeasing to God and to Nature, and all that is so displeasing is an evil, consequently it is not only better that anything should so far as possible be done by one than by many, but that it is actually good when done by one and ill when done by many. Now it is possible for the human race to be ruled by one over-lord, and therefore it is best off when it is so ruled. Thus in order that the human race should be well off, it is necessary that there should be a monarch in the world. This was also confirmed by Christ when He came into the world under Augustus; 'For when, starting from the fall of the first man as from the beginning of all our error, we regard the succession of men and their times, we shall find that only under Augustus was the world tranquil in a perfect monarchy; and that the human race was then happy in the rest of the universal peace—that all historians, all illustrious poets, yea, even the writer of the gentleness of Christ, have held it worth while to testify. Lastly, Paul also calls that happy state of things the fulness of time.'

This office of monarchy was assumed by the Roman people. On what ground? Many think that it was without justice, simply by good fortune and force of arms. Even he, Dante himself, shared this view formerly, but with the widening and deepening of his studies he afterwards arrived at the conviction that the Roman dominion was willed by God. But what God wills, that and that alone is just. How then are we to know what is God's will from His works? For though His signet may be hidden,. yet the wax which He stamps bears open testimony; and that God Himself called the Roman people to the lordship of the world appears in the first place from the fact that it was the noblest of all people, and on that account the first rank was its due. Secondly, God showed by signs and wonders that the Roman supremacy was in accordance with His will. That He wrought signs and wonders for the perfection of the Roman empire is testified by the best poets and authors. When Numa Pompilius offered a sacrifice a shield fell from heaven into the town which had been chosen by God; a goose, previously unseen, gave notice by her cry of the arrival of the Gauls, and so saved the capital; Hannibal was prevented by a sudden hailstorm from following up his victory as far as Rome; and it can only have been by miracle that Cloelia was able to break her chains and swim the Tiber. In the third place, Rome, when she had subdued the world, had in view only the good of the state, which is the aim of justice. In the fourth place, the Roman people was by nature predisposed and called to the lordship. Fifthly, it obtained and kept the supremacy by aid of divine judgments. Lastly, Christ recognised and confirmed the divine right of the Roman supremacy by being born under one emperor and dying on the Cross under another. 'Let, therefore, those who profess to be the sons of the Church cease to find fault with the Roman empire, since they see that her spouse Christ thus approved it both at the beginning and the end of His warfare. And now I think that it is sufficiently manifest that the Roman people obtained by right the empire of the world. Oh, fortunate people! oh, glorious Ausonia! if he who weakened thy empire[1] had either never been born or never been led astray by his own pious intention!'

To say that the first two books of this work affect our minds with a feeling of strangeness, and hold our interest in only a moderate measure, is not any blame to the author. He was a child of his age, and moved in its circle of thought. Nor should we probably be wrong if we assume that he himself did not attach much importance to the alleging of proofs of the necessity for the monarchy and of Rome's divine right to it. What he had really at heart was to expound the relation between Church and State, and this he undertook in his third book.

At the very outset of this he declares distinctly that here he looks to a serious contest. He says:

> Now it remains to treat of the third point, and the truth about this, since it cannot be brought forward without causing a blush to some, will perhaps be the source of some anger against me. But since truth from its immutable throne demands

---

[1] In allusion to the donations of Constantine.

it . . . I will enter upon the present conflict, and trusting in His arm who by His blood has freed us from the power of darkness, I will in the face of all the world drive the impious and the lying from the arena. Why should I fear when the Spirit, who is co-eternal with the Father and the Son, says by the mouth of David, 'The righteous shall be had in everlasting remembrance; he shall not be afraid of any evil tidings.' The present question then into which we shall inquire is concerned with two great luminaries, namely the Roman pontiff and the Roman emperor; and it is asked whether the authority of the Roman monarch, who, as has been proved in the second book, is of right the monarch of the world, depends immediately upon God or upon some vicar or minister of God, by which I understand the successor of Peter, who of a truth bears the keys of the kingdom of heaven' (iii. 1).

After this introduction, which leaves little to be wished in point of clearness, Dante enters upon the discussion of the great question that moved the world in his time. He starts from the principle that nothing can be the will of God which runs counter to Nature. After he has proved this law he remarks that the question he is treating is contentious in this respect; that when, as in other cases, ignorance is the cause of the contention, here the contention is the cause of ignorance in that even great spirits are sometimes led astray by passion, whereby error grows mighty. With regard to the truth we are seeking, three classes of men are at variance—the Pope and clergy, the decretalists, and the partisans. The Pope, to whom we do not owe what is due to Christ but only what is due to Peter, opposes the maxim that the imperial authority proceeds immediately from God out of zeal perhaps for the keys; the clergy perhaps out of zeal for Mother Church and not out of pride. 'Certain others, however, in whom inveterate cupidity has extinguished the light of reason, and who, while they are of their father the devil, call themselves sons of the Church, not only stir up strife on this question, but also, abhorring from the name of the Holy Empire, impudently deny the premisses of former questions as well as of this' (iii. 3). The decretalists, utterly ignorant of theology and philosophy, contest the divine authority of the empire out of simple covetousness. In order to get men of this kind out of the way, we must observe that Scripture is of three kinds, one taking precedence of the Church, namely, the Old and New Testaments, which are eternally valid; one equivalent, the Councils and the Fathers; one subordinate, namely, the decretals, which must rank after Holy Scripture, and receive their importance only from the Church.

So if these be excluded, others must be excluded, who being covered with ravens' feathers, claim to be white sheep in the Lord's flock. These are sons of impiety, who in order to carry out their crimes, defile their mother, cast out their brethren, and lastly will have none to judge. But why should reason be sought against them, seeing that in the snare of their own cupidity they cannot see principles? Wherefore our discussion is only with those who, led by some zeal for Mother Church, miss the truth which we are seeking. It is with these that I, relying on the reverence which a good son owes to father and mother, a good man to Christ and His Church, to the pastor and to all who profess the Christian religion, in this book enter on controversy, for the maintenance of the truth.

Who then are the opponents against whom Dante undertakes to do battle? The Pope and the better portion of the clergy, who act perhaps out of zeal for the keys and for the authority of the Church. With the bulk of the clerical faction, decretalists and partisans, he declares expressly that he will make no terms. As, however, the main part of this third book consists of the demolition of opponents' arguments, these arguments must be of Papal origin, and they are no despicable opponents whom Dante is fighting. At first he concerns himself with the well-known argument from the two lights, the Pope being the sun, while the emperor shines with borrowed light as the moon. It would be quite simple to deny that the sun was the type of the spiritual, the moon of the temporal power; and further, the moon did not spring from the sun, is not dependent on the sun, and possesses light of its own, though it receives from the sun more abundant light. 'I say, then, that the temporal power does not owe its existence to the spiritual, nor yet its strength, nor its importance, nor its operation, though doubtless it receives something from it in order that it may work more powerfully in the light of the grace which the Pope's blessing bestows upon it both in heaven and earth.' Against the second argument, that as Levi preceded Judah in birth, so the Church takes precedence of the imperial power in importance, he observes that neither does Levi typify the spiritual power nor Judah the temporal. Besides, precedence in birth in no way assumes precedence in authority, for there are many cases in which older persons do not surpass their juniors in dignity, but the contrary; as, for example, when a bishop is younger than any of his clergy. A third argument is, that Saul was chosen and appointed by Samuel. Samuel, however, was not acting as a priest but as a specially commissioned messenger of God in a particular case and for a particular end; and no conclusion can be drawn from the action of a special envoy of God to the power of the Pope, who is not a special envoy. A fourth argument is taken from the Wise Men of the East, who brought gold and frankincense to the child Jesus, showing thereby that he is Lord and Ruler in temporal and spiritual concerns. But the Pope is not Christ. No vicar's office, whether of divine or human institution, can be of equal dignity with the master's. A fifth proof: Christ assigned to Peter the power to bind and loose, the Pope has thus the power of loosing and binding the decisions and laws of the temporal authority. But the power given by Christ to Peter has no reference to temporal things, but is limited to the office of the bearer of the keys of heaven. Lastly, the two swords of Luke xxii. signify the spiritual and temporal lordship which lay in the hand of Peter, and have descended from Peter to his successors. But these two swords do not at all signify the two powers, they can in any case signify only the apostolic word and action.

After Dante has dismissed in this fashion the Scriptural arguments, he passes on to the historical, logical, and philosophical proofs. As is right, the notorious fable of Constantine's donation first comes up. Like all his contemporaries Dante has no doubt of its historical proof, but labours to show that nothing can be drawn from it favouring the claims of the hierarchy. Constantine could not alienate either the empire or a part of it, since no man can do the contrary of that to which his office binds him, and Constantine was bound by his office as Emperor to keep the realm intact. Nor on the other hand was it open to the Church to assume the imperial dignity, for by so doing it would be acting against its foundation, which is Christ alone. But the Emperor could make gifts to the Church with a view to her defence, but only so that the right of the first possessor should remain inviolate, whose unity does not allow of division, and the Church could accept the donation not as owner but only as trustee in order to spend the revenues on the Christian poor.

The second historical argument, that Pope Hadrian summoned Charles the Great to Italy and invested him with the imperial dignity, Dante dismisses with the short and appropriate remark that 'usurped right is no right.' Otherwise one could prove on the contrary side that the Emperor possessed the right to invest with the Papal dignity, inasmuch as the Emperor Otto restored Pope Leo and deposed and banished Benedict.

After dismissing the logical and philosophical proofs he passes on to the establishment of his own view, that the empire proceeds immediately from God, and therefore is not subordinate to the Church. His own thesis, as he develops it at the conclusion, is to this effect; man holds an intermediate place between the perishable and the imperishable; he participates in both by virtue of his body and his soul respectively. Accordingly he has a twofold aim towards which he must strive, and which is fixed for him by the Divine providence; happiness in the temporal life and blessedness in the eternal. The former consists in the exercise of his own powers, and is figured by the earthly paradise. The blessedness of the eternal life consists in enjoying the contemplation of God, and is therefore symbolised by the heavenly paradise. These two aims of human existence can be reached only by different means; we arrive at the happiness of this life by the way of reason, through right judgment and moral conduct; at the happiness of the next world we arrive only by the way of revelation, which excels human reason if we walk upon it in faith, in hope, and in charity. But if left to himself under the government of lower cravings, man will reach neither of these two aims; he needs therefore guidance. God in his wisdom and goodness has given him two guides, the spiritual chief shepherd whose task consists in leading mankind by the rules of divine revelation to the blessedness of the eternal life, and the Emperor, who, according to the rules of reason, that is to say according to the teachings of philosophy, is to lead mankind to the happiness of the temporal life. These two guides are not chosen by men but called by God Himself, and the human electors are only the heralds who announce the divine will. Since, however, the eternal is higher than the temporal, and revelation than reason, the Emperor is in certain points subordinate to the chief shepherd of Christendom. He is bound to show him that reverence which the first-born son owes to the father in order that he may become the fitter to exercise his no less exalted than responsible functions.

Such are in brief the contents of this work, which is important enough to deserve a more thorough-going analysis. It seems to us, however, that its aim is obvious. Some have held that it is a purely theoretic and scientific work, with no reference to the concrete circumstances of the moment or to the special conditions of the Italy of the day. And no doubt Dante declares at the outset that his purpose is to teach the ignorant and erring, and to contribute his mite towards the spreading of useful truths. One might also say that his aim was to stem the political dualism of the time, just as he has in the *Convito* and *De Vulgari Eloquentiâ* respectively combated the dualism prevailing in social and philological matters. But even a cursory inspection of the work puts it beyond doubt that we have to deal with a controversial writing in the full sense of the word. He proclaims it to be such in the introduction to the second book, and if possible still more energetically in that to the third book. That the author's desire was mainly and perhaps exclusively to enter into a thorough discussion of that question to which the third book is devoted we have already remarked, and the main object which he placed before himself in that portion of his work is obviously to combat and vanquish the arguments of opponents. But the opponents whom he combats are those who support the genuine and fundamental Guelf doctrine of the period, according to which, while all power proceeds from God, that of the Pope does so immediately, while that of the Emperor and other temporal princes comes mediately through the Pope, whence it would follow that the latter is even in temporal things subordinate to the former. To combat this doctrine and prove it to be erroneous and pernicious is plainly the actual aim of the work.

It is not easy to determine the date at which Dante can have resolved to undertake a work of this kind. As things then were in Italy repeated inducements must have presented themselves to him, one might almost say throughout his whole life. Hence there is great uncertainty with regard to the date of composition, upon which subject opinions still differ widely. Nothing of any certainty is to be got from the old biographers and commentators. Boccaccio's statement, to which we shall return again, must be only conjectural. Villani and Leonardo Bruni do not say a syllable on the point, and confine themselves to mentioning the work as Dante's. The question is, however, too important to be passed over. The purely subjective criticism of taste we may leave out of consideration, since in this matter it displays its absolute worthlessness. On the one hand it has been maintained that both in language and form the book shows clear evidence of being the work of a young beginner. On the other side it is inferred with absolute certainty — from the beauty of the language, from the practised style, and the strictly logical form, that the work was composed in the poet's later years. This controversy could only be decided by a comprehensive and tedious philological and logical comparison between Dante's two principal Latin works, such as our readers will hardly expect of us. We will therefore give the grounds for one and the other view, and after testing them, endeavour to come to an *in*dependent decision.

I. In favour of the view at present the more widely spread that the *De Monarchiâ* is one of Dante's earliest writings, composed before 1300, the following grounds are assigned:

1. With the exception of the *Vita Nuova* the *De Monarchiâ* is the only one of Dante's writings in which he does not mention his exile, although it must have offered many opportunities for this. We can only explain this by supposing that it was written before 1302. The objection that the *De Monarchiâ* was a purely theoretic work in which there would be no reason for the author to speak of himself has very little importance, for the *De Vulgari Eloquentiâ* is certainly a work of this kind, and yet Dante does not hesitate in that to refer to his exile. We must not import the rules of modern literary decorum into the Middle Ages; Dante, of all people, liked to speak of himself, and often does so in his writings. There is then something in the argument; but is it true that the *De Monarchiâ* contains no allusion to his exile? What does he mean in iii. 3, by the 'children of wickedness who drive out their brethren,' and who are the brethren that are driven out? We think that the allusion to his own fate cannot be missed. No doubt there had been banishments in former times, but in Florence, up to the end of the thirteenth century and the catastrophe of 1301-1302, Dante had no cause to complain of people being driven out, nor would he have spoken of the exiles as brethren if the like fate had not befallen him. Moreover, there is the striking fact that in the *Convito* Dante makes no reference to this work. When he has to speak of the vernacular language he refers to the *De Vulgari*

Eloquentiâ which at that time was far from being finished, perhaps indeed was not even begun. And yet where he propounds exactly the same questions as in the *De Monarchiâ* he has not a single syllable referring to a work on the same subject—which according to the hypothesis had been long finished. Even if this be possible it is highly improbable. It is far more probable that when he wrote the *Convito* he made no reference to the *De Monarchiâ*, for the simple reason that it did not then exist.

2. It has been found that the opening words have too modest a ring. To quote Witte (*Dante-Forschungen*, i. 81), 'The *De Monarchiâ* begins with the observation that it is fitting for a man, as he has himself been enriched by the work of previous generations, to work for the enrichment of his posterity. He remains far in arrear of his duty who, when he has been taught by public evidence, does not try to contribute to the common stock. Such a man is not like a tree planted by the water-side which brings forth its fruit in due season, but rather like a destructive whirlpool which is ever sucking in but never gives forth again what it has swallowed. Considering this, and in order to avoid the reproach of having buried his talent, the author desires in the common interest not merely to put forth buds, but to ripen fruit, and to set forth truths which others have not touched. How could Dante, conscious as he was of his own worth, and as far as possible from false modesty, have written thus in 1312 or later, years after he had published the four treatises of the *Convito*—that encyclopædia of the science of his time, to say nothing of the *Vita Nuova*? Or do not the words rather apply to a writer who is making his first appearance with an important work?'

To this it has been answered that in the passage cited Dante is speaking of things which are useful to the existence of a state, and that he has not touched on these in his other works. But this is a somewhat frivolous objection. Dante would hardly have said that the *Convito* and the *De Vulgari Eloquentiâ* contributed nothing to the profit of the State. But were they published before 1312? That remains to be proved. Written no doubt they were; but it is hard to believe that they were published and remained so long in an incomplete state. If, however, they were, may they not be the buds of which he speaks? As the *Vita Nuova* was the bud, of which, in the conclusion to the work, he holds out prospects of the ripe fruit, so may the *Convito* and the *De Vulgari Eloquentiâ* have been buds which were not to develop fruit till they were completed. If in 1312 Dante had not yet published them, he might well have said, without exaggerated modesty, that so far he had put forth only buds, if he had published them. He was almost bound to say so, if he were to avoid the reproach of getting no farther than the bud; that is beginning all possible subjects, and stopping short at the beginning. But is the opening of the *De Monarchiâ* over-modest? One might more justly maintain the exact contrary. A man is hardly over-modest who boasts of his love of truth, or of having been enriched by the work of his predecessors; who feels that he has a duty, a call to create something of use to posterity; who is conscious that he has a talent, and promises to bring forth fruit for the benefit of the State, and to produce something quite new, and hitherto untreated of, since he deems it beneath his dignity to handle matters which others have handled. When he boasts of being 'steeped in public documents,' which in the context can only mean experienced in political science, must he not be speaking after he has taken part in the government of Florence? And when later he refers in unmistakable terms to the change in his political views, would that be over-modest in the mouth of a young man who had hardly begun to share in political life? From the language of the *De Monarchiâ* we can draw no other conclusion as to its date than that it must belong to the later years of its author's life.

3. At the beginning of his great poem, placed in the year 1300, Dante says that he got from Virgil the beautiful style which had brought him fame. This can only refer to the *De Monarchiâ*, written as it was in the spirit of Virgil's views. But when did that work ever bring him fame in his lifetime? Never, so far as we know. The 'beautiful style' can only be the 'sweet new style' of his lyrics, referred to in Purg. xxiv. 57.

4. In the *De Monarchiâ* Boniface's notorious Bull *Unam Sanctam* of 1302 is quite ignored, therefore it must have been written before that year. How little this proves is shown by the fact that an eminent scholar, Luigi Tosti, deduces from it that Dante wrote it on purpose to controvert that Bull. In fact the argument from the two swords, which is refuted, was Boniface's main argument; and Dante would have hesitated before declaring in plain words that he was combating a papal Bull. But when he remarks, as we saw, that among all the opponents of the Ghibeline doctrine he means to consider only the Pope and the better portion of the clergy, any one who can read between the lines sees plainly enough what he means.

5. On the question of the nature of nobility there is a contradiction between *De Monarchiâ* ii. 3, and *Convito* iv. 3; while a passage on the same subject, Par. xvi. 1-9, agrees more with the view expressed in the *Convito* than with that defended in the *De Monarchiâ*. But that would only show that the *De Monarchiâ* was written before the *Convito*, *i.e.* before 1308. The contradiction is, however, more apparent

than real. In the *De Monarchiâ* he recognises hereditary as well as personal nobility. That he also does in the *Paradise*, since he states how on learning that one of his forefathers had been a knight, he gloried in his own hereditary nobility. In the *Convito* he is thinking of the nobility of the soul, which is not hereditary. But if there be any difference in his opinion about nobility, the view taken in the *De Monarchiâ* that nobility is won by a man's own prowess, and through his forefathers, is clearly riper and more practical than that taken in the *Convito* that inherited wealth confers no nobility, and this difference would be in favour of the later composition of the *De Monarchiâ*. But in the *Convito* he is speaking of the power which makes a man noble, and rejecting the base verdict of those who hold that wealth is the source of nobility; and so had in this place no occasion to treat of nobility in its significance from the statesman's point of view, a significance which in the *Commedia* he quite recognises. There is thus no real contradiction.

6. In his introduction Dante says that the subject which he is about to consider has hitherto been treated by no one. Writings of similar character had, however, been in existence since the beginning of the fourteenth century, so that the *De-Monarchiâ* must have been composed before that date. But when in Par. ii. 7, he says, 'Over the water which I take none ever sped,' it surely does not follow that no one before him had depicted the joys of Paradise, but only that in his opinion nothing that had hitherto been written on the subject was worth mentioning. A man who pitched his claims so high as Dante might easily hold a similar opinion with regard to his predecessors' works on civil law, and the relation between Church and State, assuming (what it would not be easy to prove) that he was acquainted with them.

We have thus shown that none of the arguments in favour

of the *De Monarchiâ* having been composed before Dante's exile are sufficient. Let us turn to another opinion.

II. The book is said to have been his last important work, written between 1318 and 1321. The grounds on which this is maintained are as follow:

1. In i. 14 it is said that free-will is God's greatest gift to man; the same statement as is made in Par. v. 19 *sqq*. In the majority of MSS. follow the words *Sicut in Paradiso Comediae jam dixi*. This would prove the *De Monarchiâ* to have been written after that canto. To ignore the importance of this argument would be to use our free-will in order to close our eyes. If the words are genuine, the question is settled decisively; and the fact of their occurring in the majority of the MSS. (it was thought till recently in all) is of great weight on the side of their genuineness. But no proof of it has been, or ever can be, brought forward. A full and precise account of the matter will be found in Witte's edition. The ancient translation of Marsilius Ficinus knows nothing of the words, nor has Fraticelli taken any notice of them; while Giuliani, the parent of all modern adherents of the opinion into which we are now inquiring, rejects them as spurious. His reason, that Dante would not have quoted himself in this way, is of no great importance. Dante does quote himself more than once, though perhaps not quite so pointedly as would be the case here were the words really his. But how is the fact of their absence from some MSS. to be explained? A copyist would hardly have omitted just these six words, so decisive as to the date at which the book was composed. On the other hand it is easy to imagine that a reader who was familiar with Dante's chief work might have referred in a marginal or interlinear note to the passage in the *Paradise*, and that a later copyist, altering *dixit* to *dixi*, might in all

good faith have inserted them in the text. As things are, we cannot arrive at a definite conclusion without further inquiry and collation of all the MSS.

2. In Conv. ii. 14 the poet expresses the view that the markings in the moon proceed from regions of less density in her body. In Par. ii. 58 *sqq.* he contradicts this opinion at some length as erroneous, and adheres to that of Albert the Great. In *De Monarchiâ* iii. 4 he maintains the same view as in the *Paradise*, which is taken as evidence that it was written after the *Convito*. If, which is not incontestable, we are compelled to admit that *De Monarchiâ* and *Paradise* are agreed in this matter as against *Convito*, this would be proof that the first-named work was of later date than the last, *i.e.* after 1308; but that would not necessarily bring it to the last years of Dante's life.

3. There are passages in the *De Monarchiâ* on the one hand, and in the *Paradise*, the *Letter to Can Grande* and the *Quaestio de Aquâ et Terrâ* on the other, which show points of resemblance not to be explained save on the supposition that all belong to the same period—the end, that is, of the poet's life. The *Quaestio*, however, must be left out of account, as certainly spurious; while the *Letter* is very suspicious. Taking the *Paradise* only, the resemblance can be explained by the fact that similar allied questions are being discussed. But further, as Giuliani points out in his Commentary, a little comparison will show that the similarities between *De Monarchiâ* and *Convito* are at least as marked as those between the former and *Paradise*, so that they would be consistent with the earlier composition of the Latin work.

Other arguments for this view seem hardly of sufficient importance to be set out and tested. From what we have said it must be allowed that in the present position of research it is not possible to come to a decision, but that the opinion which makes the *De Monarchiâ* to have been written before the exile rests on very dubious foundations. We may now proceed to the third view.

III. The *De Monarchiâ* was composed at the date of Henry VII.'s march to Rome. The supporters of this can appeal to Boccaccio, who states it as a simple fact. It is quite possible that, definite as his statement is, it rests on his own assumption; possible also that he took it from the tradition of the period; possible even that he had more certain information. The work is polemical in character, which renders it all the more probable that Dante had a motive for writing it; and he never had so strong a motive as at the date of the march to Rome. It would be really hard to say when else he could have had any motive for beginning the second book with the opening words of the second Psalm, and complaining that kings and people were taking counsel against the Lord's Anointed. And if Dante's letters ascribed to this period are genuine, their relation in thought and turn of expression to the *De Monarchiâ* is so close that they tell heavily in favour of Boccaccio's view.

And against this view what can be urged with any force? Let us hear Witte (*Dante-Forsch.* vol. i. p. 79): 'Our suspicions with regard to the supposition of its being a partisan pamphlet are aroused by the fact that in the whole work there is not the faintest allusion to the actual circumstances of the moment. The Emperor is always mentioned as an entirely ideal personage; but not the slightest trace can be discovered of any particular Emperor, of any Henry of Luxemburg. Nor does the writer anywhere refer to the peculiar condition of the Italy of that day.' But may he not have thought that his writing would have all the more effect in proportion as he occupied himself with a strictly scientific treatment of principles, and abstained from all allusion to the circumstances of the moment, to persons and things? At the date of Henry's march to Rome, was it in any way necessary, if he came forward in support of the Imperial rights, to mention that particular Emperor? Would not every reader understand the case for himself? and would not the work make all the deeper impression for his speaking only of the Emperor in the abstract? If he set forth how peace and justice were indispensable to the weal of mankind, might he not safely leave it to his readers to make the application to the peculiar position of the Italy of that day? And if he complains of the kings and people who stood up and took counsel against the Lord's Anointed, did not this complaint involve an unmistakable allusion to the position of Italy? To quote Witte further:

> Dante could strike quite another note when it was really his object to defend the rights of his beloved Emperor Henry. Of this we have the fullest illustration in that letter to the princes and peoples of Italy which was actually intended to do what is assumed to be aimed at in the *De Monarchiâ*. Close as may be the affinity between the points demonstrated in the two works, the tone of them is completely distinct. While in the *De Monarchiâ* everything, even the pathos of its enthusiasm, has an objective theoretic character, the reader feels in every line of the letter the reverberation of the circumstances of the moment.

Granted; but if in a scientific treatise he adopts another tone than in an apologetic letter, does it follow that they must belong to different periods? Does not the very opening of the second book of the *De Monarchiâ* contain an allusion to the address of the letter to the princes and peoples of Italy? And if fault was found with the tone of the letter, was not that very fact an invitation to adopt a calmer tone? But, says Witte once more:

There is a piece of definite evidence which is conclusive as to the impossibility of the two defences of the Empire being contemporary. The letter indicates Henry as the object of the Papal benediction; the *De Monarchiâ*, on the contrary, names the Pope among the deniers of the Empire as understood by Dante. It is apparent that Dante could not make both these statements on the same occasion, it might be said, in the same breath.

Whether he could do it in one breath we need not consider. Two years elapsed between the writing of the letter and the death of Henry, and if during this time Dante arrived at the conviction that he was mistaken in Pope Clement V., it would be quite natural that he should change his language. That he did arrive at that conviction appears from such passages as Par. xvii. 82 ; so that if there were any inconsistency it would be easily accounted for. But in fact there does not appear to be any. In the letter it is said that Pope Clement had imparted his apostolic blessing to Henry; but the *De Monarchiâ* places the Pope among the opponents of the maxim that the Imperial office was held directly from God. Clement might surely have opposed the maxim, and yet given his blessing to Henry.

After mature consideration of the whole case, the third view, viz. that the work was written at the time of Henry's presence in Italy, seems the most tenable. Most of the evidence is in favour of this, hardly anything of importance against it. But unprejudiced research is bound to admit that it is not yet in a position to speak the last word as to the date of composition of the treatise.

With regard to its genuineness no doubt can exist. Villani, Boccaccio, Bruni, all knew it and mention it. With regard to its fortunes Boccaccio tells the following tale :

This book, some years after the author's death, was condemned by Messer Bertrando, Cardinal, of Pozzetto, Papal

Legate in the parts of Lombardy, under Pope John XXII. And the cause thereof was because Lewis, Duke of Bavaria, elected by the German electors King of the Romans, coming to Rome for his coronation against the will of the aforesaid Pope John, when he was in Rome made a minor friar, Peter of Corvara, Pope, contrary to the ordinances of the Church, and made many cardinals and bishops; and had himself crowned by this Pope. Thereafter arose questions in many cases as to his authority; and when this book was discovered, he and his followers, in defence of his authority, began to use many of the arguments found therein; for which cause the book, which up till then had hardly been known, became very famous. But afterwards, when the said Lewis was returned to Germany, his followers, and especially the clerics, declined and were scattered; and the said cardinal, having none to oppose him, got hold of the aforenamed book, and publicly condemned it to the flames, as containing matters of heresy.

It has been supposed that this narrative is a little romance of Boccaccio's own invention. But proof that it is real history has quite recently come to light.[1]

[1] Guerrini-Ricci, *Studi e polemiche Dantesche* (Bologna, 1880).

CHAPTER VI

THE LETTERS

EASY would be the task of Dante-researchers if we had in his case a correspondence such as exists for his younger contemporary Petrarch. Even if he did not, like Petrarch, write letters intended for posterity, his correspondence must, in the nature of things, have been pretty extensive. But alas! very little of it has come into our possession, and of that little the greater part will not stand the test of criticism.

Dante himself, in the *Vita Nuova*, makes mention of a letter which, in the first shock of the news of Beatrice's death, he wrote to the chief men of the city, and commenced with the opening words of the book of Lamentations. But this letter was probably never sent, and never seen by any one. Villani knew of several letters, and mentions three by name, as we have already said. Boccaccio writes: 'This eminent poet wrote also many letters in Latin prose, of which a good number are still extant.' Leonardo Bruni, who has preserved for us the important fragment of a lost letter about Campaldino, and the causes of Dante's exile, recounts how the poet 'wrote more than once, not only to individual citizens, but to the people; and, among other letters, one of great length, beginning with the words, "My people, what have I done to thee?"' He states further that 'Dante was a consummate penman; his writing was long and slender, as I have seen in autograph letters of his. He wrote many letters in Latin.' What has become of them all?

Up to the end of the last century one letter only of Dante's was known in the original, viz. that to Can Grande; and this, besides being rather an introduction to the *Paradise* than a letter, is doubtfully genuine. Beyond this, the letter to the Princes and Peoples of Italy, and that to Henry VII., were known, but only in an Italian version, due perhaps to Marsilius Ficinus. In the fifth of his *Aneddoti* (Verona, 1770) Dionisi brought to light the letter to a Florentine friend—a somewhat clumsily polished bit of glass, which for some time was taken for diamond. In 1827 followed Witte's edition, containing, of hitherto unprinted pieces, the original of the letter to Henry VII., that to the Cardinals, and that to Cino of Pistoia. Ten years later Theodor Heyse found in the Palatine MS., which has since been much discussed, nine letters ascribed to Dante, seven of which had till then been quite unknown. In 1838 Witte wrote a full report of them, claiming the honour of the discovery on the ground that Heyse, who was at that time working in the Vatican Library, had at his request looked out for relics of Dante. In the joyful excitement of the discovery criticism was allowed to sleep, and the genuineness of the letters was accepted as a matter of course. Thus Alessandro Torri's edition of 1842 contained the respectable number of fourteen letters, which were taken as undoubtedly genuine. In course of time criticism awoke, and began soberly to rub its eyes. The consequence was that the abundance melted away until to-day it is seriously questioned whether we possess a single letter which can be undoubtedly ascribed to Dante. This is not the place to enter into a full inquiry on the subject;

for our purpose it must suffice to take a brief glance at the letters, and append a few remarks.

I.-III. To the Empress Margaret of Brabant, wife to Henry VII.—Three short notes, written in the name of the Countess of Battifolle who styles herself Countess Palatine of Tuscany, and so must have belonged to a branch of the 'Conti Guidi.' The first is undated, but perhaps belongs to the year 1310. It merely expresses thanks for the special favour done to the Countess by informing her of the welfare of the Emperor and Empress. The second expresses the Countess's participation in joy at the happy issue which the Empress announces to her. The third, dated at Poppi in the upper Vale of Arno, 18th May 1311, contains further assurances of her interest in the successful progress of affairs and her devotion to the cause to which, at the Empress's express desire, are appended short statements with regard to the health of the writer, her husband, and her children. Not a word is said of Dante in any of them. But he is said to have written in the name of the Countess. Whence is this inferred? Well, in the Palatine MS. they stand near other letters ascribed to Dante, and 'that Dante was the actual author is rendered probable,' says Witte, 'from the recurrence of certain words and phrases frequent in his Latin writings, coupled with the fact that at this very time the poet was staying with Count Guido in the upper Vale of Arno.' If the eminent scholar had looked at the matter from other than the discoverer's point of view he might perhaps have judged otherwise. At the present day no one believes any longer in Dante's authorship of the letters. Even Fraticelli and Giuliani have excluded them from their editions. And indeed they are not important enough to need any further discussion.

IV. To the Cardinal of Ostia, Nicolas of Prato.—This

letter is found only in the Vatican MS. It is written in the name of one A. Ca., the council, and whole party of the Florentine Whites. The writers thank the Cardinal for the trouble he has taken for the furtherance of peace in Florence and the return of the exiles, promise, as the Cardinal desires, to abstain from all hostilities against the Blacks, and beg him to continue without intermission his efforts for the good of Florence and in their favour. Now to begin with, who is A. Ca. ? It has been said to stand for 'Alexander Capitaneus,' that is, Alexander of Romena, who, as Leonardo Bruni repeats, was elected leader of the Whites; though indeed, as remarked above (p. 118), he elsewhere says that the Whites had no leader. But a Count of Romena would surely not have called himself 'Alexander Capitaneus.' Further, the writing contains neither Dante's name nor any allusion to him. It has been held that the letter was nevertheless written by him, because it stands in the MS. among some which are expressly ascribed to him; and because, according to Bruni, Dante was one of Count Alexander's twelve counsellors, and was the one among them most experienced in the use of the pen. But we have seen that Bruni's whole story is most probably fabulous. And further, the letter cannot have been written before 20th July 1304; by which time Dante had left his companions in misfortune and could therefore not have written a letter on his behalf. We must agree with Todeschini, del Luogo, and Bartoli in refusing to regard this letter as written by Dante.

V. To Oberto and Guido, Counts of Romena.—A letter of condolence on the death of Count Alexander, uncle to the persons addressed; without date. The writer says: 'Your uncle, the illustrious Count Alexander who has recently returned to that heavenly home, from which his disposition shows him to have come, was my lord and master, and his memory will possess me so long as I live in this world; for his magnanimity which now is richly rewarded with a worthy reward beyond the stars, caused me to be of my own accord devoted to him through many bygone years.' Dante is said to have written this between 1309-11. But in H. xxx. 77 *sqq*. he has put Guido and Alexander of Romena, with a brother not named, in Hell as false coiners.[1] It has been said that in the passage from the *Hell* another member of the family, of a similar name, is intended; but no one has been able to prove the existence of this second Alexander of Romena, nor is it likely that, except for the letter, he would ever have made his appearance. Witte's shift does not make the matter look any better. 'If we recollect,' he says, 'how ill those Counts responded to Dante's expressed hopes, how undecidedly, we may say in a measure hostilely, they worked in 1311 and 1312, in spite of flattering words, with regard to Dante's hero Henry VII., we can conceive that about 1314 the poet may have wielded his scourge upon men whom he had lately esteemed.'

But can we conceive that Dante can have placed in Hell on such a charge the nephew of an uncle whom he had formerly exalted to Heaven? The hand that wrote the lines of the *Hell* can never have written the letter. But its contents show it to be a clumsy forgery.

VI. To the Marquis Moroello Malaspina.—This letter too is undated. The writer informs his patron, immediately after leaving that patron's court, at which his insensibility to female charms had often been a cause of wonder, that on returning to the head-waters of the Arno he has seen a woman for whom love has irresistibly taken possession of him, has driven out all other thoughts, and entirely transformed him. It is hardly worth while to waste a word on

[1] Has he?

this ridiculous forgery. Is Dante likely to have sent such a letter to the Marquis Malaspina, a leader of the opposite party? Dante, a man over forty years old, writes to another man who has grown grey in arms to impart the weighty news that he has fallen in love! The thing is so monstrous that people have seen all manner of mysteries in the letter, such as that the woman denotes Florence. Those who like may, as the present writer has suggested in his *Prolegomeni* (pp. 383-384), see a reference to an unexpected meeting of Dante with his wife; a suggestion which a writer in the *Nuova Antologia* has taken seriously. The letter must be held for an absurd forgery until it is found in some less suspicious MS., for which we shall probably have to wait some time.

One question remains. Have we to do, in the writings, with conscious and intentional forgeries, or (as is more probable) with an innocent deception perpetrated in all good faith and in ignorance. It is a purely modern conjecture that the three notes to the Countess of Battifolle are of Dante's writing; nor was the letter to the Cardinal of Prato ever attributed to him until modern subjective criticism sought to stamp him as its author. There is therefore no question of forgery in these cases. The letters to the Counts of Romena and to Moroello Malaspina, again, do not profess to have been written by Dante, for though in the former there is talk of poverty and undeserved banishment, there were plenty of people besides Dante who had been undeservedly banished from Florence, and had consequently fallen into poverty. The headings, no doubt, ascribe them directly to our poet; but who wrote the headings? Dante himself certainly never wrote that which stands over the letter to the Counts of Romena stating the occasion of the letter and the nature of its contents. And if he did not himself write them, it is quite possible that work which was none of his may have been ascribed to him in all innocence, just as were the lyric poems found in old MSS., which can be proved to be of later origin.

VII. To Cino of Pistoia.—Without date or name of sender or receiver. It is found only in a MS. of very uncertain origin, which contains incontestable and admitted forgeries. It is a short and insignificant piece in answer to the question whether it is contrary to Love to shift from one object to another; a question which it answers in the affirmative. The heading is 'Epistola D. de Florentia.' But that D. stands for Dante, and that if it did, the Dante is our poet, he may believe who can.

VIII. To the Princes and Peoples of Italy.—This letter is found in the well-known Vatican MS., perhaps elsewhere; and is extant in an old Italian translation conjecturally attributed to Marsilius Ficinus. Until now, so far as we know, no doubt has been raised as to its genuineness. For his own part, the present writer cannot boast of the soundness of his faith in this matter. In fact, he does not believe that the letter is Dante's. To set forth the reasons would require more space than is here at his disposal; but he hopes to have an opportunity of doing so before long.

IX.-XI. To the Florentines; to the Emperor Henry VII. ; to the Italian Cardinals.—These are the three which Villani expressly mentions by name. His evidence ought to place them beyond all suspicion—but may they not have been fabricated on the strength of Villani's statement? How little was made of forgeries at one time in Italy we may see from the truly awful examples afforded by Filelfo in his so-called biography of Dante. Nor need we come down so late as Filelfo. The well-known rubbish, under the name of Frate Ilario, of which we need take no further notice, and other productions of which we shall have to speak, show what Italians were able to do in this line before Filelfo's days. As regards the letter to the Florentines, it is a suspicious circumstance that it occurs only in that Vatican MS. which we have already mentioned is questionable. That to Henry VII. is better accredited, and for the present we do not wish to hazard any doubt with regard to it. On the other hand, that to the Cardinals is highly suspicious. One strong point against it is, that it is found only in that Laurentian MS. (xxix. 8), which is of even more doubtful authority than the Palatine MS. in the Vatican.

Further, it is curious that it should begin with the same words as the letter which Dante affirms (V. N. 29) that he wrote on receiving the news of Beatrice's death. No doubt the words are those of a well-known verse of Scripture, with which Dante may at various times have opened various letters. But, as we gather from Conv. i. 1, by 1314 the *Vita Nuova* had long been published and was widely known. Is it likely that under these circumstances Dante would have selected the same verse a second time to begin a letter? If this verse had really occurred to him on the occasion of Beatrice's death, if he had really applied it to her death in the manner recorded in the *Vita Nuova*, can we not conceive that he would have deemed it a kind of profanation to apply the same words to quite a different set of circumstances? Had the *Vita Nuova* not been long well known, the idea would be conceivable; but as the case stood, hardly. Again, the words 'nunc Hannibali nedum aliis miserandam' are found almost *verbatim* in Petrarch (Canz. xi. l. 65);[1] and the statement that Uzzah gave heed to the Ark of the Covenant, but he himself to the oxen who

---

[1] So in the text; but the reference is really to Canz. vi. ('Spirto gentil, che quelle membra reggi') l. 65. The ode, it may be noted, is addressed to Rienzi.

were plunging and going astray, turns up with slight alteration in a letter of Cola di Rienzo. Did then both Petrarch and Rienzi pillage from a letter of Dante's? It is not impossible;[1] but in order to justify the assumption the letter must have better credentials than it has. Meanwhile both form and contents render it incredible that such a letter should have been written by Dante. Further research is required in regard to all these three letters.

XII. To Guy of Polenta.—In Italian: first made known by Antonio Francesco Doni, a man whom no one has ever believed. He published it 1547 in his *Prose Antiche*. No earlier traces of it have yet been discovered, and it is certain that they never will be. The letter is mere rubbish. According to it, Dante went to Venice in 1313 or 1314 as envoy from that Guido Novello of Polenta, Lord of Ravenna, who at the date in question was only *podestà* of Cesena. The object of his mission is said to have been to congratulate Giovanni Soranzo on his appointment as Doge, he having been elected in July 1312. September 1313 or 1314 would have been a trifle after date. Dante had begun, it says, to speak to the Senate in Latin, but was understood by no man; nor when, at the request of the Senate, he made use of the Italian tongue, was he more successful. And moreover he is made (not in the speech, that is, but in the letter) to quote as from Virgil words which really are Claudian's. Briefly the whole letter, though not long, consists of the merest historical and other rubbish, and it is quite inconceivable how men otherwise reasonable could suppose that such a wretched piece of patchwork could proceed from Dante.

---

[1] On the contrary, one would say, looking to the literary ways of that time, highly probable; as indeed the author himself perceived in 1890. See *Prolegomeni*, p. 128.

XIII. To his Florentine friend.—So far as our present knowledge goes, is to be found only in the Laurentian manuscript. Of this document, hitherto accepted universally as undoubtedly genuine, the present writer was the first to contest, and as he believes finally, to disprove the genuineness.[1] But as the paper in which he has done this is not easily accessible to the majority of readers, it may be as well briefly to discuss the question.

According to the style of address the receiver would be a cleric with whom Dante had a common nephew, and so either a Brunacci, a Poggi, or a Donati. But no cleric of any of these names is known to have lived at that time in Florence. The letter professes to be a reply, but we cannot make out whether to a letter of the correspondent, or of the nephew, or of the other Florentine friend, an obscurity which is not very like Dante's usual sharp distinction. The writer complains that a banished man seldom finds friends, and at the same time speaks of his many friends; that is not like Dante's logic.[2] There is mention in the letter of two ridiculous and ill-considered things, and yet mention of one only can be extracted from it, namely the folly of supposing that Dante would accept such conditions; this confusion again can hardly be Dante's. In the short letter the writer finds it necessary to impart to his correspondent the conditions of pardon which that very correspondent must have imparted to him. This betrays the later forger, who has to give the information which his reader does not possess. Nearly fifteen years after his banishment and a few months

---

[1] See *Prolegomeni*, pp. 133-138; and *Schweizerische Rundschau*, January 1891, pp. 42-73.

[2] The passages are 'Tanto me districtius obligastis quanto rarius exules invenire amicos contingit,' and 'per literas vestri meique nepotis necnon aliorum quamplurium amicorum.' The inconsistency is hardly apparent to ordinary acumen.

after the Florentines had charged him in a public document with various misdeeds and condemned him to death on that account, Dante might indeed profess his innocence, but could hardly say it was well known to all men; that was left for posterity to affirm. In the existing state of things Dante could neither look for nor await a glorious recall; it was left to an admiring posterity to speak of that. He who only writes his own name under compulsion, and thinks it necessary to excuse himself for doing so (in Purg. xxx. 55), would not as in this letter twice within a few lines write it out in full with perfect satisfaction, and quite superfluously. Nor would he himself ever have allowed such vainglory to be laid to his charge as is displayed in the letter, nor indeed did his reputation, of which the letter makes so much, stand at that time so very high; this again is the language of admiring posterity. The proud and self-conscious confidence which the letter breathes throughout was quite foreign to our poet in the years immediately succeeding the death of Henry VII., and the idealistic language which rings out in the conclusion of the letter is not that of the hardly-tried man inwardly yearning after his native city, but that of the scholar who sits tranquilly at his desk and meditates upon the way in which in a given case it befits a philosopher to speak and to act. Upon internal evidence the letter betrays itself in every sentence and every line for a rhetorical exercise, a clumsy patchwork of later times.

As for the external evidence for its genuineness, this is if possible even in a worse position than the internal. As regards manuscripts the character of the only one which contains the letter is such as to make it highly suspicious. The amnesty granted to the Florentine exiles in 1316, which forms the historical occasion of the letter, is not an established fact, nor is it at all probable that a few months after the poet and his sons had been condemned to death he would have been allowed to return to Florence under the same conditions as all the other exiles. But with regard to the alleged fact all contemporaries are absolutely silent. Dante himself, often as he complains of his exile and of the injustice done to him, often as he gives touching expression to his burning desire of returning to his beloved city, nowhere in his writings gives the least hint that he might have returned had not his sense of honour prevented him from accepting the humiliating and undignified conditions which were set before him. Yet he would have had plenty of opportunity for doing so. In P. xvii. the sorrows of exile are depicted at some length, and the poet's own feeling finds vigorous expression. Was not this passage obviously the place at which to mention the shame devised for him by the harsh conditions connected with the amnesty, and the noble pride with which he had rejected the proffered grace? Why then did he preserve absolute silence about it? especially when he had thought it his duty not to pass over in silence matters of far less importance. Again the touching lamentation over his banishment in P. xxv. 1 *sqq*. is quite inconceivable in the form in which we have it if under whatsoever conditions the gates of the poet's city had been open to him. If that had really taken place an allusion to the unacceptableness of the conditions could have been lacking here all the less that the verses of reproach and yearning are directly addressed to the Florentines, and he must have seen what an obvious retort they would have had. They could have maintained with obvious justice that the cruelty of which he complained was already overcome, and that it now rested with him to overcome his own pride. From their point of view they would have been justified in replying, 'We have permitted you to return to Florence under the usual conditions with which all amnestied exiles must comply. If your pride does not allow you to accept these conditions like the rest, or if you imagine that we shall make an exception favourable in your case and recall you with honour, that is your fault not ours. The cruelty which keeps you out and is not yet overcome is simply and solely the cruelty of your own unbending pride!' Such a man as Dante would surely have foreseen so easy and so apparently well-grounded an argument, and would certainly have forestalled it; but this he has not done. The passage is thus irreconcilable with the contents of the letter, and as it was undoubtedly written after 1316, it follows logically that the letter cannot have been written by Dante, and that the poet knew nothing of any amnesty being offered him under any conditions whatever.

Nor does Villani know anything of it By his honourable recognition of Dante's innocence he tacitly admits that his fellow-citizens and the members of his party were guilty of a grave injustice towards the poet. Why does he not mention that they had tried at least partially to remedy the injustice, and that the gates of the city had been re-opened to him, though he himself, from pride or from a noble self-respect, had rejected the proffered favour. Villani had a double motive for drawing attention to the matter. In the first place he would be doing some little towards rehabilitating the Florentines, and further he would have a characteristic instance to illustrate the charge which he brings against Dante of being conceited and sensitive. And yet he is here as completely silent as he was at an earlier point, when mentioning the summons to Count Guy of Battifolle, and the reforms carried out by him in 1316. This silence is eloquent,—that Villani, who in 1316 was a man of mature years, knew nothing of an amnesty offered to the poet is hardly conceivable, that he knew of it and said nothing about it is still less so.

Boccaccio, in the part of his work where he is talking about Dante's characteristics and faults, tells the following anecdote:

> Our poet was of a lofty disdainful spirit, insomuch that when efforts were being made by a certain friend of his, who was acting at Dante's instance and request, to obtain permission for him to return to Florence, which thing he desires greatly beyond all else, and no means being found of dealing with those who at that time had the government of the republic in their hands, save only the following: that he should stay for a certain space in prison, and thereafter should in some public solemnity be presented as a subject for mercy to our principal church, and should consequently be free and clear of every condemnation previously passed upon him; the which thing appeared to him to be fitting and usual in the case of degraded and infamous men and not of others, wherefore, contrary to his own greatest desire, he preferred rather to stay in exile than to return home by such a road.

Between this anecdote and our letter there exists a connection so close that even verbal coincidences are not lacking. Therefore one of three things: Boccaccio knew the letter and used it as genuine, or the letter was fabricated later on the basis of Boccaccio's anecdote, or Boccaccio knew it and did not consider it genuine.

The first view cannot be held; Boccaccio's anecdote is merely intended to give an example of Dante's lofty and unbending spirit, and can therefore claim no higher historical value than other anecdotes of the same biographer. In the part of his work which was to be strictly biographical, Boccaccio does not say a syllable about this affair, nor does he do so in his later commentary. This silence, just at the point where there would have been a good opportunity of telling the story, is made all the more suspicious by the fact that his long and eloquent invective against the Florentines for banishing the poet and not recalling him would have been impossible in its extant form if he had known anything of the offer of an amnesty. In that case a man like Boccaccio would surely not have missed the opportunity of presenting his readers with some elegant rhetoric quite after his own style concerning the unworthy conditions which the Florentines required from Dante. This silence of Boccaccio at a decisive point shows that he knew nothing of the proposed amnesty.

Nor is Boccaccio silent merely. He speaks also, and where he speaks he himself supports the spuriousness of the letter. He, too, mentions the hope which the poet had nourished for years of returning to Florence, but adds quite plainly that this hope was for ever frustrated by the death of the Emperor Henry VII. He writes, 'By reason of this death all those who had held by him lost in common all these hopes; but, above all, Dante, who, without taking any thought of return, went over the Apennines into Romagna, where the last day of his life, which was to put an end to all his troubles, awaited him.'

On Boccaccio's own testimony, then, after Henry's death, there was no more talk of a return to Florence, and Dante himself gave up all hope. How rightly he judged we may see from the sentence of November 6, 1315. In order to save the historical accuracy of the anecdote given above, we need only assume that Boccaccio is recounting an incident which took place before Henry's march to Rome. But at that time Dante could not speak about his exile of nearly fifteen years, therefore he could not have written this letter. It might indeed be attempted, in order to save the letter and the story, by making a small alteration in the reading, to change the three lustres to two; but not only does history know nothing of any amnesty offered to the poet before the date of Henry's march to Rome, but the documents of 1311 and 1315 prove just the contrary.

Leonardo Bruni agrees with Boccaccio. 'When the Emperor Henry died at Buonconvento, Dante had no further hope left. He had cut off for himself the path of mercy by his contemptuous outcries against the government of the republic, and there was no longer any power upon which he could base his hopes. Therefore he let every hope go, and passed the rest of his life in poverty in Lombardy, Tuscany, and in Romagna under the protection of various lords, until he went to Ravenna, where his life terminated.' That is clear enough, and agrees with all the facts known to us; but if, as necessarily results from this, the amnesty of 1316, so far as concerns Dante, is a simple fable, the poet was not in a position to refuse it nor consequently to write the letter.

Whether it was forged on the basis of Boccaccio's anecdote we cannot venture to affirm. According to the letter, the conditions of the amnesty were first the payment of a certain sum, and secondly the undergoing of the disgrace of offering the penalty in conjunction with a confession of guilt. The second condition we find in Boccaccio; but in the place of the money fine, he speaks of a certain term of imprisonment. The similarity of the *certam quantitatem* of the letter with the *certo spazio* of Boccaccio is surely not accidental, though a money fine and a term of imprisonment are different things. Since, however, the connection between the anecdote and the letter is undeniable, we ask how the variation arose. The answer to this might be 'from more mature consideration.' The poet, exiled and deprived of his goods, who was going about almost in a state of mendicancy, would hardly have any sum of money at his disposal, and thus the payment of a fine came to be changed to a term of imprisonment. This touch seems to betray the later reflection, for it is impossible to see on what grounds any one inventing the letter afterwards should have converted Boccaccio's imprisonment to the payment of a fine. At any rate this contradiction shows how untrustworthy is the whole story of the amnesty.

There is yet one more view to be considered, that Boccaccio knew of the letter but regarded it as spurious. But can we not go a step farther? May we not raise a question whether Boccaccio had not some share in the composition of this letter and others which exist in the same Codex? Our letter and that of the so-called Frate Ilario are simply fancy exercises in rhetorical style. Both appear in the germ, no doubt, but still in their complete substance in Boccaccio's biography of Dante, and the one manuscript in which both are maintained is closely connected with Boccaccio, some having thought that it was actually written by him, others that it belonged to him. Are we, however, therefore to suspect Boccaccio of having himself been the forger? Certainly not. No one who knows the honourable and excellent author of the *Decameron* but is aware that he was certainly incapable of forgery. Yet how, if the letters really owe their origin to him? Suppose they were merely preparatory exercises to the composition of the biography, written, not the least in the intention of forging and deceiving, but as harmless rhetorical exercise, just as ancient and modern historians have freely composed countless speeches and addresses of princes or generals. It is possible that future researches, and more especially a thorough, careful, and scientific testing of the manuscript in question, may some day give a decisive answer to this. It must suffice here to have shown that the famous letter to the Florentine friend was not and cannot have been of Dante's writings, and that the touching chapters in former biographies which have been based upon it are simply and solely the creation of fancy.[1]

XIV. To Can Grande della Scala, Lord of Verona.—As has been already remarked, this is rather a dedication of the *Paradise* than a letter in the strictest sense. The author begins with relating how Can Grande's wide-spread fame had moved him to visit the court of Verona in order to convince himself of its truth, and that he had there found something greater and of more renown than he had heard at a distance, and that had made him Can Grande's most devoted friend. He excuses himself for using the word friend, standing as he did so far below the prince, since true friendship can exist between men of very unequal social rank. His desire is to preserve this friendship, his most precious treasure, and he wishes for this reason to offer the prince something of value. But he had found nothing suitable except that exalted division of the *Commedia* which is adorned with the title of the *Paradise*, and which he proposes by these presents to assign to him. Then follows a pretty full introduction to the *Commedia* in general, and of the *Paradise* in particular, which is of great importance to the interpretation of the poem, and to which we shall recur in the next part. The opening verses of the first canto of the *Paradise* are then expounded, and the writer excuses himself for being compelled for private reasons to pretermit any further commentary, and much else that may be of use to the public. Meanwhile he hopes that the prince will grant him the means of proceeding hereafter to this useful explanation.

With regard to the genuineness of this piece there has been more controversy than about any other writing of or ascribed to the poet. Yet the discussions have not yet led

[1] See note, p. 158.

to an even approximately certain result. Unfortunately the battle has not always been conducted in a fashion such as science would approve. The letter contains a pretty complete system for the explanation of the *Commedia*, and accordingly those who maintained this system were always throwing it in the teeth of their opponents that they attacked the genuineness of the piece solely on the ground that if it were once admitted their whole interpretation was condemned, while the others could reply with equal justice or injustice that interest in the system of interpretation was the sole motive for defending the genuineness. When we on our side express clearly the view that we hold the system of interpretation formulated in the letter for the only one that is right and genuinely Dantesque, but that none the less we are unable to convince ourselves that the thing is genuine, we venture to hope that no reproach can touch us from one side or the other. If it ever comes about that the genuineness is certainly established and all doubt on the matter completely discarded, we shall, in the event of our living to see it, rejoice with our whole heart, therefore obviously we can only touch upon the question here; any one who wants to go into it fully must look into the works of such people as Ferrazzi, Scolari, Giuliani, Scheffer-Boichorst, and Bartoli. The attack upon its genuineness was headed by Scolari, who has published a long list of works both large and small on the subject; while Giuliani is among its defenders, and with him may be mentioned Blanc and Witte.

Against this genuineness it used to be loudly asserted that no thirteenth-century manuscript of it was known; this objection, however, may now be dismissed. According to a document discovered by Giuliani, Philip Villani, the historian's nephew, when he entered in 1391 upon the office of Dante professor at Florence, began by expounding the letter to Can Grande. Moreover the letter itself was found in a MS. which belongs undoubtedly to the end of the fourteenth century, while the Munich MS. which contains the first portion of it appears to be not much later in date. But even though it be established that the piece existed by the end of the fourteenth century, it does not absolutely follow that it was really composed by Dante. In the half-century and more after his death many things may have been written and ascribed to him. Besides in the fourteenth century it was thought a very harmless matter to ascribe to an author writings which did not belong to him, and it is foolish to begin talking about forgery.

The internal character of the letter, and the spirit in which it is written, tell heavily in favour of its genuineness, but the older commentaries are written in much the same spirit, and a fragment of a commentary might easily be cast into the form of a dedication. It has been said that the old commentators such as the so-called *Ottimo*, or Dante's son Peter, knew the letter, since passages occur in them which agree precisely with certain passages in it. This is quite true, but the inexplicable and suspicious point is that those old commentators should have known the piece and used it without naming it. Why did not Jacopo della Lana or Boccaccio appeal to Dante as their authority if they were making use of one of his writings? Ought we not to look at the matter from the other end, and hold that the letter was put together on the basis of the old commentaries? In this connection Boccaccio's commentary is instructive. We find in it long passages which, if the exact contrary is not the fact, were simply translated from the Latin dedication. Yet Boccaccio never appeals to Dante's authority, just as in his biography he is absolutely silent about the letter to Can Grande, which surely deserved to be named among Dante's work. What is yet more curious, if it be genuine, Boccaccio had it under his eyes and made a diligent use of it. But he explains the title of the poem in agreement with the explanation which is given in the letter to Can Grande, yet instead of appealing to the poet's own authority he introduces his explanation with the word 'credo,' 'I believe.' But why 'believe' if he had Dante's own statement before his eyes? Thus it is by no means proved that the old commentators knew and used the letter to Can Grande. A fact on the other side is that up to the present day the letter has never been found mentioned by biographers or commentators until we come to Philip Villani in 1391. Those who accept it as genuine regard it as having been composed in 1318 or 1319. But could Dante then have said that he was still a novice in the favour of Can Grande as he does in the letter? And could he well dedicate the *Paradise* in 1318 or 1319 when it was perhaps begun, but certainly far from being finished?

Section vii. of the dedication is taken, even to the illustrations, from *Convito* ii. 7, which is not generally Dante's way. Just as little is he accustomed, in the explanation of his own poems, to speak of himself in the third person. Yet we will not here go farther into the question, the limits of this work do not allow of it, and we are not at present in a position to express a definite judgment. The question like so many others is still in suspense.

Lastly we have to mention a poetical correspondence in Latin. A young admirer of our poet, nicknamed from his efforts to imitate Virgil 'Joannes de Virgilio,' being at that time a teacher at Bologna, addressed to him, somewhere about the summer of 1319, a Latin poem. He invites

Dante to Bologna, and expresses his astonishment that Dante should have undertaken to write in the vernacular a work of the dignity of the *Commedia*. The young man was modest enough to exhort the old poet to set forth more suitable matter in a more noble and classical draping. He carried his artlessness to the point of suggesting to Dante a list of subjects for poetic treatment. In reply Dante sent him a pastoral poem in which he professes to have read the verses sent to him while staying with a friend beside the pasturing flocks. He calls himself Tityrus, his friend Dino Perini, Meliboeus, and Joannes, Mopsus. In playful style Dante praises his young admirer on account of his poetic studies, approves his learning, and goes into abundant eulogy of his studies and their success, with a side stroke at those who busied themselves with jurisprudence. Then striking a more serious note, he complains that in this unreceptive time not only poetic ornament, but the very name of poet is as good as forgotten, so that the muse had scarcely succeeded in making Mopsus a poet for all his nightly watching. For himself, indeed, he longs for the laurel wreath, but hesitates to accept it in Guelfic Bologna with no taste for poetry. It were better and more fortunate if he should ever return home to adorn his hair, once blonde now grey, for his triumph and to conceal it under the laurel. He does not know whether his life will last long enough to see the wish fulfilled, for not until the completion of the *Commedia* will the time arrive, with Mopsus' permission, to crown his head with ivy and bay. With proud self-knowledge Dante passes briefly over the reproach of writing in the vulgar tongue and does not deign any refutation of his young critic's reasons, but in order to content him he sends him this Latin eclogue, which concludes with an allusion to the hard lot of exile and to the poverty of the poet.

Joannes de Virgilio adopted the note struck by Dante, and cast his reply also into the form of a pastoral poem. In this he applauds Dante's Latin verse, encourages him to hope for a speedy return to Florence, and invites him in the meantime to Bologna, where scholars will await him with eagerness, and where he will make the acquaintance of Albertino Mussato. In a second poem Dante declines the invitation with the remark that he must beware of King Robert of Naples. There is no lack in it of instruction or of smart hits, but the young Virgilian enthusiast made no reply, and the correspondence came to an end. An unknown contemporary states that Dante let his second rejoinder wait for over a year, and that not till he was dead was it found and forwarded by his son.

Villani has not mentioned our poet's eclogues, whence one must conclude that he did not know of them. Boccaccio and Bruni, however, knew them. The former writes, 'Besides this, Dante composed two very beautiful eclogues which he addressed to the teacher Joannes de Virgilio, in reply to certain verses which the latter had sent him.' Bruni, after remarking that Dante had more talent for writing in the vernacular than in Latin, says, 'A proof of this are his eclogues composed in hexameters, which, allowing that they are beautiful, are not so good as plenty that we have seen.' After this evidence, to which may be added that of the unknown contemporary, there can be no question of their genuineness. All the same, doubts, by no means unfounded, have been cast upon them. For our part we hold them for genuine, but must admit that our belief in them is by no means equal to a rock in firmness.

CHAPTER VII

APOCRYPHAL WORKS

BESIDES those works that we have discussed there are sundry others attributed to our poet with which he had nothing to do. Even of the fourteen letters ascribed to him, more than half, as we have seen, are decidedly spurious, and nearly all the others more or less doubtful. As we have also mentioned, people regarded these in former times otherwise, we might say in more childish fashion, than is now the case. But history teaches by only too many examples that mistakes are easily possible even in the times of most enlightened criticism.

The research of the present day takes very justly no longer any account of such statements as those of Filelfo, according to whom Dante composed a history of the Guelfs and Ghibelines, and heaven knows what besides. That very many lyric poems in manuscript and editions have been wrongly assigned to our poet can no longer be doubted, though it is not always easy in particular cases to distinguish between genuine and spurious. How the most acute critics can go astray in such matters is proved by the history of the sonnets exchanged between Dante and Forese Donati. We have, however, said all that is necessary about the lyric poems, nor need we waste any time over such works as the *Laude in onore di Nostra Donna*, published by Bonucci in 1584, or Mainardi's *Nuovo Credo di Dante*, since nobody regards them as genuine. We must, however, make a few remarks on the *Penitential Psalms*, the *Creed*, and the treatise *De aquâ et terrâ*.

The *Penitential Psalms* and the *Creed* are in *terza rima ;* the former consist of rather free paraphrases of the seven Psalms known by that name. To all appearance the poet used the text of the Vulgate, but also borrowed from ancient and mediaeval expounders certain dogmatic expansions. Of these it is sufficient to say that the sixth Psalm is expanded to sixteen tercets, the thirty-second to twenty-six, and so on, so that each psalm makes a complete canto.

The *Creed* consists of eighty-three tercets and contains an introduction, a paraphrase of the Apostles' Creed, and some tercets on the seven sacraments, the ten commandments, the seven deadly sins, *Pater Noster*, and the *Ave Maria*. In order to see the difference between Dante and the anonymous poetaster, we need only compare the *Pater Noster* as here given with that of the opening of Purg. xi., the latter being magnificent poetry, the former a tedious rhyming paraphrase.

According to an anecdote contained in a manuscript in the Riccardian library at Florence, Dante had, by reason of his stinging references in P. xii. to the Franciscans of his day, incurred the dislike of that order. Some of the friars accordingly collected the alleged heretical passages from the *Commedia*, and denounced the poet to the Inquisition as a man who did not believe in God and cared nothing for the articles of the faith. When summoned before the Inquisition, Dante begged for a night's respite in order to set forth his confession of belief, and on the following morning showed up these eighty-three tercets to the satisfaction of the spiritual court and to the confusion of his accusers. No comment is needed on this anecdote; at the present day nobody regards these rhymes as Dante's work, though they are common enough in manuscripts. Formerly they were accepted by such people as Rossetti, Artaud, and Balbo.

The work to which we now have to refer was till lately, on the contrary, universally received as genuine. In 1508 Manfredo da Monteferrato published at Venice a quarto volume, the long-winded title of which we may give in the original :

Quaestio florulenta at perutilis de duobus elementis aquae et terrae tractans ; nuper reperta, quae olim Mantuae auspicata Veronae vero disputata et decisa ac manu propriâ scripta a Dante florentino poetâ clarissimo. Quae diligenter et accurate correcta fuit per reverendum magistrum Joannem Benedictum Mancettum de Castilione Arretino regentem Patavinum ordinis eremitarum divi Augustini sacraeque Theologiae doctorem excellentissimum.

For shortness' sake this work is quoted simply under the title *De aquâ et terrâ*. It is a report written, as alleged, by Dante himself of a public disputation which he held at Verona on Jan. 20, 1320, and relates to the question with regard to the position and figure of the two elements of earth and water. The object is to inquire whether the water, namely, the sea, is at any part of its sphere higher than the land which comes out of it, a question to which great importance was assigned, and which in Dante's day was generally answered in the affirmative, as for instance by Brunetto in his *Trésor*. The treatise, on the other hand, after examining the more important arguments for the affirmative, answers it decisively in the opposite sense. The question may strike us at the present day as strange ; but if the treatise—which, so far as its form goes, follows throughout the scholastic method, but in the views expressed is far in advance of the ideas of Dante's time, and approaches those of recent science—was really composed by Dante, we are here in presence of a miracle. Dante must have known the theory developed two hundred years later by Leonardo da Vinci, or must at least have had a clear presentiment of it. He must have been in possession of discoveries which future generations were the first to make. Stoppani has discovered that the little work contains nine truths of cosmology hitherto undreamt of which were in part foreseen, in part distinctly asserted, and in part proved, and which form the bases of modern science, namely, (1) the moon is the main cause of ebb and flow, (2) equality of the level of the sea, (3) centripetal force, (4) spherical form of the earth, (5) that the dry land is merely excrescences from the earth's surface, (6) the grouping of continents towards the north, (7) universal attraction, (8) the elasticity of steam as a motive power, (9) upheaval of the continents. Dante must indeed have been a wonderful man![1]

This time even the most credulous will be tempted to unbelief, and will ask whether it is really certain that Dante, who died in 1321, can have known all this, or, in other words, whether the genuineness of the treatise was open to no doubt. Torri, Fraticelli, Giuliani, and others have replied that it cannot be, for it bears Dante's name; he designates himself expressly as the author, accurately describes the place, time, and reason of its composition, and even adds the precise information that he wrote out the treatise with his own hand. But is not this circumstantiality of itself suspicious and quite contrary to Dante's style?

[1] It may be worth while to point out that we have other evidence to show that Dante was not ignorant of some of the most important among these physical facts.

Does not deliberate intention come too abruptly to view, and would not all this detail be sufficient to arouse suspicions of a forgery? 'But,' replies Giuliani, 'the thoughts, the mode of expression, the style, the manner of the demonstration all betray the spirit of the great poet who wrote also the books upon monarchy and upon the vernacular speech.' This is a subjective reason which has not the shadow of objective value. We who have searched through Dante's works no less frequently and industriously, find in the treatise nothing whatever of his style and yet less of his spirit, and if, as has been further urged, passages of this work agree with others from the *De Monarchiâ*, this proves in any case only that the forger had read and made use of that treatise.

It is just the 'new cosmologic truths,' as we said, which awaken doubt, and raise it to a certainty that, at the beginning of the fourteenth century, such things could not be and were not stated, and if we try to come to terms with the assumption that Dante was announcing beforehand discoveries of the future, the miracle would become yet more miraculous. For if Dante delivered that treatise before all the learned world of Verona, it is obvious that its contents must have aroused very considerable notice, and yet not a word was said about it. No single chronicler, no single member of the audience, no single contemporary writer has, so far as we know, taken the very slightest notice of these new facts of cosmology. No word, no sound was uttered against it in spite of the many opponents who are spoken of in the treatise. No report, direct or indirect, has been preserved of a fact of such importance which took place in the presence of the whole city of Verona, and it would have remained for ever forgotten had not the good Father Moncetti, two hundred years later, produced and made known the treatise which, according to him, had rested for many olympiads in the bookcase.

Of all the biographers and commentators, no single one has any knowledge of this work which ought to have done more, if possible, for the poet's fame than the *Divina Commedia* itself, nor has had a single syllable to say about it; and of this work, for its date an epoch-making one, not one single manuscript has been preserved except the one which lay for many olympiads in the bookcase, which Father Moncetti produced, and which from that time appears, alas! to have been again lost.

To those—and there are such—who still believe in the genuineness of this compilation, which rests entirely upon a theory, or, if you like, discovery of Leonardo da Vinci, we may tranquilly say 'show us a single manuscript of the treatise belonging to the fourteenth or even the fifteenth century and we will do our very best to believe;' but the appearance of any such manuscript may be awaited calmly without any agitation. Until that time there can be no talk among reasonable men of seeing in Moncetti's publication a work by our poet. He himself, the fortunate discoverer and editor, testifies that the manuscript which he produced was in many places corrupt; but if the treatise was up to that time wholly unknown, and he was the first to discover a manuscript of it, how could he possibly know that it was corrupt, or in what places it was so? Again, at the end it was expressly said that the treatise has been emended, polished, and set in order by Moncetti. Now, assuming that he had a genuine work of Dante before him, how far did his emendations and improvements extend? How much of the treatise as we now know it belongs to Father Moncetti and how much to Dante? If Moncetti's emendations and embellishments introduced into it the new facts of cosmology which had been discovered shortly before his publication of it, what remains for Dante? and who was Father Moncetti? Torelli tells us—one of the most distinguished and eminent mathematicians and astronomers of his time, which seems sufficient. It is really extraordinary with what carelessness this palpable forgery has been accepted for a genuine production of Dante's, and has served as a foundation for biographical and other structures. Still more wonderful and truly touching is the naïveté with which, on the strength of this fabrication, people have tried to fix Dante's position in the history of cosmography. Let us give credit to Tiraboschi and Pelli, Troya and Foscolo, Balbo and Bartoli, as well as to later inquirers, who have not nibbled at this bait.

PART V
THE 'DIVINA COMMEDIA'

CHAPTER I

ORIGIN OF THE POEM

IN the first ode of the *Vita Nuova*, § 19, Dante, to the glorification of his Beatrice, sings that the angels in Heaven are wishing to have her there, and pray God to call her back from earth, since she is the one thing lacking to Heaven. But God in His mercy replies, 'Have patience; let her remain in the world below so long as pleases Me. There is one there that fears to lose her who will say to the lost ones in Hell, "I have seen the hope of the Blessed."'

In these last words is plainly expressed the intention of some day celebrating his beloved in a poem, the outward form of which was to be a pilgrimage through the realms of the next world or at least through that to perdition. And here we have the first perceptible germ of the idea of the *Divina Commedia*. Any other interpretation of the words appears artificial and far-fetched. It has been suggested that the poet merely wished to bring into prominence the distance between himself and his love without any thought of a future poem—to represent her as a saint destined for and desired in Heaven while he was a poor sinner deserving Hell. But nowhere in the *Vita Nuova* is there the least trace of this miserable sinner feeling. On the contrary a feeling of peace as of a child of God breathes all through it. Besides, however sinful he may have felt, Dante would never have descended to the monstrous blasphemy of designating himself in his youth as one of the lost. Indeed in the very next strophe he says just the contrary: 'Whoso has spoken with Beatrice can come to no ill end.' Nay, the *Vita Nuova* concludes with the expression of the hope to see her again in the glory of Heaven. A not less questionable solution is that which understands by Hell and the lost folk this sinful world with its, for the most part corrupt, inhabitants, a conception which is quite foreign to the *Vita Nuova*. These interpretations owe their existence to the fact that it seems incredible that Dante can have formed an idea of the *Divina Commedia* before 1290, the date of Beatrice's death. Accordingly people have tried to get out of the difficulty by supposing the ode to have been recast afterwards, and in its original form to have been without the second strophe. This theory, however, has been once for all upset by the manuscript of the notary Peter Allegranza of Bologna, dated 1292; but not much is gained thereby, for it cannot in any case be denied that the conclusion of the *Vita Nuova* points to the great poem which was to come.

It would thus be a wilful closing of the eyes to light if we refuse to admit that, even before Beatrice's death, Dante had formed the idea of his great poem. We must not, however, understand this as meaning that he had at that time already begun to lay down the plan of it. We have only to deal with the first germ from which long afterwards the noble tree grew. It is quite certain that at that time the poet had not dreamt of such a work as the *Commedia*. He could not, indeed, have any notion of such a work, since he was still only in the first of his three stages of development. Nothing further was in his intention, nothing more is promised in the conclusion of the *Vita Nuova* than a poem to the glorification of Beatrice. At that time his insight reached no farther than to see that, if he were to carry out his idea worthily, he needed studies quite other than he had hitherto followed, and the determination to pursue them with all his power. Accordingly, as the conclusion of the *Vita Nuova* proves beyond a doubt, he postponed the execution of the work with full knowledge of what he was doing. The *Convito* tells of the studies with which he occupied the interval, and puts off still farther the execution of the old idea, but declares that it is by no means abandoned. In this work Dante will say no more about the blessed Beatrice; he will do this in another work hereafter to be written. But at the time when he wrote the *Convito*, the plan of this work hereafter to be written must have been pretty narrowly limited. At that time he certainly did not think of a universal all-embracing poem. He had just begun a work, the dimensions of which, in the event of its being completed, could not be calculated. Simultaneously he had announced another work, the *De Vulgari Eloquentiâ*, the execution of which would also be the work of years, and it is self-evident that he could not at that time have been thinking of a work like the *Divina Commedia*, even though we were unaware that, when he wrote the *Vulgari Eloquentiâ*, he did not even dream of dealing in poetry with the matters of which he treated in the *Commedia*. We thus arrive at the result, rendered certain, we think, by Dante's own declarations and indications, that before 1290 he had formed the idea of a poem, to take the form of a spiritual pilgrimage through the realms of the dead, with the aim of glorifying the love of his youth; that he held fast to this idea, consciously and with a firm intention of carrying it out; that this idea, originally limited, expanded itself more and more into the mighty plan which reached its fulfilment in the *Commedia*.

Now, however, the question arises, When was the plan matured, and when did the poet set to work to carry it out? In any case, as we may see with certainty from the allusions in both works, this did not take place until after Dante had begun to occupy himself with the composition of the *Convito* and of the *De Vulgari Eloquentiâ*.

Next, let us see what we can get from history towards the answering of the question. At the very beginning, in the introductory canto, there appears the mysterious form of the *Veltro*, who is prophesied of as the saviour of Italy. The great majority of commentators see in this an allusion to Can Grande della Scala. If this interpretation is correct, it follows that the canto in its present form cannot have been composed before the death of Henry of Luxemburg. Up to 1309 Can Grande had achieved nothing to induce the hope that he might be the saviour of Italy. Up to that time he had been only co-regent with his elder brother Alboin, and was in no way specially eminent. But up till the date of Henry's march to Rome, Dante expected the salvation of Italy to come from him and not from any Italian prince. It was not until Henry's death, when Can Grande became sole ruler and imperial vicar, that he could draw any attention to himself, and justify the hopes which find expression in the first canto of Dante's *Commedia*. This argument is equally good for those who think that we ought to see Uguccione della Faggiuola in the *Veltro*, but in any case the argument applies to all those for whom the *Veltro* imports either Can Grande or Uguccione.

In the sixth canto of the *Hell* Dante foretells, through the mouth of the Florentine Ciacco, the important events of the year 1301, and all that followed until the final banishment of the Whites in 1304, whence it necessarily follows that this canto must have been written after that date. But it is also said of the Black party that they would carry their heads on high for a long time, an expression obviously denoting a long series of years. Thus several years after 1304 must have elapsed when Dante wrote this canto, a conclusion which another passage places out of all doubt. In H. xix. 76 *sqq*. Dante makes Nicolas III., Pope from 1277-1280, say that Boniface VIII. will relieve him, but will not brandish his feet in the third *bolgia* as long as he himself has done—meaning that he will in turn be relieved by Clement V., Pope from 1305-1314. In the year 1300, when Dante's vision is feigned to take place, Nicolas had been in that position for twenty years. Now, if Dante knew that Boniface, who reigned from 1294-1303, would not remain so long in that painful situation, but be sooner relieved by Clement, he must, when he wrote the canto, have known of Clement's death [1]; for we can hardly assume him to have had a prophetic knowledge of the date when a Pope would die. There can then be no doubt that the nineteenth canto of the *Hell* was written after April 1314; and as it is hardly a likely coincidence that Dante should have been engaged upon that canto at the very time when he heard of the Pope's death, we may put the date of its composition even somewhat later.

In Purg. vii. 96, Dante says that Henry's exertions to heal Italy and restore the imperial power would come too late. We need no further proof that these lines were

---

[1] This does not absolutely follow. With the exception of Innocent III. (1198-1216) no Pope for many centuries had held the see for anything like eighteen years; so it would be a pretty safe prophecy that Clement would replace Boniface before 1323. From the moment of Clement's election Dante would assuredly have destined him for Malebolge. If we suppose the three years which Nicolas still had to spend in his inverted attitude to be taken into consideration, the prophecy becomes still safer.

written after the Luxemburg Emperor's departure from the scene.

Boccaccio is able to relate that at the poet's death the *Commedia* lay still incomplete, since the last thirteen cantos of the *Paradise* were lacking. All search for them was fruitless, and only a miraculous dream led to their discovery. Whatever may be thought of this anecdote, it is clear from it that the poet completed his great work only just before his death, and was not permitted himself to publish the final cantos; for if they had appeared in his lifetime, the story of the discovery would be unintelligible.

We are thus on firm historical ground when we say that Dante began to work at the *Divina Commedia* as we now have it after the death of Henry VII., and completed it in the last months, perhaps the last days, of his life. Research is not as yet in a position to enable us to fix more accurately the date at which the whole or individual portions came into existence. If the poetic correspondence with Joannes de Virgilio is genuine, it follows that by 1319 the *Hell*, and perhaps also the *Purgatory*, were completed and even published—a view which other evidence (given by Witte, *Dante-Forschungen*, xi. 137 *sqq.*) confirms. It is hardly likely that, in the deep depression following Henry's death, and the ruin of his own hopes, Dante would have applied himself to the great work in the later months of 1313; so that we seem forced to the conclusion that the *Commedia* came into existence between 1314 and 1321. If it is objected that such a work could hardly have been produced in the last seven or eight years of a broken man's life, we can merely ask for proof of the possibility that Canto xix. of the *Hell* can have been written before 20th April 1314,[1] and for any evidence that Dante was by

[1] See note on last page.

his forty-seventh year a worn-out man or verging upon senility.

But Dante has referred to the year 1300 the vision described in his sublime poem; and why should he have done this when he did not set to work upon it till fourteen years later? No doubt he had good reasons, though we do not know them. We must, however, entirely reject the notion that there is any question of an actual vision which took place in that year. Dante was no visionary enthusiast; the vision is merely the poetic form selected by him in which to clothe his thoughts. He no more experienced actually the visions of the *Commedia* than those of the *Vita Nuova*. He may well have had reasons for putting the fictitious vision in the period before his exile. The year of Jubilee may have produced upon him, as upon the whole Christendom of the time, a mighty and ineffaceable impression, and this may have continued to form a motive for his poetic fiction. Besides, if he wished, as indeed he did, to depict his own spiritual development glorified in poetry, it is obvious that he could not represent it as beginning with the death of Henry VII. Inward revolutions are accomplished gradually; even Saul did not become Paul between to-day and to-morrow. Saul withdrew for three full years into the desert, and then, but not till then, did he return to the scene as Paul. Dante reproaches himself with the fact that many impressions produced either no result, or, at any rate, not such as was wished and intended. Like other men, he had his transition period, which he has indeed depicted at the outset of his poem. At the starting-point of the vision—that is, according to his poetic fiction, in the year 1300—the poet first becomes aware, with horror, that he has gone astray in a dark and savage forest. He sees the hill-top illumined by the sun, and sets out to climb the hill. But he is hindered by the three wild beasts, and is only delivered from his difficult position by Virgil, and that not until he has fought out the fight with his own cowardice. That inward experiences of long duration are here depicted is no less obvious than that the poet represents them as the experiences of one day. Thus, the very beginning of the poem refers us, for the real action of the grand drama, to a date which is separated from the year 1300 by a long period of transition, and so far from this opening postulating an earlier composition of the cantos in question, it rather serves to establish the result we have already obtained.

But this result—namely, that the *Commedia* in its present form was begun in 1314 and finished in 1321—must not be understood as implying that the poet had not up to that time written a single verse. The actual working out of the poem was preceded by a long period of preparation. We have seen that the first idea of it goes back to the year 1290, and that he was at work upon it thenceforward, he says plainly at the end of the *Vita Nuova*. Indeed, according to his plain declaration in all his studies of that time, he had nothing in view but the lofty aim of the future poem. That he afterwards went aside from this aim we have plain proof in the *Convito* and the *De Vulgari Eloquentiâ*, and it is plainly enough stated for all who can read it in the concluding vision of the *Purgatory*. Yet it appears, from various passages, that he never quite lost sight of this aim. In Conv. ii. 9, he intimates his purpose of speaking again in another place of the departed Beatrice. In Purg. xxx. 129, he allows himself to be reproached with a diminution in his love for Beatrice, but not with having totally forgotten her.

But if he did not lose sight of his aim, it follows that he must have been working towards it. We can indeed only conjecture and form more or less sure conclusions as to the actual nature of the preparatory work. In a wider sense all Dante's smaller writings may be called preparatory works, since their material, his own experience of life, his philosophy, and his statesmanship were transmuted into precious metal in the great poem. In a narrower sense we may regard the preparatory work as a kind of collecting of materials, whereby the materials for the great structure were worked up and got ready beforehand. There is some truth in the objection that a work like the *Commedia* could not have come into existence in the last seven or eight years of the poet's life. It would be inconceivable if we had to assume that when he was working up the first canto in the year 1314 no one of the 14,233 lines of which the poem consists was written. We must assume that thousands of verses and tercets, entire episodes, similes, and descriptions were all ready when the poet at length set seriously to work upon the execution of his mighty plan. Those were the materials which he converted into the structure, just as men convert building materials. To keep up the metaphor, we must say that one stone fitted here, another there, a third elsewhere with a little previous chipping. Many stones would not fit the structure, and had to be laid aside as useless; others needed to be freshly shaped and made ready for their purpose, for the building was carried out with so great care that every stone had to be employed in the right place, and to be accurately suited to the whole.

The image here employed must be intelligible, and may serve to illustrate the fashion in which the great poem grew up. In much the same way does every poet and every artist work. We do not, indeed, possess the outline sketch of the *Commedia*, but we have such in the case of more recent works, and these are not, as a rule, mere skeletons. Even in the sketch the bones are now and again clothed with flesh; here one thing, there another is versified; and in the final work the verses are sometimes used as they stand, sometimes recast and modified, sometimes discarded altogether. Just in this fashion, like works of art in all times, must the *Divina Commedia* have come into existence.

Nor are tokens wanting to show that it really was so; certain episodes look as if they had been composed under the fresh impression of a recent event. For example, it would be hard to believe that the powerful episode of Count Ugolino came into existence a quarter of a century after the event. It tells the tale of a heart overpowered by that which it is describing. Further, the poem is rich in local touches, which look like photographs taken on the spot—so much so that people, starting from the assumption that when Dante began the first canto not a single verse had yet been written, have wished to turn the *Commedia* into a journal of travels, and calculate where the poet was when he composed this or that canto. This perverse imagining is based on the perfectly accurate observation that many descriptions of landscape in the *Commedia* must plainly have been sketched on the spot. The objection that Dante cannot have visited all the countries and regions of which he speaks, since, in order to do so, he must have travelled nearly all over the world, is too childish. There is a distinction between mentioning and describing. Dante does not give descriptions of the coasts of Flanders or of the deserts of Libya; what he says about them by no means implies ocular observation. On the other hand, there can be no difference of opinion as to many descriptions in the poem, which not only absolutely imply ocular observation, but which must have been produced on the spot, and not merely from recollection. That we may fully admit, but we must further remark that these descriptions were sketched as opportunity served, and afterwards made available for the great poem.

Boccaccio tells us, both in his biography and in his commentary, that Dante had written the first seven cantos before his exile, but left the manuscript behind in his flight from Florence, and therefore gave up the entire plan. It was not till some time afterwards that the manuscript was discovered at Florence and sent to the poet, whereupon he resumed the work. For the truth of his statement the writer appeals to two witnesses, Dante's nephew, Andrew Poggi, and his friend, Dino Perini. But in his commentary doubts had occurred to him, which is a proof that he did not invent the anecdote; and since the two witnesses contradicted each other, each ascribing to himself the merit of finding the manuscript, it follows that we have not to deal with an invention either of Poggi or of Perini; for if two different witnesses agree exactly, either their story is true, or they must have made it up in confederation. But in the present case confederation is excluded by the contradiction; therefore, so far as they agree, the tale must be true, though not indeed in the sense that the rediscovered MS. actually contained the first seven cantos. The sixth, as we have seen, cannot have been written till many years after the catastrophe. The view that that manuscript contained lyric poems is inadmissible, for there can have been no confusion between any such and the first cantos of the *Hell.* It must have contained something in poetical shape which the witnesses afterwards recognised in those cantos. It may have been the description of the *sciagurati*, it may have been the scene with Francesca, or what not; in any case, the manuscript can have only contained outlines or rough drafts, and have been a preparatory work or collection of materials. It is quite conceivable that, if Dante mislaid this manuscript, he would have let the plan fall through for the time, resuming it when he recovered the manuscript. Boccaccio can hardly have invented the story, but he may very well have worked it up, after his fashion, into a dramatic scene.

If, however, it was a collection of materials, whence did the poet get them? He is certainly not original in the sense of having created his materials any more than Erwin von Steinbach created the materials of which he built the Cathedral of Strasburg. Dante drew in the first instance upon his own heart and his own rich experience of life. With admirable intelligence he searched through the mysterious book of the human heart, and took from it the best part of his song. He also read carefully in the great book of nature, which indeed lies open to every man, but which only the few elect know how to read like him with acute understanding. A deep student of the soul, a keen observer, he drew plentifully from the inexhaustible well of human history. A consummate artist, he turned to account experience and fortune, character and morals, joy and sorrow, love and hatred, virtue and vice, life and death; and added thereto the collected wisdom of his age. He drew copiously on the one hand from the Bible, the Fathers, the scholastics, the mystics; on the other hand, from the classical authors of antiquity, Aristotle and Plato, Virgil, Ovid, Lucan, Statius, and Boëthius; in philosophy he is the faithful follower of Plato, Aristotle, and their commentators, in theology of Peter Lombard, Albert, and Thomas. So copiously has he drawn from these sources that the best commentaries of the *Commedia* are more than half made up of quotations illustrating the passages under discussion. The form of a journey through the realms of the next world was suggested to him by the age in which he lived; the literature of that age is so full of visions of the future state, of descriptions in prose and poetry of the torments and the bliss of eternity, that it were childish to ask which of these visions and legends Dante may have known and used. No doubt he knew many of them, but we can hardly trace anything of their influence upon his poem. He is thoroughly independent and original all the while that he is taking materials wherever he finds them.

CHAPTER II

CONTENTS

I. *Introduction.* Half-way upon the road of human life, that is to say in his thirty-fifth year, the poet wakes from a protracted slumber and observes with horror that during his sleep he has gone astray in a dark and fearful wood which is as bitter as death. How he came into it he does not know, for he was then too much overcome with sleep. He leaves the wood and reaches the foot of a hill whose summit is gilded by the morning sunlight. His fear vanishes, he rests and looks back upon the wood, then sets to work to climb the hill. But presently he sees a leopard light and fleeting, which bars his way in such fashion that he is often disposed to turn back towards the wood of terror. Presently he plucks up courage and hopes to get the better of the leopard, but he is met by a lion spurred with fierce hunger, and immediately after by a lean and ravening she-wolf. Through the horror which issues from her gaze she causes him to think the labour of climbing so great that he gives up all hope of the ascent, and is driven back more and more towards the place where the sun gives no light. As he is rushing down to lower ground there appears to him the shade of the Roman poet Virgil, who on being appealed to for help by Dante tells him that he must take another road, since that on which he is belongs to the wolf, who slays all that betake themselves to it. Her existence will continue for a long time yet, until the hound appears who shall put her to a painful death, and send her back to Hell, whence envy first called her forth. He will also be the deliverer of Italy. The way which the poets had to take leads through Hell and Purgatory, and here Virgil offers himself as guide; if Dante will ascend from the region of purification to Heaven a worthier soul will guide him, since to himself as a heathen the gates of Heaven are closed. Dante accepts the offer thankfully, and follows his leader. But when evening comes he again loses heart, and asks timidly if he be really the man to undertake such a journey. Virgil informs him that three blessed ladies, Beatrice, Lucy, and one who is unnamed, but by whom the Blessed Virgin is meant, care for him in the court of Heaven. The unnamed one has summoned Lucy. Lucy has summoned Beatrice to hasten to his help; whereupon Beatrice has descended into the nether world in order to send Virgil for his deliverance. Dante again takes heart, and follows his guide with fresh courage.

II. *Hell.* They have reached the entrance; over the gate of death Dante reads the terrible inscription: "Through me ye pass into the city of woe." It is an inscription which announces no hope of salvation. Dante shrinks again, but Virgil bids him follow without fear and without shrinking, saying that they are come to the region of the lost. He takes Dante in kindly fashion by the hand, and leads him in—

> Where sighs, with lamentations, and loud moans
> Resounded through the air pierced by no star.

They are in the outer court of Hell. In this region a banner is flying round, never resting, and after it without resting speed countless troops of spirits stung by wasps and gadflies till the blood flows mingled with their tears to their feet, and is there licked up by loathsome worms. These are the cowards, the undecided, the nonchalant; Heaven has rejected them, Hell will none of them. Among them Dante recognises one, him who 'through cowardice made the great renunciation,' and when he has recognised him he straightway knows what folk these are. The pilgrims come to the bank of Acheron, and Charon, the boatman of Hell, hesitates about ferrying a living man across. Then comes a storm with lightning, and Dante falls senseless.

On recovering consciousness, he finds himself on the farther bank of Acheron, in the first circle of Hell; the *Limbus* of mediaeval theology, where are the spirits of the virtuous persons who died unbaptized, and where also the holy men of the old dispensation resided until delivered by Christ immediately after His death. The great poets of antiquity—Homer, Horace, Ovid, Lucan—greet Dante and receive him into their company. In the second circle Hell proper begins. At the entrance is Minos, the awful judge of Hell. In this circle are punished carnal lust and unlawful love. A whirlwind drives the spirits about incessantly, up and down, hither and thither; nor can they indulge any hope of ever attaining rest. In words of touching tenderness Francesca of Rimini relates the history of her unhallowed love and her tragic end.

In the third circle are those whose god was their belly. They lie in the mud, guarded by Cerberus. Ciacco prophesies to the poet the events of 1301 and the following years. At the entrance to the fourth circle Plutus[1] blusters in unintelligible noises, to scare the pilgrims from farther progress. In one half of the circle the misers are going

---

[1] More probably Pluto is meant.

round, in the other half the spendthrifts. They howl out bitter blasphemies, come into collision at the end of the half circle, bellow one at another, and then return again in an everlasting dance of colliding and rebounding. On this text Virgil instructs his pupil with regard to Fortune, the heavenly dispenser of earthly prosperity. Hence by a dismal path the poets descend to the fifth circle, and see in the swamp of Styx the ill-tempered, all naked and covered with mud. Across Styx the ferryman is Phlegyas, who in rage against Apollo set the temple at Delphi on fire. While they are crossing spirits emerge from the marsh and stretch out their hands towards the boat, but are beaten off by Phlegyas. Dante recognises his fellow-townsman Filippo Argenti, to whose brutal rage he opposes his own righteous wrath, and is praised and congratulated for it by Virgil. Next he sees in the distance, like a mediaeval fortress, the infernal City of Dis, surrounded by deep moats, with its towers glowing red, and walls like iron. This city bounds the sixth circle, and forms the division between the upper and the nether Hell; on one side the sins of intemperance, on the other those of malice and a corrupt heart. Thousands of fiends defend the entrance to the city; high above on the top of the towers stand the Furies, calling Medusa to turn the poet to stone with the sight of her. Warned by Virgil to turn his back, Dante presses in terror close to his guide, who covers his eyes with his own hands. Earthquake and thunder follow, amid which a heavenly messenger[1] appears, before whom the devils fly affrighted. He opens the door with a wand, and vanishes without a

---

[1] Spoken of as *lautlos* in the original; but the 'heavenly messenger' delivers a speech of eight lines. Perhaps the author was misled by 'non fe motto *a noi*.' But there are several inaccuracies in this summary.

sound. The poets enter, and find that the City of Dis is a vast graveyard. Heretics and teachers of error, with their disciples, lie in red-hot tombs, whose lids are off. There is the magnanimous Farinata degli Uberti, who talks with Dante of affairs at Florence, and prophesies his banishment; Cavalcante Cavalcanti, who inquires after his son Guido; there are a Pope and an Emperor, Anastasius II. and Frederick II.; all who held that the life of the individual ended with the grave lie in red-hot graves. At the Last Day the lids will be closed, and they will lie for ever in darkness and separation from God.

Before they descend into the nether Hell, Virgil expounds the system on which the punishments are graded; so that Dante may henceforth have no need to ask, but only to look. They then go down by a slope covered with rocky *débris*, the result of the earthquake whereby all Hell was shaken when Christ descended. The way is guarded by the Cretan Minotaur, the fruit of Pasiphae's vile passion, whom Ariadne, herself half-sister to the monster, delivered into the hands of Theseus. In the three rings of this circle are punished those guilty of violence against their neighbour, against themselves, and against God. Centaurs guard the murderers and tyrants, who occupy the first ring, being plunged, more or less deeply according to the measure of their guilt, into a stream of boiling blood. Among the tyrants of antiquity are Alexander of Pherae [1] and Dionysius of Syracuse; among the more recent, the savage Ezzelin, and Obizzo, Marquis of Ferrara. All alone, sunk up to the neck in the scalding torrent, is Guy of Montfort, who killed Henry, son of Richard Earl of Cornwall. Then come Attila, Pyrrhus of Epirus, Sextus Pompey the pirate, and

---

[1] According to the older, and perhaps better, opinion the *Alessandro* of II. xii. 107 is Alexander the Great.

two dreaded highwaymen of the thirteenth century, Rinier of Corneto and Rinier "the Mad." Crossing the stream of blood on the back of Nessus, the Centaur who died on account of Deianira, the pilgrims reach the second ring of the circle, where the souls of suicides are confined in uncanny trees (preserving sensation for the purposes of their punishment), so as to form an extensive wood, in which the Harpies roost. Peter de Vineis, the Chancellor of Frederick II., relates his fate and asserts his innocence. Those who have taken their own lives[1] after squandering their possessions are hunted through the thorny wood and torn to pieces by black hounds. In the third ring, a desolate sandy plain, are found, under an eternal rain of fire, the naked shades of blasphemers, unnatural offenders, and usurers. There is Capaneus, one of the "Seven against Thebes," the derider of the gods, whose punishment even in Hell is made sharper by his unbending pride. There is Brunetto Latini, who speaks to Dante with thoughtful fatherly love, and like Farinata before him, prophesies the poet's exile. There at the extreme inner edge of the ring sit the usurers ever looking at the money bags which are hung round their necks.

From this inner edge Phlegethon falls far down to the eighth circle. Dante undoes the cord which he has round his waist, and gives it to his guide, who hurls it into the abyss, in order to entice up the monster Geryon, the hateful image of fraud, that he may carry the pilgrims down on his back. In the eighth circle are the Evil Pits, Malebolge. These are ten concentric trenches, in each of which is placed one special class of deceivers. In the first panders and seducers go round in opposite directions, incessantly

[1] Suicide forms no necessary part of the spendthrifts' qualification. Jacopo di Sant Andrea is not known to have killed himself.

scourged onwards by devils. In the second flatterers grout like pigs in filth reaching to their mouths, and beat themselves with their fists.

As the representatives of this fraternity are mentioned the smooth-tongued Florentine, Alessio Interminelli of Lucca, and the Thais of Roman comedy. In the third *bolgia* we find the simoniacs sticking head downwards in shafts in such a way that only their feet, red-hot and moving convulsively, emerge from the opening. The Popes are fully represented here, and Dante hurls words of fiery wrath against their simony and nepotism, comparing the see of Rome with the harlot of the Apocalypse, and lamenting Constantine's donatism as the beginning of corruption. In the fourth pit soothsayers, magicians, and astrologers go with melancholy and slow paces, twisted round between the chin and the trunk, grisly caricatures of the human form in one great and revolting procession. The fifth pit is marvellously dreary—corrupt officials lie in a lake of boiling pitch, and as often as they try to emerge from it they are harried and slashed by devils. The two poets also are deceived, derided, and put in fear by these devils, who ultimately fall to quarrelling among themselves. They belong to a special class, the *Malebranche* or Evil Claws. Some of them are actually mentioned by name, and the grisly comicality reaches its highest point in these cantos, xxi. and xxii.

In spite of the treachery of the devils, Dante, carried by Virgil, reaches the sixth *bolgia*. Here the hypocrites, groaning under the terrible burden of the leaden copes in which they are clad, go slowly and drearily, passing by, standing on Caiaphas and his colleagues of the Sanhedrim, who lie crucified on the stony ground, with sharp stakes. In the seventh pit Dante sees terrible crowds of strangely-fashioned serpents, among whom naked people run, their hands bound behind their backs by snakes, who pursue them and pierce them through and through. These are the thieves, and as down there there is nothing else to steal they steal each other's human shape. Men become snakes, snakes men again, in horrible, never-ending transmutations. Among them Dante finds Vanni Fucci, a church-robber from Pistoia who, in order to vex him, prophesies the speedy overthrow of the Whites. Five Florentines of noble families appear, all thieves, and form worthy representatives of both parties. Dante cannot refrain from an ironical apostrophe to Florence. The eighth pit is filled with countless flames, in which are concealed and consumed to all eternity those who have given wicked advice. Ulysses and Diomed make themselves known, also Guy of Montefeltro, whom Boniface VIII., here called the 'Prince of the new Pharisees,' had by a shameful misuse of his Papal authority cast into eternal damnation. The ninth pit contains those who have caused dissension, and sectaries of all kinds. A devil cuts the limbs from their bodies, slicing them down with a sword, tongues are cut out, heads and hands hewn off, so that one of them, Bertrand de Born, who had stirred up a son to revolt against his own father, carries his head in his hand like a lantern. In the tenth and last pit dwell the counterfeiters; they lie there covered with eruptions and tormented with loathsome diseases; coiners swelled up with dropsy, liars and slanderers raging with fever. Shades as in wildest delirium rush along raging in fiendish madness, biting and wounding other shades. Quarrels go on with language so foul that Virgil has to warn his pupil that it is unseemly to listen, since whoso delights in hearing such things enjoys a base pleasure.

In the ninth circle is punished treachery, the most grievous of all crimes. All round the pit giants lofty as towers stand for guardians, with their feet at the bottom and rising by half their bodies above the edge. One of them, Antaeus, takes the pilgrims in his hand and sets them down far below on the floor of the circle. Cold and congelation reign here, the four divisions of the circle form a great sea of ice in which the souls are sunk proportionately to the blackness and unnaturalness of their treason. Their tears become ice, which torments them by closing up their eyes. They freeze to one another, and mutually hate and betray. In Caïna are the traitors to their own relations, in Antenora traitors to their country, in Tolommea those who have betrayed their friends, in Giudecca those who have betrayed their benefactors. Here is Ugolino who gnaws the skull of Ruggieri, and relates the terribly grand history of the starvation of himself and his children. There is Alberigo dei Manfredi whom, by words of double meaning, Dante persuades to relate his own misdeeds. In the middle of the Giudecca and at the centre of the earth stands Lucifer the prince of Hell, half on this side of the central point, half on that, lacerating with his three mouths Judas, Brutus, and Cassius. His shaggy body, fifteen hundred feet long, serves them as a means of climbing down and past the centre; and thus after three days' wandering they leave Hell through the tunnel made by Beelzebub, and reach the surface of the other hemisphere, where they again behold the stars.

III. *Purgatory.* They have reached the foot of the mount of purification. Dante rejoices at the sight of the sweet hue of Oriental sapphire, of the fair planet Venus which kindles love, of the constellation of the Fish, and the four wondrous stars seen by no man since the first pair. A venerable old man, Cato of Utica, his head illumined by the gleam of the four wondrous stars, comes to meet the pilgrims, and bids Virgil take his pupil to the sea-shore, wash off from him the traces of the journey through Hell, and gird him with a smooth rush. A boat comes up swiftly from the sea guided by an angel who, instead of rudder and sail, uses his own wings. It is laden with spirits who are chanting the psalm of deliverance; among them Dante recognises his friend Casella, who affectionately intones one of Dante's own odes. Cato warns them to make haste, and they set out on their journey up the mountain. In contrast to Hell, where, as the road proceeds downwards, it becomes more difficult and dangerous, the ascent here grows more easy as they proceed. The mountain is so shaped that it offers the greatest labour at the beginning, and becomes less difficult the farther they climb. In the ante-Purgatory are found the four classes of the negligent, waiting to be admitted into Purgatory proper, the place of penance and purification. Those who have died under the ban of the Church must wait thirty times as long as their excommunication lasted. If in over-confidence in God's mercy they have postponed repentance until the time of their death, they have to wait there until a period equal to their delay. If they have died by a violent death they have to wait as long as their life had lasted. If they have postponed their repentance by reason of earthly cares, they are delayed for a period equal to twice their lifetime.

Among those who died under the ban of the Church Dante finds Manfred, son of the Emperor Frederick II., who begs him to inform his daughter Constance, wife to Peter of Aragon, that he is among the saved, since the curse of priests cannot exclude from Heaven. As the pilgrims pass farther they meet with Belacqua, the guitar maker of Florence, as phlegmatic and indolent in the next world as he had been in this. Among those who had died by a violent death are mentioned Jacopo del Cassero of Fano, a former *podestà* of Bologna, who, in the language of Leviticus xvii. 11, speaks of his blood as that wherein he dwelt; Buonconte of Montefeltro, the commander of the Aretines, slain at Campaldino, who relates how an angel and a devil contended for his soul, and how his body fell to the disposal of the latter; Pia of Siena, who alludes to her tragic end in brief words which will never lose their pathos; Benincasa of Arezzo, murdered by the sons of a robber knight whom he had, as *podestà* of Siena, caused to be executed; Ciacco dei Tarlati of Florence, drowned with his horse in the Arno; the good Frederick Novello, murdered by an opponent in 1291; and others, such as the son of Marzucco of Pisa, Count Orso, and Peter de la Brosse. All these souls, as soon as they perceive that Dante is yet alive, crowd round him with the entreaty that on returning to earth he will persuade the survivors to pray for them. This causes him to inquire whether the prayers of the living can, in any way, affect the fate of the dead, a question which is answered in the affirmative so far as concerns the denizens of Purgatory only. Towards evening they meet the troubadour, Sordello of Mantua, whose cordiality towards one whom he only knows as his fellow-countryman gives Dante the cue for his grand and famous apostrophe to Italy in general and Florence in particular. After sunset farther progress is impossible, and they pass the night in a flowery hollow of the mountain, where the sides of the path widen out into a valley. Kings and princes occupy this, among them Rudolf of Habsburg, Ottocar of Bohemia, Philip the Bold, Henry the Fat of Navarre, Peter of Aragon, Henry III. of England, and many others, including Nino Visconti and Conrad Malaspina. Two angels appear and drive away a serpent which seeks to glide into the valley during the night. When Dante at last falls asleep he imagines himself in a dream to be borne aloft by an eagle; when he awakes he is actually before the gate of Purgatory proper. Virgil informs him that Lucy has descended from Heaven and borne him aloft while he slept.

Three steps lead up to the gate of Purgatory, where stands an angel with gold and silver keys, who, with the point of his sword, traces on the poet's forehead seven P's, sign of the seven deadly sins, and bids him wash them off in the seven circles of Purgatory. From the gate a steep and narrow way between the walls of rock, winding like the waves of the sea, leads to the first of the seven circles of Purgatory which, like the rest, is a level terrace circling the whole mountain, in which the sin of pride is purged away. The souls move along bearing, like Caryatids, heavy burdens, and contemplate images setting forth examples of humility on the one hand, and on the other of the sin which is being punished. Here, as in all the other circles, the first instance of the virtue is the Virgin Mother greeted by the angel as Blessed, and humbly acknowledging herself as the handmaid of the Lord. A second image of humility is presented by King David dancing before the Ark of the Covenant, while his wife Michal looks at him in foolish pride from a window. A third image is offered by the Emperor Trajan alighting, in friendly fashion, from his war-horse in order to do justice to the suppliant widow. The images of pride punished are Satan falling from Heaven, the hundred-armed Briareus struck by lightning, the giants conquered by the gods, Nimrod, Niobe, Saul falling on his sword, Arachne changed to a spider, Rehoboam in flight, Eriphyle slain by her own sons, Sennacherib slaughtered by his sons in the Temple, Cyrus with his head cut off and immersed in the vessel filled with blood, and the host of Holofernes fleeing with the carcass of their beheaded general. In this circle we meet with Umberto Aldobrandeschi, one of the Counts of Santafiore, assassinated in 1259 at the instigation of the Sienese, the famous miniaturist, Oderisi of Agubbio, who now humbly places Franco of Bologna above himself, and gives occasion to Dante to dilate upon the transitory fame of artists and poets, little thinking that his own fame would be imperishable; Provenzano Salvani, the Sienese potentate, who fell into the hands of the Florentines in 1269, and was murdered by an enemy from his own city. The mention of a noble deed done by Salvani gives Oderisi occasion to prophesy the poet's exile in enigmatic words.

During every passage from one circle to another one of the Beatitudes, contrasting with the sin of the last circle, is uttered by angelic voices, and as Dante leaves each circle an angel fans his brow and thus wipes out one of the P's, indicating that he is now purified from the sin which is expiated in that circle, whereby he ascends to the next lighter than before.

In the second circle the envious are punished. Here there are no sculptures and no pictures; all is smooth, the rock is of a livid colour, and the road by which the pilgrims go is monotonous. They go for about a mile without noticing anything, then spirit-voices flit past them urging to neighbourly love of friends and foes alike. Pictures and sculptures would here be useless, the penitents can see nothing, since their eyelids are fast sewn together with wire. The voices recall the Virgin Mother taking thought for the good of others at the marriage in Cana, and of Orestes, the unselfish friend of Pylades.[1] Meanwhile, other voices in the opposite direction call to mind those whom envy brought

[1] As a matter of fact, the unselfish action recorded is that of Pylades.

to destruction, such as Cain, the fugitive murderer of his brother, and the Athenian Aglauros, who was turned to stone for envying her sister the love of Mercury. Dante speaks with Sapia of Siena, who recounts her own sinful envy, causing him to confess that he is himself not free from this sin, but that he has laid upon himself a far heavier load of pride. Then he meets two deceased noblemen of Romagna, Guido del Duca and Rinieri dei Calboli, who enter into a conversation with him which develops into a bitter lamentation over the political condition of Tuscany and of their own province. 'Mankind,' says Virgil, 'seek only after the bait; in the sky above Heaven calls them in vain, displaying to them its beauties; their eye gazes only to earth, and therefore God chastises them.'

The angel of love with his wings fans the second *P* from the poet's forehead, and accompanied by the chant 'Blessed are the merciful,' they ascend to the third circle, where anger is purged away amid a dense and pungent smoke. Here the lesson is given by ecstatic visions, partly showing examples of gentleness and placability—Mary, who does not chide when she finds the Child Jesus in the Temple; Pisistratus of Athens refusing to take vengeance on the youth who has kissed his daughter; Stephen praying for his murderers,—partly the evil consequences of wrath: Procne, who in revenge has set before Tereus his own child to eat, changed into a swallow; Haman hanging on the gallows; and the wife of Latinus who has over hastily slain herself, and left her daughter Lavinia lamenting, on a false report of the death of King Turnus. Marco Lombardo directs the poet in the way upwards, and discovers to him the reason why the world is so deserted by all virtue and so teeming with wickedness. It is not the influence of the stars, but the powerless state of the empire caused by the confusion of the spiritual and temporal powers which is responsible for the melancholy condition of Italy. Dante's whole theory is here developed in summary, after which the angel of peace fans away the third *P* from Dante's forehead, and escorted by the chant 'Blessed are the peace-makers,' they mount up to the fourth circle where the sin of *accidia* is punished.[1]

Night prevents farther progress, and Virgil employs the time in explaining the various modes in which men sin. With slight differences of detail he sets forth the teaching of St. Thomas upon the nature of the seven deadly sins and expounds the nature of human freedom. The souls who are doing penance spur each other on in rapid course, calling out to each other instances of zeal—Mary going to Elizabeth with haste, Caesar marching quickly into Gaul, and examples of dilatoriness punished—the Israelites in the desert, and the companions of Aeneas who remained behind in Sicily. In a dream Dante sees a woman, the symbol of false goods on which a man sets his heart, to whom his own glance of love lends the appearance of loveliness, but who when the mask is taken from her reveals herself as a loathsome form. As they mount up they hear the song, 'Blessed are they that mourn,' and the fourth *P* is fanned away from Dante's forehead. The fifth circle is occupied by the avaricious lying with their faces to the earth, bound hand and foot, and stretched out motionless, weeping and singing the verse, 'My soul cleaveth to the dust.' Among them is Pope Hadrian V., who when the poet would kneel before him in reverence shows him that in the next world there are no popes, and laments that of all his still living relations only his niece Alagia takes thought for the good

[1] The original word has been kept because 'indolence' only represents one side of the sin denoted by it.

of his soul. Avarice is the accursed old she-wolf who in her never-sated greed swallows more than all the other beasts, and Dante sends up to Heaven the question, When he is to come before whom the monster will give way? The souls in their weeping by day call to recollection examples of poverty and liberality, the poverty of Mary, the contempt of the Roman Fabricius for gold, the liberality of St. Nicholas: while at night they set forth instances of avarice—Pygmalion, who killed his brother-in-law for greed; Midas, who starved in the midst of his gold; Achan, who earned for himself stoning with the booty of Jericho; Heliodorus, who found his death in an attempt to plunder Sion; Ananias and Sapphira, who through covetousness lied to the Holy Ghost; Hecuba, who in her rage scratched out the eyes of King Polymnestor; and the Parthians who dipped the head of Crassus in molten gold. Here they find Hugh Capet, the butcher's son, who became King of France, who laments the corruption which has made its way into his house, and in ever-memorable words brands the ill-treatment of the prince of the new Pharisees at the hand of his descendant, Philip the Fair. The mountain shakes, a chant of *Gloria in excelsis Deo* resounds all about them, showing that a soul has completed its penance. Statius appears and attaches himself to the two poets and explains to them the reason of the shock and of the chant, informing them at the same time that in this circle not only the avaricious but spendthrifts like himself have to purge their sins, and relating on what road he himself found salvation. After the angel of this circle has wiped yet another of the marks of sin from Dante's forehead, all three proceed upwards to the sixth circle.

Here they see copies and off-shoots of the tree of knowledge of good and evil from which Eve plucked the forbidden fruit. The two trees which they see at the entrance to the circle, and at the exit from it, have their roots upwards [1] while their tops lessen downwards like fir-trees turned upside down. Those who are punished in this circle who formerly had been the slaves of gluttony, but now utter the praises of God, are horribly wasted so as to be unrecognisable, while the hunger which torments them is sharpened by the sight and the odour of the fruit. From the leaves of the first tree come voices recalling the frugal life of Mary, of the Roman women of old, of the prophet Daniel, of the men of the golden age, and of the forerunner of the Saviour who lived on locusts and wild honey. In the top of the other tree a voice warns to beware of the sin of Eve, calling to mind the race of the Centaurs born of Ixion and a cloud, and Gideon's warriors, who on account of their lack of moderation were excluded by divine command from taking part in his victory. Here Dante finds Forese Donati, his former friend and companion in sin, who with burning words chastises the immorality of the women of Florence, and names to him some of the penitents, the poet Bonagiunta of Lucca, Pope Martin IV., Ubaldino of Pila, Boniface, Archbishop of Ravenna, the merry toper Marchese of Forlì, and Fiesco of Genoa. Bonagiunta prophesies to the poet that for a noble lady's sake he will one day hold dear the city of Lucca which some despise. In conversation with him Dante characterises his own poetic style in brief but cogent terms. Forese prophesies the speedy fall of Corso Donati the chief of the Black party. When they leave this circle the angel of moderation wipes the last *P* but one from the poet's forehead, and during the climb Statius, in a long and connected speech, unfolds the Thomist

---

[1] All that the text says is that the branches diminish from the top downwards.

doctrine of the soul, differing from the master only in giving the departed soul an ethereal body.

In the seventh and last circle, where sins of lust are cleansed, the souls are moving in the flames which issue from the precipice, so that the poets have to pass along the outermost edge. In the flames the penitents are singing the hymn of the divine clemency and quoting the example of the pure Maid of God who could testify her purity before the angel, and also the warning given by the instance of the nymph Callisto seduced, and then so terribly punished. The crowds of penitents meeting from either direction express by the cries of Sodom and Gomorrha, and Pasiphae, their loathing of the sin to which they had given way in life. Among them Dante finds the poets Guido Guinicelli and Arnald Daniel, the latter of whom announces himself in beautiful Provençal verses. On the other side of the flames stands the angel of chastity, who with the cry 'Blessed are the pure in heart,' invites the poet to go through the fire. Dante trembles and shrinks, even Virgil's exhortations are in vain, and it is not till he is reminded of Beatrice, from whom he is now separated only by the fiery wall, that he hastens towards the flames, while from above is heard, 'Come ye blessed of my Father.' When the farther side is reached the last P is wiped away; Virgil takes his leave, he can guide Dante no farther since he himself can henceforth discern nothing more. Dante's will is now free and sound; he can follow it without needing further guidance.

IV. *The Earthly Paradise.* On the summit of the mountain Dante enters a beautiful wood through which a clear stream flows. Beyond the brook singing and gathering flowers appears Matilda radiantly beautiful, and instructs the poet about the place in which he is. Next appears a magnificent mystic procession—seven golden candlesticks go in front, while from behind their flames bands issue which tint the air with the colours of the rainbow. Four-and-twenty dignified elders follow, and then comes a triumphal car drawn by a marvellous gryphon, on which is enthroned the glorified Beatrice adorned with heavenly beauty. Three maidens dancing on the right and four on the left escort the car, and after it come four mysterious animals. The rear is brought up by two elders, four men of humble appearance, and one other elder sleeping, though with the air of one in thought. Beatrice, who is veiled, addresses first indirectly, then in direct speech, stern reproaches to the poet for his infidelity to her, and after he has bitterly lamented and made straightforward confession, she unveils herself so that he can refresh his ravished soul by the sight of her beauty.

The mystic procession moves forward to the tree of knowledge and of obedience, to which the gryphon fastens the car by its pole; whereupon the tree which had hitherto seemed withered begins again to grow green and to blossom. The gryphon with the elders now departs and ascends to Heaven, while Beatrice with the seven maidens and the seven candlesticks remains on guard by the car. Then suddenly an eagle swoops upon the car and makes it totter, then a lean fox glides into it, then a dragon rises up through a cleft in the earth between the two wheels and tears part of the car away. The eagle comes again and endows the waggon with his feathers, upon which a horrible transformation takes place in the car. From different parts of it arise seven heads with ten horns; no longer Beatrice, but a wanton harlot is seated upon it, and by her side a giant who first caresses and then beats her, and finally unfastens the car now changed into a monster, and drags it away into the wood. Beatrice prophesies the coming deliverer; Matilda, who has already dipped the poet in Lethe, leads him to the spring Eunoe. He drinks of it and returns pure and ready for his flight to the stars.

V. *The Heavenly Paradise.* Beatrice turns to the left and gazes at the sun; Dante gazes on Beatrice, and presently sees an ocean of light shed all about him, and perceives the sweet harmony of the celestial spheres. Beatrice tells him that he is no longer on the earth, but has ascended with lightning swiftness to Heaven, borne by the innate longing of the purified soul for God. From sphere to sphere Beatrice's beauty becomes ever nobler, her smile ever more enchanting. In the first sphere, that of the Moon, Beatrice instructs the poet concerning the markings on the moon and the power of the stars to effect changes. Like pale reflections, as hard to recognise as a pearl on a white skin, appear here the first of the blessed souls; they are the souls of those who in life had failed to keep a vow. Among them is Piccarda Donati, who had been torn from her cloister by men more accustomed to evil than to good, and married by force. Next to her appears Constance, mother of the Emperor Frederick II. The poet learns from Beatrice that the souls show themselves to him in localised appearances, but are in reality outside of space, with God in the highest or motionless heaven. Then she teaches him concerning the nature of a vow and the possibility of offering a substitute for it. Next they ascend to the second heaven, the sphere of Mercury, as swift as an arrow which strikes the mark before the bow-string is at rest. The blessed spirits greet Dante with the cry that the sight of him, as of one to whom God is gracious, will increase their love, and press round him in order to be of service to him by imparting of their light. These are the souls of persons who on earth had employed themselves in the attainment of honour and renown. Here is the Emperor Justinian, who in a long speech relates with consummate art the history of the Roman eagle from the foundation of Rome to Charles the Great, and adds a denunciation of the Ghibelines, who pursue their partisan aims under the imperial standard, and of the Guelfs, who are hostile to the empire as such. Here is Romeo, who having been requited by Count Raymond Beranger with black ingratitude for his noble and unselfish help, went away poor and old and begged his living bit by bit.

Immediately after the history of the Roman eagle follows that of the Redemption, the secret of which Beatrice unfolds to the writer as they soar to a higher sphere. It is a secret which is hidden to the eyes of all whose spirit has not been fortified in the flames of love. In the third heaven, or sphere of Venus, appear the blessed spirits of those who had formerly devoted themselves to earthly love, which, however, is not to be ascribed to the influence of the star of Venus. The poet is here first addressed by Carlo Martello, the titular King of Hungary, who upon his inquiry explains to him how it happens that goodness is not inherited, but that often an evil man springs from a good man and *vice versâ*. Then speaks the once so amorous Cunizza, the sister of the terrible Ezzelino of Romano, who describes her ancestral castle by its situation, points out the troubadour Folco of Marseilles, and announces the coming chastisement of Padua, of Richard of Cammino, lord of Treviso and of Feltro—chastisements which he can read in the mirror of the divine justice. Rahab of Jericho, too, is here, who once assisted Joshua in the conquest of that promised land whereof the court of Rome, whose thoughts are set only on the gold florin, takes little heed; but thereto God will shortly come to help.

They now fly to the fourth heaven, that of the Sun, where teachers shine like the brightness of heaven, and those who have turned many to righteousness like the stars for ever and ever. There they are satiated with God, who permits them to gaze upon the essence of the Trinity and other theological mysteries. Thomas Aquinas appears with his master, Albert the Great, with Gratian of Bologna, Peter Lombard, King Solomon, Dionysius the Areopagite, Orosius, Boëthius, Isidore of Seville, the Venerable Bede, Richard of St. Victor, and Siger of Brabant. All these he introduces and describes, and delivers a brilliant eulogy of St. Francis of Assisi, ending with a sharp invective upon the deterioration of his own brethren, the Dominicans. Then appears a second ring of blessed spirits—Augustine, the provincial of the Franciscans; Illuminatus, the disciple of St. Francis, and his companion to Egypt; Hugh of St. Victor; Peter the 'Eater,' chancellor of the university of Paris; Peter of Spain, afterwards Pope John XXI.; Nathan the prophet, Chrysostom, Anselm, Donatus the grammarian, Rabanus Maurus, Abbot of Fulda and afterwards Archbishop of Mainz, and Joachim of Flora, Abbot of Curazzo. With them is the Franciscan general, St. Bonaventura, who announces the praises of St. Dominic, and laments the falling off of discipline among the Franciscans. At Dante's request St. Thomas instructs him as to the manner of the risen bodies of saints, the others express their agreement in an 'Amen' full of longing, and Dante and Beatrice soar up to the fifth heaven, or sphere of Mars.

In a group of flashing jewels which form a cross, upon which Christ is gleaming, appear the spirits of those who have borne arms in the service of the Lord. Dante is affectionately greeted by his ancestor Cacciaguida, who describes the good old times of Florentine citizenship, relates his own history in that of his house, prophesies the poet's coming exile and poverty, exhorts him to publish all his vision with a fearless spirit, and points out his companions, the heroes of the faith—Joshua, Judas Maccabaeus, Charlemagne, Roland, Godfrey of Bouillon, and Robert Guiscard.

As they ascend from the fiery red light of Mars to the white Jupiter, the contrast of colours is reflected in the countenance of Beatrice. In the sixth heaven appear the blessed spirits of upright kings, who chant the hymn of righteousness as they move about like glowing sparks; presently shaping themselves into the figure of an eagle, which replies to Dante's inquiry touching the divine justice and the grant of eternal salvation, scourges with burning words the greed of the Popes and the unrighteousness of kings and princes, and makes known to Dante some of the spirits composing it. Its eyebrow is formed of the glorified souls of King Hezekiah, the Emperor Constantine, William the Good, king of Sicily, the Emperor Trajan, and Rhipeus of Troy; while the spirit that gleams in the pupil of the eye is David, who here is aware of the reason of his salvation. Finally, the eagle explains how it comes that heathens like Trajan and Rhipeus are found among the elect; incidentally to which Dante is instructed upon faith, salvation, and predestination.

In the seventh heaven, or sphere of Saturn, appear in glory the saints of the contemplative life; among them being Peter Damian, who refers the poet to the secret of the Divine selection, whereby its own guides and guardians are assigned to each individual soul; and lashes the luxury of unworthy worldly-minded clerics, upon which all the souls pray aloud for the punishment of such. Then appears St. Benedict, founder of the order called after him, and of the convent of Monte Cassino; relates his life, speaks of his foundations, and laments that his order too has deteriorated.

In the eighth heaven, that of the fixed stars, Dante sees Christ in all the brightness of His glorified manhood; and around Him the Virgin Mother and the Apostles. After He has returned on high Dante (who has been unable to endure the sight of Him) has to undergo a threefold examination. Peter tests him for faith, James for hope, John for love. After his well-sustained trial Adam appears and instructs him upon original sin, the original time, language, and abode of the human race. There rings through Paradise a sweet enrapturing song. Peter changes colour in wrath, and delivers a terrible and crushing denunciation against him who has usurped his seat, which in the sight of God is vacant, and has turned his burial-place into a sewer full of blood and foulness. At this fiery speech all heaven grows dark, and Beatrice changes like a modest woman, who, though assured of herself, shows herself abashed at the mere hearing of another's transgression. After this speech the blessed spirits fly up to the empyrean, filling the air like snowflakes when the sun is passing into the sign of Capricorn.

Having risen to the ninth or crystalline heaven, Dante at first beholds its glories only in the eyes of Beatrice, whose beauty is further heightened. Then he gazes on the nine choirs of angels, who move in concentric circles around God as their centre. He is instructed concerning the angels, their creation and fall, their nature and operation, their order and hierarchy. This teaching ends with the condemnation of the vain fruitless fashion of preaching then in vogue, and Dante ascends with Beatrice to the empyrean, where is the heavenly zone, the actual seat of the Godhead and of all the blessed. Here Beatrice's beauty reaches such a height that human words are powerless to give even a pale image of it. In the heavenly zone Beatrice shows him the throne whereon the Emperor Henry VII. will sit; then she leaves him and resumes her position among the blessed. Her place is taken by St. Bernard de Clairvaux, who guides the poet to the final aim of man. He shows him Mary, the Queen of Heaven, Eve, Rachel (next to whom Beatrice is sitting), Sarah, Rebecca, Judith, and Ruth; then the archangel Gabriel, Adam, Moses, Peter, John, and other heroes of the faith. In a noble prayer Bernard beseeches the intercession of the Queen of Heaven on the poet's behalf. Dante obtains grace to plunge himself in the contemplation of God, therewith he has reached the highest and final aim of man —the pen falls from his hand, the poem is ended.

CHAPTER III

THE FORM

THAT there is here no question of a comedy, in the modern sense of the word, will have been obvious from the summary which we have given of the contents. In Dante's time quite another notion was conveyed by this term, which he twice applies to his poem, while he calls Virgil's *Aeneid* a tragedy. We possess an explanation of it, which may pass for authentic, even though criticism should ultimately arrive at the result of showing that in the form in which we have it, it is not due to Dante himself. In the epistle to Can Grande, section x., we read :

The title of the book is, 'Here beginneth the Comedy of Dante Alighieri, a Florentine by birth, not by character : to the understanding of which it is to be known that *Comoedia* is so called from *Come*, a village, and *ode*, which is a song. Thus *comoedia*, as it were, the *song of villagers*. Now a comedy is a kind of poetic narration, differing from all others. It differs from tragedy in its matter for this reason, that a tragedy is in its beginning admirable and tranquil, but in its end or event is foetid and horrible. . . . But a comedy introduces the difficulty of some subject, while its matter ends happily, as Terence shows in his comedies, and therefore some writers have been accustomed in their letters of greeting, in the usual place of greeting, to say, Wishing a tragic beginning and a comic ending. So, too, they differ in their style—tragedy is exalted and sublime, comedy careless and humble. . . . Hence it is clear that the present work is called comedy, for if we consider the matter of it in the beginning it is horrible and foul, as Hell; in the end it is prosperous, desirable, and pleasing, as Paradise. If we consider the style this is careless and humble, as being the vernacular tongue in which even women converse.'

This exactly agrees with the views and expressions customary in the Middle Ages; the terms *tragic, comic, elegiac*, did not indicate the manner of poetic representation, but referred rather to the matter which was poetically treated. Wherefore Virgil's *Aeneid* is called *tragedy*. On the other hand everything which turned out happily was called *comedy*, even though subject and treatment were anything but comic. The *Orlando Furioso* would in Dante's time have been called tragedy, the *Gerusalemme Liberata* comedy; which according to modern ideas sounds indeed comical.

The term *divine* was first applied to this poem by an admiring posterity, agreeably to the Italian usage, according to which anything noble, beautiful, or sublime is styled briefly *divino*. The term was applied at first to the poet himself and then transferred to his work; yet the title *Divina Commedia* did not become usual until the middle of the sixteenth century. Before that the poem was styled simply *La Commedia*, or still more briefly *Il Dante*. But indeed the title of the work was long undecided, although the poet's contemporaries adhered to that which he himself had selected. Thus the famous Aldine editions of 1502 and 1515 bear the title, *Le terze rime*, regarding only the metrical form. Two of the three editions of the seventeenth century are intituled *La Visione*, in this case with reference to the poetic garb of the contents. In our century, as in the last, the title *Divina Commedia* has been exclusively employed.

For the title *Visione* one may appeal to the poem itself in which it is twice expressly indicated as a vision, and indeed, according to the poetic disposition of the matter, it is a vision—the vision of a pilgrimage through the three realms of the next world. This form of representation, so popular in the Middle Ages, having been once selected, the poet found himself compelled to consider the external shape of the next world and to draw up a plan of it—at least in his own mind. Dante has done this with such careful accuracy, not forgetting the very smallest detail, that fully-specified descriptions have been given from his data, and people have now and again taken ruler and compass in order to draw out ground plans and elevations of the invisible world. In this matter the poet in no way relied on his own powers of invention and imagination; he found plenty of precedents. Never has the thought of the future life been so wide-spread and influential as in the Middle Ages; the Christian religion in the West had progressed to the point of denying visible reality, so that spirit and fancy were thrown back upon the necessity of occupying themselves closely with the invisible hereafter which alone was regarded as veracious. If man in this world was only as it were in a waiting-room expecting every moment to have to start for his journey to another world, where he would remain for eternity, it was surely natural for him to interest himself seriously in the topography of that other world. On this subject the records of revelation imparted nothing certain and decisive except that there were in the future two worlds, one of endless ineffable joy for the good, one of endless ineffable torments for the wicked. But since the conditions of Heaven and Hell were absolute, the question must press itself even upon untrained thinkers whether the eternal destiny of the individual was finally decided at death, which is dependent on countless accidents. The idea of a further development, and therewith the possibility, that a man might decide for himself beyond the grave, was wholly foreign to mediaeval thought. But experience of life could not fail to point out that most men, when they leave the world, are not bad enough for Hell or good enough for Heaven—a thought which, if we once admit the absolute character of Hell and Heaven, can never be confuted. Thus as a natural consequence there arose the doctrine of Purgatory, according to which every soul which had departed in the faith and was destined for bliss had to undergo purificatory punishment in a definite place common to all for sins insufficiently expiated on earth, a punishment which could be mitigated and shortened by the pious activity of survivors. Once granted the premiss, which neither the Middle Ages nor indolent popular belief up to our time ventured to controvert, of the absolute contrast between Heaven and Hell, the doctrine required nothing but an appeal to sound human understanding; and an appeal to the Bible was all the more superfluous and imprudent that it could never boast of success. Judas Maccabaeus may, on finding idolatrous amulets hung about the necks of his dead on the battlefield, have sent a sin-offering on their account to the priests at Jerusalem; but it would require the most audacious exegesis to find in this any trace of a belief in Purgatory. Or if a proverbial expression of the Apostle Paul (1 Cor. iii. 14), which has nothing whatever to do with the next world, be appealed to, it is only necessary to read in St. Augustine, who has quite rightly understood the passage in question of earthly trials, by which all that is vain and small in a man's life is destroyed as straw by the fire, while the soul is saved as from the fire. But since, as we have already shown, the doctrine of Purgatory is postulated by reason no less than by humanity and religion, it was firmly held by the scholastics of the thirteenth century and was energetically maintained against the Greeks, while nothing but the misuse which was gradually made of it could have induced the reformers to reject it. Thus our poet found the three divisions of his poem ready to his hand, Hell the realm of never-ending torments, Purgatory the realm of purificatory and temporary pains, and Paradise the realm of everlasting joy and bliss.

Next arises the broader question as to the topographical position and form of these realms. Here too it may be seen that Dante did not rely wholly upon his own invention. Scholasticism had brought within its scope the bright regions of Heaven no less than the darkness of Hell. Thus Heaven was divided into three parts, the visible part or firmament, the spiritual, in which angels and saints dwell, the intellectual, in which the saints enjoy the contemplation of God. Further, the schoolmen taught that there were four places of abode for departed souls, Hell proper where the devils abide, and whither those who have sinned mortally go at once; Purgatory, which lies next to Hell, the *Limbus puerorum* in which are children who have died unbaptized, and the *Limbus patrum*, called also Abraham's bosom, the abode of pious men of old time, whither Christ descended in order to preach redemption to the spirits in prison. In opposition to these statements mysticism rose to a spiritual interpretation, and treated as an inward condition that to which the schoolmen gave a local habitation. This view was not unknown to our poet, and its influence is shown in the chastisements of Hell no less than in the pains resulting from the penances of Purgatory. But for the articulation of his poem he had no reason to refer to the views of the mystics.

But even the scholastic topography of the next world could not be adopted and improved in value by Dante without additions, since his visionary journey would have brought him first to the regions of expiation, and not till after this among the lost, which could not be brought into harmony with the idea of the poem. Taking a genial view therefore he removed Purgatory from the regions below the earth and formed a far less dismal plan of it, namely a mountain rising exactly opposite the hill of Golgotha, the only land in the farther hemisphere which since Adam's fall no living eye yet has seen and no vessel has navigated. This island-mountain rising up from the broad seas, bears upon its summit the earthly Paradise where the first of mankind dwelt in happy innocence. By this means the three realms were sharply divided from each other, and it became possible to begin the symbolical journey into Hell, continue it through Purgatory, and to bring it to an end in Heaven.

'God,' says the author of the Book of Wisdom, 'has ordered all things in measure and number and weight.' With this text in his mind Dante has built up architecturally the three realms of the next world. At the base of this arrangement is his numerical symbolism which has its roots in the Bible, and, as we have seen, plays so important a part in the *Vita Nuova*. The numbers which determine and govern the architecture of the whole poem are 3, 9, and 10; there are three main divisions corresponding to the three realms. The rhyme is governed by three, since the poem is composed in tercets. Each of the three parts has thirty-three cantos, being the number three multiplied by ten and increased by itself. The first canto is to be regarded as an introduction or prelude so as to complete the number one hundred which is the square of ten, the perfect number. Each part falls into nine divisions; in Hell we have an outer region with nine actual circles of *Hell*; in *Purgatory* an *ante-Purgatorium*, seven circles, and the earthly *Paradise*; in *Paradise* the seven Heavens of the planets, the Heaven of the fixed stars, and the *Primum mobile*, outside of which is the empyrean or immovable seat of the Godhead. Each part can also be divided by the number ten; in *Hell*, the outer region and the nine circles; in *Purgatory*, three sub-divisions of the ante-Purgatory and seven circles; in *Paradise*, nine heavens and the empyrean. Even in subordinate matters numerical symbolism appears; the three beasts who oppose the poet, three blessed ladies who take thought for him in Heaven, three guides, Virgil, Beatrice, St. Bernard, who take charge of him; three faces of Lucifer, three sparks which have set men's hearts on fire, three Furies on the towers of the city of Dis. To regard this as accidental is prohibited by the fact that Dante has obviously marked out the plan of his poem down to the smallest detail, as the wonderful symmetry of the whole and of the parts leaves no room to doubt. According to accurate division each part should have contained 4744 lines; *Hell*, however, has 4720, *Purgatory* 4755, *Paradise* 4758. Though it cannot be proved, it is highly probable that Dante made these differences in length intentionally; at any rate, looking to Purg. xxxiii. 136, we cannot doubt that he had at least approximately settled the number of lines beforehand.

So far as the locality is concerned, Dante's Hell is generally identical with that of the schoolmen. Its architecture on the other hand is his own creation, even if he has borrowed somewhat from the numerous existing visions and descriptions of the other world. Hell then is depicted as an enormous inverted cone, or a funnel, diminishing in ever-narrowing circles till it ends in a point, alike the seat of Lucifer and the centre of the universe. We might say that as the circles of Heaven grow wider as they approach God, so the circles of Hell become narrower as they recede from Him. But this ingenious notion, propounded by Hettinger,[1] will not hold in face of the arrangement of Purgatory, where the circles equally narrow in proportion as they are nearer to God. We must therefore regard the realms of eternal and temporary torment as constructed on purely aesthetic and architectonic principles and views. A funnel must narrow as it descends, a mountain as it rises; while the circles of heaven can only be conceived as widening, since each encloses all below it.

The poet's most original creation is the ante-chamber to Hell, the abode of the unstable; and we may add, the division of Hell into sundry concentric circles, rendered necessary by his classification of sins and sinners. The journey goes down from circle to circle to the centre of the earth, above which, in a vertical line equal to half the diameter, lies Jerusalem, with Golgotha, the scene of the atonement.[2] As to the position of the entrance-gate of Hell, the poet gives us no indication; but it would appear to be conceived as lying not far from Florence; in any case in Italy, where also is Rome, then held to be the centre of the Christian world. In order to avoid a return to the surface through Hell, which would have been at once unpoetical and opposed to the aim and genius of the poem, Dante has invented a cavern leading from the centre back to daylight, opening in the other hemisphere and at the foot of the mount of purification. The final canto of the *Hell*

---

[1] P. 105 of the English edition.
[2] Do not all points on the earth's surface lie vertically above the centre?

gives the following explanation of the origin of this cavern. Satan fell from heaven upon the earth at a point antipodal to Jerusalem, and was hurled into the earth like an arrow, so that by his own gravity he remained fixed at the middle point of the earth. The land which formerly covered the other hemisphere, as it does ours, through terror at the catastrophe, hid itself under the waves of the sea, and fled to our hemisphere. But the portion of the earth which was forced aside by Satan's fall, which also caused the passage above mentioned, spouted up behind him as he fell, and formed the mountain of Purgatory in the other hemisphere. Thus the antipodal hills, that of purification and that of atonement, were both caused by Satan's fall from heaven; so that Satan in a certain way brought about the remedy for the corruption arising from him.

The Purgatory, which so far as form and position go is a creation quite of the poet's own, is regarded as a mountain presenting itself in the form of an erect cone, rising in terraces. Its height, which no earthly mountain attains, is probably equal to the depth of hell, or a half diameter of earth. Just as Hell is built in three main divisions, so is Purgatory; with the ante-Purgatory corresponding to the outer region of Hell, its seven circles of expiation to the circles in Hell where sins of incontinence and malice are punished, and the earthly Paradise to the lowest gulf or Giudecca. But other parallels are not wanting. To the fearful dark wood corresponds as its opposite the divine forest on the summit of the mountain; to Charon the ferryman of Hell, the angel who ferries the souls of the redeemed across to the land of penance; to the green meadow of *Limbus*, the valley blooming with flowers; to the defended gate of the city of Dis, the locked door into Purgatory proper. In the ninth canto of *Hell* appears the heavenly messenger who opens the city to the pilgrims; in the ninth of *Purgatory*, Lucy, who carries the poet up while he dreams. Such parallels, which may easily be multiplied, are assuredly not accidental. That Purgatory, considered as a whole, forms a counterpart to Hell is obvious. In the one it is constant descent, in the other constant ascent; in the one devils terrify and torment the souls, in the other the souls are summoned and encouraged by angels; in the one all is shrouded in night, in the other are sunlight and the friendly lustre of stars; in the one are curses and revilings, in the other hymns and blessings; in the one the whole apparatus of torture is calculated to excite disgust, in the other a penitent can use such terms as:

> Torment I say, yet I should call it solace.

As to the construction of Paradise, we have from another quarter the poet's own dictum. He says in Conv. ii. 3, 4, that according to Ptolemy, and as appears from the principles of astronomy and philosophy, there are nine moving heavens:

> And the order of their position is as follows: the first that is reckoned is that of the moon; the second, that in which Mercury is; the third, Venus; the fourth, the sun; the fifth, Mars; the sixth, Jupiter; the seventh, Saturn; the eighth is that of the stars; the ninth is that which can only be perceived by the movement above mentioned, which is called the crystalline or diaphanous, or wholly transparent. But outside of these Catholics suppose the empyrean Heaven, which is as much as to say the heaven of flame, or the luminous; and they suppose this to be immovable, since it has in itself in respect of every part that which its matter requires. And this is the reason why the *Primum mobile* has most rapid movement; because by reason of the fervent longing which every part of it has to be joined to every part of that most divine

motionless Heaven, it revolves within that with so great desire that its velocity is as it were incomprehensible. And this motionless and peaceful Heaven is the place of that Supreme Deity which alone fully beholds itself. This is the place of the blessed spirits, according as Holy Church, who cannot lie, will have it; and this Aristotle, to whoso understands him aright, seems to mean, in the first book *De Caelo*.

Here we have the whole architecture of Dante's Paradise. But there was in it a difficulty for the poet which had to be overcome. As his journey was performed from Heaven to Heaven, if all the angels and all the blessed inhabit the empyrean, the highest motionless heaven, it follows that the nine lower heavens are uninhabited; and in contrast to Hell and Purgatory, where every circle is occupied by a special class of sinners, the journey through Heaven would have to be lonely and monotonous, lightened only by conversation between Dante and Beatrice. This would have destroyed the wonderful symmetry of the poem. But his genius did not desert the poet here. He had learnt from his master Aquinas that there are various degrees or stages of blessedness. He assumed nine of these, corresponding to the nine lower heavens, and made the blessed, who really dwell all together in the one motionless heaven, appear in every case in that heaven which corresponds to the degree of this blessedness according to the principle stated in Par. iv. 28 sqq.

> Of seraphim, he who is most ensky'd,
> Moses and Samuel and either John.
> Choose which thou wilt, nor even Mary's self,
> Have not in any other heav'n their seats,
> Than have those spirits which so late thou saw'st;
> Nor more nor fewer years exist; but all
> Make the first circle beauteous, diversly
> Partaking of sweet life, as more or less

Afflation of eternal bliss pervades them.
Here were they shown thee, not that fate assigns
This for their sphere, but for a sign to thee
Of that celestial furthest from the height.

A different question arises with regard to the principle upon which Dante has gone in classifying sins and punishments; since Purgatory and Hell seem to differ widely in this respect. Going downwards in either case, we find at first complete agreement; lust, gluttony, covetousness, are the first three. After these we find in Hell, anger, which in Purgatory is separated from the others by sloth; but after this there is no further similarity. Where, in Hell, are envy and pride punished? In Purgatory, where are expiated all the sins which we find in Hell within the city of Dis? Are sinners of this kind all eternally damned, the proud and the envious all saved?

In Dante's view the gaps caused by guilt will be filled again by the punishments, a thought which had already been fully developed by St. Thomas Aquinas.[1] In Hell naked justice ruled, in Purgatory justice combined with mercy. The aim of punishment can only be one of the following: to anticipate or prevent transgressions, to atone for injustice committed by punishment inflicted, or to reform the evil-doer through suffering; or, in other words, punishment must be either preventive, retributive, or reformative. The preventive aim is clearly out of place in eternity, since no fresh transgression can be committed which could be checked by means of punishment; nor, again, in the case of Hell, can there be any question of reformation, there is no question there of repayment, repentance, or reform, the lot has fallen for good and all, and the destiny is immutably fixed for ever. Thus, for the punishments of Hell,

[1] S. T. ii. 1; Q. 87, A. 1.

the only object left is retribution; there the *jus talionis* alone passes current, which has found its popular expression in the well-known words, 'an eye for an eye, a tooth for a tooth.' In Dante's Hell the punishments are allotted strictly according to this law, but, according to this law, it is obvious that only the positive deed, the actually committed crime, and not the thought of transgression or the inclination thereto, can be reckoned, that is punished. The very idea of requital excludes this. Thus, *accidia*, slothfulness, does not consist in the commission of positive harm, but rather in the doing nothing, either good or evil, the living without praise and without blame. Obviously, however, not doing, or sins of omission, cannot be punished in the same place as sins of commission. It is, therefore, a vain undertaking to search for the circle of Hell in which this class of sinners are hidden. Their place can only be in the ante-Hell, the abode of the cowards, the half-hearted, those who from indolence are neutral angels as well as men.[1]

Pride and envy are sinful inclinations and feelings, the sources of many sins in act, but much or everything depends upon whether they actually come to these sins in act, or whether the man succeeds in suppressing his inclinations and feelings sufficiently to prevent the smouldering spark from breaking into flame. If he does so he is not far from the kingdom of God, and will attain to the grace of penance, so that his soul, on the departure from the body, may take its way to the mountain of purification. But if the evil germs of pride and envy have borne their fruit in active

[1] This is the view taken by Daniello in contradiction to all his predecessors. On the other hand, it should be said that the words of H. vii. 121-123 distinctly indicate that the *accidiosi*, no less than the *iracondi*, are to be found in the Stygian marsh; as the author clearly saw when he wrote his commentary. *Accidia* is a great deal more than indolence.

sins, it is these latter and not their roots that will be considered in the apportioning of the punishment; the intention being regarded only, as Witte says, so far as an earthly judge is obliged to do the like in deciding the responsibility of the doer or the special nature of the transgression.

This simple and obvious solution of the apparent difficulty was discovered by Giambullari as early as the sixteenth century. He rightly recognised that all the sins which are punished in Dante's Hell, from the sixth circle downwards, may be referred to their roots in pride or envy, or both together. Satan's fall is ascribed in P. ix. 129 to envy, in xxix. 59 to pride; and it has been supposed that Dante takes him as representative of both these sins in Hell. But seeing that he has indicated both of these and covetousness besides as the chief vices of the Florentines, and as the vices which have inflamed all hearts, he might easily have found proud and envious persons among his contemporaries enough to people his poetic Hell. Satan, however, became, through these sins, a traitor to his highest benefactor, and it is these active sins which are punished in the lowest Hell, as may be clearly seen in the case of Cain, who is punished not on account of his envy, the sole root of his sin, but on account of the sin of action, namely, fratricide.

Thus Dante could not create a special circle of Hell for pride and envy, since in Hell naked justice prevails; the fundamental principle for the punishments is then retribution only, and retribution cannot be applied to inclinations but only to deeds.

In Purgatory things are on a different footing. No doubt, the principle of retribution is not wholly excluded even here, the idea of it was, in the Middle Ages, too deeply rooted for any one to be able to tear himself free of it. Reformatory schools were not invented till the nineteenth century; the views upon which they were founded were absolutely unknown in the Middle Ages, and even Dante had no prophetic intimation of them. But in Purgatory the principle of reformation and purification is so predominant that the other falls into the background. Purgatory is, therefore, described as the realm in which man's spirit is cleansed and becomes worthy to ascend to Heaven. Therefore, it is said of the souls who have found grace that they go thither in order to become more fair, and not in order to atone or do penance. Therefore, some of the purgatorial punishments, as, for example, in the circle of the gluttonous, are strictly wholesome exercises rather than the endurance of positive pains. Therefore, again, the purification consists not only in the endurance of pain, positive or negative, but in the absorbed contemplation of manifold examples of that virtue which forms the contrast to the sin which is being expiated. Reformation and cleansing, however, demand not only that the sin which has been committed in act should undergo retribution and atonement, but also that the roots of the evil should be torn up, the evil inclinations overcome, and that the heart should recover its purity which had been stained.

Hence it is clear that in Purgatory the violent, the traitors, and so forth, could not have any special place beside the proud and envious, since the external action, which in Hell is punished as a sin of act, is here expiated as a sin of thought. And just because in Purgatory the object aimed at is the extermination of the roots, the special circles of the indolent, the proud, and the envious could just as little be lacking here as they could be looked for in Hell, for the very reason that there the sins of act are themselves punished but the roots remain. In Purgatory the penitent souls gradually wash away all uncleanness, in Hell they remain bad to all eternity, and their eternal badness forms an important aggravation to their torments. Thus in the pit they revile and ill-treat and mutilate each other, while the souls in Purgatory lovingly stimulate each other to speedy purification. Sapia, in canto xiii., had committed the sin of blasphemy; if she had died impenitent she would have taken her place beside Capaneus in Hell, but as she had done penance she is found in the second circle of Purgatory cleansing herself from the envy which had formerly made her a blasphemer. So in canto xi., Umberto of Santa Fiore had committed many violent actions through pride; dying impenitent he would have come to the stream of boiling blood, but through penance he is enabled to purge himself of the pride which had made him a man of violence. And since, according to Christian teaching, all sins, even the most grievous, can be forgiven, even heretics and traitors who died penitent can be purified in those circles of Purgatory where penance wipes out those sins which had been the roots of their sinful actions. It is clear, therefore, that Dante's division and distribution of punishments in the *Hell* and in the *Purgatory* is based upon a profoundly-thought-out and accurately-executed system.

Perhaps even more marvellous than the peculiar poetical energy or the wonderfully symmetrical power of imagination, is the daring boldness with which Dante set to work in his great poem. If it were to be anything besides a dry enumeration of sins and punishments, a barren description, a rhyming handbook to the geography of the next world, or a treatise on its penal law, the poet was bound to people the various regions of the three realms of eternity. That was clearly obvious, and even in the older and contemporary visions of the next world inhabitants are not lacking.[1] But

---

[1] Compare, for example, the recently-discovered *Apocalypse of Peter*.

these are the merest shadows without individual characteristics, and therefore tedious in the highest degree. Dante has rightly recognised that if he had only represented the damned, the penitent, and the blessed in general, his poem would have turned out so dry and monotonous that no man would have tested his patience in reading or understanding it. The whole object was to individualise, and Dante is the first who did this. With such mastery has he done it that it is just the most personal episodes which have become the most popular. Francesca of Rimini, Farinata, Ugolino, Pia, Sordello, Piccarda, Francis of Assisi, Cacciaguida, and all the rest are familiar figures to every educated person. On the other hand, the dissertations upon legal, philosophical, theological questions interest only the professed Dantist who wishes to know his author to the very bottom.

Dante thus found himself compelled to people the regions of the next world not with mere general types, but with a special and definite list of individuals, with individuals, moreover, clearly characterised and adapted to attract the interest of his readers. Thus, too, he was compelled to exercise the rights of the eternal judge, and to allot rewards and punishments, salvation and damnation to particular individuals. It was, therefore, very venturesome to draw for this purpose upon the contemporary world, which might even seem not strictly necessary. Mythology, sacred and profane history, offered personages in abundance quite individual enough to be brought successfully into his drama of the future, and, as a matter of fact, he has taken from these sources no small number of the persons who appear, speak, or act in his work. But if he had confined himself to this all the persons in the poem would have belonged to mythology, to the ancient worlds of Judea, Greece, and Rome, or to the earlier Middle Ages. The *Commedia* would have become a poem, rich, perhaps, in poetic beauties, and would have fallen into oblivion as completely as Petrarch's *Africa* or Trissino's *Italia Liberata*.

But Dante was determined to paint a complete picture of the real world in which he lived, he would draw his age as it thought and felt; in its knowledge and its conceptions, in its enjoyments and renunciations, in its joys and sorrows, in its hopes and fears, in its efforts and weariness, in its morality and immorality, in its virtues and vices. Boldly, audaciously, according to our modern ideas, he seized upon the circles of real life in which he moved, took out of them the most prominent personages, condemned them to Hell, transferred them to Purgatory, or exalted them to Paradise, and made them all immortal in his immortal verse. There in the eternal world they had to meet him, the mystic pilgrim, to inform him concerning their lives, their deeds, and their sufferings, to relate the past and foretell the future, to depict the place where, and the men with whom, they had lived. It is for this reason that the great canvas is so magnificently full of life, so inimitably attractive. Nor has the poet spared the highest heads; popes, emperors, kings, princes, cardinals, bishops, potentates—he hurls them all pitilessly into Hell and tears the mask from their faces. Even upon still living men he accomplishes his terrible judgment. Down in the lowest Hell the souls of traitors are already dwelling, while here on earth their bodies are in the possession of devils.

Did Dante select his personages and distribute them among the three realms of the next world upon any fixed principle? Seeing that the method of his work rests strictly on principles, we cannot answer this question in the negative. It is, however, not easy to decide what the principle is upon which he made his selection. Some have thought that it was personal, and that he allowed himself to be guided throughout by motives of personal liking or hatred. That is, in any case, a serious exaggeration. Of many persons, whom he has immortalised by introducing them into his poem, we have no knowledge at all whether he ever came into any personal relation with them or theirs, or if he even knew them personally. But the notion cannot be entirely rejected. Dante certainly mentions a person here and there mainly, if not exclusively, from personal motives. What did the world at that time know of one Cacciaguida, about whom no chronicler has anything to say, and whose name appears only in unimportant documents? Did the Florence or Italy of that day trouble itself about the late Forese Donati? In these cases a personal motive clearly governed the selection, and so, too, doubtless, in the case of other persons. But this is far from saying that the selection was chiefly decided by personal motives, in general Dante followed another principle.

In the first place it was obvious that where there were no direct personal motives to affect or decide the choice, it must fall upon persons who were known, or in some respect conspicuous, and thus familiar to contemporaries. The poem would have had little interest for contemporaries, and still less for posterity, if the personages introduced had been merely Toms, Dicks, or Harrys, of whom, in their own day, the world knew nothing and cared less. No doubt, many persons would have been, long ago, quite forgotten if Dante's verses had not endowed them with immortality; but we must remember that six centuries separate us from Dante's time. When we reflect that in less than a hundred years nothing will be known of many people whose names we are now constantly seeing in the newspapers, we can understand that in Dante's time there must have been persons widely known, concerning whom even his oldest commentators have nothing certain to tell us. We are not justified by their ignorance, still less by our own, in concluding that the persons in question were obscure in Dante's time.

Thus some other consideration must have prevailed in the selection of the personages. The *Commedia* contains the whole science of the age, in the shape of information imparted to the reader in the course of his mystic pilgrimage. In order to avoid monotony, which might ultimately become wearisome and tedious, the poet places these expositions and teachings in the mouth not only of his guides, but of the spirits whom he meets on his journey. For this purpose he was compelled to select suitable persons. It would have had a strange effect if any chance deceased person had unfolded the deepest problems of the scholastic philosophy and theology, or if some founder of an order had related the history of the Roman eagle. This is the reason of the fact that so few of the poet's contemporaries are mentioned in the *Paradise*. In order to discuss the questions which are there raised it was natural that the chief representatives of early Christian and mediaeval philosophy should, as is actually the case, be chosen.

In the next place, the poem is unusually rich in descriptions of places and of the political and moral conditions of Italian cities and districts, which again would necessarily condition the selection of persons. Florence could be described only by a Florentine; Bologna and Siena only by their own citizens. Lastly, some persons have obviously been selected as being specially adapted for presentation, as types of entire classes whether of sinners, penitents, or saints. Judas, Brutus, and Cassius are obvious instances, but many others could easily be indicated.

We must not, however, assume that every personal selection can be explained in this way without going farther. Under this head much remains problematic in a poem so prolific of problems. In the case of Francesca da Rimini, indeed, there is nothing striking about her being placed in Hell, much in her being made a type of loving graciousness and tender womanliness; an unfortunate victim of a noble passion whom we admire and envy, lament and pity, weep for and excuse. If one remembers that when she maintained those illicit relations, she was a wife and mother, her paramour a married man and father, it is simply inconceivable how a man of so strict notions could in this way have glorified an adulteress, and still more that he should have condemned to the deepest Hell, simply for avenging his own honour, her brave husband, who only did what every honourable man would do under similar circumstances. Still more problematic is it, how Dante could have branded with so fearful a crime the 'dear paternal image' of Brunetto Latini, who in this life had taught him day by day how man rises to immortality. Brunetto may have been notoriously guilty, but why did Dante play the part of Ham, instead of following the example of Shem and Japheth? It is indeed the fact that nothing would have been known of Brunetto's shame if Dante had not revealed and perpetuated it. Some secret must be concealed behind his words.

It would be superfluous to adduce further instances. Only an accurate inquiry bringing to the test even the minutest details with regard to the system which Dante followed in selecting his personages, combined with precise statistics as to such of the inhabitants of the three realms as are named, may perhaps contribute to render the solution of the riddle possible. That in the thousand and more volumes—dissertations, pamphlets, treatises—which we reckon in Dante literature, no single work of the kind is to be found, deserves special mention as a remarkable feature.

In an overwhelming majority, the inhabitants of the next world in Dante's poem belong to Italy. The work is no doubt universal; it is the epic of Revelation and at the same time a comprehensive picture of the age. But even a Dante could only know his own age in a limited degree, and he was therefore compelled to seek for his personages, his heroes if you will, in circles which were known to him. Even if he had been in Paris, or even in Oxford, his knowledge of land and people, history and manners, in France or England, or elsewhere, can have been, according to modern conceptions, but scanty. Of the Germans he knew little more than he read in Tacitus. On the strength of this, and perhaps on the behaviour of the few Germans whom he may have known as mercenary soldiers in Italy, he has judged or rather condemned the whole nation. His judgment is no whit better founded than that of uncultivated folk in Switzerland, who form their judgment of all Germany from the numerous vagabonds from whom we suffer, or from the restless chatterers who take refuge among us, and in return for the bread which we give them, disturb our country by the declamations with which they favour the world; these are not the German people, only its offscourings. That Dante was not only the first poet, but also the first *savant* of his time, is beyond question, but he was not omniscient. So far as regards the history, the manners, the whole life of his time, his knowledge did not extend far beyond the frontiers of Italy; and any one who undertakes to convict him of having occasionally formed his judgment upon very superficial information will have no difficult task. In saying this, however great an outcry may be raised in Italy and elsewhere upon these remarks, we do not think that we are taking the least liberty with the poet. Dante was no doubt a man of great character, a great poet, a great scholar, a man who was materially in advance of his time; but, for all that, he was always a child of his time.

In the mediaeval visions of the next world, such as were then current, whether the seer looks into the future in a dream, or talks with the dead and gets his information from them, or goes into the next world and wanders through its regions, he is as a rule quite alone. A journey without companions is however somewhat tedious. In this respect, Dante's creative and original power was especially shown. He adopted another fashion of travelling. In carrying out his great journey he is not alone; he has always with him one or two companions acquainted with the way. Virgil, who is well informed upon all questions of reason, is beside him for a time; Statius supplements Virgil; Beatrice leads him from the summit of the mount of purification to the final height of Heaven; and the holy mystic of Clairvaux aids him to the contemplation of the Godhead. That Virgil and Beatrice are both alike his guides, rather has to do with the aim than with the form of the poem. But even in the matter of its form, the poem gains much in living interest through this invention. Dante asks; his guides reply and instruct him. Either on their demand, or himself in doubt, he states a point, expresses an opinion, and his guides confute what is wrong and give the reason for the right view. The poem thus gains dramatic life, and the serious reader never feels the slightest sensation of tedium. Even where abstruse questions of scholastic theology, alien to us moderns, are discussed, the poet knows how to hold our attention at full stretch.

In order to complete our consideration of the form of the poem, it remains to cast a glance upon the guardians of the various regions of the next world. The gruesome entrance to Hell is unguarded; any one who will can go in so long as he is not scared away by the terrible inscription which bids him on entering abandon every hope. This conception of the open gate is borrowed from Virgil (*Aeneid*, vi. 127). The fearful inscription, meant perhaps to take the place of a warder, is Dante's own invention. But what is the purpose of the inscription? It cannot be to frighten away the souls of the damned, for they are compelled to enter; nor does it need any inscription to tell them that they are going to eternal woe and among the lost folk, and also that there is no hope for them. Can its object be to frighten away those who have no business there from visiting the place of sin and torment? or does it symbolise the voice of conscience which warns off the man from sin, and utters its grave *principiis obsta*? The ante-Hell, again, has no guardian; it would seem that the office is performed by the unresting banner; and besides, what need would these good-for-nothing cowards have of a guardian? They remain inactive and unenterprising, doing nothing to which they are not driven, forced, and compelled. No doubt they are envious of every other lot, and would sooner be in the lowest Hell than where they are, but people of their stamp never pull themselves together with any vigour to change their condition. A guardian for them would be unnecessary luxury, they are sure not to run away.

From this point onwards every circle of Hell has its appointed warder. Charon the ferryman, Minos the judge, Cerberus the hound with the three mouths who tears and rends the unhappy souls; Plutus (or Pluto) the accursed wolf, who bellows in so terrifying a fashion and is understood by no one; Phlegyas the boatman of the Stygian swamp, who offers a grisly welcome to the souls; the demons and furies who tried to forbid entrance to the fiery city; the Minotaur, the infamy of Crete, raging in impotent wrath; Geryon the monster with the pointed tail, the foul image of fraud; the giants tower high with their terror-striking figures; and below, at the centre and in a pit, the horribly comic figure of Lucifer, the emperor of the kingdom of woe. And in order to complete the dismal picture, the Centaurs, beasts inflamed with anger, stand as arrow-armed sentries over the stream of boiling blood. Such are the guardians of the realm of sorrow.

As we see, with the exception of the demons, the poet has taken them all from Greek and Roman mythology. There is no need to say much on this point,—for the whole Catholic middle age, the gods of the heathen were but devils; and by adhering to this universal belief of his time, and using the figures of mythology as guardians of Hell, Dante gained a considerable poetic advantage. Abstract figures of devils cannot be so easily and so sharply characterised as are these mythological beings whose clearly-defined traits were ready to his hand.

But what exactly have these guardians of Hell to do? Have they to see that the souls do not escape to higher circles, and ultimately get out of Hell altogether? It might appear so, but it is not so. Nowhere can we find the faintest trace of any impulse on the part of the lost souls to make their way upwards; nowhere anything to show that if the two pilgrims had tried to turn back, the road would have been closed to them or rendered in any way difficult. On the contrary, the guardians as a rule make a difficulty about letting them proceed, whence it follows that their function is to hinder the lost from leaving the place assigned to them in order to descend any deeper.

This may seem a paradox, but it is really a marvellously

profound purpose on the poet's part; there is no change in Hell, the souls make no effort to go back, they are far more likely to be dragged down by the weight of their own sins as a stone is attracted to the earth. The power of moving, even if it were ever downwards from circle to circle and from step to step, would introduce variety into the life of Hell, and thereby make it more tolerable. So we, disregarding all terrors, accommodate ourselves willingly to the journey in company with the poet; but in Hell every situation is eternal, and this fearful monotony makes the horrible torments of Hell inconceivably more horrible. If the cowards in the ante-Hell envy every other lot, they would clearly be glad to go farther down and share the lot of the blackest souls in the lowest pit; but this cannot be. They must for ever pursue the unresting flag and ever be stung by gad-flies and wasps. Also from another point of view we recognise that it is the office of the guardians of Hell to hinder the souls from leaving their appointed circle and pressing on to a lower point. The tendency of sin in its essential nature is downwards into the nearest proximity to its originator, and in this very fact is shown its terrible power to drive the man ever forwards till he turns to a devil. The evil-doer finds his pleasure in ever accomplishing new and blacker misdeeds, hence arises the natural effort of the entire world of Hell to press nearer to the Prince of Hell; but as the tree falls so it must lie. Eternal damnation knows no progress even in wickedness; the lost see in front of them only an accession of their torments at the resurrection of the body, a frequently-recurring thought in Dante.

If evil tends downwards like water, good tends upwards like flame; the one yearns to be near the devil, the other to be near God. Accordingly we find a contrary state of

things in Purgatory,—while the guardians of Hell are demons, ✓
those of Purgatory are angels; and while the former shriek
curses at the soul, the latter encourage them with hymns
and beatitudes; while the former hinder the damned from
leaving their circle and constrain them to a ghastly eternal
monotony, the latter lovingly urge them on, and invite
them as soon as they are purified to come higher and press
forward to the beatific proximity of God. Accurate comparison shows that even in details Purgatory is diametrically
opposed to Hell.

The guardians of the circles of Purgatory are angels, and ✓
for that very reason have no individual features. They are
ethereal beings whom, as a rule, we do not even see, but
only hear their beautiful voices and feel the healing breeze
of their wings. Even the porter at the entrance gate of
Purgatory proper is not an individualised form; we cannot
rightly look at him, for his countenance shines like the
sun, so that we cannot endure it. We see only the flaming
sword in his hand and his ashy-coloured raiment, from
which he draws forth two keys, and hear his serious words,
full, nevertheless, of heavenly kindness. It is only of the
ante-Purgatory that the guardian is an individual figure, the
younger Cato, the suicide of Utica.

Much has been written upon the fact that Dante makes
this heathen and suicide the warder of Purgatory. In the
first place, we must remark that Cato was not what may be
called an ordinary suicide; he renounced life of his own free
will because he could and would only live as a free man.
In spite of his deed, antiquity has agreed in esteeming and
honouring him highly. Even many fathers of the Church
have done so, and their opinion has descended to Dante,
so that he even declares him to be the most worthy of mankind to pass for a type of God upon earth. 'What man,' he

says in Conv. iv. 28, 'was more worthy than Cato to symbolise God? Surely none.' Elsewhere, too, Dante speaks of Cato with respect and admiration. Thus Conv. iv. 5:

> Oh, most sacred heart of Cato, who shall presume to speak of thee! Certainly I cannot speak of thee better than by holding my peace and following Jerome when, in his preface to the Bible where he touches upon Paul, he says that it is better to say nothing than too little. Certainly it must be manifest when one remembers the life of these and other godlike citizens that it was not without some light from the divine goodness over and above their own noble nature that such wonderful achievements came to pass, and it must be manifest that these most excellent men were instruments whereby the Divine Providence proceeded in the Roman empire where many times we see the hand of God to have been present.

Now it is obvious that Dante could not have placed the godlike citizen Cato in Hell, and equally that in his universal poem he could not have passed him over in silence. Where, then, was he to place him? in Heaven? But to this his ecclesiastical views as a Christian would be opposed. If in one of the seven circles of Purgatory, in which? Of which of the seven deadly sins had Cato been guilty? Not even of pride, for it was not pride but pure love for freedom which made him a suicide. It has hitherto been unnoticed that in making Cato the guardian of Purgatory, Dante has judged him with terrible severity. He has to wait thousands of years below the region of penitence and perform his office until the day of judgment. Like a second Ahasuerus he must wait until the Lord return. All other souls who have found grace purify themselves in a longer or shorter time, and then enter into the joy of Heaven, there to await in glory and bliss the resurrection day and the last judgment. But to Cato Heaven remains until then closed. Through the ages, like another

Moses on Nebo, he sees the Promised Land from afar and is unable to enter it himself. All the redeemed come from south and from north, from east and from west, and after a period which, in comparison with eternity, is less than a moment, they receive the beatific call, 'Come ye blessed of my Father, inherit the kingdom which is prepared for you from the beginning of the world.' But for the godlike citizen this call will never resound until the end of time. And yet we wonder that Dante has made Cato the warder of Purgatory; nay, it is rather the case that the poet has judged with marvellous severity a man whom he so honoured. Cato is the very last of all those who will come to bliss; at the great day indeed, but not before, will the 'husk which Cato left in Utica' shine brightly, and not till then will he enter into the joys of Paradise.

After the last circle of Purgatory no guardian is found. We cannot suppose that Matilda discharges this function for the earthly Paradise; there is no indication of this; rather she is there obviously only on Dante's account. We might perhaps have expected to find here the cherubim with the flaming swords whom God placed east of the Garden of Eden to keep the way to the Tree of Life. But they are not found there, and probably we must look for them in the two angels who come down in Purg. viii. to guard the beautiful dell of Purgatory against the serpent which tries to glide into it. Indeed Dante could not consistently with his own system allow any guardians to appear beyond the region of penance; for when the soul leaves the seventh and last circle of Purgatory its will is free, right, and sound, and therefore in accordance with the will of God. Thus there is no more need of a guardian, and accordingly neither in the earthly nor the heavenly Paradise do we meet with any.

X

CHAPTER IV

THE PURPORT OF THE POEM

DANTE repeatedly calls attention to the fact that his verses conceal a deeper sense than appears in the letter of them. In Conv. ii. 1, he writes:

> It is to be known that writings can be understood, and should be expounded chiefly in four senses. The first is called the literal, and this is that which does not extend further than the very letter. . . . The second is called the allegorical, and this is that which is hidden under the cloak of these fables, and it is a truth concealed under a fair falsehood. . . . The third sense is called the moral, and this is that which readers should go intently gathering through the writings to the profit of themselves and their pupils, as may be gathered in the Gospel when Christ went up into the mountain to be transfigured, and of the twelve apostles took only three with him, wherein we may understand morally that in our most secret doings we should have but few companions. The fourth sense is called anagogic, that is supràsensual . . . as we may see in that hymn of the prophet which says that when the people of Israel came out of Egypt, Judah became holy and free. Now, albeit this is manifestly true, according to the letter the spiritual meaning is no less true, namely, that when the soul issues forth from sin it becomes holy and free under its own control.

We meet with just the same thought in the letter to Can Grande, illustrated too by the same example. This example may be called the very programme of the *Com-*

media, for the poem shows how man becomes free and pure by leaving his sins, as indeed is plainly stated in the last lines of Purg. xxvii.

As we saw, Dante selected for his poem the form, at that time current, of a vision, but it is clear that the vision itself was not the end but only the means; to use his own words, the beautiful fable under which the truth is concealed.

And what is this truth? What is the aim and at the same time the fundamental thought of the poem?

The original purpose of the poet was, as the *Vita Nuova* places beyond doubt, to celebrate and renown the glorified love of his youth. It was fortunate for his fame, still more fortunate for posterity, that he did not at once proceed to carry out his plan, for at that time he could not have written the *Divine Comedy*. It was through his experience of life in the long and eventful years which elapsed between his writing the last words of the *Vita Nuova* and the beginning of the *Commedia* that his original plan underwent a mighty extension. The glorification of the pure maiden so early lost was not forgotten; she appears again in the poem as the real love of former days, but at the same time as an exalted symbol, the last indeed so predominantly that people have now and again deemed in her sublime image no traces are to be found of earthly and human reality. But the glorification of Beatrice has now become a secondary aim, subordinated to one infinitely more comprehensive and more sublime. In the letter of dedication to Can Grande it is said, 'The aim of the whole and the individual parts is twofold, a nearer and a farther; but if we seek into the matter closely we may say briefly that the aim of the whole and the individual parts is to bring those who are living in this life out of the state of misery, and to guide them to the state of happiness.' That also is the chief aim of the poem, but the subsidiary aims which are subordinate to the chief aim have also attention expressly called to them. Such are, in the first place, the glorification of Beatrice, and then the intention of addressing serious lectures to certain cities and individual potentates, discussing grave problems of science, and, perhaps not least, achieving re-admission through the fame acquired into the gates of the beloved mother city. But all these are only side aims which pass entirely into the background in comparison with the chief aim, namely, redemption in the most comprehensive sense of the word. At any rate it is quite possible that Dante did not himself write the letter to Can Grande, in which case we cannot appeal to his own testimony. But we have the testimony of all the old commentators up to the end of the eighteenth century; these, with unusual unanimity, indicate redemption as the end of the poem, and occasionally say almost in so many words what we read in the letter of dedication. What is still more significant, the poem itself as we have it from beginning to end points to this aim, and Dante himself says quite expressly that the purpose of his vision is the salvation of this sinful and therefore unhappy world. The sole source of the modern discussions, whether the main objects of the poem are political, moral, or religious, is to be found in the fact that in modern times people set a great gulf between matters which for mediaeval men, and for Dante among them, form one great unity. If his object was the redemption of men from misery and the guidance of them to happiness, the poem must have been at once religious, ethical, and political.

What, according to Dante's conceptions and ideas, is the happiness of mankind? In this life a peaceful and orderly life, in eternity the joy of Heaven. He says, *De Monarchiâ* iii. 15:

The ineffable Providence has set forth two ends to be aimed at by man, namely the happiness of this life which consists in the operation of his own virtue and is figured in the terrestrial Paradise; and the happiness of eternal life, which consists in the fruition of the divine countenance, to which man's own virtue cannot ascend unless aided by divine illumination, which is to be understood by the heavenly Paradise. To these two forms of happiness indeed, as to various ends, it behoves us to come by various means, for we come to the first through the teaching of philosophy, so only that we follow it out by operating according to the intellectual and moral virtues. But to the second we come through spiritual teachings which transcend human reason, so only that we follow them by operating according to the theological virtues, namely faith, hope, and charity. But these ends and means, although they have been displayed to us, the first by human reason which has indicated them all to us through the philosophers, the second by the Holy Spirit, who through the prophets and the sacred writers, through Jesus Christ the Son of God co-eternal with Himself, and through His disciples, has revealed supernatural truth necessary to us, these human covetousness would cast aside were not men like horses straying in their own brutishness restrained in the right way by bit and bridle. Wherefore man had need of a double guidance according to the twofold end, namely the chief Pontiff who should lead the human race in the way of revelation to eternal life, and the Emperor, who according to the teachings of philosophy should direct it to temporal happiness.

Here we have the master key to the understanding of the poem. In it we see a pilgrim who first arrives at the earthly Paradise; but the earthly Paradise according to Dante's express declaration is the symbol of earthly happiness, whence it follows that the poem is intended to show by what road a man can arrive at the happiness of the earthly life. At the same time we see in the poem a pilgrim who presses forward to the highest Heaven, the seat of the Godhead; and since the heavenly Paradise, as we have equally heard from Dante's own mouth, is a symbol of eternal bliss, it follows that the poem is at the same time intended to show how a man arrives at eternal bliss. But the pilgrim in the poem does not travel alone, Virgil leads him to the earthly Paradise; and since according to Dante's clear explanation it is the emperor whose business it is to lead mankind to earthly happiness, it follows with absolute necessity that Virgil is the symbol of the Roman universal monarchy according to Dante's universal conception of it; or to put the matter more generally still, we may say that Virgil is the symbol of temporal sovereignty. To the heavenly Paradise the pilgrim is led by Beatrice, and Dante has taught us that the heavenly Paradise, Jerusalem which is above, typifies the blessedness of eternal life, to guide men to which is the function of the Pope. Thence it follows with equal necessity that Beatrice is simply and solely the symbol of the papacy according to Dante's ideal conception of that; or again to put it in the most abstract terms, the symbol of spiritual authority. That is the sum of the matter; everything else is valueless. Null and void, useless exercises of fancy, are the countless dissertations and inquiries ancient and modern as to the allegorical significance of Dante's guides. We would not here enter into them even if the aim of this work and the space at our disposal allowed of a discussion no less wearisome than discursive. In regard to this matter we have Dante's own declaration which is fully sufficient for us, and therewith disregarding all learned and unlearned chatter, we may let the subject rest.

The question why Dante should have selected Virgil and Beatrice as the symbols respectively of the ideal temporal and ecclesiastical government is essentially otiose. The poet could choose as he pleased, and was under no necessity to ask permission of his future commentators. The choice of Beatrice was based on exclusively personal grounds; by choosing her to play the part which he assigned to her, Dante has brilliantly redeemed the promise given at the end of the *Vita Nuova* to say of Beatrice what had never yet been said of any mortal woman. The choice of Virgil too must have been decided from personal motives. It was to the study of his works that Dante owed his instruction in poetry, for which reason he calls him his master and exemplar, from whom he has taken the beautiful style which has earned him honour; while of the *Aeneid* he testifies that he knows it through and through, a statement which can only mean that he had learnt the whole of it by heart, incredible as that may seem to those who in the modern fashion of desultory reading do not know what true mental concentration is. If Dante had derived peace of mind and a certain amount of earthly happiness from occupying himself with poetry in general and Virgil in particular, it was quite natural that he should honour as the founder of his happiness the master who had led him deeper into poetry, and should select him as his guide to the earthly Paradise. For the function assigned to him in the poem Virgil was specially adapted as having sung the foundation of the Roman monarchy, as a witness for the vocation, the office, and the power of the Roman Emperor, and also as the prognosticator and unwitting herald of Christianity. Besides, if Virgil was imagined by the Middle Ages on the one hand as a magician, on the other hand he was also imagined as an ideal man who ranked not only as the greatest scholar, but also as the purest soul of antiquity.

Thus Dante's poem pursues a twofold aim: the guiding of mankind to external and internal, temporal and everlasting happiness; from which it follows that it is not a political nor an ethical nor a merely religious poem, but all these together in a higher unity.) We must, however, add another element, the personal. The *Divina Commedia* is indeed at one and the same time the poem of human redemption in a far wider sense than Klopstock's *Messiah* and Milton's *Paradise Lost* and *Regained*, and the most universal among all poems of all ages and nations. It is equally, what may seem almost a contradiction, the most individual and the most subjective. No great poet has ever been so subjective as Dante. He is himself the chief hero of his epic, he is Man, who is set free from the misery of the vale of woe and led by faithful guides to the blessedness of temporal and eternal life.¹ He is the centre about which the whole mighty structure of the poem revolves; for his sake Beatrice descends from the highest Heaven and seeks the portal of the dead, for his sake Virgil leaves limbo and hastens to save him, at his request the souls speak and make answer, to him they give such information as he desires, he it is who receives from the spirits—from Virgil and Statius, from Matilda and Beatrice, and from the blessed in Heaven—instruction upon all manner of questions and problems temporal and eternal. (He is in the poem not only *a* man, but *Man*, the representative of all mankind in a state of misery and sighing for redemption and happiness.) He is at the same time the one definite individual who, sometimes justifying, sometimes blaming himself, relates his own past, who makes mention of his own ancestors, friends, and enemies, and esteems it a matter of sufficient importance to weave in special events from his own life. We must therefore distinguish in the poem an individual and a universal element.) In many places this is easy. When Dante speaks of his relations with Brunetto Latini, with poets and musicians, when he mentions the basons in his own beautiful St. John's, one of which he once broke to save the life of a child, or the men-at-arms whom he saw coming out of the fortress of Caprona; when he repeatedly brings in prophecies of his own banishment, it is clear that we have before us purely individual matters. On the other hand the two elements are frequently fused together in such fashion that a distinction between them is impossible. So it is at the very beginning in the fundamental allegory of the poem; no doubt the poet astray in the wood who wishes to climb the sunlit hill, but is hindered therefrom by the three beasts, and then is saved by the aid which is unexpectedly offered, is the image or symbol of man in general who would gladly flee from his misery but cannot do it without the assistance of prevenient grace. But who can deny that even in this allegory an individual element is equally contained, and that Dante is here depicting in allegoric form experiences of his own outward and inward personal life. Contrariwise the striking scene of Dante's meeting and reconciliation with his glorified Beatrice is undoubtedly of a highly individual character. Yet no less undoubtedly is this same scene, and indeed the whole sublime concluding vision of the Purgatory, one of the most universal that poetry has ever produced.

Since the fundamental allegory, as contained in the first two cantos of the poem, forms the main theme which is afterwards developed and set forth in all directions in the poem itself, the objects to be sought in the explanation of the whole naturally are concerned in the first place with the explanation of these first two cantos. Here the aim, the fundamental idea of the whole composition, must primarily be sought and established. Among the old commentators we find an astonishing unanimity, but we must certainly allow that no one of them in his exposition presents a full understanding of the whole and the details, and that none of them has recognised and brought out anything but the one no doubt predominant aim, namely the ethical and religious. They leave almost entirely out of notice the political aim, subordinate indeed, but yet not to be ignored. For all of them Dante is the sinner, who having gone astray in the forest of wickedness, is struggling after salvation, and, when opposed by the sins which lie at the root of all wickedness, can only find it on the road of contrition and penance through the opposition of the divine grace. All this is no doubt quite correct, but it is not the whole truth, and therefore we cannot wonder, especially when we consider the political conditions of Italy in their time, if since Dionisi, and still more since Marchetti, the contrary opinion that the aim of the poem is purely political, has been maintained and has found adherents.

According to one party the dark wood is the image of the state of error and of sin; according to the other, of political tumult and passion. Taken generally, the wood is the symbol of human misery in the most comprehensive sense, internal and external, spiritual and bodily. But since all inward and spiritual misery is brought about by means of error and sin, and very much outward and physical evil by political disorder and social mismanagement, the wood may be taken to be both in one. The sunlit hill is in one view the heights of truth and virtue, in the other the state of peace and prosperity. But if the wood was the symbol of human misery in the widest sense, so the hill being its counterpart, must be the symbol of human happiness inward and outward, bodily and spiritual. But again the inward and spiritual can only thrive in the soil of truth and virtue, the physical only in peace and in well-ordered political and social conditions. Thus the hill also comprehends both, and is the symbol of truth and virtue, and yet at the same time of good order in the political world. The poet who is striving for higher ground is mankind, which from its state of wretchedness yearns after twofold happiness. The three beasts which hinder the poet's ascent represent in one view the three chief vices, lust, pride, avarice; according to the other, three powers—the Florence of 1300 with its Black and White parties, proud France, and insatiable Rome. Both interpretations are one-sided. Fused in one they give pretty generally the right notion, although with regard to the exact signification of each of the three beasts, at any rate in the religious and moral sense, various features can be observed. According to Boccaccio they denote the flesh, the world, and the devil; according to the view taken in the present writer's *Prolegomeni* they are unbelief, pride, and false teaching.

Our task here, however, is not to write a commentary upon details but only to develop the aim or fundamental thought of the whole; and next to show how this thought is expressed in the fundamental allegory. Leaving details to the commentator, we will endeavour to obtain a comprehensive view, to which end it appears profitable to keep apart the two elements, the individual and the universal; while, on the other hand, it is hardly possible to sever the other two—the moral or religious and the political.

1. Before Dante's thirty-fifth year there had been a period in his life when he felt indefinably miserable within and unhappy without. How he came to this extremity he himself could not say, as though overcome with sleep he had for a long time abandoned himself to a sinful life and conduct, to such a degree that in later years it was painful to him to remember it. In the year of jubilee 1300, for whatsoever reasons and inducements, he awoke from his sleep, and recognised that he had gone astray, and was

unhappy both in body and spirit. In body, because as the conditions of the time were he could feel neither happy nor safe in his own city, nor find any satisfaction in political activity. When he arrived at self-inspection he recognised the misery and the danger of his position, and took up a firm determination to order his life quite otherwise. This, however, was not quite so easy as he at first thought. In political matters he might indeed hope, if he made his whole influence available, and used his time prudently, to preserve quiet and peace in Florence, and not to allow matters to come to war between the two parties. But what could he do against the proud house of Valois, and, even more, what against the tricky, insatiable greed of the Roman court? Yet less easy was it to attain to the higher, the inward happiness. He made attempts no doubt over and over again, but without success; no doubt he lifted his eyes to the hills from whence comes help, turned his back upon his former life, and strove after a life of virtue, the peace of the soul, the repose of the heart, reconciliation with God. But then he struck into a false road—the road of the she-wolf, when he followed a school whose teaching is not God's teaching. Then he had to fight against lack of faith, which cannot put its trust in God's all-powerful help, since it fixes its eye only upon itself and its own strength. Then he, the philosopher, somewhat fastidious through his own learning, had to struggle with the pride which holds that in order to reach the final aim of human existence, there is no need of any aid from above. Then he had to fight against the teaching, at that time so widely diffused, of practical materialism which seeks the final aim of human life, not in the eternal, but in the temporal only. Thus he could not work his way out of his misery; after each effort he fell back again. But grace from above stretches out her arms to him and comes to his help. The blessedness of the temporal, and still more of the eternal life must be reached by quite another road than he had hitherto supposed. This is at first made clear to him. He wavers, he hesitates; can he enter upon this road? Under encouragement he forms this resolve, and starts at once to carry it into effect.

2. 'All we like sheep have gone astray,' but with few exceptions man in his youth is not, when overcome with sleep, aware that he has gone astray, and how and where. Dreaming, unconscious, without purpose or insight, he leaves the right way. Not till the time of youth is past and the blood is grown cooler does awakening generally follow, and well is it for him to whom this occurs no later than in the middle of his life. No sooner is he awake than the wish and effort to leave the condition of misery and to attain to that of bliss are there. This is bound up with great difficulties, as the individual commonly deems at the beginning. He cannot change the course of the external world, he is warned to wait patiently until God shall send the *veltro* to save him. In the best possible case he can, if like our poet he has a call to it, utter strict judgments about persons and abuses. But even his own small inward world he cannot so easily alter. If he is not deaf towards the call of grace he really strives for improvement; and after reaching salvation, and therewith inward peace and rest of the soul, he has yet to undergo many conflicts against inward and outward foes. Three beasts (and here we need not consider the signification of each; here they can be the lust of the flesh, the lust of the eyes, and the pride of life; there they are lust, pride, and avarice; elsewhere the world, the flesh, and the devil; or again, unbelief, proud self-confidence, and false teaching or

principles) oppose themselves to his exit from the dark wood of human sin and misery, and it needs the voice of grace, which indicates to him, now awakened, how he is to take the only way of redemption,—encouraging and strengthening when his own courage fails and his own heart recoils.

The fundamental allegory of the *Divina Commedia* then, as it is contained in the first two cantos, shows how man, after his awakening, strives in vain to reach the heights of spiritual and bodily blessedness, and how he then only becomes able to do so when the eternal grace points out to him the only path which leads to his aim.

What then is this path? How does man succeed in passing over from the condition of misery to that of happiness? The answer to that question is given by the whole poem. At first the path leads down into the depths of self-consciousness, and then to the consciousness of sin in its true nature as well as in its terrible consequences. Only then does the path lead upwards through penance and purification, first to the earthly then to the heavenly Paradise; that is to say, to the blessedness of this life and of life eternal.

The source of all unblessedness, whether temporal or eternal, is sin in its manifold forms. What is sin, and what are its consequences? To this question the *Hell* gives the answer. Sin is the absence of holiness in time, and brings forth a complete unholiness in eternity. God is the source of all blessedness; man, when separated and estranged from God, is wholly deprived of it. That which separates and estranges him from God is sin in its hundredfold forms. The heavier the sin the wider is the separation from God, the deeper the misery. Therefore Satan, the original sinner, the originator of all sins, is held fast at that point to which weight is attracted from all sides, and which in the region of existence is the point farthest from God. To fall deeper is impossible. Sinners are nearer to him, or farther from him, according to the weight of the guilt which has separated him from God. All suffer, but what they suffer is their sin itself.

In the letter to Can Grande (chap. 8) we read: 'In the allegorical sense the subject of the whole work is man, according as by virtue of his own free will he is subjected through merit or demerit to rewarding or chastising justice.'

In the margin of an old manuscript we find to this passage the words, 'Thus the author of this *Hell* is speaking here according to the allegorical sense, in which we as pilgrims on our pilgrimage can incur merit or guilt.' Very true.

The temptation must occur to the merely superficial observer to envy the earthly happiness of evil-doers, and to find it irreconcilable with the divine justice. Then the balance will be sought in the next life, and perhaps, on the authority of Luke xvi. 25, the gulf between this world and the next made as broad as possible, by establishing the retributory contrast—prosperity here, misery there; misery here, blessedness there. So, with few exceptions, held the entire Middle Age; so, too, do unthinking people at the present day who have no training in philosophy. Perhaps Dante is nowhere greater than in setting himself entirely free from this imagination, and in endeavouring to show how sin carries its damnation in itself, and even here condemns the guilty to a life of Hell. Dante's Hell shows us, in all the manifold subdivisions of its torments, the truth of the inner life unmasked, in strict accordance with the law stated in Wisdom xi. 16, that wherewithal a man sinneth by the same also shall he be punished. The indolent, lukewarm coward who seeks his enjoyment in undisturbed comfort and repose, and thereby places himself in an unnatural condition, nowhere finds firm ground beneath his feet, and floats equidistant between heaven and hell, condemned for that reason to envy every other lot, since it is at any rate better to be something complete than half and half. The commonplace, the debased temperament which cannot battle, strive, struggle, endure, or hope is a torment of Hell to itself. Such characterless beings must perpetually turn with the wind running after the ever restless banner; and every trifle about which only the most contemptible commonplace nature distresses itself, be it only the stings of insects, becomes an unendurable torment. Want of faith is the inseparably twin sister of want of hope, and where hope is wanting there is Hell. Thus the inhabitants of Limbo are condemned to hopelessness, and cannot rejoice in the light of revelation from above, but only at the very best in the faint light of human reason.

Sensual passion is a storm which whirls the man to and fro without resting, and therein he undergoes his torment. Even if, as in the case of Paolo and Francesca, it obtains its desire of everlasting union with the beloved one, this, if the love has been true and deep, tends to increase the torment. It is keener torture than suffering oneself to see those suffer whom one truly loves without being able to obtain for them any alleviation. For the glutton whose God is his belly his position in Hell is the punishment. These lie in a gloomy atmosphere filled with stench on a miry soil, wallowing ever in the mire. It must have been of set purpose that Dante has in this circle named only one sinner—Ciacco the 'Hog.' The servant of Mammon is condemned for ever to roll along his master as an unendurably heavy burden. To the angry and the proud anger and pride are at once crime and torment, sin and punishment. Indeed in the case of Capaneus the poet has expressly indicated that the sin is its own penalty.

In this way we can go through all the forms of punishment in Dante's Hell, finding everywhere that the sufferings graded by the poet's fancy in such astonishing variety are the sensible images of the state of the sinner's soul and the expression of the particular sins, while he aims at and in masterly fashion hits the mark of showing the sinners in their essence, in their true form, stripped of all treacherous and lowering masks, and in this way giving the final answer to the question what sin actually is. At the same time the poet wished to show to what sin leads. For the poem contains not only the naked truth of the inner man but also, at any rate, in the intention of the poet, the naked truth of the next world, both in the most intimate organic connection. In regard to a Christian poet whose poem takes the form of describing the condition of departed souls in the next world, we are compelled to assume without hesitation that he really believed in an invisible spiritual world, in an immortal life, in future reward and punishment. And if he did believe in this he must have pondered deeply over the position of departed souls, and his descriptions are to be accepted as the result of his pondering. Much no doubt has been influenced and conditioned, in some cases decided, by aesthetic and poetic considerations. It is so at any rate with the topography and constructive arrangement of the three realms, which he doubtless himself would wish to have regarded as the poetic shell; since he can hardly have really imagined the abodes of the damned or the penitent as he has constructed them for the purposes of his poem. But as regards the status of the souls in the next world we can hardly go wrong if we assume that he has described it as he really imagined it. On this showing, the future life is not something different, but is the direct and uninterrupted continuation of the present, and the completion of what has been prepared and developed in the earthly life, the flowering of what has sprung here, the fulfilment of what has here been threatened or promised. There appearances melt away, shells fall off; there the hidden treasure is brought to light, the dross sinks down and froth evaporates. The pure light of truth which here was bound in the mists of the earth and could not make its way through the coarse earthly senses, shines there like the midday sun, and either warms the unclad souls with love or burns in their wounds like fire. Punishments are developed into logical consistency from the sin itself, wherefore the lost souls in Hell are just the same men that they were upon earth, with the same impulses, tendencies, and passions by which on earth they allowed themselves to be guided and ruled. In contrast to all his predecessors without exception no single punishment has been described by Dante solely in order to stimulate the fancy and inspire terror, but only such as result, with the necessity of natural laws, from the nature of the sins. That he, a child of the Middle Age, should have risen to a conception which even at the present day is philosophically incontestable, shows his true greatness, and makes him stand alone in his own time, which indeed could not understand him. He wished to show to a generation, which had formed the wildest conceptions of the next world, that Heaven and Hell are in truth only the poetic side of the belief in immortality, and that man carries them here in his own heart, while in the next world he merely continues and completes what he began here; and lastly, that there is only one blessedness, namely, godliness, and only one damnation, godlessness.

Thus Dante's *Hell* proposes to answer the question, what sin is in its essence, and what fruit it bears in time and eternity. If a man has once recognised that sin is a hateful thing which deforms body and soul, and at the same time a horribly cruel tormentor which tortures the sinner without remission in time and eternity, the yearning after redemption must awaken in him, so that in anxiety for his own salvation he asks, 'What must I do to become free from sin?' To answer this question is the aim of the *Purgatory*.

It thus becomes clear that the sufferings in Purgatory must have quite a different character from those in Hell. While there they consisted in the everlasting endurance of the sin itself with its fearful consequences, here they must consist of exercises by means of which the sin is not only expiated and atoned for but also torn up by the roots. Accordingly the souls must exercise themselves in just that virtue which forms the contrary to the sin in which they had indulged. Thus the proud man who bore his head so high must learn under a heavy burden to bow himself in humility. The envious man whose eye looked with disfavour upon others' fortune and prosperity must expiate his sin with his eyes closed by force, and study no longer to look askance when God is good to his brother. The angry, wrapt in a dense smoke, reap what they have sown while the smoke of their wrath is become their dwelling-place and their torment; at the same time they exercise themselves in the virtue of gentleness and kindness. The lazy exercise themselves in busy activity, the miserly and extravagant learn, while lying fettered hand and foot on the ground, to estimate rightly the value of earthly things. The gluttonous are practised in abstinence, and it is only the lustful who are purified by means of the flame of their own passions. All have deterrent examples of the vice as well as encouraging examples of the virtue brought to their remembrance which can only have a meaning in a place where the sufferings aim at improvement and purification. Thus Purgatory answers the question how man is to become free from sin and its consequences, by showing that it has first to be expiated through the endurance of appropriate suffering and then by being eradicated from the heart, which comes to pass by means of an active exercise in the virtue as well as by the consideration of deterrent and stimulating examples.

In this way, man comes at last to the earthly Paradise, that is, according to Dante's interpretation, to happiness in this life. It may appear remarkable that Dante's earthly Paradise is uninhabited. We should have expected to find here a tabernacle of God among men, the pattern of a well-ordered happy state, a people from whom we might see and recognise what the essence of earthly happiness is; instead of this the poet finds only the solitary Matilda. Afterwards appears the mighty mystical procession, but this quickly vanishes again. Has not the poet made himself guilty of an inconsistency? We hear him say repeatedly that the earthly Paradise is the place where man is happy, but where are the happy ones? What is the use of a happy land if it is uninhabited? Dante must surely have put these questions to himself, but the difficulty was one that could not be got over. He could not people the earthly Paradise with men living in the body, for it is placed not in this world but in the next; nor could he people it with departed souls, for they, when their purification is completed, enter the higher happiness of Heaven. Besides that departed souls would not be appropriate to be put forward as examples of the happiness of this life. Moreover, he would doubtless have been led to the same result from another point of view. Since sin entered into the world there has never been any perfect earthly happiness, and what does not exist cannot be described. This thought is practically expressed in Purg. xxix. 22, where Dante says that he felt moved to blame the rashness of Eve,

> for that there, where earth
> Stood in obedience to the heavens, she only,
> Woman, the creature of an hour, endur'd not
> Restraint of any veil; which had she borne
> Devoutly, joys ineffable as these
> Had from the first, and long time since, been mine.

This was no doubt the chief ground on which Dante, instead of here describing earthly happiness, left the earthly Paradise uninhabited. After the fall mankind were driven out of it, and so man can no longer inhabit it. We find in another place a description of earthly happiness in a well-ordered state, namely where Cacciaguida draws the idyllic picture of the Florentine life in his day in contrast to its later corruption.

Instead then of the inhabitants who would here be out of place, we have in the earthly Paradise besides Matilda the grand procession of the Christian Church, by means of which the divine scheme for the redemption of sinful mankind is displayed, and at the same time it is shown what man has to do in order to be a participator in the redemption. Here, too, the redemption of the symbolical pilgrim is repeated after he has, in accordance with the prescriptions of the Church, finished his penance and reconciled himself with his Beatrice.

In the third and last portion of his poem, the *Paradise*, Dante has to draw a picture of eternal happiness. He must have felt a strong temptation to describe paradisal enjoyments of a refined sensuous nature in infinite multiplicity and variety, so as to display a counterpart to the *Hell.* Even the scholastics and mystics had not been wholly able to resist this temptation, with all the pains that they took to represent their Heaven under a worthier and more spiritual aspect than that of the Mussulman's Paradise. Dante's junior contemporary, Heinrich Suso (1300-1365), who represents poetic mysticism in the Middle Ages, gives the following picture of the bliss of Heaven:

Rise up and go with me. I will lead thee into contemplation, and will make thee give a distant glance after a rough similitude. Look beyond the ninth Heaven, which is times untold farther than a hundred thousand times as far as any kingdom of the earth. There is another Heaven which is called *caelum empyreum,* the fiery Heaven so named not from fire, but from the immeasurable brightness that glows through it which it has by its nature immovable and unchangeable; and that is the Lord's court wherein the heavenly host dwells, wherein the morning stars sing praises together and all the sons of God shout for joy. There stand the eternal thrones surrounded with light inconceivable, from which the evil spirits were cast down and where the elect belong. See, the beautiful city shines here with streams of gold. It beams with precious pearls inlaid with precious stones transparent with crystal, reflected from red roses, white lilies, and blooming flowers of every kind. Now look upon the fair fields of Heaven. Ha! here is all the beauty of summer; here the meadows of bright May; here the true veil of joy; here one sees joyous glances passing from love to love; here harp and viol, here singing, dancing, and cherishing of joys entire; here the wish has full power; here love without suffering in ever-enduring security. Now look about thee at the untold multitude, how they drink after the whole desire of their hearts at the living fountains that flow trickling forth. Look how they gaze on the clear bright mirror of the unveiled Godhead, in which all things are plain and open to them. Next steal farther and look how the sweet queen of the heavenly land of whom thou art so enamoured in thy heart soars with glad dignity above all the heavenly host, inclining tenderly towards her wooers surrounded with the flowers of the rose and the lily of the valley. See how her lovely beauty causes love and joy and wonder to all the heavenly host; how the bright Cherubim and their company have a bright influence and effluence of My eternal ineffable light: how the thrones and squadrons on high have sweet rest in Me and I in them; how My elect disciples and My beloved friends sit in so great repose and honour upon their honourable judgment-seats; how the martyrs shine in their rose-red garments, the confessors beam in their green robes of beauty; how the tender virgins sparkle in angelic purity; how all the heavenly host flows along in Godlike sweetness. Ha! what a company! What a mirthful land!

There is no lack here of sensuous traits such as at times come out pretty strongly in the schoolmen. So do strict monks speak of the sweet joy and bliss of lying in Heaven on the breast of the Holy Virgin. Feasts and music and beautiful raiment and social pleasures are not lacking in many a mediaeval description of heavenly bliss. Nothing of this kind is to be found in Dante's *Paradise*.[1] If in the *Hell* we marvel at the inexhaustible fertility of his fancy, we wonder even more at its austerity in the *Paradise*. People have indeed found this most sublime portion of the poem less fascinating than the first, and have thought to explain the fact by the commonplace observation that since on earth there are so many sufferings and so few joys, pain is much easier to describe than happiness. But if Dante had wished to describe pleasures of sense he would surely not have been puzzled to invent and describe them in great variety. The truth is that as a true Christian he wished to depict the Christian Heaven in which the enjoyments of the senses have no place.

Even in Christian antiquity blessedness was regarded as a painless state, one of perfect knowledge, and contempla-

[1] One would say rather that Suso must have had Par. xxx. before him.

tion, and fruition of God. According to St. Augustine, the blessed life is eternal peace, the perpetual sight of God, and the recognition of Him as the ultimate and supreme goal for man. The schoolmen, whose chief bliss in this world consisted in subtle distinction, placed the bliss of Heaven principally in a sharpened intelligence. Thus Duns Scotus, among others, held it for an important question, whether the soul could recognise the quiddities of things. Peter Lombard declares the knowledge of God to be eternal blessedness. (Dante himself says (Conv. iii. 8) that blessedness is contentment—at which all else aims as the noblest state. Elsewhere (iii. 15) he writes: 'The eyes of wisdom are her proofs, with which the truth is most surely seen; and her smile is her persuasion, wherein the inward light of wisdom is seen as under a veil; and in these two is perceived that highest pleasure of blessedness, which is the chief good in Paradise.')

It is not then because his fancy lacked power, or that he found himself incompetent to describe a variety of joys and raptures, but with full deliberate purpose, that (Dante has rejected in his *Paradise* any picture of enjoyments that could bear even a distant relation with those of sense.)(His aim was not to charm and delight the fancy, but to show the reader in all earnest how man arrives at the blessedness of life eternal.)(But if this consists in knowledge, it is obvious that in Paradise no gradation of pleasures and enjoyments, but a graded increase in knowledge alone can find a place.) If in Hell and Purgatory we have two systems of sins and punishments, and therewith gradations of guilt, and of retribution or purification, in Paradise it is a system of cognitions. (The raptures of Dante's Heaven are of a purely spiritual and intellectual sort, while the torments of Hell and the pains of Purgatory are physical. In direct contrast to the everlasting monotony, the eternal, unchanging sameness, which makes Hell yet more hellish, we have in Heaven eternal progress, eternal ascent from knowledge to knowledge, whereby Heaven becomes more heavenly. Starting with questions of cosmology, such as that of the markings in the moon, we advance to the highest and gravest questions of philosophy and theology, upon which the pilgrim receives information. The nature and value of free will, merit, and recompense; the nature of men and angels, creation, sin and redemption, providence, the government of the world, grace and justice, faith, hope, and charity, resurrection and judgment,—the highest or final problems of science and knowledge are here solved, and with each solution comes an increase in blessedness, which reaches its completion and culminating point when at length the spirit looks upon the mysteries of the Trinity in Unity and the Incarnation.

CHAPTER V[1]

EXPOSITION AND DISSEMINATION

HAD the poet been permitted to live longer, he would probably have himself undertaken the task of expounding his great poem. If the letter to Can Grande be really his, he actually began the work, and regretted that he could not at that time go on with it. In chapter xxxii. we read: 'This is the general sense of the second part of the Prologue; but I shall not now expound it in detail. For my domestic needs constrain me, so that I must needs leave alone this and other things useful to the commonweal. But I hope that of your munificence I may at another season be permitted to proceed to a profitable exposition.' If he wrote this, he must himself have perceived the need and the use for a commentary to the *Commedia*, and purposed himself to write one; as he undoubtedly would have done if his premature death had not put an end to all plans and projects.

It is a pity that it never got beyond the preface. Even if the commentary had turned out as exhaustive as that to the odes expounded in the *Convito*, and consequently con-

---

[1] The latter portion of this chapter (which represents two of the original) is of the nature of a paraphrase; as it was thought that a good deal of the matter would hardly interest English readers.

sisted of a stately army of volumes, we should have gained much, apart from the absolute certainty with which we should have understood the whole and the details, in being saved the thousands of volumes which have been devoted to the exposition of the text and of individual passages. Or may we regard it as fortunate for the poet and his work that he was unable himself to write the commentary? Difficult problems tempt us to solve them; what is dark and mysterious exercises upon us a special force of attraction. If everything in the *Commedia* had been from the first made clear by an explanation of the highest authenticity; if all problems had been solved by the author himself, few would have been the minds, in all probability, who would have occupied themselves with the sublime poem.

The work of comment and exposition began immediately after Dante's death—perhaps even during his life—and to-day, after six centuries, flourishes more vigorously than ever. Even as these lines are being written, a commentary which is to be completed in three folio volumes is in course of appearing.[1] If we count partial and complete commentaries, we run into hundreds; while explanations of individual passages are to be reckoned by the thousand. The value of many among these is, however, questionable. Less numerous is the tale of original expounders of Dante. Of many so-called commentators one may safely say that they are in fact merely compilers—in many cases simple excerptors and copyists. This began very early. Jacopo della Lana, the 'Ottimo,' the Anonymous Florentine, give their names to three commentaries, each consisting of three stout volumes; but at bottom they form but a single commentary, which in later times was copied with the addition of little

[1] I cannot identify the edition referred to.

fresh matter. A genealogy of Dante-commentaries would be a very interesting piece of work, which would lead to a result very similar to that of modern inquiries into the origin of mankind.

Of commentaries at present known, that of Graziuolo de' Bambaglioli, chancellor of Bologna, passes for the oldest, having been written in 1324, three years after the poet's death. It is written in Latin, and does not extend beyond the first division of the poem. Later commentators have used it freely, and it was translated into Italian before the end of the fourteenth century. We owe the publication of this translation to Lord Vernon, the Maecenas of Dante-study. The Latin original was long thought to be lost. It was only after fifty years' research and inquiry that Witte discovered the earliest MS. of it: but he never had the opportunity to edit it as it deserved. Between 1880 and 1890 a second MS. was discovered by him, and soon after a third; and at the present moment (June 1891) Antonio Fiammazzo is engaged in editing this earliest of commentaries on Dante in its original Latin form.

Not very much later is the anonymous Italian commentary to the *Hell*, edited by Francesco Selmi in 1865. Indeed, in the editor's opinion, this is the oldest, and written in the year of the poet's death; though Carducci assigns it to 1328. The unnamed commentator announces himself as a Florentine of the Black party, and is therefore by no means enthusiastic in favour of the poet. He must have worked independently, for he was no scholar, but a commercial man, and was not likely to have known of other comments if any such existed. The work is of interest considering who the author was, and the date of its composition; but of small value in respect of the understanding of the poem. The writer does not seem to have known the poet personally, and has often failed to understand the poem which he is by way of explaining.

Both Dante's sons, James and Peter, are reckoned among his commentators. A comment written in 1323 or 1324 is ascribed to the former; but its value is scarcely higher than that of those already mentioned. Its genuineness has been seriously doubted. But in the preface the author distinctly names himself as James, son of Dante, and it is hard to imagine that a forger would have ventured to do this at a time when the real owner of the name was living. No doubt in this commentary we find no information with regard to Dante's personal fortunes, and the commentator shows no intimate acquaintance with the position of circumstances at Florence. But that the son should say little or nothing about his father beyond what arose immediately out of the poem on which he was commenting is very natural, while it is extremely doubtful whether he would have had any acquaintance with Florentine affairs. We do not know at what age he left Florence, but we know that after 1315 he must have been among the exiles, so that his notes cannot have been written there. Thus we may provisionally regard the commentary as being by him.

Of incomparably more importance is the commentary which embraces the whole poem by Peter, probably the elder son of the poet. This is composed in Latin, and is distinguished by theological, philosophical, and scholastic learning, not taken at second hand, but the result of individual study and reading. Even of this work the genuineness has been doubted or even positively denied, as by Tiraboschi and still more by Dionisi and his followers. But as the commentary was written in 1340, we can say also in this case that a forger would not have given himself out as Petrus Dantis, and spoken of the poet as his father at a time when the real Petrus Dantis was still alive. With regard to his want of acquaintance with matters at Florence, the same is to be said as in the case of James, and if Petrus accuses the poet of sundry vices he does not do it from want of filial piety, but simply because in his day people thought themselves bound to find in Dante's verses confessions of sins on his part whether he was expressing pity for the lost and penitent or severely blaming particular sins. These were simply the principles of interpretation in vogue at the time, and if a commentator was unable to burst these fetters, this is no reason for thinking that he cannot have been the poet's own son. This commentary is almost exclusively concerned with the allegorical meaning of the poem, while the literal explanation is for the most part neglected.

Earlier and even more important is the Italian commentary upon the whole poem by Jacopo della Lana of Bologna. This was written between 1321 and 1333; it became one of the chief sources from which later expounders drew, and was twice printed before 1500. It is not wanting in mistakes, misconceptions, and blunders of all kinds, but the commentator clearly takes pains to understand the poem on all sides and to explain it correctly, so that in a certain sense he may be called the Father of Dante-commentators. The anonymous author of the so-called *ottimo comento*, which was written not much later, has borrowed from him to a degree which it is difficult to reconcile with modern notions of literary propriety, but in those days people's views on this subject were different. The *ottimo* is not the only one who, setting to work with the best intention of being independent, has used his predecessors freely in the first part, has grown weary in his exposition of the *Purgatory*, and has ended by copying the commentary to the *Paradise* almost word for word. Thus this *ottimo comento* is in the first portion borrowed from Lana, Bambaglioli, and others, but still may be called an independent work in which the writer now and again appeals to his personal acquaintance with Dante and to information received from him. In the second part, as we proceed, his dependence upon Jacopo della Lana appears more and more, and in the third part we get simply a new and very slightly altered edition of his predecessor's work, so much so that the most recent editor of Lana's commentary saw reason to declare 'The *ottimo* is Lana.'

At Boccaccio's instance the Florentines, in 1373, founded a professorial chair of Dante, that is to say they made a special post for the public exposition of the *Commedia*. Boccaccio himself was the first to be entrusted with this office, and out of his public lectures a commentary grew; or rather his commentary is the text-book to his lectures. This, however, contains only the first half of the *Hell*, since lectures and commentary were interrupted by his death. The claim of this work to independence cannot be denied, though the author has used his learning and his reading in a way which, usual as it was at that time, appears to us too free. Boccaccio's wearisome garrulousness is shown here in all its extent, and the scholastic divisions and distinctions hardly make the commentary other than tedious reading. Boccaccio apparently had Dante's *Convito* before his eyes as a model; still, in spite of all defects, this commentary is highly important, even indispensable, both on account of the historical, biographical, and literary references and from a linguistic point of view. Like Dante himself in the *Convito*, Boccaccio has kept apart the literal and allegorical sides of his explanation, and therewith has shown the right road. He cannot, however, be acquitted of the charge of having, in the allegorical explanation, imported more than he found.

Another Italian commentary has been ascribed to Boccaccio, but, as the glaring contradictions between the two works place beyond doubt, erroneously. This embraces the whole poem, and has been edited by Lord Vernon. It was written in 1375 by some person unknown, who does not even put on the mask of Boccaccio, and is generally known as the false Boccaccio. Some few historical notices, now and again rather questionable, are found for the first time in this; otherwise this work is of little value.

Benvenuto Rambaldi of Imola is beyond all question the most important and the most eminent of all commentators on Dante in the fourteenth century. His comprehensive Latin commentary is the result of lectures delivered by him in Bologna beginning in 1374. Benvenuto speaks of Boccaccio as his master, perhaps on account of having attended the lectures delivered by him in St. Stephen's Church at Florence. Benvenuto is the historian among Dante commentators, and in this respect is so important that Muratori made extracts from his commentary on the score of purely historical interest, and published them in the first volume of his *Italian Antiquities.* He is thoroughly conscientious, and as trustworthy as a scholar could be in the fourteenth century, when historical criticism had not yet come into existence. It is only recently that we have been able to honour him as he deserves, since with the exception of Muratori's extracts, his great work was only to be found in MSS. to which few had access. It was even almost brought into discredit during the sixties by the publication of an ignorantly-fabricated work which passed itself off as a translation. Now through the munificence of Mr. William Warren Vernon, himself a distinguished commentator, who has inherited from his father Lord Vernon his enthusiasm for Dante and his liberality in the service of learning, this important commentary in its complete form has been made accessible to all. In 1887 it appeared at Florence in five handsome volumes.

Almost simultaneously Francesco da Buti (1354-1406) was lecturing on the *Commedia* at the University of Pisa. On these lectures is based his Italian commentary, equally comprising the whole poem, and completed in 1385. If Benvenuto is the historian among expounders of Dante, Buti is the grammarian. At the same time his historical equipment is at times defective, and Foscolo was not altogether wrong when he said that Buti was rich in anecdote but too credulous. His importance, however, as we have said, lies in the philological direction, and here the learned professor of grammar is in his element. These two, Benvenuto and Buti, worthily close the list of the fourteenth-century commentators.

To the same century possibly belongs the Italian commentary of the 'nameless Florentine,' which was edited and highly esteemed by Fanfani, but is a compilation of doubtful origin and of no original value. The unknown compiler has borrowed freely in his exposition of the *Hell* from Boccaccio and Peter, Dante's son, with additions of his own in which he appears as neither a good philologer nor a trustworthy historian. He soon lost patience with his work. In the *Purgatory* he pillages from Lana, and in the *Paradise* simply copies him verbatim. Probably this work dates from the beginning of the fifteenth century.

During the same century three more commentaries were written. The first by Guiniforto degli Bargigi of Bergamo, in the Italian language, extends only to the *Hell*, and is devoid of any original value, being almost servilely dependent on his predecessors. Moreover, we have only a mutilated edition of it, since the editor thought fit to cut out all the theology as being too rigidly orthodox. Far more important is the commentary by Cristoforo Landino of Florence upon the whole poem, completed in the year 1480, and representing the culture of the Renaissance. This commentator has special merits as a purifier of the text, but his exposition plunges too deep into mysticism, and achieves far too much in the way of allegorising. For this reason the learned commentary, which for more than half a century had complete possession of the interpretation of the poem, stands for us in a decidedly lower position than those of the predecessors of whom its author made use. The list of the commentaries written in Latin is closed by that of Stefano Talice da Ricaldone, which consists of lectures published in 1474. It is little more than an epitome of Benvenuto, for which reason it remained unnoticed, and passed completely into oblivion, until it was recently rediscovered, and edited at the instance of the present King of Italy.

· The sixteenth century produced three new commentaries, not reckoning either the paradoxical work of Vincenzo Buonanni upon the *Hell*, nor the scanty notes which Lodovico Dolce of Venice (who was the first to assign the epithet *Divina* to the *Commedia*) appended to the poem. In 1544 Alessandro Vellutello of Lucca published his commentary. He, though standing on the shoulders of his predecessors, especially of Landino, is far more sober, reasonable, and reserved in the matter of allegorical interpretation. The commentary of Bernardino Daniello, also of Lucca, which appeared in 1568, though containing little new matter, is distinguished by careful grammatical interpretation of the text, while Ludovico Castelvetro, in his exposition of the first twenty-nine cantos of the *Hell*, displays himself only too often as an offensive criticaster.

In the seventeenth century the study of Dante fell to pieces all over Italy. Only three small and worthless editions of the *Commedia* appeared in this century. An age which delighted in empty bombast and childish metaphor was naturally unable to sympathise with Dante's massive style. As nobody read Dante, it was natural that nobody should comment on him. Yet even the ill-famed *seicento* did not venture to bring him into ridicule, as Voltaire, Bettinelli, and others chose to do in the last century, with the result of making themselves ridiculous for ever.

The study of Dante gradually revived in the eighteenth century, but the oldest commentators were now forgotten. People knew only Landino and Vellutello, or by great good luck Daniello, who had been but once printed. Thus to some extent the work had to be begun again from the beginning. Giovanni Antonio Volpi of Padua (1686-1766) published his *Indici*, a kind of commentary in dictionary form, which in its day was often printed and much used, but has now been superseded by better work. The Jesuit Pompeo Venturi of Siena (1693-1752) put forth a compressed exposition of the poem limited to elementary explanations, which in many cases looks like a citation of the poet before the inquisition. The Franciscan Bonaventura Lombardi, a man of small intelligence, but of great mechanical industry, about the end of the century wrote one of the most serviceable commentaries to the *Commedia*. Of him Witte says that he had the qualification of a great love for the poet, and a persevering industry. In his verbal explanations he holds with the predecessors of Venturi, basing them more completely than any other writer on works treating of the language in general. The list of his new explanations is not very great, and deals for the most part with subordinate matters; while it cannot be denied that they are frequently unfortunate, and bear in a curious degree the stamp of the narrow mind which forces itself to have an opinion. Still this commentary, both at home and abroad, was rightly received with approbation as the most careful, most industrious, and most serviceable for immediate wants.

Most of the so-called commentators of the nineteenth century have subsisted on the provision made by Lombardi with occasional contributions from Venturi. The most honourable have been those who have reprinted Lombardi's commentary with more or fewer additions of their own. Thus De Romanis, in the two Roman editions of 1815 and 1820, and the Paduan editors in the famous five-volume edition of 1822. The reproduction of this work in one volume by Passigli of Florence (1838 and 1847-1852) is still the most serviceable edition for ordinary use, and its value is increased by the appendix, which gives an abundance of explanatory matter in extracts from fifty-two not easily accessible works.

Other commentators, as Portirelli, Poggiali, Costa, Fraticelli, Bianchi, borrow from Lombardi, with some additions from their own and other sources. Giosafatte Biagioli wished to walk on his own lines and thought no little of his own independence, but produced from his own resources little more than dull trivialities. To quote Witte: 'He flatters himself that his explanations are all his own. Indeed he has already been found fault with for devoting very little attention to the older commentators. Yet we find that he repeats just those opinions of his predecessors which are most obvious, and what is worse, others which are often unreal enough, are attacked in a haughty fashion quite out of proportion to the dignity of the subject. The very inelegant and at times colloquial language makes the book almost unreadable.' Antonio Cesari proposed, as the modest title of his work imports, to give only an aesthetic commentary, yet his performance is pretty thorough and complete, and forms still a serviceable and very readable exposition. Gabriele Rossetti filled two volumes with his own wild fancies, and put them forth as an 'analytical commentary' to the *Hell*. Niccolo Tommaseo, with a wider if not always deeper equipment of scholarship, and making more diligent use than had hitherto been done of his earlier predecessors, wrote a commentary which is still indispensable to the student. We will not speak here of the innumerable commentators of recent times, since it is hardly becoming to pass judgment upon one's fellow-labourers in the same field.

Hitherto we have spoken only of commentators in the more limited sense, that is to say of scholars who have explained the poem in the whole or in parts. If we reckon in the writers of brief notes, their number for Italy alone may reach more than a hundred. But we come then to the immeasurable host of those who, without actually writing commentaries, have devoted themselves to the study and exposition of Dante, and have made more or less important contributions to the understanding of the *Divina Commedia*. To reckon them all, and give even the briefest estimate of their works, would require a special and very comprehensive book; even the bibliography of them would fill a stout volume. It is therefore obvious that we must quite decline to give even in outline the scantiest picture of the magnificent activity which has been shown in the domain of Dante research, an activity which, at the present day, is assuming ever larger dimensions.

Foreign countries, too, have taken a vigorous part in the work. In former times the general aim was to introduce the poet in each case into the literature of the country, so that the foreign Dante literature of former days consists of little more than translations, paraphrases, summaries, biographies, and the like. But when Dante had been made known, then began the serious task of penetrating deeper into the understanding of the poem, and with such success that even in Italy at the present day it is not permissible to ignore what foreign nations have done in this respect. France has been worthily represented by Ozanam, Fauriel, Ampère, and De Batines, whose works are among the gems of Dante literature. France, too, had her Rossetti in Eugène Aroux, who outdid the Neapolitan in bold unreason, and involuntarily indeed did much to draw a wider attention to the poet. In England the two Vernons, father and son, have, by publishing the old commentaries, done more than many professed editors of Dante to help readers to understand the *Commedia*, and they will be mentioned with gratitude and honour when many recent editors have fallen into oblivion. Neither, however, has confined himself to the editing of hitherto unprinted commentaries. Lord Vernon produced the most magnificent work on the *Hell* that has ever been printed. His son William Warren Vernon holds a distinguished place among expounders of Dante by reason of his remarkable commentary, which is not yet finished. Beside him stand Butler and Plumptre, as well as the American Longfellow, whose commentaries are well worth consideration. If it be said that they rely materially upon other, and especially upon the old commentators, this is literally correct; but if it be meant as a reproach it is quite unreasonable. Any one who at the present day wished to explain Dante without a profound study of the old commentators, and a consultation of the more eminent among the new, would only make himself ridiculous, and waste his time and trouble. A thorough commentary upon the *Commedia* must henceforth be grounded upon the presentation, observation, and critical testing of the material which already exists in such abundance; and its original value will be great in proportion as the commentator has conscientiously consulted all that has hitherto been done in this line.

The science of Dante has to thank the English-speaking peoples for a work which up to the present is unique of its kind, the use and value of which can only be recognised and estimated after a lengthened use of it. We mean the concordance of the *Divina Commedia* compiled by Professor Edward Allen Fay, with astounding labour and admirable diligence. This has lately reached us from America, the new Ravenna of the great poet, whither his children in the shape of bibliographical curiosities follow him one after another so long as they are not kept shut up in public or private libraries. Fay's work is as yet little known on the Continent, but will without doubt gradually become recognised as one of the most indispensable aids to the study of the great poem. Even the present writer, who has long had the whole poem stamped on his memory, admits with gratitude that he has occasion every day to take down this book. It is certain that this at any rate will never grow dusty in the library of a student of Dante.

In the field of Dante-research, Germany at present takes incontestably the first rank, considering what it has done for the explanation and profounder interpretation of the *Commedia*. The commentaries of Kannegiesser, Streckfuss, Kopisch, and others, have no need to fear comparison with those most generally in use in Italian,

French, and English; while those of Philalethes and Witte remain unrivalled. Independently, moreover, of continuous commentaries, we may say, without hesitation, that no nation has penetrated so far into the comprehension of the sacred poem or rendered it such prominent services. One can hardly particularise individuals without the risk of doing injustice to others. We may, however, mention Blanc's Dante dictionary, a work such as only German scholarship and German industry could have produced, and which Italy, as she has admitted by translating it, has nothing to match; Hettinger, the venerable theologian of Würzburg, who has been able almost more than any one else to interest cultivated readers in Dante and make his poem comprehensible at all points to them; Pauer, Ruth, and Schlosser, and above all Carl Witte who devoted wholly and entirely the gifts which fell to his lot as a marvellous child [1] to the poet who sang the marvels of eternity, labouring more than half a century with marvellous diligence, and recognised throughout the educated world as the prince of Dante scholars. Many other names could be cited from Germany but we may be content with these. The *History of Dante Literature in Germany* was written and printed nearly ten years ago, and we may be allowed to refer our readers to it.

A poem like the *Divina Commedia* may be explained and rendered intelligible not only verbally but by pictures. It has exercised a powerful influence upon art, especially in Italy, and art has on its side taken trouble to interpret the poem in its own language. This is not the place to enter into details with regard to Dante's influence upon the

[1] In the *Annual Register* for 1811 will be found mention of 'a boy ten and a half years old, who is a real phenomenon. His name is Charles Witte. At eight years he possessed Greek, Latin, French, English, and Italian.' Three years later it is recorded that he had taken his Doctor's degree.

pictorial arts; the works of Giotto and Giovanni Pisano, Taddeo Gaddi and Andrea Orcagna, Fra Angelico, Leonardo da Vinci, Raphael, and so many others belong to the history of art and cannot here be spoken of. Just as little can we enumerate the illustrations and miniatures contained in old manuscripts of the *Commedia*. The history of Dante's influence upon the arts would be the subject for a separate work which does not as yet exist, but for which it may be hoped the world will not have much longer to wait. Here we have but to mention briefly the more important artists who have endeavoured to translate Dante's verses into the language of art by the representation of the whole poem or individual scenes.

The first illustrator of the *Commedia* was Sandro Botticelli (1447-1515). Formerly the only fruits of his zealous study of Dante that were known were the eighteen engravings found in some rare copies of the edition with Landino's commentary published at Florence in 1481. The engraving of these was by some attributed to the artist himself; but others, with more probability, assign the work to Baccio Baldini. It is only quite recently that the full importance of Botticelli as an illustrator of Dante has become known through the manuscript formerly in the Duke of Hamilton's collection, now at Berlin, which has been made accessible in a handsome reproduction by Lippmann. His younger contemporary, Michelangelo Buonarroti, holds also an honoured place. His enthusiasm for Dante is well known, as also the fact that his famous Last Judgment owed its inspiration to the poet. But he had also prepared a noble collection of illustrations to the *Commedia*, which, to the grievous injury both of art and of the study of Dante, were lost at sea between Civita Vecchia and Leghorn.

Federigo Zuccaro (1560-1610) executed some hundred

illustrations to the *Commedia*, which exist in Florence, but have not been edited. Those of Jan van Straet, or Stradanus, of Bruges (1536-1604), a pupil of Vasari, have recently been reproduced. Neither the last-mentioned nor others of the sixteenth and seventeenth centuries have any particular merit—Zatta's large edition of 1757-1758 being rather well meant than successful; and it is not until we come to John Flaxman (1755-1826) that we find any artistic illustrations of the poem that are in any way worthy of the original. With less precise execution, the designs of William Blake display, as might be expected, an even higher artistic inspiration.

In the present century, artistic activity started with the Florence folio of 1817-1819, known as the 'Anchor' edition, containing one hundred and twenty-five copper-plate engravings. It had a great reputation in its day, but is now almost forgotten; largely for the reason that the artists did not take the trouble to form a conception of Dante's thoughts, but evolved their beautiful pictures from their own fancy. The hundred outline drawings by Sofia Giacomelli, which were issued with Artaud's translation (Paris 1813), and the hundred and one by Giangiacomo Macchiavelli in the Bologna editions of 1819-1823 and 1826, are best passed over in silence. Pinelli made a vain attempt to rival Flaxman; but Genelli's sketches are more satisfactory. Joseph Anton Koch, a Tyrolese, designed frescoes illustrative of the *Commedia*, some of the cartoons for which are preserved in the Royal Library at Dresden, and have been photographed. Cornelius's outlines are good, and were honoured with an explanatory text by Döllinger.

Of all recent illustrations those by Gustave Doré have met with most success,—to an extent, it must be said, beyond their merits. It cannot be denied that they possess a certain grandeur; but they, again, rarely embody Dante's conceptions, and are, on the whole, only fancy pictures suggested by the poem. By far the finest and most intelligent work in this line has been done by the late Francesco Scaramuzza of Parma. Posterity will perhaps be astounded to find how little was known of his great work in the last decade of the nineteenth century. The charming little designs of Mrs. Traquair (Edinburgh, 1890) should not pass unnoticed.

In our days Dante-societies for the study and interpretation of the poem have arisen. The first was started in Dresden in 1865, under the patronage of 'Philalethes.' The *Jahrbuch* (Leipzig, 1867-1877) contains a mass of valuable material, but has now ceased to appear: whether the society itself exists or not, no man seems to know. Another society was founded in 1881 at Cambridge, Massachusetts. Its yearly transactions, less voluminous than those of the German body, appear with great regularity; and we have to thank it for the production of such a work as Fay's *Concordance*. An Italian society has recently been set on foot in Florence by Carlo Negroni, an indefatigable student; but beyond its bibliographical bulletin it has so far produced nothing. Fanfani's plan of a periodical was only carried out after his death, by the publication at Verona of a monthly journal, *L' Alighieri*, which may be expected to do useful work.

One of the most difficult questions with which research has to deal is that of the text. We cannot, alas! accept Dumas's view that 2000 copies of the poem were produced at Ravenna under Dante's supervision. Even one per cent of that number would have much lightened the task of the textual critic. But as a matter of fact, there is not one MS.

of which we are entitled to assume that it even existed in the poet's lifetime. Consequently the received text has been corrupted in many places; and from Landino onwards, commentators have endeavoured to purify it. Unfortunately they have never been clear as to the principles to be followed. The older critics sought, no doubt, to support the reading they adopted by the authority of one or more MSS. But their actions as to the comparative value of the authorities were primitive, and too frequently most votes were allowed to carry the day; with the result that the collection of a few more MSS. might upset the previous judgment. The unsoundness of this principle is clear, when we consider that no number of copies made from a given MS. can have any more authority than the original one. It is related of one scribe that he made a hundred copies of the *Commedia*, and earned enough thereby to portion his numerous daughters. Now, as a poor man, he is not likely to have possessed more than one early MS.; and if we know which this was, why need we search after the hundred? Our first task must therefore be to establish the pedigree of our MSS., after which few will remain of the existing five hundred with which criticism need trouble itself.

This work, however, is at present far from being finished. Witte began upon it half a century ago, but came to no certain results, chiefly no doubt because he chose a too lengthy and too uncertain road. Since his death the task has been seriously approached by Mussafia, Negroni, and others; while the works of Moore and Täuber justify a hope that we may be nearing the goal of a definitive critical edition of Dante. Nothing of the kind exists so far. Not one of the four hundred or so editions of the poem can claim to satisfy the first demands of criticism. The first eight, which appeared between 1471 and 1480, give each the text of some one MS., retaining even the most obvious blunders. Landino's text, which came out in 1481, was purged of gross errors; but was superseded by the Aldines (1502-1515), which followed one, and that a somewhat late codex. This practically fixed the text for three centuries. With the exception of the Giunta edition of 1506, based on a good, but not immaculate MS., and Vellutello's of 1544, which was the result of a collection of several MSS., every edition of the sixteenth century rests upon this. Even Landino and Vellutello had to resign themselves to seeing their comments printed with it. The Cruscan of 1595, in spite of the misleading boasts of the Academicians, is really based on the Aldine; and from this no one for the next two centuries ventured to depart. Not till the end of the eighteenth century did Dionisi and Lombardi venture to shake themselves free of its fetters, and as Witte (*Dante - Forschungen*, i. p. 253) says, 'to doubt the infallibility of the Academy.'

Dionisi submitted to the imagined authority of the MS. in the Santa Croce convent at Florence; Lombardi venerated the Nidobeatine edition of 1477-78, and partly adopted its variants. Portirelli followed Lombardi faithfully in his text, Poggiali in his commentary; while the Paduan editors manfully continued his work. Fantoni's edition of 1820 is an accurate copy of a good MS. which claims to be the autograph of Boccaccio. Viviani's is a worthless and dishonest compilation. That of the four Florentines, Becchi, Nicolini, Capponi, and Borghi, is based on twenty MSS., but the readings are selected without any principle save the taste of the editors. Much was expected in the way of textual criticism from Ugo Foscolo, but when his edition appeared it was a disappointment. Witte reconstructed the text, adhering closely to four of the best and earliest MSS., and allowing no word to appear that was not supported by at least one of them. His work has been both praised and depreciated beyond its deserts; but must be regarded as, though not conclusive, yet the first really critical edition, and to that extent a pioneer. The edition of the Codex Cassinensis, produced with admirable monastic industry, offers a mass of critical material nowhere else obtainable with equal completeness. Scarabelli's publications are inconceivably superficial, and have fallen into oblivion after an existence of hardly twenty years. In the author's own edition the principle of taking into account not only the MS., but the earliest commentators, has been adopted. Some commentaries are, it will be admitted, older than any extant MSS., and even in the case of others we may assume that Dante's own sons, for instance, had probably seen his autograph; while Jacopo della Lana, the 'Ottimo,' and others doubtless had access to MSS. earlier than any which we now possess. The definitive edition will unquestionably have to be based on information drawn from both sources; but the editor's private taste must have no place.[1] Apart from the fact that our taste is not that of the Middle Ages, our business is to inquire, not what Dante ought to have written, but what he really did write.

A few words should be said about translations. In Dante's own day, as we learn from his correspondence with Giovanni del Virgilio, learned men were of the opinion that he ought to have written his great poem in Latin. Naturally, therefore, as soon as it became famous, people set to work to turn it into that language. The first to do

---

[1] As will readily be seen, this doctrine, though sound in the main, may be pushed too far. Dante certainly did not write nonsense; but of no copyist can we be sure that he always knew nonsense when he saw it.

this appears to have been Matteo Ronto, a monk of Siena († 1443). Several MSS. exist of his work, which is thought to have been composed in 1381; but only fragments of it have been printed. In the eighteenth century Carlo d' Aquino, a Jesuit, published a Latin translation (Naples, 1728); and several have appeared since 1800. At present these are of course merely the recreations of scholars, but in the Middle Ages it was otherwise. Learned men who despised the vulgar tongue may even have found it hard to bring themselves to read Dante in the original; but in any case, as the example of John of Serravalle shows, they wished to make his work accessible to foreign scholars.[1] Next, for its further dissemination, would follow translations into foreign vernaculars. Then we have Provençal renderings before the middle of the fourteenth century. Little more than a century after Dante's death the whole poem was translated into Catalan by Andreas Febrer;[2] and the *Hell* into Spanish by Villegas (Burgos, 1515). In the present century several Spanish translations have appeared; one at Buenos Ayres.

France has produced many translations of the *Commedia*. Specimens of two, dating from the fifteenth and sixteenth centuries respectively, were given by Littré in the preface to his Old French version of the *Hell*. The first printed was that by Grangier in 1596—a mere paraphrase, and a tasteless one. France has indeed been unfortunate in her translations of the *Commedia*, the best being Fiorentino's, in prose, published 1843, and frequently reproduced. Lamennais' is too literal; Ratisbonne's probably the next best to Fiorentino's.

---

[1] It may be here mentioned that Serravalle's commentary has been recently edited by order of Pope Leo XIII.
[2] First published Barcelona, 1878.

It was not till more than four hundred years after Dante's death that Germany began to pay attention to his works; but the delay has been amply atoned for. The first complete translation, in prose, by Lebrecht Bachenschwanz, appeared in 1767-69 at Leipzig. This has no great merit, and we must come down to the present century before we find any worthy of record. Karl Ludwig Kannegiesser published his version in *terza rima* between 1809-21; and it has since gone through frequent editions, the last under the auspices of Witte (Leipzig, 1873). The style is dignified, and the commentary valuable; but the language is often obscure and somewhat rough. The version of Streckfuss, likewise in *terza rima*, which also has been often printed between 1824 and 1871, is fluent, readable, and clear, but modernised to the point of occasional triviality. But all these were far surpassed by the blank verse rendering due to the late King of Saxony, then Prince John, who used the pseudonym of Philalethes. This appeared first at Dresden between 1828 and 1849, and has been reprinted at intervals till 1891. It is distinguished by admirable fidelity and a masterly command of language; while the commentary is a gem of Dante literature which Italy herself must envy, and which she now for the first time is making her own by means of a translation. Ludwig Gottfried Blanc at the age of eighty-three published a translation of the entire poem into blank verse (Halle, 1864); but in this case the work was injured by the author's fame as a scholar, which led to higher expectations than his poetical ability was adequate to fulfil. His notes, moreover, were far too scanty. Witte was more successful. His version (Berlin, 1865 and 1876), also in blank verse, showed more poetic skill, and was provided with a commentary, which in point of usefulness stands next to that of Philalethes. Altogether Germany possesses at the present moment seventeen complete translations of the *Divina Commedia*; and, reckoning in the various editions through which some of these have passed, it has been printed no less than forty-one times in the German language. Besides these there are partial translations in great numbers. Considering that in addition several editions of the original text have appeared in Germany, it may safely be said that hardly any foreign poet is so well known and so diligently read by Germans as Dante.

Among English-speaking nations the *Commedia* is perhaps even more widely known. At any rate, if we reckon complete and partial versions, English possesses more of them than German. The first, of the *Hell* only, by C. Rogers, was published in 1782. The Rev. Henry Boyd followed with a similar work in 1785; and in 1802 produced a translation, in six-line stanzas, of the entire poem. It cannot be said that his version possesses any merit; while his notes are scanty and unintelligent. Three years later appeared the first instalment (*Hell*, i-xvii.) of Cary's rendering in blank verse; and in 1814 the entire work, in three pocket volumes. From its appearance the serious study of Dante in England may be said to date. It has been repeatedly reprinted, and may be said to have become, in its way, a classic. The notes, for the most part historical and literary, are admirable; and the book will always be indispensable to students of Dante. Of other verse translations the most important are Dayman's in *terza rima* (*Hell*, 1843; entire poem, 1865); Pollock's, in blank verse (1854), with outline illustrations, and notes few but useful; Longfellow's (Cambridge, Mass., 1867), perhaps the most popular of any in blank verse, with copious notes and illustrative extracts; Plumptre's (1886-87) in *terza rima*, with copious introductions and notes, distinguished by independent and thorough research, but suffering a little from the translator's readiness to accept almost any theory if sufficiently picturesque; and Haselfoot's (1887), also in *terza rima*, an excellent version, with short but valuable notes, modelled apparently on those of Cary. Prose translations are few. Dr. J. A. Carlyle's admirable rendering of the *Hell* remains a fragment. The *Purgatory* has been well translated by W. S. Dugdale. The present translator has published an edition of the whole poem (1880-1892), with a prose version and notes; and Mr. C. E. Norton of Cambridge, Mass., a prose translation. Another, by Sir E. Sullivan, has just appeared. On the whole it may be said that since Blanc, Witte, Philalethes, and Hettinger have departed, England and America have entered into Germany's inheritance of Dante-research.

It would be hard to find any literary language into which the *Commedia* has not been rendered during the second half of the present century. Russia has a prose version of the *Hell* by V. van Dima, and one in verse by Dmitri Min. Molbech has translated the whole poem into Danish in *terza rima*. Portugal, Sweden, and Greece have their versions, the last-named by Musurus Pasha. Holland possesses several; Armenia, Poland, Bohemia, Hungary, are all represented. Others may have escaped our notice; but we may safely say that with the exception of the Bible no book has been so often printed, none so often translated into other languages, as Dante's *Divina Commedia*. The fame for which he so eagerly longed has fallen to his lot in a measure which in his boldest dreams he can never have ventured to anticipate.

INDEX

ABATI, Durante degli, 49
—— Neri, 114 n.
Acquasparta, Matthew of, Cardinal of Ostia, mission to Florence, 12, 89, 91, 95, 98
Acre, loss of, 10
Adam, 409, 410
—— of Brescia, 9
Adimari, the, 8
Adolf of Nassau, Emperor, 143, 256, 298
Aglauros, 399
Agubbio, Oderisi of, 398
Aguglione, Baldo d', 151
Albert of Austria, Emperor, 143, 256, 298; death of, 13
—— the Great, 9, 407
Alberti, Neri degli, Prior of Florence, 81
Aldighieri, Dante's surname derived from, 32
Aldobrandeschi, Umberto, 398
Alessandria, battle of, 16
Alexander, in Hell, 390
—— IV., Pope, 7
Alfani, Gianni, 272
Alighieri, family, rank of, 36-39
—— Antonia, 72, 73, 164
—— Beatrice, 72, 73, 76; her existence doubted, 164
—— Dante, v. Dante
—— Francesco, 38, 49, 50, 94
—— James, 72, 73, 76, 164; commentary ascribed to, 467
—— Peter, 72, 73, 76; at Ravenna, 162, 164; his commentary on *Div. Com.*, 467

Alighiero, Dante's ancestor, 34
—— Dante's father, 34, 47-50; supposed exile, 43-45
Allegranza, Peter, his MS. of *Vita Nuova*, 374
Altoviti, Palmiero degli, Prior of Florence, 81
Amaury of Narbonne, 62
Amelia, Carlo d', 13
Amidei, the, 5
Ampère, 476
Anastasius II., 390
Ancona, Bishop of, mission to Germany, 88
Anjou, Charles of, v. Charles
Anonymous Florentine, commentary by, 465, 471
Antæus, 394
Apocryphal works ascribed to Dante, 364-70
Apothecaries' guild, Dante a member of, 81
Apulian dialect, Dante's remarks on, 313
Aquinas, Thomas, death of, 8; in Paradise, 407; his influence on Dante, 248, 421, 422
Aquino, Carlo d', translation of *Div. Com.*, 485
Arachne, 397
Architecture, Dante's knowledge of, 59
Arco, Moronto de, 33
Arezzo, wars with Florence, 9, 10, 13-15, 61-62; factions in, 9, 14, 61
—— Benincasa of, 396

Argenti, Filippo, 389
Aristotle, referred to by Dante, 231, 384, 421
Aroux, E., 245, 476
Ascoli, Cecco of, Dante's letter to, 163
Attila, 390
Augustine, Provincial of Franciscans, 407
—— St., 414; his conception of bliss, 461
Auvergne, Peter of, 312
Avellana, Dante's alleged retreat to, 154
Averroes, quoted by Dante, 231
Avignon, Papal See removed to, 13
Azzo VIII. of Este, 307

BACHENSCHWANZ, Lebrecht, translation of *Div. Com.*, 486
Bacon, Roger, 3
Balbo, Cesare, life of Dante, 29
Bambaglioli, Graziuolo de', commentary, 466
Bardi, Simone de', 10; his wife supposed to have been Dante's Beatrice, 187-97
Bargigi, Guiniforto degli, commentary, 471
Bartoli, Adolfo, 70 *n*., 158 *n*., 266; life of Dante, 30; unfairness to Bruni, 66; his views disputed, 163, 182, 284
Batines, De, 476
Battifolle, Countess of, letters to the Empress Margaret, 343
—— Guy of, 15, 353
Beatrice, the story of Dante's love for, 175-87; wrongly identified with Beatrice Portinari, 187-97; birth of, 41; death of, 41, 180, 191, 274, 285; influence of her death on Dante, 54, 58, 198, 240; appears in *Purg.* as symbol of the Church, 200, 444; vision of, in *Vita Nuova*, 202; her reproof of Dante, 218-24; in Paradise, 387, 403-10; Dante's works in honour of, 279, 373, 441; supposed portrait of, 29

Becchi, ed. of *Div. Com.*, 483
Bede, Venerable, 407
Beelzebub, 394
Belacqua, 68, 395
Bella, Giano della, 10, 11, 88
Bellarmine, Cardinal, 244
Bellincione, Dante's grandfather, 34
Bello, Dante's great-uncle, 34
—— Gieri del, 34
Bembo, Bernardo, repairs Dante's tomb, 167
Benedict XI., intervenes in Florentine affairs, 12, 113
—— St., 409.
Benevento, battle of, 7
Benvenuto, *v.* Rambaldi
Beranger, Count Raymond, 406
Bernard, St., 217; Dante's guide in Heaven, 410, 433
Bertrand, Cardinal, *v.* Poyet
Biagioli, Giosafatte, commentary, 474
Bianchi, commentary, 281, 474
Bilenchi, Biondo, Prior of Florence, 86
Biographies of Dante, 19-30
Biondo, Flavio, 139
Biscioni, Anton Maria, his theory regarding Beatrice, 182, 194
Blacks and Whites, origin of, 12, 86, 143, 251; strife between, 12-13, 87, 89-99, 112-20, 135; also *v.* Whites
Blake, William, illustrations of Dante, 480
Blanc, Ludwig Gottfried, Dante-dictionary, 478; translation of *Div. Com.*, 486
Boccaccio, life of Dante by, characterised as romantic, 20, 25, 253; copied by later biographers, 26-28; commentary, 102, 469; another commentary wrongly ascribed to, 470; his writings quoted, 74, 92, 99, 103, 126, 152, 161, 167, 176, 252, 260, 297, 339, 354, 355, 363; referred to, *passim*; perhaps the author of the "Letter to a Florentine Friend," 357; his gift to

Dante's daughter, 73; appointed Dante-professor, 469; copy of *Div. Com.* said to be in his handwriting, 483
Boëthius, studied by Dante, 55, 56, 211, 220, 384; idea of *Vita Nuova* taken from, 280, 283; in Paradise, 407
Bologna, factions in, 8, 13, 115, 135; Dante's visit to, 24, 125-31, 134-37; dialect of, 313
Bonafedi, Noffo, Prior of Florence, 86
Bonagiunta of Lucca, 402
Bonareddita, 34
Bonaventura, St., death of, 8; in Paradise, 407
Boniface, Archbishop of Ravenna, 402
—— VIII., pontificate of, 11-12; intervention in Florentine affairs, 87-96; policy of, 87-89, 251; alleged mission of Dante to, 100-105; death of, 113; indulgence granted by, 282; bull Unam Sanctam, 252, 333; mentioned in *Inf.*, 377, 393
Borghi, ed. of *Div. Com.*, 483
Born, Bertrand de, 393
Botticelli, Sandro, illustrations of Dante, 479
Boyd, Henry, translation of *Div. Com.*, 487
Brescia, siege of, 14, 145, 147, 151; revolt in, 14, 146
Briareus, 397
Brosse, Peter de la, 8, 396
Brunacci, Pietra, 277
Brunetto, Dante's uncle, 34
Bruni, Leonardo, life of Dante by, 27; his writings quoted, 37, 62, 63, 81, 90, 92, 100, 116, 118, 141, 148, 341, 356, 363; referred to, *passim;* alleged letter from Dante quoted by, 62, 65-66
Brutus, 394
Bull Unam Sanctam, 252, 333
Buonanni, Vincenzo, commentary, 472
Buonarroti, Michelangelo, 43; illustrations of Dante, 479

Buondelmonti, the, 5
Buti, Francesco da, life of Dante, 26, 198; lectures and commentary, 471
Butler, commentary, 476
Buto, Johannes di, document written by, 116

CACCIAGUIDA, 31-35, 120, 159, 408, 429, 459; his speech quoted, 5, 32
Caiaphas, 392
Cain, 399, 424
Calboli, Fulcieri da, 12
—— Rinieri da, 399
Cammino, Gherardo da, 298
—— Richard of, 406
Campaldino, battle of, 10, 62; Dante's presence at, 62-69
Can Grande, 15, 16, 146, 154; head of Ghibeline League, 16, 156; Dante's patron, 122, 134, 157-60, 163-64; supposed identity with the Veltro, 376
—— letter to, 158, 159, 336, 342, 440, 442; contents of, 358; of doubtful genuineness, 358-61; quoted, 5, 411, 441, 453, 464
Canaccio, Bernardo, epitaph on Dante by, 166
Cancellieri, house of, divisions in, 86
Cantelm, James of, 153
Canzoni pietrose, 277
Capaneus, punishment of, 391, 426, 455
Capponi, ed. of *Div. Com.*, 483
Caprona, siege of, 10; Dante's presence at, 69
Cardinals, Italian, letter to, 342, 347-49
Carducci, 466
Carlyle, J. A., translation of *Inf.*, 488
Carpentras, conclave at, 156
Carrières, criticism of Dante by, 21
Cary, translation of *Div. Com.*, 487
Casella, 68, 395
Cassano, battle of, 7

Cassero, Jacopo del, 396
Cassius, 394
Castelvetro, Ludovico, commentary, 472
Castracani, Castruccio, 15, 16
Cato, in Purgatory, 394, 437-39
Cavalcanti, the, banished, 14, 114
—— Cavalcante, in Hell, 390
—— Guido, his intimacy with Dante, 53, 178, 272, 278; banishment and death of, 90, 95; a freethinker, 217, 235
Celestine V., 11
Cerchi, the, leaders of faction in Florence, 87, 89, 116
Cesari, Antonio, commentary, 475
Charlemagne, 408
Charles I. of Anjou, King of Naples, 7-9
—— II. of Anjou, King of Naples, 9, 10, 14; visits Florence, 61; grants to, opposed by Dante, 82, 95; occurs in Dante's works, 299, 307
—— of Valois, his interference at Florence, 12, 81, 90, 97-98, 103, 112; Dante's opposition to, 95, 105, 106
—— Martel, titular King of Hungary, 11; his friendship with Dante, 36, 82; in Paradise, 406
Charon, 388
Chrysostom, 407
Church and State, Dante's views on, 318-28
Ciacco, 454; predictions put in his mouth, 376, 388
Cialuffi, Lapa, 49, 50
Ciangulo, Nicolaus, ed. of *Inf.*, 4
Cicero, studied by Dante, 55, 211, 220
Cino of Pistoia, *v.* Sinibaldi
Cione, Dante's uncle, 34
Cipolla, 140
Clement IV., 26
—— V., 155, 252, 339, 377; pontificate of, 13-15
—— VII., 169
Clemenza, daughter of Charles Martel, marriage of, 15

Codronchi, Archbishop, 170
Colle, battle of, 7
Colonna, the, 11
Colonne, Guido dalle, 6
Comedy, definition of, 411-12
Compagni, Dino, chronicle of, 99, 100
Conrad III., 32
—— IV., reign of, 6
Conradin, defeat and death of, 7
Constance, mother of Frederick II., 405
Constantine, 408; donations of, 322 *n.*, 326, 392
Convito, compared with *Vulg. El.*, 131, 303-307; with *Vita Nuova*, 186, 204-11, 292-93; with *Div. Com.*, 223-24; Witte's explanation of, 227; Dante's faith as shown in, 231, 232-36; date of composition, 273, 297-99; odes intended to have been included in, 274-76; aim of, 289-92; title, 293; contents, 294-97; language, 295; remarks of Villani and Boccaccio on, 297; reason for its unfinished state, 299; quoted, 55, 57, 122, 133, 193, 204, 205, 208, 210, 211, 220-22, 232, 233, 235, 237, 286, 289, 290, 291, 298, 302, 303, 420, 437-38, 440, 462
Convivio, alternative title of *Convito*, 293
Cornelius, outlines, 480
Corneto, Rinier of, 391
Corsi, Domenico, Dante's tomb repaired by, 167
Cosmology, Dante credited with miraculous knowledge of, 367
Costa, commentary, 474
Creed, paraphrase of, apocryphal, legend as to its composition, 365
Cremona, engaged in civil wars, 14 16, 145-46
Crusca, Accademia della, ed. of *Div. Com.*, 483
Cunizza, 406
Curzola, sea-fight off, 11
Cyrus, 397

INDEX 493

DANIEL, Arnald, 403
Daniello Bernardino, life of Dante, 27, 42 ; commentary, 423 *n*., 472
Dante Alighieri, ancestry of, 31-39 ; date of birth, 7, 40-46 ; birthplace, 43-45 ; parents, 47-50 ; studies, 51-60 ; military service, 62-70 ; family life, 71-79 ; public career in Florence, 23, 80-96 ; alleged employment on missions, 82-86, 100-105, 157, 349 ; banishment, 12, 15, 99, 104-108 ; reason for his banishment, 94-96, 105-107 ; life in exile, 111-65 ; at the universities, 125-32, 134-37, 140 ; death, 16, 24, 42, 160, 165 ; treatment of his remains, 165-71 ; story of his love for Beatrice, as told by himself, 175-80 ; its meaning discussed, 180-97 ; episode of the "noble lady," 186, 192, 200-13, 220 ; his spiritual wanderings, 198-238 ; alleged scepticism, 226-36 ; spiritual development, 239-50 ; attitude towards the Church, 231, 233, 235, 243-50 ; towards political parties, 251-59 ; personal appearance, 260-63 ; portraits, 263 ; character, 264-66 ; instances of his alleged self-conceit and pride, 103, 354 ; condemned after death as a heretic, 167 ; tradition that he joined the Franciscans, 198 ; his rank in literature, 1-4 ; biographies of, 19-30 ; various writings concerning, 1-4, 464-78, 481-88 ; epitaphs on, 166
—— Lyric Poems, 272-78 ; letters, 341-61 ; eclogues, 361-63 ; apocryphal works, 364-70. For his other works, see their respective titles
—— professorship founded at Florence, 469
—— societies, 481
—— of Majano, 274, 278
Dantino (= Dante ?), resident at Padua, 135-37
David, King, 397

Dayman, translation of *Div. Com.*, 487
De aquâ et terrâ, spurious, 160, 336, 367-70 ; purport of, 366
De Monarchiâ, contents of, 318-28 ; aim, 328 ; date of composition, 257, 329-39 ; condemned as heretical, 167, 339 ; not the work of a sceptic, 235 ; quoted, 236, 254, 320, 322, 323, 324, 325, 443
De Vulgari Eloquentiâ, perhaps the basis of a course of lectures, 131 ; probably written soon after Convito, 239, 302-308, 332 ; genuineness, 308 ; title, 309 ; contents, 309-17 ; quoted, 270, 303, 306, 310, 311, 312, 313, 314, 316
Dima, V. van, translation of *Inf.*, 488
Diomed, 393
Dionisi, 225, 342, 467, 483
Dionysius of Syracuse, 390
—— the Areopagite, 407
Divina Commedia, original idea of, 373-75 ; date of composition, 376-80 ; preparations for, 380-83 ; sources, 384-85 ; contents, 386-410 ; title, 411-13, 472 ; topography, 413-21 ; classification of sins and punishments, 422-26 ; peopling of next world, 421, 426-33 ; guardians of the various regions, 433-39 ; purport of the poem, 440-63 ; general remarks on, 1-5, 379, 382 ; anecdote of first seven cantos, 137-39, 383 ; introductory cantos of, 218, 238, 240, 447-52 ; commentaries on, 464-78 ; lectures, 469, 471 ; dictionaries, 473, 478 ; concordance, 477 ; illustrations, 478-81 ; manuscripts and editions, 1, 4, 480, 481-84 ; translations, 484-88. See also *Inferno*, *Purgatorio*, and *Paradiso*
Dolce, Lodovico, 42 ; notes on *Div. Com.*, 472
Dolcino, Fra, sect of, 13
Döllinger, writings on Dante, 4, 480

Donati, family of, concerned in Florentine factions, 5, 8, 89
—— Corso, leader of Blacks, 87, 402; sentenced to death, 89; returns to Florence, 97; summoned before Benedict XI., 114; death, 13
—— Forese, interchange of sonnets with Dante, 48, 207, 219, 272; in Purgatory, 68, 213, 402, 429
—— Gemma, Dante's wife, 72-79, 164; supposed identity with the "noble lady," 208-12
—— Maria, Dante's mother-in-law, will of, 72
—— Nella, 78
—— Piccarda, 78, 405
Donatus the Grammarian, 407
Doni, Antonio Francesco, 349
Doré, Gustave, illustrations of *Div. Com.*, 480
D'Ovidio, note on a passage in *Convito*, 303
Duca, Guido del, 399
Dugdale, W. S., translation of *Purg.*, 488
Duns Scotus, on the future life, 462

ECLOGUES exchanged by Dante with Joannes de Virgilio, 162, 362-63
Edward I. of England, accession, 8
Elisei, Dante's supposed kinship with the, 33-34
Eliseo, brother of Cacciaguida, 32, 33
Emperor, Dante's ideal of an, 143-44, 254-56; his conception of the Emperor's divine authority, 318-29
Enzo, son of Frederick II., death of, 7
Eriphyle, 397
Erlangen, Ebrard of, claims Dante as an opponent of Rome, 247
Eschenbach, Wolfram von, 21
Este, House of, becomes supreme in Ferrara, 16
Eve, 410

FAGGIUOLA, Uguccione della, lord of Pisa, 15, 16, 153-54, 156, 157; takes refuge at Verona, 15, 154, 157, 160; death of, 16; supposed identity with the Veltro, 376
Falconetti, Ricco, Prior of Florence, 86
Fantoni, ed. of *Div. Com.*, 483
Fauriel, 281, 476
Fay, Edward Allen, Concordance of *Div. Com.*, 477
Febrer, Andreas, translation of *Div. Com.*, 485
Feletti, Pio, Dante's bones discovered by, 171
Ferrara, captured and re-captured, 14; revolution in, 16
Fiammazzo, Antonio, 466
Fiesco of Genoa, 402
Figueira, Guillem, 270'
Filelfo, Giovanni Maria, life of Dante by, 27, 83, 347; his theory of Beatrice, 182, 194
Fiorentino, translation of *Div. Com.*, 485
Flacius, Matthias, claims Dante as a witness against Rome, 244
Flagellants, rise of, 14
Flanders, Henry of, 153
Flaxman, John, illustrations of *Div. Com.*, 480
Florence, summary of events in, 5-16; conditions of nobility in, 37-39; mode of recording births, 40; qualifications for full citizenship, 42, 81; law concerning minority, 46; street improvements, 59; Bruni's history of, 66, 93; priors of, 9, 81, 86; guilds, 81; prevalence of materialism, 217; origin of Guelf and Ghibeline parties, 5; of White and Black parties, 12, 86; war with Arezzo, 9, 10, 13-15, 61-62, 115, 117; with Pisa, 8, 10, 15, 69, 153-54; civil strife in, 5-15, 87-105, 142-43, 251, 256; fires in, 9, 10, 114; amnesty to exiles, 151; Papal intervention in, 8, 12-13, 87-92,

INDEX

95-98, 103, 113-15; laid under interdict, 13, 89; intervention of Charles of Valois, 12, 90-92, 97-98, 103, 112; conflict with Henry VII., 14, 145-48, 151; Dante born in, 43-45; his public life in, 80-96; his banishment from, 12, 15, 95, 99-100, 102, 104-108, 151, 153, 156, 288; his love for, 78, 133, 148, 152, 310; his fame in, 288; posthumous honours paid him by, 168-69, 171; fresco portrait of him found in, 263; Dante professorship founded at, 469; edd. of *Div. Com.* published at, 479, 480, 483
Florentine, Anonymous, commentary by, 465, 471
—— friend, letter to a, 158 *n.*, 342, 350-58
Florentines, chief vices of, 424
—— letter to, 148, 149, 341, 347-49
Folco of Marseilles, 406
Forese, Peter, 82
Forli, battle of, 9; Dante's alleged visit to, 139
—— Marchese da, 402
Foscolo, Ugo, 245, 471; ed. of *Div. Com.*, 483
Francesca da Rimini, 388, 431, 454
Francis of Assisi, St., eulogy on, 407
Franciscans, Dante's bones concealed by, 169-71; Dante supposed to have joined, 198; his alleged conflict with, 365
Franco of Bologna, 398
Frangipani, 7; Dante's supposed descent from, 33, 37
Fraticelli, 281, 474; life of Dante, 29; ed. of Dante's works, 158 *n.*, 276
Frederick II., Emperor, reign of, 6; patron of Sicilian poetry, 6, 270; "last emperor of the Romans," 143, 256, 298; in Hell, 390
—— King of Sicily, 11, 12, 16; refuses lordship of Pisa, 15, 153

Frescobaldi, Dino, 272
Fucci, Vanni, 393

GABRIEL the Archangel, 410
Gabrielli, Cante de', Podestà of Florence, 104, 105
Galileo, 43
Gambaro, Gherardino di, Podestà of Florence, 116
Ganghereta, attack on, 116
Gemma, Dante's wife, *v.* Donati
Genelli, illustrations of Dante, 480
Genoa, 9-12, 14-16, 157; Henry VII. at, 145-46
Germans, Dante's judgment of, 432
Geryon, 391
Gherardesca, Ugolino della, 8-10, 69; Dante's treatment of the story of, 3, 382, 394
Gherardi, Simone, 88
Gherardini, the, banished, 114
Gherardo, Dante's uncle, 34
Ghibelines, leaders of, 35-36, 67; crushed at Campaldino, 62; expelled from Pistoia, 86; allied with Whites, 12, 13, 112-16, 135, 256; Dante's connection with, 115-22, 155-57; divided into Green and Dry, 251; also *v.* Guelfs
Giacomelli, Sofia, illustrations of Dante, 480
Giambullari, interpretation of *Inf.* by, 424
Gianni, Lapo, 272
Gietmann, theory regarding Beatrice, 183
Giotto, portrait of Dante said to be by, 263
Giudice Alberti, Neri del, Prior of Florence, 86
Giuliani, 281; maintains genuineness of *Aq. et Ter.*, 367-68
Giunta ed. of *Div. Com.*, 483
Giusti, Giuseppe, 263
Gloria, Andrea, on Paduan documents, 136
Godfrey of Bouillon, 408
Goethe, remarks of, quoted, 3, 214
Gonzaga, Cardinal Luigi Valenti,

2 K

Dante's tomb restored by, 167, 169
Grangier, translation of *Div. Com.*, 485
Gratian of Bologna, 407
Graul, Karl, claims Dante as a forerunner of Luther, 246
Greek, Dante ignorant of, 58, 157
Gregory X., pontificate of, 7-8
Grion, Giusto, theory as to Dante's birth, 46 *n.*
Gubbio, Dante's supposed stay at, 157
Guelfs, Dante's connection with, 43-45, 81; banished from Florence, 43-45; divided into Black and White, 86, 143, 251
—— and Ghibelines, origin of, 5, 142, 251; strife between, 6-16, 61-62, 69, 112-16, 135, 153-54; ensigns, 6; list of families belonging to, 36; Dante's attitude towards, 252-59
Guerini, 46 *n.*
Guidi, Counts, 150
Guinicelli, Guido, 8, 271, 403
Guiscard, Robert, 408

HADRIAN V., 8, 400
Haselfoot, translation of *Div. Com.*, 488
Hegel, 4
Henry VII., Emperor, career of, 14-15, 144-46, 298; character, 144-45; Florence hostile to, 14, 119, 145-48, 151, 256; Dante's hopes in, 140-41, 146-51, 298-300; *De Mon.* probably written on the occasion of his march to Rome, 337-39; Dante's hopes crushed by his death, 152, 154, 161, 200, 240, 242, 351, 355-56; *Div. Com.* written after his death, 376-78; throne prepared in Heaven for, 410; Dante's letter to, 147-51, 156, 342, 347-49
—— III. of England, 8, 396
—— son of Richard of Cornwall, 7, 390
—— the Fat of Navarre, 396

Herzog, claims Dante as an opponent of Rome, 247
Hettinger, commentary on *Div. Com.*, 4, 418, 478; Dante's philosophical difficulties set forth by, 233
Heyse, Theodor, letters discovered by, 342
Hezekiah, 408
Holofernes, 398
Homer, used by Dante, 53, 177; in Limbo, 388
Honorius IV., 9
Horace, used by Dante, 53; in Limbo, 388
Hugh Capet, 401
Humboldt, Alexander von, on dogmatic religion, 214

ILARIO, Frate, spurious letter of, 85, 139
Ildefonso, Father, *v.* San Luigi
Illuminatus, 407
Imbriani, Vittorio, 30, 46 *n.*
Imola, Benvenuto of, *v.* Rambaldi
Inferno, quoted, 47; interpretation of the first two cantos, 218, 376, 379, 447-52; anecdote of the first seven cantos, 137-39, 383; contents, 386-94; also *v. Div. Com.*
Innocent IV., 7
Inquisition, anecdote of Dante's citation before, 365
Interminelli, Alessio, 392
Isidor of Seville, 407
Italian dialects, Dante's knowledge of, 306; his remarks on, 312-14
—— poetry, beginning of, 6, 270-72
Italy, Princes and Peoples of, letter to, 149, 342, 347

JAMES, St., 409
Joachim of Flora, 231, 407
John, King of Saxony, *v.* Philalethes
—— I. of Montferrat, 307
—— XXI., Pope, 407
—— XXII., Pope, 15, 156; conflict with Lewis of Bavaria, 340

John, St., Apostle, 409, 410, 421
—— —— Baptist, 421
Joshua, 408
Jubilee, in 1300, 11, 282; Dante's vision supposed to be in year of, 379
Judas Iscariot, 394
—— Maccabeus, 408, 414
Judith, 410
Justinian, 406

KANNEGIESSER, Karl Ludwig, translations and notes by, 276, 477, 486
Klopstock, 446
Koch, Joseph Anton, illustrations of Dante, 480
Kopisch, commentary by, 477

LAMBERTACCI, the, expelled from Bologna, 8
Lamberti, Mosca dei, 5
Lamennais, translation of *Div. Com.*, 485
Lana, Jacopo della, commentary by, 33, 465, 468
Landino, Cristoforo, life of Dante, 27, 42; notes on, and ed. of *Div. Com.*, 472, 483
Lapa, wife of Alighiero, 49, 50
Lastra, battle at, 115, 118
Laterino, castle of, captured by Aretines, 13
Latini, Brunetto, 11, 391, 431; supposed to have taught Dante, 54, 60
Latino, Cardinal, 8
Laude in onore di Nostra Donna, spurious, 364
Laurentian MS., 348, 350, 351
Lausanne, Henry VII. at, 14, 145
Lentino, Giacopo da, 6
Leo X., 168
Lerici, battle of, 16
Lessing, 284
Letters ascribed to Dante, 62, 65-66, 341-361; also *v.* Can Grande, etc.
Lewis of Bavaria, Emperor, 15, 144; in conflict with the Popes, 167, 252, 340

Lewis X. of France, 15
—— of Savoy, 14
Lippmann, 479
Littré, Old French versions of *Inf.* ed. by, 485
Lombard, Peter, 384, 407, 462
Lombardi, Bonaventura, ed. of *Div. Com.*, 473, 483
Lombardo, Marco, 399
Longfellow, translation of *Div. Com.*, 476, 487
Löscher, Valentin Ernst, 246
Lucan, used by Dante, 53, 384; in Limbo, 388
Lucca, 8, 10, 12, 13, 15; occupied by Uguccione, 15, 153-54; Dante's stay at, 155, 160
—— Gentucca of, 277
Lucia, 387, 397
Lucifer, 394
Lungo, Isidoro del, 30
Luni, Archbishop Antonio of, 137
Lunigiana, Dante in, 137, 139, 299
Luther, Dante claimed as a forerunner of, 246
Lyons, Council of, 8

MACCHIAVELLI, Giangiacomo, illustrations of Dante, 480
Maestro Bandini, Domenico di, life of Dante, 27
Malaspina, the, Dante's hosts, 137-39, 299
—— Albert, poet, 270
—— Conrad, 396
—— Moroello, letter to, 212, 345-47
—— Spinetta, 16
Malatesta of Rimini, 8
—— Paolo, 454
Manetti, Gianozzo, life of Dante by, 27
Manfred, King of Naples, 6, 7; patron of Sicilian poetry, 271; in Purgatory, 395
Manfredi, Alberigo dei, 394
MSS. of *Div. Com.*, 481-84
Margaret of Brabant, Empress, 146; letters to, 343
Marradi, Tommaso, sacristan at Ravenna, 169-70

Martin IV., Pope, 9, 402
Mary, St., the Virgin, 387, 397, 399, 401, 409, 410, 421
Marzucco, of Pisa, 396
Matilda, Dante's guide, 403, 405, 439, 458, 459
Medusa, 389
Meloria, battle of, 9
Messer Giardino, Piero di, 42
Mezzano, Menghino, epitaph on Dante, 166
Micciole, Fazio of, Gonfalonier of Florence, 86
Michael Angelo, v. Buonarroti
Milan, 8, 12; Henry VII. crowned at, 14, 145
Milanesi, Gaetano, 85 n.
Milton, 446
Min, Dmitri, translation of *Inf.*, 488
Minos, 388
Missirini, life of Dante, 29
Molbech, translation of *Div. Com.*, 488
Monarchy, Dante on, v. *De Monarchiâ*
Moncetti, first ed. of *Aq. et Ter.*, 366, 368-70
Montaccianico, captured, 115
Montaperti, battle of, 7
Montecalvi, captured, 13
Monte Catini, battle of, 15, 154
Montefeltro, Buonconte di, 62, 67, 396
—— Guido di, 8, 9, 10, 393
Monteferrato, Manfredo da, *Aq. et Ter.* published by, 366
Montegranaro, Johannes de, statutes compiled by, 46
Monte Sommano, captured, 154
Montferrat, William, Marquis of, 10
Montfort, Guy of, 7, 390
Moon, markings on the, 336, 405
Moore, 66 n., 482
Mordani, Filippo, 170
Mornay, Du Plessis, 245
Moronto, brother of Cacciaguida, 32
Moses, 410, 421
Munich MS., 360
Muratori, extracts from Rambaldi's commentary, 470

Mussafia, 482
Musurus Pasha, translation of *Div. Com.*, 488

Naples, taken by Conrad IV., 6
—— King of, v. Charles
Nathan, the prophet, 407
Negroni, 482
Nella, 78
Nello, Prior of Florence, 86
Nessus, 391
Nicholas III., Pope, 8, 9, 377
—— IV., Pope, 9, 10
Nicolini, edition of *Div. Com.*, 483
Nimrod, 397
Niobe, 397
Nobility, conditions of, at Florence, 37-39; Dante's views on, 333
Norton, C. E., translation of *Div. Com.*, 488; of *Vita Nuova*, quoted, 179
Novello, Federigo, 396
—— Guido, defeated, 7
—— —— of Polenta, Dante's host, 157, 160-63, 165-66; letter to, 162, 349
Nuovo Credo di Dante, spurious, 365

Obizzo, Marquis of Ferrara, 390
Oltrarno, fire in, 10
Ordelaffi, Scarpetta degli, leader of the Whites, 12, 119, 139
Orestes, 398
Oria, Branca d', 8
—— Lamba d', 11
Orlandi, Guido, 272
Orosius, 407
Orsini, Cardinal, envoy to Florence and Bologna, 13
Orso, Count, 396
Ostia, Cardinal of, v. Acquasparta, Matthew of; and Prato, Nicholas of
Ottimo Comento, 35, 465, 468-69
Ottocar, King of Bohemia, 9, 396
Ovid, used by Dante, 53, 384; in Limbo, 388
Oxford, tradition of Dante's visit to, 125, 126
Ozanam, 476

PADUA, revolt against Henry VII., 14, 145, 146; conflict with Can Grande, 15, 16; Dante's alleged visit to, 128, 129, 131, 135-37, 139, 141
Palatine MS., letters found in, 342-48
Palermo, Italian poetry fostered at, 6, 271
Paradise, Earthly, 403-405, 443, 458-59
Paradiso, quoted, 5, 32, 421; contents, 405-10; reference to, in *De Mon.*, 335-36; also *v. Divina Commedia*
Paris, Dante's visit to, 24, 125-31, 140, 147, 299
Parma, revolt against Henry VII., 146
Passerini, 48
Passigli, 474
Pauer, 478
Paul, St., doctrine of Purgatory based on a passage from, 414
Paur, 23
Pazzi, family of, 8, 12, 14, 116
Pegolotti, family of, 10
Pelli, Giuseppe, life of Dante by, 28, 29
Penitential Psalms, paraphrase of, 365
Perez, Francesco, 182
Perini, Dino, authority for anecdote of Dante's MS., 138, 383
Perot, François, 244
Peter, brother of Robert of Naples, 15
―― III. of Aragon, 9, 396
―― Damian, 408
―― of Corvara, Anti-Pope, 340
―― of Spain, 407
―― St., 409, 410; Apocalypse of, 426 *n*.
―― the Eater, 407
Petrarch, 25, 217, 348
Philalethes (=John of Saxony), commentary and translation by, 478, 486
Philip of Valois, 16
―― the Bold, 396
―― the Fair, 9-11, 15, 251

Pia of Siena, 396, 427
Piantrevigne, captured, 112
Piccarda, 78, 405
Pinelli, illustrations of Dante, 480
Piper, Ferdinand, 246
Pisa, events in, 8-11, 14-16; conflict with Florence, 8, 10, 15-16, 69, 153-54; Henry VII. at, 14, 146; Dante's supposed stay at, 157
Pisistratus, 399
Pistoia, earthquake in, 11; Black and White feud in, 12, 86-87, 143; war with Florence, 12, 13, 112, 115; joins Guelfic league, 153
―― Cino of, *v.* Sinibaldi
Plato, works of, used by Dante, 293, 384
Plumptre, commentary and translation by, 476, 487
Plutus (= Pluto?), 388 and *n*.
Poetry, growth of, in Provence and Italy, 6, 270-72
Poggi, Andrew, referred to by Boccaccio, 102, 138, 383
―― Leone, 50
Poggiali, 474, 483
Polenta, Guido of, *v.* Novello
―― Ostagio da, 167
―― Ostasio da, 168
Pollock, translation of *Div. Com.*, 487
Pontedera, captured, 10
Poppi, Dante's supposed stay at, 150
Porciano, lords of, 150
Porta San Pietro, patrician quarter of Florence, 32, 81
Portinari, Folco, his daughter said to have been Dante's Beatrice, 176, 187-97; his will and death, 191
Portirelli, 474, 483
Portraits of Dante, 263-64
Poyet, Bertrand du, burns *De Mon.* as heretical, 167, 339
Prato joins Guelfic league, 153
―― Nicholas of, Cardinal of Ostia, intervenes in Florentine affairs, 12, 13, 113-15; praises Henry VII., 144; letter to, 343

Preitenitto, son of Cacciaguida, 34
Princes and Peoples of Italy, letter to, 149, 342, 347
Procne, 399
Provençal, Dante's knowledge of, 52, 53
—— poetry, 269-70
Psalms, Penitential, paraphrase of, 365
Puliciano, battle of, 12, 113
Purgatorio, quoted, 62, 144, 155, 459; contents of, 394-405; concluding vision in, 224, 229, 238, 241; also *v. Divina Commedia*
Purgatory, growth of doctrine of, 413-15
Pylades, 398
Pyrrhus of Epirus, 390

QUINTAVALLE, Noffo, 88

RABANUS Maurus, 407
Rachel, 410
Rahab, 406
Rambaldi, Benvenuto, life of Dante, 26, 48, 69; commentary, 470
Ratisbonne, translation of *Div. Com.*, 485
Ravenna, plague at, 162; Dante said to have taught in, 130-32, 161, 164; his stay at, 157-65; his death at, 16, 24, 42, 152, 160, 165; his tomb at, 166-67; dispute with Florentines as to his bones, 168-71
Rebecca, 410
Reggio, revolt against Henry VII., 146
Rehoboam, 397
Religion, in conflict with science, 214, 218; Dante's religious opinions, 218-38
Renier, Ridolfo, 70 *n.*, 183
Reuter, on the conflict between faith and science, quoted, 216-17
Rhipeus of Troy, 408
Ricaldone, Stefano Talice da, commentary, 472
Riccardian MS., portrait in, 264
Rienzo, Cola di, 349

Rieti, earthquake in, 11
Rimini, Bishop of, *v.* Serravalle, John of
Rinier the Mad, 391
Robert, King of Naples, 14-16, 146; lord of Florence, 15, 153; Dante's distrust of, 363
Rogers, C., translation of *Inf.*, 487
Roland, 408
Romanis, De, notes on *Div. Com.*, 474
Romano, Ezzelin of, 7, 390
Rome, jubilee in, 11, 282; Henry VII.'s march to, and coronation at, 14, 145, 146, 298, 299, 337-39, 376; Dante's supposed mission to, 83, 100-105; Church of, Dante's attitude towards, 231-35, 243-50; dialect of, 313; Empire of, Dante's belief in its divine sanction, 254-55, 319-22
Romena, Alexander of, said to have been leader of Whites, 117-20, 344; letter supposed to be from, 344; in Hell, 345
—— Counts of, 119, 345; letter to, 344
Romeo, 406
Ronto, Matteo, translation of *Div. Com.*, 485
Rossetti, Gabriele, 182, 245, 475
Rudolf of Habsburg, Emperor, 8, 143, 256, 298, 396
Ruggieri, 394
Rusticucci, Giacopo, 75
Ruth, in Paradise, 410
Ruth writings on Dante, 478

SACCHETTI, 34
St. John's Church at Florence, baptisms at, 40, 43
St. Victor, Hugh of, 407
—— Richard of, 407
Salerno, university founded at, 6
Salvani, Provenzano, 7, 398
Salvatico, Guido, 150, 299
Salviati, 278
Salvini, 278
Samuel the prophet, 421
San Brocolo, battle of, 8

San Gemignano, Dante's supposed mission to, 82-86
—— Godenzo, agreement of, 116
——Luigi, Ildefonso da, document published by, 84-85
Sant Andrea, Jacopo di, 391 *n*.
Santa Croce, church of, at Florence, founded, 11
—— Fiore, Umberto of, 426
—— Maria Novella, church of, at Florence, meeting in, 97
Santi, Antonio, 170, 171
Sapia, 399, 426
Sarah, 410
Satan, example of pride, 397, 424
Saul, 397
Savoy, Count of, 15, 153
Saxo-Ferrato, Bartolo a, 168
Saxony, Elector of, 88
Scala, Albert della, 111, 122
—— Alboin della, 122-23, 134
—— Bartholomew della, Dante's host, 122-24, 134, 135, 160
—— Gianfrancesco della, *v.* Can Grande
Scarabelli, 484
Scaramuzza, Francesco, illustrations of Dante, 481
Scartazzini, life of Dante, 29 ; ed. of *Div. Com.*, 484
Schelling, 4
Schlosser, 478
Schwarz, Johannes, 244
Scrovigni, Pietra, 277
Selmi, Francesco, 466
Sennacherib, 397
Serravalle, captured, 112
—— John of, 485 ; narrates Dante's visits to the universities, 126-27, 130, 140
Sesto, Cambio di, 88
Sextus Pompey, 390
Sicilian Vespers, 9
Sicily, poetry of, 6, 270-71 ; dialect of, 270, 313
Siena, Ghibelines supported by, 7 ; rising in, 16 ; allied to Florence, 61
Siger of Brabant, 127, 231, 407

Sinibaldi, Cino, of Pistoia, 272, 277, 312 ; sonnet to Dante, 278, 284 ; letter to, 342, 347
Solomon, King, 407
Soranzo, Giovanni, Doge of Venice, 349
Sordello, 9, 270, 396
Spinoli, Ubizzino, 14
Spires, Henry VII. at, 298
Spoleto, earthquake in, 11 ; Guelfs expelled from, 14 ; outrage in, 16
Spreti, Cami lo, opening of Dante's tomb described by, 169
Statius, used by Dante, 384 ; in Purgatory, 401, 402, 433
Stephen, St., 399
Stinche, Le, castle of, captured, 13
Stradanus, *v.* Straet
Straet, Jan van, illustrations to Dante, 480
Streckfuss, 477 ; translation of *Div. Com.*, 486
Strocchi, Dionigi, 170
Studies, classification of, 51-52
Sullivan, Sir E., translation of *Div. Com.*, 488
Suso, Heinrich, his conception of heaven, 460-61

TAGLIACOZZO, battle of, 7
Tarlati, Ciacco dei, 396
Täuber, 482
Templars, suppressed, 13
Thais, 392
Theophrastus, 25, 78
Tiraboschi, 28, 467
Todeschini, writings of, 29, 30, 84 ; quoted, 119
Tognocchi, Antonio, 199
Tommaseo, Niccolo, commentary, 475
Torre, Della, family of, 8
Torri, Alessandro, editor of Dante's letters, 342
Tosa, Pino della, 167
Tosinghi, the, 8
Tosti, Luigi, 333
Tragedy, definition of, 411-12
Trajan, example of humility, 397 ; in Paradise, 408

Travelling, difficulties of, 163, 165
Trinity, Church of the, at Florence, meeting of Blacks in, 89, 92, 95
Trissino, Gian Georgio, suspected of having forged *Vulg. El.*, 308
Trivulzio, Gian Giacomo, 83
Troya, Carlo, writings of, 28
Tuscan poets, list of, 272
Tuscany, Countess Palatine of, *v.* Battifolle

UBALDINI, the, 13; indemnity to, 115
Ubaldino of Pila, 402
Uberti, the, 6, 116
—— Farinata degli, Ghibeline chief, 7, 35, 390
Ubertini, the, 116
Udine, Dante's supposed stay at, 157
Ugolino, Count, *v.* Gherardesca
Uguccione, *v.* Faggiuola
Ulysses, 393
Unam Sanctam, Bull, 252, 333
Urban IV., 7, 26
Urbiciani, Bonagiunta degli, 155

VASARI, 263
Vatican MS., *v.* Palatine
Vellutello, Alessandro, writings of, 27, 140, 472, 483
Veltro, interpretation of, 376
Venice, at war with Genoa, 11; with Ferrara, 14; Guelfs expelled from, 14; Dante's alleged mission to, 83, 157, 160, 165, 349
Venturi, Pompeo, notes on *Div. Com.*, 473
Vernon, Lord, 137, 466, 470, 476
—— William Warren, 470, 476
Verona, Uguccione takes refuge at, 15, 154, 157, 160; Dante's stay at, 111-12, 122-24, 134, 135, 141, 157-60, 163-64
Veronica, exhibition of the, 282
Vicenza, taken by Henry VII., 14, 145; battle near, 15
Vidal, Peire, 270
Villani, John, the first biographer of Dante, 24; present at the entry of Charles of Valois, 97; at the battle of Lastra, 118; quoted, 5, 6, 81, 91, 98, 112, 113, 114, 125, 135, 145, 146, 148, 153, 160, 165, 265, 273, 297; referred to, *passim*
—— Philip, life of Dante by, 26, 35, 64, 165; Dante-professor at Florence, 359
Villegas, translation of *Inf.*, 485
Vinci, Leonardo da, 367, 369
Vineis, Peter de, 6, 391
Virgil, studied by Dante, 53, 333, 384, 445; Dante's guide, 386-403, 433, 444-45; symbolical of temporal sovereignty, 444
Virgilio, Joannes de, poetical correspondence with Dante, 162, 361-63, 378, 484
Visconti, the, 8, 12
—— Galeazzo, 16
—— Marco, 16
—— Nino, 68 *n.*, 77, 396
Visione, title formerly given to *Div. Com.*, 412-13
Vita Nuova, sole authority for Dante's youth, 52; compared with *Convito*, 186, 204-11, 292-93; Witte's explanation of, 225; origin of, 279; idea of, borrowed from Boëthius, 280, 283; date of composition, 52, 183, 272-74, 280-83, 284-85; early MS. of, 374; title, 279; contents, 175-203, 280; historical value, 180-86, 283-86; Dante's own opinion of, 204, 286; germ of *Div. Com.* contained in, 179, 373, 380; quoted, 177, 178, 179, 180, 184, 185, 189, 196, 200-203, 269, 373
Viviani, ed. of *Div. Com.*, 483
Volpi, Giovanni Antonio, commentary by, 473
Voltaire, his remarks on Dante, 245

WHITES, allied with Ghibelines, 12, 13, 112-22, 135, 256; amnesty to, 151; alleged mission from, to Boniface VIII., 100-105; letter

in the name of the, 343-44; Dante's connection with, 95, 99-107, 112, 115-22, 124, 135, 256-58; also v. Blacks
William I., Count of Poitiers, 269
—— the Good, King of Sicily, 408
Witte, Karl, works of, criticised, 478, 482, 483, 486; quoted, 19, 225-29, 231-33, 331, 337-39, 343, 345, 474; referred to, 20, 28, 42, 46 *n.*, 158 *n.*, 199, 243, 272, 276, 294 *n.*, 303, 335, 359, 424, 473; Dante's letters ed. by, 342; MSS. found by, 466; precocity of, 478 *n.*

ZACCARIA, Ranieri di, 156
Zanche, Michael, 8
Zatta, illustrations to Dante, 480
Zuccaro, Federigo, illustrations to Dante, 479

THE END

Printed by R. & R. CLARK, *Edinburgh*

www.ingramcontent.com/pod-product-compliance
Lightning Source LLC
Chambersburg PA
CBHW020858020526
44116CB00029B/343